MATRIX POPULATION MODELS

Matrix Population Models

Construction, Analysis, and Interpretation

Hal Caswell

Biology Department
Woods Hole Oceanographic Institution

Sinauer Associates, Inc.   Publishers
Sunderland, Massachusetts

MATRIX POPULATION MODELS

Library of Congress Cataloging-in-Publication Data
Caswell, Hal.
Matrix population models: construction, analysis, and
interpretation / Hal Caswell.
    p.   cm.
Bibliography: p.
Includes index.
ISBN 0-87893-094-9
ISBN 0-87893-093-0 (pbk.)
1. Population biology—Computer simulation. 2. Matrices—Data pro-
cessing. I. Title.
QH352.C375   1989
574.5′248′0113–dc20   89-31516
CIP

Printed on paper that meets the guidelines for permanence and durability
of the Committee on Production Guidelines for Book Longevity of the
Council on Library Resources.

Printed in U.S.A.

4 3 2 1

To my mother and father

Contents

Preface

In 1969, having been told that matrix algebra would someday be useful in ecology, I enrolled in a course in the subject. It was a standard undergraduate matrix algebra course, no better and no worse than countless others, but I found it frustrating because I couldn't see *how* it was going to be useful. Only after suffering through the course did I stumble upon P.H. Leslie's papers on matrix population models. I began investigating them; this book is the result.

I am convinced (obviously) that matrix models are a powerful and useful tool for investigating population dynamics. My goal in this book is to make them more widely available.

Writing a book is like holding an imaginary conversation. My partner for most of this conversation has been a graduate student in population biology who, having been told that matrix models are useful in ecology, wants to see how. Sometimes in the later chapters I have found myself talking to an older version of this student, say, one who had become sufficiently fascinated with the topic to try to write a book on it. Throughout, though, I have tried to write the book that I would have liked to have available to me.

I have assumed very little by way of mathematical background. Appendix A provides a brief overview of matrix algebra for the reader whose first question is, "What's a matrix?" I have done my best to help such a reader make it as far as possible through this materisl.

I owe a great debt to the many colleagues and friends with whom I have worked on matrix population models over the years. They have made great contributions to my understanding. Portions of the manuscript were critically read by Joel Cohen, Robert Desharnais, Terry Hughes, Clifford Katz, Mark Kot, Michael Lynch, James McGraw, Andrew Solow, Vicki Starczack, and Shripad Tuljapurkar; their comments were very helpful, and the remaining errors should certainly not be held against them. Students at the University of Connecticut, the University of Tennessee, and Woods Hole Oceanographic Institution were subjected to earlier versions of this material; their feedback was useful and their patience appreciated. I am also grateful to P. Bierzychudek, J. Connell, K. Gross, T. Hughes, J. McGraw, and P. Werner for providing unpublished data, to Sue Volkmann for her TEXpertise, to Beth Goff for clerical assistance and to Dan Smith for programming. It is also a pleasure to discharge some old debts by acknowledging my teachers: William Cooper, William Kilmer, J. Sutherland Frame, Oscar Ichazo, and Patrick Watson. The staff of Sinauer Associates has been most helpful throughout the production process.

Yale University Press, Springer-Verlag, the University of Chicago Press, the Ecological Society of America, and the American Mathematical Society kindly gave permission for use of previously published materials.

My research on matrix population models would have been impossible without the generous and continued support of the National Science Foundation. The production of this book was aided by a Science Alliance Visiting Professorship at the University of Tennessee and a grant from the Independent Study Program of the Woods Hole Oceanographic Institution. I am grateful to all these sources of support.

Woods Hole, Massachusetts
March, 1989

MATRIX POPULATION MODELS

Chapter 1

Introduction

1.1 Demography and the Life Cycle

The life cycle is the fundamental unit of description of the organism. Bonner (1965) has gone so far as to identify "the organism" with its life cycle:

> Not only the adult, but the whole life cycle will be considered the organism. This is an ancient notion, for philosophers have often pointed out that an *individual* conventionally means an organism in a short instant of time. ...For example, if we refer to a "dog" we usually picture in our minds an adult dog momentarily immobilized in time as though by a photographic snapshot. ...[but] is the dog not a dog from the moment of fertilization of its egg, through embryonic and foetal development, through birth and puppyhood, through adolescence and sexual maturity, and finally through senescence? (Bonner 1965, p. 7)

Ecology, genetics, evolution, development, and physiology all converge on the study of the life cycle. This book is an extended look at one way — a particularly powerful way — of analyzing the demographic consequences of the life cycle. The vital rates (i.e., birth, growth, development, and mortality rates) on which demography depends describe the development of individuals through the life cycle. The response of these rates to the environment determines population dynamics in ecological time and the evolution of life histories in evolutionary time.

1.2 Demography

By focusing on the vital rates in the context of the life cycle, demography addresses both the dynamics and structure of populations. The most fundamental fact of population dynamics is the potential for exponential growth.

1

This potential was known as early as the sixteenth century (Cole 1958). John Graunt in 1662, Linnaeus in 1742, and Benjamin Franklin in 1751 all wrote of exponential population growth. Malthus, whose "Essay on the Principle of Population" appeared in 1798, is sometimes credited with discovering the principle of exponential increase, but it was actually known long before.

The second fundamental fact of population dynamics is that populations do not continue unrestricted exponential growth for long. Models for restricted populations were first derived in the mid-nineteenth century by the Belgian mathematician Pierre-Francois Verhulst, who derived the logistic equation in 1838 (Hutchinson 1978). It was eventually rediscovered and popularized by Pearl and Reed (1920; see Kingsland 1985). Extensions to interspecific competition and predator-prey interactions soon followed (Lotka 1924, Volterra 1926, Gause 1934, Kostitzin 1939).

The logistic equation and its relatives ignore population structure by treating all individuals as identical. The existence of demographically important differences among individuals is obvious. In humans, the most obvious factors are age, sex, and location. The economics of annuities and life insurance led to an early concern with mortality differences as a function of age. The Romans attempted to calculate the change in mortality with age in the third century A.D. (Hutchinson 1978). John Graunt compiled age-specific mortality data from birth and death records in London in 1662. Shortly after, the astronomer Edmund Halley in 1693 presented the first thoroughly modern treatment of a life table. In 1760 Euler (Euler 1970) showed that a fixed life table and constant birth rate implied convergence to a stable age distribution (i.e., a constant proportion of the population in each age class), with a constant exponential growth rate.

Modern demography rests on the work of A.J. Lotka, who in the early twentieth century developed what is now known as stable age theory: the theory relating the structure and dynamics of a population classified by age groups and living in a constant environment.

The potential for exponential growth applies to animal and plant populations as well as human populations. Darwin (1859) saw in this unrealized potential an inevitable "struggle for existence," and thus an automatic natural selection of the individuals most well adapted to the prevailing conditions. However, serious demographic work on animals did not begin until the 1920s. Pearl (e.g., 1928, 1940) constructed life tables for laboratory *Drosophila* populations, investigating the effects of density, starvation, genetics, and other factors on the survivorship curve. Bodenheimer (1938) summarized life tables and age distributions for several species, and by the time of Deevey's (1947) classic paper, life tables were available for rotifers, mammals, and birds. The influential textbooks of Allee et al. (1949) and Andrewartha and Birch (1954) contained extensive discussions of life table methods.

The matrix population models that are the subject of this book date from the mid-1940s. They integrate population dynamics and population structure particularly clearly. Although they are only one of several mathematical frameworks for demographic modeling (Chapter 2), they are particularly useful when the life cycle is most appropriately described in terms of size classes or developmental stages, rather than age classes (Chapter 3).

Chapters 2–6 examine time-invariant, density-dependent matrix models — the case that leads to exponential growth. Age-classified models are discussed in Chapter 2. Chapters 3 and 4 present the stage-classified models of which the age-classified model is a special case. Chapter 5 shows how to derive important properties of the matrix model directly from a graphical description of the life cycle. Chapter 6 investigates sensitivity analysis and its connection with life history evolution.

Chapter 7 considers some statistical issues that arise in comparative studies, when one wants to assess the significance of differences among a set of matrix models. Chapters 8–10 relax the limitations of Chapters 2–6, considering stochastic models, density-dependent models, and frequency-dependent two-sex models, respectively. Results in these areas are much more recent, and examples of their application are correspondingly fewer than in the earlier chapters.

1.3 Construction, Analysis, and Interpretation

The construction, analysis, and biological interpretation of models go hand-in-hand. A model must be constructed before it can be analyzed. Model construction requires not only knowledge of the analytical tools that will eventually be applied to the model, but also a concern for the necessary data and for the manipulations needed to transform the data to the required form. Once constructed, a model must be analyzed to derive its conclusions. Here mathematical tools, from numerical simulation to more sophisticated analytical approaches, become important. Once a model has been constructed, its consequences are there for the taking. Many published studies have barely scratched the surface of the consequences implied by their demographic models. This is particularly unfortunate as demographic data are not easy to collect. Data of such value should be analyzed in as much detail as possible.

Finally, the results of an analysis must be interpreted in biological terms. This requires an understanding of the way the model was constructed, especially its assumptions and the problem context in which the data were collected. The comparative approach is particularly important. A single value of a transition probability, a population growth rate, or a sensitivity may mean relatively little; the comparison of two or more of these quantities is of much greater significance. Many of the methods to be described in this book have been applied so infrequently that there is little or no background available for comparative analysis. It is partly to stimulate such comparisons that I have undertaken to write the book.

1.4   Mathematical Prerequisites

My goal is to make matrix population models accessible to the biologist who wants to use them. I have assumed that you, the reader, are familiar with classical age-structured demography (the life table, the calculation of the intrinsic rate of increase, and the stable age distribution). These topics are now covered in most introductory ecology texts. Some knowledge of matrix algebra will be helpful, but I have included (Appendix A) a survey of the basics that are needed for the development and analysis of the models. Even with no background in matrix algebra, I hope that much of the material in the book will be intelligible based on the material in the Appendix. A generous sprinkling of examples is intended to show the mathematical results in action. The material in Chapters 8–10 is more technically difficult, but I have done my best to make it accessible.

1.5   Notation

Chapters, sections, and subsections are referred to by number. Equations, examples, figures, and tables are numbered within chapters. Equations are referenced in parentheses, i.e., (4.2) refers to the second equation in Chapter 4.

Matrices are denoted by upper case boldface letters and their entries by lower case letters with subscripts; thus, a_{ij} is the entry in the ith row and jth column of the matrix $\mathbf{A}$. Vectors are denoted by lower case boldface letters and their entries by lower case letters with subscripts; thus, v_i is the ith element of the vector $\mathbf{v}$. Complications arise when both vectors (or matrices) and their entries must be distinguished. My convention is to denote the (i,j) entry of matrix $\mathbf{A}_k$ by $a_{ij}^{(k)}$.

Vectors are column vectors by default. The transpose of a vector or matrix is denoted by a prime, thus $\mathbf{A}'$ is the transpose of $\mathbf{A}$. The complex conjugate transpose of $\mathbf{A}$ is denoted by $\mathbf{A}^*$. The scalar product of two vectors is denoted by $\langle \mathbf{x}, \mathbf{y} \rangle = \mathbf{x}^* \mathbf{y}$. The Kronecker product of two matrices is denoted by $\mathbf{A} \otimes \mathbf{B}$.

The probability of an event x is denoted $P(x)$, the conditional probability of x given y is denoted by $P(x|y)$, and the expectation of a random variable x is denoted by $E(x)$.

Chapter 2

The Age-Classified Matrix Model

2.1 The Life Table

Classical demographic analysis is based on a system of tabulating age-specific survival and reproduction known as the life table.[1] Life table analysis, based on the work of A.J. Lotka (Lotka 1924), is now included in most introductory ecology texts. A good discussion oriented toward animal populations and emphasizing estimation problems is to be found in Caughley (1977); a very thorough treatment in the context of insect populations is in preparation by J. R. Carey (in preparation). Standard sources in the human demographic literature include Keyfitz (1968, 1977), Keyfitz and Beekman (1984), Pollard (1973), and Shryock and Siegel (1976).

2.1.1 Survivorship

The basic entry in the life table is the *survivorship* function

$$l(x) = P[\text{survival from birth to age } x]$$

The survivorship function is monotonically nonincreasing, with $l(0) = 1$. (It is often rescaled so that $l(0) = 10,000$ or some such number, rather than 1, and interpreted as the number of survivors out of an initial cohort of 10,000, rather than as a probability.)

A variety of other life table statistics (survival and mortality rates, the distribution of age at death, life expectancies, etc.) can be calculated from

---

[1]The life table *sensu stricto* deals only with death (an interesting euphemism), but in a broader sense it can be taken to include the maternity function, giving the age-specific rate of reproduction.

$l(x)$. Particularly important to us will be the "force of mortality" or instantaneous mortality rate, $\mu(x)$, which is defined by

$$\mu(x)dx = P[\text{death in } (x, x + dx)| \text{survival to age } x] \qquad (2.1)$$

The probability of surviving from x to $x + dx$ is $l(x + dx)/l(x)$. Expanding $l(x + dx)$ in a Taylor series, ignoring second-order and higher terms, gives

$$l(x + dx) = l(x) + dx\frac{\partial l(x)}{\partial x} \qquad (2.2)$$

so that the probability of surviving from x to $x + dx$ is

$$\frac{l(x + dx)}{l(x)} = \frac{l(x) + dx\frac{\partial l(x)}{\partial x}}{l(x)} \qquad (2.3)$$

Subtracting this quantity from 1 gives the conditional probability of dying in $(x, x + dx)$:

$$P[\text{death in } (x, x + dx)| \text{survival to } x] = 1 - \frac{l(x) + dx\frac{\partial l(x)}{\partial x}}{l(x)} \qquad (2.4)$$

$$= -dx\frac{\partial \ln l(x)}{\partial x} \qquad (2.5)$$

Thus $\mu(x)$ is given by the negative of the slope of the survivorship curve on a semilogarithmic plot.

It is often useful to hypothesize a constant force of mortality over an age interval Δx and use (2.5) to calculate the probability of survival over that age interval as

$$\frac{l(x + \Delta x)}{l(x)} = e^{-\mu(x)\Delta x} \qquad (2.6)$$

2.1.2 Reproduction

Reproduction is described by the *maternity* function

$$m(x) = E(\text{offspring per individual aged } x \text{ per unit time})$$

In sexually reproducing species, $m(x)$ is usually expressed in terms of female offspring per female. This convention must be relaxed in two-sex models (Chapter 10).

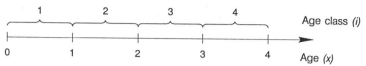

Figure 2.1: The relation between the continuous age variable x, used in the life table functions $m(x)$ and $l(x)$, and the discrete age classes i, used in the projection matrix parameters P_i and F_i.

2.2 Formulation of the Matrix Projection Model

2.2.1 Age Classes and the Projection Matrix

We begin by dividing the continuous age variable x into discrete *age classes*, $i = 1, 2, \ldots$, all of the same duration, following the scheme shown in Figure 2.1. Note that age class i corresponds to ages $i-1 \le x \le i$. This convention has the advantage of numbering the age classes, and the rows and columns of the matrix model, beginning with 1 rather than 0. The definition of age classes in the literature is inconsistent, and often confusing (cf. Michod and Anderson 1980 and Goodman 1982, who discuss this issue with some care. The former choose to begin numbering age classes at 0, the latter at 1).

Next, we define a *projection interval*, or time step, of the same duration as the age class width. We then project the abundance of each age class from one time to the next. Let $n_i(t)$ denote the abundance of age class i at time step t. Leave the first age class aside for the moment. The individuals in any age class other than the first at time $t + 1$ must be the survivors of the previous age class at time t. Thus

$$n_i(t + 1) = P_{i-1} n_{i-1}(t) \qquad \text{for } i = 2, 3, \ldots \tag{2.7}$$

where P_{i-1} is the survival probability of members of age class $i - 1$.

Individuals in the first age class cannot be survivors from a previous age class at $t - 1$; they must have originated by reproduction during the time interval $(t, t + 1)$. Thus we can write

$$n_1(t + 1) = F_1 n_1(t) + F_2 n_2(t) + \cdots \tag{2.8}$$

where the *fertility*[2] coefficients F_i give the number of age class 1 individuals at time $t + 1$ per age class i individual at time t.

The relationship between the projection coefficients P_i and F_i and the life table functions $l(x)$ and $m(x)$ is considered in Section 2.3. At this point it is enough to realize that, given the abundance of each age class at time t

---

[2]In this text, I follow the usage of human demographers, and use *fertility* to describe actual reproductive performance and *fecundity* to denote the physiological maximum reproductive output.

and enough survival and fertility information, one *could* make a projection of the population at time $t + 1$, using expressions of the form (2.7) and (2.8).

The system of equations (2.7) and (2.8) can be written in matrix form (see Appendix A):

$$
\begin{pmatrix} n_1 \\ n_2 \\ n_3 \\ \vdots \\ n_s \end{pmatrix} (t+1) = \begin{pmatrix} F_1 & F_2 & F_3 & \cdots & F_s \\ P_1 & 0 & 0 & \cdots & 0 \\ 0 & P_2 & 0 & \cdots & 0 \\ \vdots & \ddots & \ddots & \cdots & \vdots \\ 0 & 0 & \cdots & P_{s-1} & 0 \end{pmatrix} \begin{pmatrix} n_1 \\ n_2 \\ n_3 \\ \vdots \\ n_s \end{pmatrix} (t) \qquad (2.9)
$$

or, more compactly

$$
\mathbf{n}(t+1) = \mathbf{A}\mathbf{n}(t) \qquad (2.10)
$$

The matrix $\mathbf{A}$ is a population projection matrix. This special, age-classified matrix is often referred to as a *Leslie matrix*, in recognition of P.H. Leslie's (1945, 1948) role in its development. It is nonnegative (since negative elements would imply the possibility of negative numbers of individuals), with positive elements only in the first row (fertilities) and in the subdiagonal (survival probabilities).

2.3   Parameterization of the Matrix Model

The entries in the population projection matrix are usually derived from the life table. Much confusion has been created by misunderstanding this derivation. Caughley (1977) went so far as to dismiss matrix models as useless because one of the parameterizations in the literature seemed unreasonable. We will thus take some care with the problem here.

We begin by making an important distinction (Caughley 1977) between *birth-flow* populations, in which births occur continuously over the time interval, and *birth-pulse* populations, in which reproduction is concentrated in a short breeding season. Humans are an example of a birth-flow population, whereas mammals, birds, and many other organisms in seasonal environments are more accurately described as birth-pulse populations. These patterns of reproduction produce very different distributions of individuals within age classes, and lead to different approximations for the survival probabilities and fertilities.

And there must be approximations. It must be recognized that $l(x)$ and $m(x)$ are continuous functions, whereas the entries in the projection matrix are discrete coefficients. Some degree of approximation is unavoidable; the important thing is to realize just how the approximations are being made.

2.3.1 Birth-Flow Populations

Birth-Flow Survival Probabilities

P_i is the probability that an individual in age class i will survive from t to $t+1$. This depends on the age of the individual within the age class; the probability of survival from precise age x to $x+1$ is $l(x+1)/l(x)$. However, in forming age classes, we have given up all knowledge of age within the age class. Therefore, we approximate $l(x)$ within each age class by its mean over the interval $i-1 \leq x \leq i$, so that

$$P_i = \frac{\int_i^{i+1} l(x)dx}{\int_{i-1}^i l(x)dx} \tag{2.11}$$

$$\approx \frac{l(i)+l(i+1)}{l(i-1)+l(i)} \tag{2.12}$$

(In practice, human demographers may take into account more detailed information on the distribution of deaths within the age interval, especially for infants. This adds a term for the average number of years lived by the individuals dying within the age interval to their calculations; here I am assuming in effect that all deaths occur at the midpoint of the age interval. See Keyfitz 1968.)

Other alternatives are possible, but I have never seen them used. Assuming a constant force of mortality within the age interval suggests using the geometric rather than arithmetic mean as the approximation within the interval, in which case

$$P_i = \left(\frac{l(i)l(i+1)}{l(i-1)l(i)} \right)^{1/2} \tag{2.13}$$

$$= \left(\frac{l(i+1)}{l(i-1)} \right)^{1/2} \tag{2.14}$$

A second alternative is to calculate the probability of survival for each age and then average over the age interval:

$$P_i = \int_{i-1}^i \frac{l(x+1)}{l(x)}dx \tag{2.15}$$

$$\approx \frac{1}{2} \left(\frac{l(i)}{l(i-1)} + \frac{l(i+1)}{l(i)} \right) \tag{2.16}$$

Comparison of (2.12), (2.14), and (2.16) for several life tables suggests that the differences in the P_i are small (e.g., less than 2% in a life table for United States females using 5-year age classes), and probably irrelevant for most applications.

Birth-Flow Fertilities

The calculation of the fertilities F_i is more complex than the calculation of the survival probabilities. Again the formulas hinge on the distribution of births and deaths within an age class (Keyfitz 1968).

The F_i are defined by the first row of the projection matrix:

$$n_1(t+1) = \sum_i F_i n_i(t) \tag{2.17}$$

The first step in deriving the F_i is to derive an expression for $B_{(t,t+1)}$, the total number of births in the interval $(t, t+1)$. Let $n(x,t)$ denote the number of individuals aged $(x, x+dx)$ at time t (remember that x is a continuous variable). Then

$$B_{(t,t+1)} = \int_0^\infty \int_t^{t+1} m(x)n(x,z)\, dz\, dx \tag{2.18}$$

However, we are ignorant of the detailed dynamics of $n(x,t)$ within the time interval, so we approximate $\int_t^{t+1} n(x,z)dz$ by the arithmetic mean of $n(x,t)$ and $n(x,t+1)$. With this approximation,

$$B_{(t,t+1)} \approx \int_0^\infty m(x) \left(\frac{n(x,t) + n(x,t+1)}{2} \right) dx \tag{2.19}$$

Next, we approximate the continuous variables $m(x)$ and $n(x,t)$ by constant values (e.g., their means) m_i and $n_i(t)$ over the age interval $i-1 \leq x \leq i$. Given these approximations,

$$B_{(t,t+1)} \approx \frac{1}{2} \sum_{i=1}^\infty m_i[n_i(t) + n_i(t+1)] \tag{2.20}$$

However, $n_i(t+1) = P_{i-1}n_{i-1}(t)$ for $i \geq 2$. Substituting this into (2.20) and rearranging terms yields

$$B_{(t,t+1)} = \frac{1}{2} \sum_{i=1}^\infty (m_i + P_i m_{i+1}) n_i(t) \tag{2.21}$$

Comparing (2.21) with (2.17), we see that $(m_i + P_i m_{i+1})/2$ is close to F_i. However, $B_{(t,t+1)}$ is not quite equal to $n_1(t+1)$; some of the offspring born during the interval will not survive to time $t+1$. Those born just after t

must survive almost an entire projection interval to be included in $n_1(t+1)$. Those born just before $t+1$ are at risk of mortality for only a brief time. An average individual must survive for one-half of the projection interval, the probability of which is $l(0.5)$. Thus

$$F_i = l(0.5)\left(\frac{m_i + P_i m_{i+1}}{2}\right) \tag{2.22}$$

If $l(0.5)$ is not known directly, it can be estimated using linear interpolation (Keyfitz 1968):

$$l(0.5) \approx \frac{l(0) + l(1)}{2} \tag{2.23}$$

Most organisms, however, have relatively high neonatal mortality: in such cases logarithmic interpolation is more accurate:

$$l(0.5) \approx [l(0)l(1)]^{1/2} \tag{2.24}$$

According to (2.22), the typical individual in age class i produces offspring at a rate that is the average of the maternity function for that age class and the subsequent age class, the latter weighted by the probability of survival to the subsequent age class. The offspring produced must survive for one-half time unit to be counted in the population at time $t+1$. An alternative interpretation of (2.22) is in terms of a typical individual in the center of age class i. It spends half of the time interval producing offspring at the rate m_i, and, if it survives, ages into the next age class and produces offspring at the rate m_{i+1} for the rest of the time interval.

2.3.2   Birth-Pulse Populations

The maternity function and age distribution of a birth-pulse population are discontinuous. The maternity function $m(x)$ is shown in Figure 2.2. Individuals reproduce on their birthday each time unit (let us use years for the sake of discussion). We assume $m(0) = 0$; otherwise newborn individuals would begin reproducing on the day of their birth.

The age distribution (and the formulas for P and F) depends on when the pulse of breeding falls, relative to the time at which the population is counted (Figure 2.3). Let p $(0 < p < 1)$ denote the fraction of the time interval that elapses between the pulse of reproduction and the census. At census time, the age distribution consists of a series of pulses of individuals aged p, $1+p$, $2+p$, ...

In many studies (e.g., birds, large mammals; see Caughley 1977) censuses are carried out either just before or just after breeding. These cases correspond to the limits as $p \to 1$ and $p \to 0$, respectively.

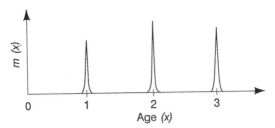

Figure 2.2: The maternity function for a birth-pulse population. Individuals reproduce only on their birthday.

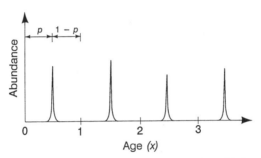

Figure 2.3: The age distribution at the time of census for a birth-pulse population. The time of the census is defined by p, the proportion of the time interval elapsing between the pulse of reproduction and the census.

Birth-Pulse Survival Probabilities

In calculating birth-pulse survival probabilities, we no longer have to approximate to obtain survival probabilities for "typical" individuals within the age class; every individual in age class i is identical, aged $i-1+p$. Thus

$$P_i = P(\text{survival from age } i-1+p \text{ to } i+p) \qquad (2.25)$$

$$= \frac{l(i+p)}{l(i-1+p)} \qquad (2.26)$$

For a postbreeding census $(p \rightarrow 0)$,

$$P_i = \frac{l(i)}{l(i-1)} \qquad (2.27)$$

and for a prebreeding census $(p \rightarrow 1)$,

$$P_i = \frac{l(i+1)}{l(i)} \qquad (2.28)$$

Mortality during the first age interval (say, the first year) appears in two different forms in prebreeding and postbreeding censuses. For a postbreeding census, $P_1 = l(1)/l(0)$, and includes first-year mortality. For a prebreeding census, $P_1 = l(2)/l(1)$, and excludes first-year mortality; in this case the missing mortality is incorporated into the fertility coefficients.

Birth-Pulse Fertilities

Again, we seek a set of F_i satisfying (2.17), beginning with an estimate of $B_{(t,t+1)}$. Since all the births within the interval $(t, t+1)$ occur at precisely $t + 1 - p$, it follows that $B_{(t,t+1)} = B(t + 1 - p)$, which is given by

$$B(t + 1 - p) = \sum_{i=1}^{\infty} n_i(t)m_i\phi_i \qquad (2.29)$$

where m_i is the reproductive output of an individual of age class i upon reaching its ith birthday and ϕ_i is the probability that an individual in age class i at census time survives long enough to reproduce on its next birthday, i.e., the probability of survival from age $x = i - 1 + p$ to age $x = i$. In a birth-pulse population at time $t + 1 - p$ the survivors of those individuals alive at time t celebrate their birthdays and reproduce.

The probability ϕ_i of surviving from census to reproduction can be approximated by assuming a constant force of mortality over the interval $(t, t+1)$, in which case the probability of surviving for a fraction $1 - p$ of a time unit is P_i^{1-p}. (Detailed information on seasonal mortality rates within the year can, of course, be used if it is available.)

Once reproduction has taken place, the offspring must survive a fraction p of a time unit to time $t + 1$ in order to be counted in $n_1(t + 1)$. That probability is given by $l(p)$; it may be estimated by interpolation, as $l(0.5)$ was for birth-flow populations [Equations (2.23), (2.24)]. Thus the fertility coefficient for a birth-pulse population is given by

$$F_i = l(p)P_i^{1-p}m_i \qquad (2.30)$$

For a postbreeding census $(p \to 0)$,

$$F_i = P_i m_i \qquad (2.31)$$

whereas for a prebreeding census $(p \to 1)$,

$$F_i = l(1)m_i \qquad (2.32)$$

Note the appearance of first-year mortality in F_i for the prebreeding census case.

Example 2.1 Parameterization of an age-classified matrix

Consider the following hypothetical life table for a population in which all individuals die by the time they reach four years of age.

x	$l(x)$
0	1.0
1	0.8
2	0.5
3	0.1
4	0.0

Application of (2.12), (2.27), and (2.28) yields the following estimates for the P_i:

		Birth-Pulse	
i	Birth-Flow	$p \to 0$	$p \to 1$
1	$\frac{0.8+0.5}{1.0+0.8} = 0.722$	$\frac{0.8}{1.0} = 0.800$	$\frac{0.5}{0.8} = 0.625$
2	$\frac{0.5+0.1}{0.8+0.5} = 0.462$	$\frac{0.5}{0.8} = 0.625$	$\frac{0.1}{0.5} = 0.200$
3	$\frac{0.1+0.0}{0.5+0.1} = 0.167$	$\frac{0.1}{0.5} = 0.200$	$\frac{0.0}{0.1} = 0$
4	0	0	—

Notice that in the prebreeding census ($p \to 1$) there is no survival from the third to the fourth age class, because individuals in the fourth age class at the time of the census would be beginning to celebrate their fourth birthday, but the life table implies that none of them survives to do so. In the postbreeding ($p \to 0$) case, however, individuals in the fourth age class have just celebrated their *third* birthday; hence $P_3 > 0$.

Given the hypothetical set of reproductive outputs for each age class, i.e., the m_i of (2.22), (2.31), and (2.32), we can calculate the fertility coefficients F_i:

			Birth-Pulse	
i	m_i	Birth-Flow	$p \to 0$	$p \to 1$
1	0	$0.9\left(\frac{0+2(0.722)}{2}\right) = 0.650$	$(0.8)(0) = 0$	$(0.8)(0) = 0$
2	2	$0.9\left(\frac{2+6(0.462)}{2}\right) = 2.052$	$(0.625)(2) = 1.250$	$(0.8)(2) = 1.6$
3	6	$0.9\left(\frac{6+3(0.167)}{2}\right) = 2.926$	$(0.200)(6) = 1.200$	$(0.8)(6) = 4.8$
4	3	$0.9\left(\frac{3+0(0.000)}{2}\right) = 1.350$	$(0)(3) = 0$	$(0.8)(3) = 2.4$

The parameterization of the matrix affects the results of the analysis. For example, the eventual rates of exponential growth (calculated using the methods of Section 4.3) implied by the three matrices in this example are

Birth-Flow	1.793
Birth-Pulse, $p \to 0$	1.221
Birth-Pulse, $p \to 1$	1.221

The birth-pulse model yields the same growth rate regardless of the time of census, but the birth-flow and birth-pulse models predict quite different dynamics.

2.4 Projection: The Simplest Form of Analysis

Having constructed a projection matrix from age-specific life table data, the next step is to explore its consequences by analyzing the matrix. The results will depend on our hypotheses about the coefficients P_i and F_i. They are certainly affected by external environmental factors, by density, by sex ratios, by other species, and by other factors as well. Although the coefficients can be written as functions of these factors (see Chapters 8–10), we will begin with the simplest idealized situation, in which the coefficients are constant. The relevance of this assumption will be discussed in some detail in Section 2.5.

The simplest form of analysis is suggested by the matrix projection equation $\mathbf{n}(t+1) = \mathbf{A}\mathbf{n}(t)$. Beginning with an initial age distribution vector $\mathbf{n}(0)$, the subsequent state of the population is projected by repeated matrix multiplication:

$$\begin{aligned}
\mathbf{n}(1) &= \mathbf{A}\mathbf{n}(0) \\
\mathbf{n}(2) &= \mathbf{A}\mathbf{n}(1) = \mathbf{A}^2\mathbf{n}(0) \\
&\vdots \\
\mathbf{n}(t) &= \mathbf{A}\mathbf{n}(t-1) = \mathbf{A}^t\mathbf{n}(0)
\end{aligned}$$

It is an easy and instructive exercise to program this repeated multiplication on a small computer (among other things, writing a program for it guarantees that you understand the rules for matrix multiplication).

Example 2.2 Some experiments with projection

As an example, consider the following numerical experiments with the projection matrix

$$\mathbf{A} = \begin{pmatrix} 0 & 1 & 4 \\ .7 & 0 & 0 \\ 0 & .5 & 0 \end{pmatrix} \tag{2.33}$$

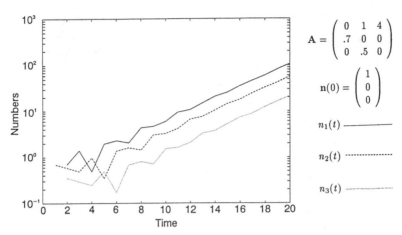

$$A = \begin{pmatrix} 0 & 1 & 4 \\ .7 & 0 & 0 \\ 0 & .5 & 0 \end{pmatrix}$$

$$\mathbf{n}(0) = \begin{pmatrix} 1 \\ 0 \\ 0 \end{pmatrix}$$

$n_1(t)$ ———————

$n_2(t)$ ···············

$n_3(t)$ ··············

Figure 2.4: Numerical projection of an initial population consisting of a single individual in age class 1.

According to this matrix, the probability of surviving from the first age class to the second is 0.7 and the probability of surviving from the second age class to the third is 0.5. Individuals in the three age classes produce 0, 1, and 4 surviving offspring per projection interval.

Figure 2.4 shows the results of applying this matrix to the initial population vector

$$\mathbf{n}(0) = \begin{pmatrix} 1 \\ 0 \\ 0 \end{pmatrix}$$

The relative abundances of the three age classes fluctuate initially, but eventually each age class, and thus total population size, grows exponentially, with the three age classes in constant relative proportions.

Further experimentation suggests that this result is independent of the initial population vector $\mathbf{n}(0)$. Figure 2.5 shows the dynamics of three populations beginning with single individuals in each of the three age classes. All three populations eventually grow at the same rate, but there are differences in population size at any given time. One might suspect (given some foresight about the concept of reproductive value, to be introduced in Chapter 4) that this results from the timing of events in the life cycle. Individuals in the third age class begin reproducing immediately, whereas individuals in the first age class must wait, with an attendant probability of mortality, one time step before they begin to reproduce and two time steps before they reach their maximum fertility. Thus the population started with age class 3 indi-

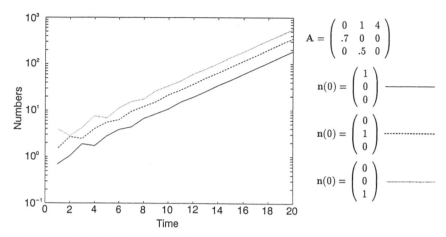

Figure 2.5: Projection results using the projection matrix of Figure 2.4 and three different initial populations. Total population size is plotted.

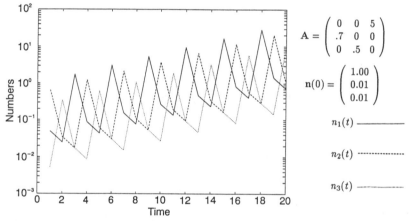

Figure 2.6: Numerical projection results when all reproduction is concentrated in the last age class.

viduals has, and maintains, a head start over the others.

Although eventual exponential growth and convergence to a stable age distribution seem to be independent of initial conditions, they are not independent of the form of the projection matrix $\mathbf{A}$. Figure 2.6 shows the results of modifying the first row of $\mathbf{A}$ in (2.33) so that all reproduction is concentrated in the last age class. Instead of converging, the age structure now oscillates with a period of three time units.

The differences between Figures 2.4 and 2.6 suggest that the concen-

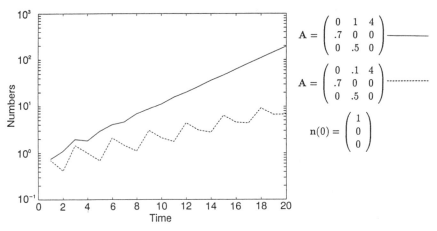

Figure 2.7: Projections of total population size varying the concentration of reproduction into the last age class.

tration of reproduction within a single or a few age classes influences the rate of convergence to the stable age distribution. This hypothesis is supported by Figure 2.7. The dynamics resulting from the original matrix are compared with those resulting from reducing F_2 from 1 to 0.1, thereby increasing the concentration of reproduction in the last age class. Both populations converge to exponential growth, but the second, with reproduction more concentrated, converges much more slowly.

It is also apparent from Figure 2.7 that reducing F_2 from 1 to 0.1 decreased the eventual rate of population growth, which is to be expected. Making similar changes elsewhere reveals that their effect on growth rate depends on their timing. For example, suppose we change fertility in the basic matrix **A** by adding one offspring. Figure 2.8 compares the results of adding this offspring to F_1 and to F_3. The impact on population growth rate is much greater in the first case than the second.

The conclusions suggested by these experiments (exponential growth, convergence of the age structure, the value of different initial populations, the effect of the concentration of fertility on convergence, the sensitivity of growth rate to life history changes) can all be investigated analytically. As we shall see, the resulting conclusions are more general and more powerful than what could be obtained by numerical projections alone.

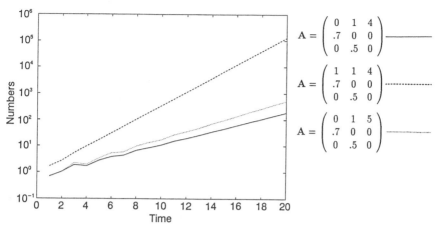

Figure 2.8: Projections of total population size, comparing the projection matrix of Figure 2.4 (solid line) with the results of adding 1 surviving offspring to F_1 and F_3.

2.5 Assumptions: Projection vs. Forecasting

What assumptions are required by the analysis so far? First, the construction of the model assumes implicitly that it is appropriate to classify individuals by age. As we will see in the next chapter, this is equivalent to assuming that properties other than age are irrelevant to an individual's demographic fate. If any other properties are relevant, they must be highly correlated with age, or the distribution of individuals among those categories must be stable. This is not an innocuous assumption; the demography of many organisms depends on size or developmental stage much more than on age, and these variables are often only poorly correlated with age (Chapter 3). Second, the discrete nature of the model discards all information on the age dependency of vital rates within age classes. The choice of a set of age classes makes an implicit assumption that this approximation is adequate.

Our analysis in Section 2.4 *seems* to assume that the fertilities and survival probabilities remain constant over time. This requires the vital rates to be independent of density and have no inherent time variation. At first glance, this seems ridiculous. The vital rates of most organisms vary conspicuously in time and space, and the effects of density on population dynamics are well documented. How, then, can one justify analyses such as those we have just discussed? Worse yet, how can one justify carrying out the more complex analyses to be presented in subsequent chapters?

The answer to this question is fundamental to the interpretation of demographic analyses, regardless of whether they use matrix models. It turns on an important distinction between *projection* and *forecasting* or prediction (Keyfitz 1972a). The failure to recognize this distinction has led to unfortunate confusion in the ecological literature.

A forecast is an attempt to predict what *will* happen. A projection is an attempt to describe what *would* happen, given certain hypotheses. Grammatically, forecasting uses a matrix model in the indicative mood and projection in the subjunctive. For example, specifying a projection matrix **A** implies an eventual population growth rate and structure. A population described by **A** would eventually grow at that rate with that structure, if nothing happened to change the vital rates. Ecological use of this purely analytical result is often criticized for assuming that the environment *is* constant and that density effects *are* unimportant. However, one must assume these conditions as facts about the world only if the model is being used to forecast actual future population dynamics. No such assumptions are required to interpret the growth rate and population structure as answers to the hypothetical question "how *would* the population behave *if* the present conditions were to be maintained indefinitely?" To assert that "the present demographic properties of this population are such that, were they to remain constant, the population would eventually grow at such-and-such a rate with such-and-such a structure" is not to claim that the first, hypothetical clause is true.

Interpreted as projections, the results of demographic analyses reveal something about present conditions (more precisely, about the relation between present conditions and the population experiencing them), *not* about the future behavior of the population. As Keyfitz (1972a) has pointed out, one of the most powerful ways to study present conditions is to examine their eventual consequences were they to remain as they are. The speedometer in a car fulfills an analogous function. A reading of 60 miles per hour *predicts* that, in one hour, the car will be found 60 miles in a straight line from its present location, 120 miles in two hours, and so on. As a forecast, this is almost always false. But as a projection, it provides valuable information about the present situation of the automobile.

So it is with demographic projections. They are particularly revealing because they integrate the impact of environmental conditions on vital rates throughout the life cycle. To know the survival probabilities and fertilities of every age class under a particular set of circumstances is to possess a great deal of biological information about those circumstances. This information is most valuable when coupled with a comparative approach, in which the vital rates are measured under two or more different conditions (e.g., Section 6.1.9). The use of demographic analysis in these studies does not depend on assumptions of density independence or environmental constancy.

2.6 Other Models

In this section, we consider the relation of the Leslie matrix model to two other frequently used models for age-classified populations: Lotka's integral equation and the McKendrick-von Foerster equation.

2.6.1 Lotka's Integral Equation

Lotka's model (Sharpe and Lotka 1911, Lotka 1939) follows the dynamics of births; the rest of the age distribution at any time can be obtained from the birth function and the survivorship function.

Let $B(t)$ denote the number of births occurring at time t, and $n(a, t)$ denote the number of individuals of age a at time t. By the definition of the maternity function,

$$B(t) = \int_0^\infty n(a, t)m(a)\, da$$

Suppose that the population has been in existence long enough for the initial population at time $t = 0$ to have died out. Then the individuals of age a at time t are survivors of the $B(t - a)$ individuals born a units earlier.[3] Their probability of survival to age a is $l(a)$. Thus $B(t)$ can be written

$$B(t) = \int_0^\infty B(t - a)l(a)m(a)\, da \qquad (2.34)$$

If (2.34) can be solved to find $B(t)$, the number of individuals at any age a can be found as $n(a, t) = B(t - a)l(a)$.

Lotka solved (2.34) by conjecturing that population growth would eventually become exponential, and trying a solution of the form $B(t) = \exp(rt)$. Substituting this into (2.34) yields

$$e^{rt} = \int_0^\infty e^{r(t-a)}l(a)m(a)\, da$$

Dividing both sides by $\exp(rt)$ yields

$$1 = \int_0^\infty e^{-ra}l(a)m(a)\, da \qquad (2.35)$$

This is Lotka's well-known equation for calculating the intrinsic rate of increase of a population from $l(x)$ and $m(x)$. There are an infinite number of solutions to (2.35), so the general solution for the birth series can be written

$$B(t) = \sum_{i=1}^\infty Q_i e^{r_i t} \qquad (2.36)$$

---

[3] If survivors of the initial cohort still remain, they will add a term $G(t) = \int_0^\infty n(a, 0)\frac{l(t+a)}{l(a)}m(a)\, da$ to the right-hand side of (2.34). However, if there is a finite maximum life span, $G(t)$ eventually declines to zero, and thus does not affect the long-term population dynamics.

where the coefficients Q_i depend on the initial conditions (see Keyfitz 1968 or Coale 1972 for details of their calculation).

It is not hard to show that there is only one real root of (2.35) (call it r_1), and that it exceeds the real part of any of the complex roots. Thus, as $t \to \infty$, r_1 dominates the solution, and the population eventually grows exponentially at that rate.

The integral equation (2.34) is a continuous time version of the first row of the Leslie matrix:

$$
\begin{aligned}
n_1(t+1) &= F_1 n_1(t) + F_2 n_2(t) + F_3 n_3(t) + \cdots \\
&= F_1 n_1(t) + F_2 P_1 n_1(t-1) + F_3 P_1 P_2 n_1(t-2) + \cdots
\end{aligned}
$$

If the age and time intervals are made smaller and smaller, this expression will eventually approach an integral equation of the same form as (2.34). As we will see in Chapter 4, the solution for $\mathbf{n}(t)$ from the matrix model also involves a sum of exponential terms, obtained as the solutions to an equation of the same form as (2.35).

2.6.2   The McKendrick-von Foerster Equation

The McKendrick-von Foerster equation (McKendrick 1926, von Foerster 1959) is a partial differential equation in which age and time are both continuous. Let $n(a, t)$ denote the age distribution at time t. The number of individuals in the age interval $(a, a + da)$ is given by $n(a, t)da$. Suppose for the moment that there is no mortality. Then at time $t + dt$ these individuals will be alive and aged $a + dt$:

$$
n(a, t) = n(a + dt, t + dt)
$$

Mortality results in the loss of some of these individuals during the interval $(t, t + dt)$. Let $\mu(a, t)$ denote the per capita mortality rate at age a and time t. Then

$$
n(a, t) - n(a + dt, t + dt) = \mu(a, t) n(a, t)\, dt \tag{2.37}
$$

If we expand $n(a + dt, t + dt)$ in a Taylor series, ignore terms of order dt^2 and higher, and substitute into (2.37), we obtain

$$
n(a + dt, t + dt) \approx n(a, t) + \frac{\partial n}{\partial a} dt + \frac{\partial n}{\partial t} dt \tag{2.38}
$$

from which

$$
\frac{\partial n(a, t)}{\partial t} + \frac{\partial n(a, t)}{\partial a} = -\mu(a, t) n(a, t) \tag{2.39}
$$

Equation (2.39) is the McKendrick-von Foerster equation. It expresses the dynamics of the population under the impact of aging and mortality, but does not include reproduction. Reproduction appears as a boundary condition, defining the abundance of age zero individuals:

$$n(0,t) = \int_0^\infty m(a,t)n(a,t)\,da \qquad (2.40)$$

When both $m(a,t)$ and $\mu(a,t)$ are time-invariant, solution of (2.39) subject to the boundary condition (2.40) yields the same exponential growth pattern, and the same equation for r, as the integral equation approach (see Roughgarden 1979, p. 351).

Equations (2.39) and (2.40) together constitute a continuous version of the entire Leslie matrix (Sinko and Streifer 1967). Equation (2.40) corresponds to the first row of the matrix. To show the correspondence between the rest of the matrix and (2.39), consider the equation for one age class, say n_i:

$$n_i(t+1) = P_{i-1}(t)n_{i-1}(t)$$

where the survival probability has been written as an explicit function of both age and time. Rewriting this in terms of $\Delta n_i = n_i(t+1) - n_i(t)$ yields

$$\Delta n_i = P_{i-1}(t)n_{i-1}(t) - n_i(t)$$

If the time interval is small, the survival probability $P_{i-1}(t)$ is approximately $1 - \mu(i-1,t)$, so

$$\Delta n_i = [1 - \mu(i-1,t)]n_{i-1}(t) - n_i(t)$$

or

$$\Delta n_i + [n_i(t) - n_{i-1}(t)] = -\mu(i-1,t)n_{i-1}(t)$$

The first term on the left-hand side is the change in n_i with time; the second is the change in $n(t)$ with age, so we can write this expression as

$$\frac{\Delta n_i}{\Delta t} + \frac{\Delta n}{\Delta a} = -\mu(i-1,t)n_{i-1}(t)$$

Letting the time and age intervals Δt and Δa shrink toward zero yields the continuous form (2.39). [For more detailed discussion, see Liu and Cohen (1987) and De Roos et al. (1989).]

Choosing a Model

Comparisons of the various approaches (Keyfitz 1967, Goodman 1967, Sinko and Streifer 1967, Roughgarden 1979) indicate that they are essentially equivalent descriptions of population dynamics. Charlesworth (1980) used integral equations in his analysis of the genetics of age-structured populations. Roughgarden (1979) has argued the merits of the McKendrick-von

Foerster equation. The integral equation has been generalized to density-dependent populations (e.g., Swick 1976, 1981, Rorres 1976, Botsford and Wickham 1978, Charlesworth 1980). The McKendrick-von Foerster equation has been generalized to deal with size-classified populations (Sinko and Streifer 1967, 1969, Oster 1976, Botsford 1984), with populations classified by physiological age (van Sickle 1977a,b), and with density dependence (e.g., Gurtin and MacCamy 1974, Oster and Takahashi 1974, Oster 1976, Hastings 1978b). Metz and Diekmann (1986) provide a detailed treatment of partial differential equation models for age- and size-classified populations.

The choice of a modeling framework is somewhat a matter of personal taste. Personally, I prefer matrix algebra to the solution of integral equations or partial differential equations. Moreover, it is easy to generalize matrix models to complex life cycles, in which individuals are classified by factors other than age. The formulation of the McKendrick-von Foerster equation requires the variable a in $n(a,t)$, whether it represents age, size, or some other quantity, to be continuous. Many life cycles contain inherently discrete stages (instars, metamorphic stages, reproductive vs. vegetative stages, etc.) that are not susceptible to this approach, but are easily expressed in matrix terms. Matrix models are also ideally suited to numerical calculation; the numerical solution of partial differential equations requires discrete approximations essentially identical to the Leslie matrix (Streifer 1974).

2.7   Historical Notes

Matrix population models are a relatively recent development in demography. They were independently developed in the 1940s by Bernardelli (1941), Lewis (1942), and Leslie (1945, 1948), but were not widely adopted by human demographers until the late 1960s, and by ecologists until the 1970s.

Leslie's papers (1945, 1948) were by far the most influential of the early developments. Patrick Holt Leslie (for some reason, everyone knew him as George) had studied physiology at Oxford in 1921, but was prevented by a severe case of tuberculosis from pursuing a medical career. In 1935 he joined the Bureau of Animal Population at Oxford, under the direction of Charles Elton. Elton suggested to him that it would be valuable if the mortality and fertility schedules of an organism could somehow be combined into a single expression, and he began a search through the human demographic literature for appropriate techniques. One result was the first application of Lotka's equation for the intrinsic rate of increase to an animal population (Leslie and Ranson 1940). The other was his development of the matrix model.

Leslie, a self-taught mathematician, had taught himself matrix algebra to pass the time while hospitalized with lung problems. His 1945 paper began by expressing the basic age-specific projection equations (2.7) and (2.8) in matrix form. He went on to consider the eventual rate of increase and the stable age distribution, and the relation to the usual methods of computation. In a second paper (1948), he elaborated the matrix analysis to include the relation of matrix models to logistic population growth and predator-prey interactions.

Two other workers had independently used matrix algebra in projection models. The first was Harro Bernardelli (1941), who had published a paper in 1941 in the *Journal of the Burma Research Society* with the title "Population Waves." Bernardelli's paper was unusual in focusing not on the eventual stability of population structure, but on intrinsic oscillations in population structure. He had observed oscillations in the age structure of the Burmese population between 1901 and 1931. As an abstract model for such oscillations, he proposed a matrix projection model with

$$\mathbf{A} = \begin{pmatrix} 0 & 0 & 6 \\ 1/2 & 0 & 0 \\ 0 & 1/3 & 0 \end{pmatrix}$$

and showed by numerical calculations that this gave rise to apparently permanent oscillations in the age structure (cf. Example 2.2 and Figure 2.6). He argued that fluctuations in economic and ecological systems might be produced by such a mechanism, and that attempts to find external causes for the oscillations might be misguided.

Matrix population models had also been suggested in a short paper by Lewis (1942) in the *Indian Journal of Statistics*, which covered much the same ground as Leslie's 1945 paper, but in more concise form. Leslie was unaware of this paper until after his 1945 paper was published, but acknowledged it in his 1948 paper.

Although Leslie's papers presented the basics of the matrix approach, and although Leslie had close working relationships with (and was highly regarded by) some of the most prominent population ecologists of the time, there was essentially no response from ecologists. Matrix models are not mentioned in the treatise of Allee et al. (1949), or in Smith's (1952) critique discussion of population models, or in Andrewartha and Birch (1954), or in Slobodkin's (1961) influential population ecology text. Human demographers seemed largely unaware of matrix models until after Keyfitz's (1967) and Goodman's (1967) demonstration of their equivalence to integral equation and difference equation models, and Keyfitz's influential 1968 book.

Only a handful of ecological papers used matrix models prior to the 1970s (Lefkovitch 1963, 1965, Pennycuick et al. 1968, Rabinovich 1969, Usher 1966, 1969a,b, Williamson 1959). Stage-classified matrix models (Chapter 4) were first introduced during the 1960s (Williamson 1959, Lefkovitch 1965, Rogers

1966, Usher 1966, Goodman 1969) and were adopted by plant population ecologists in the 1970s to describe populations classified by size rather than age (e.g., Sarukhan and Gadgil 1974, Hartshorn 1975, Werner and Caswell 1977, Caswell and Werner 1978, Enright and Ogden 1979).

The delay in the adoption of matrix population models by biologists reflects the perception of matrix algebra as an advanced and esoteric branch of mathematics – a perception that is now changing. It is also partly due to one of Leslie's other major contributions to ecology: the introduction of life table methods. While developing matrix models, Leslie was also collaborating with L.C. Birch and Thomas Park on the application of Lotka's life table methods to insect populations. The resulting papers (Birch 1948, Leslie and Park 1949) were very influential in introducing this method to population ecologists. Allee et al. (1949) and Andrewartha and Birch (1954) also included extensive discussions of life tables and their analysis. The mathematics of life table analysis were more accessible to ecologists at the time. Moreover, before the advent of computers, there was little that one could do with a matrix model that could not be done just as easily with a life table. Indeed, much of Leslie's (1945) paper is spent developing transformations of the projection matrix for which hand calculation was feasible. Thus there was little impetus at that time for ecologists to adopt matrix methods.

Chapter 3

Stage-Classified Life Cycles

The age-classified model developed in Chapter 2 assumes age-specific survival and fertility rates are sufficient to determine population dynamics. This is not always true. Even in human populations, for which age-classified demography was originally developed, factors other than age (sex, marital status, location) are known to affect the vital rates. In organisms with more complex life cycles age is even less adequate, and demographic models must be developed in terms of a classification by some more appropriate set of life cycle stages.

In this chapter we consider the choice of a variable in terms of which to describe population structure. We begin with a consideration of the formal notion of "state" in dynamical system theory. This will provide criteria for choosing among possible variables; we will then consider statistical techniques for making such choices.

3.1 State Variables

The notion of the "state" of a system is pervasive in system theory. In Newtonian mechanics, for example, the state of system is defined by the positions and momenta of its component particles. In ethology, the ideas of "motivation" or "drive" are used to describe the state of individual organisms. Ecosystem ecology relies heavily on models in which the state of an ecosystem is specified by the amounts of material or energy contained in each of a set of compartments. In demographic models the state of the population is given by the distribution of individuals among a set of categories (e.g., age classes).

3.1.1   Zadeh's Theory of State

The starting place for the formal analysis of the notion of state (Zadeh and Desoer 1963, Zadeh 1964, 1969, Resh 1967a,b) is the idea of an *abstract object* $\mathcal{O}$. This object interacts with its environment through a set of stimulus or *excitation* variables $\mathbf{e}$ and a set of *response* variables $\mathbf{r}$. Let $\mathbf{e}(t_0, t_1)$ and $\mathbf{r}(t_0, t_1)$ denote time series of $\mathbf{e}$ and $\mathbf{r}$ over the interval $t_0 \leq t \leq t_1$. Then the object $\mathcal{O}$ is defined in terms of its dynamics; to be precise, it is defined as the set of all the stimulus-response time series it produces:

$$\mathcal{O} = \{\mathbf{e}(t_0, t_1), \mathbf{r}(t_0, t_1)\} \tag{3.1}$$

Experimental study of an object consists of applying excitation series $\mathbf{e}(t_0, t_1)$ and noting the resulting responses $\mathbf{r}(t_0, t_1)$.

If we consider complete stimulus histories, over the entire lifetime of the object, it is reasonable to demand that the object be determinate, i.e., that the response be uniquely determined by the excitation.[1] It is then possible in principle to replace the catalog of behaviors (3.1) with a stimulus-response function

$$\mathbf{r}(t_0, t_1) = f[\mathbf{e}(t_0, t_1)] \tag{3.2}$$

The function $f(\cdot)$, relating as it does entire time series of responses and excitations, is difficult to work with.[2] An obvious simplification is to try to work with the instantaneous values $\mathbf{e}(t)$ and $\mathbf{r}(t)$:

$$\mathbf{r}(t) = g[\mathbf{e}(t)] \tag{3.3}$$

The problem is that such an instaneous stimulus-response equation is almost never determinate, because the response to an excitation is seldom uniquely determined by that excitation.

> It is a common observation that the same stimulus given to the same animal at different times does not always evoke the same response. Something in the animal must have changed and we invoke an 'intervening variable'. This is something which comes between the two things we can measure — in this case the stimulus we give and the response we get out — and affects the relationship between them. (Manning 1972)

The "intervening variable" of the ethologist is the state variable of the system theorist, which is introduced to make the stimulus-response relationship determinate. Consider a variable x, ranging over some set X. The variable x is a state variable (and X the state space) if it satisfies the following two requirements:

---

[1] The corresponding condition for stochastic systems is that the probability distribution of the response be uniquely determined.

[2] Although frequency-domain methods for linear systems in effect do just this.

1. There must exist a function $G(\cdot)$ which uniquely determines the response at any time t as a function of the stimulus *and the state* at t:

$$\mathbf{r}(t) = G[x(t), \mathbf{e}(t)] \tag{3.4}$$

   The function $G(\cdot)$ is known as the stimulus-state-response function.

2. There must exist a function $F(\cdot)$ which uniquely determines the state at any time as a function of the state at any earlier time and the stimulus sequence from the earlier time to the present:

$$x(t + \Delta t) = F[x(t), \mathbf{e}(t, t + \Delta t)] \tag{3.5}$$

   for any t, Δt, and $\mathbf{e}(t, t + \Delta t)$. The function $F(\cdot)$ is known as the state transition function. It appears as a differential equation in continuous systems and as a difference equation in discrete systems.

The stimulus-state-response equation, the state transition equation, and the specification of an initial state at time t_0 completely determine all subsequent dynamics. As the stimulus sequence unfolds, the state variable changes according to (3.5), and the responses are determined, moment by moment, by (3.4). The adequacy of a potential state variable is assessed by the information it contributes to the specification of the response to the environment.

3.1.2 State Variables in Population Models

Formal state theory was introduced into population ecology by Caswell et al. (1972), Boling (1973), and Metz (1977; see Metz and Diekmann 1986). Metz and Diekmann (1986) introduced a useful distinction between the state of an individual (an *i-state*) and the state of a population (a *p-state*). Examples of *i*-state variables include age, size, hunger, and a variety of physiological measurements. The *p*-state variable is a density function; it describes the state of the population by specifying the numbers of individuals in each *i*-state (e.g., the age distribution, the size distribution, etc.).

The simplest population models use the total number of individuals $N(t)$ as a *p*-state variable (Caswell et al. 1972). This would be acceptable if all individuals were identical. If the individuals differ, however, populations of the same size but with different internal structures will behave differently under the same conditions (e.g. Figure 2.5), violating the state axioms.

Classical demographic theory uses age as an *i*-state variable, and the age distribution (as in the Leslie matrix, the Lotka integral equation, and the McKendrick-von Foerster equation) as a *p*-state variable. For many organisms, however, the age of an individual provides little or no information about its demographic properties. Thus knowing the distribution of individuals among age classes tells little or nothing about the behavior of the population, and the age distribution is an inadequate p-state variable.

Alternatives to age as an i-state variable include size and various measures of developmental stage (instar, etc.). Or, the i-state may itself be multidimensional (e.g., age *and* size, or age *and* spatial location), in which case the p-state variable is a multidimensional density function.

A successful i-state variable permits prediction of an individual's fate, or at least improves such prediction over that possible without knowledge of the state. To test the adequacy of a potential i-state variable one classifies individuals by the variable, and examines their fate after exposure to a given environment, and sees whether knowledge of the state variable improves the prediction of the individual's fate.

It is difficult to carry out such tests at the population level. One would have to establish populations with different p-states (e.g., different size distributions) and see if the p-state determined the response to the environment. Fortunately, Metz and Diekmann (1986) show that, under most conditions, a density function over an adequate i-state variable is automatically an adequate p-state variable. Thus, potential p-state variables can be tested by measuring the amount of information they provide about the demographic properties of individuals, rather than populations. The next section provides a number of examples.

3.2   The Inadequacy of Age as a State Variable

The adequacy of age as a state variable depends on how much information it provides about the demographically relevant aspects of individual development. Several circumstances combine to limit this information and make other state variables more suitable than age. These circumstances include the combination of size- or stage-dependent demography with plastic growth, the existence of multiple modes of reproduction, and (in a broad sense) environmental heterogeneity.

3.2.1   Size-Dependent Vital Rates and Plastic Growth

If the vital rates depend on body size and growth is sufficiently plastic that individuals of the same age may differ appreciably in size, then age will provide little information about the fate of an individual. The same argument applies to stage-dependent demography coupled with plastic development (e.g., instars of variable duration).

Size-dependent demography is probably the rule rather than the exception, and is especially pronounced in species with a large range of adult body size as a result of indeterminate adult growth. Some examples follow:

- Some species must achieve a threshold size before beginning to reproduce. Examples include monocarpic perennial plants (Werner 1975, Gross 1981, Hirose and Kachi 1982, Klinkhamer et al. 1987a,b), trees (Zon 1915), salps (Heron and Benham 1985), echinoderms (Lawrence 1987), crabs (Somerton 1981, Somerton and MacIntosh 1983, Campbell and Eagles 1983), and fish (Alm 1959).

- Arthropods that develop through a series of discrete developmental stages (instars) must reach a certain stage before becoming sexually mature.

- Once reproduction begins, reproductive output is strongly dependent (usually allometrically) on adult body size in herbaceous plants, trees (e.g., Forbes 1930), kelp (Chapman 1986), molluscs (Thompson 1979, Peterson 1986), crabs (Hines 1982), insects (Tantawy and Vetukhiv 1960, Palmer 1985), isopods (Sutton et al. 1984), fish (Weatherley and Rogers 1978, Hourston et al. 1981), amphibians (Salthe and Mecham 1974), and turtles (Gibbons et al. 1982).

- Closer examination of data on reproductive maturity often reveals complicated interactions of several factors, of which age is only one. For example, see Haig et al. (1941) for effects of size and vigor on reproduction in white pine, Klinkhamer et al. (1987a,b) for effects of size, age, and growth rate on flowering in monocarpic perennial plants, and McKenzie et al. (1983) for effects of age, size, and genotype on sexual maturity in fish.

- Size-dependent mortality has been documented in herbaceous plants (e.g., Harper 1977, Solbrig 1981, Cook 1980, Sarukhan et al. 1984), trees (e.g., Jiminez and Lugo 1985), corals (Hughes and Jackson 1985), and marine invertebrates in general (Jackson 1985). In modular organisms, mortality usually decreases dramatically with size (measured as the number of ramets or modules); very large genets of such organisms may be nearly immortal (Cook 1985).

- Size affects sex change in both plants and animals (Policansky 1982, Charnov 1982).

Although size-dependent demography is often linked with indeterminate growth (see Sebens 1987 for a discussion of the confusion surrounding this term), it is not limited to species with such growth. Sauer and Slade (1987), for example, have documented effects of body size on survival and reproduction in vertebrates, and have used size-based demographic models for small mammals (Sauer and Slade 1985, 1986). Weight and body composition are known to affect the age at reproductive maturity in humans (Frisch 1984).

Size- or stage-dependent vital rates by themselves are not enough to render age inadequate as a state variable. If growth is so tightly regulated that age is a good predictor of size, then even if fecundity and mortality depend on size, age will work as an i-state variable. A number of authors (e.g., Stearns and Koella 1986) have used this approach to develop models phrased in terms of size, but using age-classified demography. Let x and s denote age and size, respectively, and suppose that reproduction $[m(s)]$ and mortality $[\mu(s)]$ are functions of size, while size is a function of age

$$s = g(x) \tag{3.6}$$

where $g(\cdot)$ is a growth function. Then reproduction and mortality can be written as $m[g(x)]$ and $\mu[g(x)]$, and survivorship written as

$$l(x) = \exp\left(-\int_0^x \mu[g(z)]dz\right) \tag{3.7}$$

The intrinsic rate of increase r can then be found from Lotka's equation, $1 = \int l(z)m[g(z)]dz$.

This approach relies on the growth function $s = g(x)$, and fails when size-dependent vital rates are coupled with plastic growth, so that an individual's age reveals little about its size. Such plasticity is widespread, although it is sometimes disguised by the questionable practice of fitting growth curves to *mean* size-at-age data. It is not restricted to continuous growth; the development rate of arthropods with discrete instars varies dramatically in response to temperature (e.g., Brown 1927 for cladocera, McLaren 1978 for copepods, Wagner et al. 1984 for insects). Even at constant temperatures, variability in developmental rates leads to appreciable variance in instar durations (Bellows 1986).

3.2.2   Multiple Modes of Reproduction

Many organisms exhibit both sexual and vegetative or clonal reproduction (Jackson et al. 1985). Sexual and vegetative offspring of the same age may differ markedly in their demographic properties. Cook (1985), for example, summarizes data on several clonal plant species showing that the probability of successful establishment for vegetative offspring is from 3 to 30 times higher than the corresponding probability for offspring produced from seed. To the extent that individuals of the same age have different vital rates, age is an inadequate i-state variable for such species.

3.2.3   Population Subdivision and Multistate Demography

A third situation leading to inadequacy of age as an i-state variable results from population subdivision, when the subpopulations are exposed to different environments. Specification of an individual's state in such a population requires specification of its age *and* its environment. Spatial subdivision is an obvious example; if individuals migrate between regions characterized by different vital rates, the age × region distribution is required to specify the state of the population. There is a large literature on such "multiregional" models (e.g., Rogers 1975, 1985). More recently, demographers have realized that these models also apply when individuals are classified by age and sex, age and marital status, age and employment status, etc. The term "multistate demography" is used to describe models in which individuals are classified by multiple i-state variables (Land and Rogers 1982, Schoen 1988).

3.3   Statistical Evaluation of State Variables

We turn now to the statistical problem of choosing among two or more potential i-state variables. The appropriate methods differ for continuous and discrete data.

3.3.1   Continuous Demographic Data

Standard statistical methods (regression, analysis of variance) can be used to evaluate the contribution of potential state variables to knowledge of continuous demographic traits, especially reproductive output.

> **Example 3.1 Age, size, and fecundity in the Pacific herring**
>
> Hourston et al. (1981) report on the fecundity of 23 stocks of the Pacific herring (*Clupea harengus pallasi*) in waters off British Columbia. Weight, length, and age were measured for each individual, and fecundity was measured by counting eggs in the ovaries. Regression equations were calculated for each stock relating fecundity to (log-transformed) age, length, weight, and combinations of the variables. The mean R^2 values, indicating the proportion of variance in fecundity explained by each variable were

Variable	R^2
Age	0.392
Length	0.606
Weight	0.705
Length + Age	0.615
Weight + Age	0.713
Weight + Length + Age	0.719

Clearly, either length or weight does a better job of predicting fecundity than does age. Note that age *is* significant, however, implying that it does indeed contribute to knowledge of fecundity. This does not imply that both age and size should be included in a demographic model. A clearer picture is obtained by comparing the R^2 values for Length + Age and Weight + Age with those for Length and Weight alone. This shows that the age of an individual contributes very little to knowledge of its fecundity, once its length or weight is known. The coefficients of partial determination $R^2_{FA|W}$ and $R^2_{FW|A}$, which measure the proportion of the variance in fecundity accounted for by age and weight, controlling for the other variable, are

$$R^2_{FA|W} = 0.027$$
$$R^2_{FW|A} = 0.582$$

That is, once weight is known, age explains only an additional 2.7% of the variance in fecundity, whereas weight explains an additional 58.2% beyond that explained by age. These data suggest that weight is a much more important state variable than age for this species. (See Peterson 1986 for a similar analysis of the clam *Mercenaria mercenaria*.)

3.3.2 Categorical Demographic Data

Matrix population models deal with individuals in discrete categories. Discrete categorical data are most appropriately analyzed using loglinear models (Bishop et al. 1975, Fienberg 1977, Fingleton 1984); the use of these models in choosing i-state variables was suggested by Caswell (1986, 1988).

Consider a data set in which the initial states of a set of individuals are defined by two or more criteria (e.g., age and size), and the fates of those individuals are recorded at a later time. The fate categories may or may not be the same as the state categories (e.g., death often appears as a fate, but not as an initial state). Such a data set can be described by a multiway contingency table; the examples to follow (from Caswell 1986, 1988) produce tables classified by age (A), size (S), and fate (F). The entry m_{ijk} in cell

(ijk) of the table gives the number of individuals starting in age class i and size class j at time t and ending up in fate k at time $t + 1$.

Loglinear analysis is based on a linear model relating the logs of the table entries to the categorical variables defining the table. The complete model for the three-way tables considered here is

$$\log m_{ijk} = u + u_{A(i)} + u_{S(j)} + u_{F(k)} + u_{AS(ij)}$$
$$+ u_{AF(ik)} + u_{SF(jk)} + u_{ASF(ijk)}$$

where u is the log of the total number of observations in the table, $u_{A(i)}$ the effect of the ith age class, $u_{AS(ij)}$ the effect of the interaction of the ith age class and the jth size class, and so on.

The parameters in the loglinear model can be estimated by maximum likelihood methods.[3] The goodness of fit of the model is then assessed by the log likelihood ratio

$$G^2 = -2 \sum_{\text{cells}} (\text{observed}) \log \left(\frac{\text{observed}}{\text{expected}} \right) \qquad (3.8)$$

which is asymptotically distributed as χ^2 with degrees of freedom equal to the difference between the number of cells in the table and the number of parameters fitted in the model.

The statistical significance of an interaction is assessed by examining the change in G^2 following the addition or deletion of that term from the model.[4] This change in G^2 is distributed as χ^2 with degrees of freedom equal to the increment in degrees of freedom in the two models being compared.

The significance of an interaction is always measured relative to the model to which it is added. This requires the choice of an appropriate "null model" against which to test any interaction. In the present context, age and size are explanatory variables, and fate is a response variable. The appropriate null model is thus AS, F (Fingleton 1984), asserting that the structure of the table reflects the age-size distribution of the tested individuals and the frequency of different fates, but that fate is independent of age and size. Against this null hypothesis, we can evaluate the effects of adding terms representing the interaction of explanatory and response variables: AF (the effect of age on fate), SF (the effect of size on fate), and ASF (the effect of age-size combinations on fate).

---

[3]The estimates often require iterative calculation, but are readily available in most statistical software systems.

[4]Following standard practice, we consider only hierarchical models, in which the presence of an interaction (e.g., u_{AS}) implies the presence of all lower order interactions involving those variables (e.g., u_A and u_S). A hierarchical model can be conveniently specified by writing down the highest order interactions necessary to imply all terms actually present, e.g., the model AS, F contains the terms A, S, F, and AS.

Table 3.1: Results of loglinear analysis of age and size effects on fate of *Dipsacus sylvestris* and *Verbascum thapsus* (Caswell 1988).

Model	Dipsacus sylvestris			Verbascum thapsus		
	df	G^2	P	df	G^2	P
AS, F	46	1253.19		22	648.8	
AS, SF	36	55.04		12	20.1	
SF	10	1198.15	0.0001	10	628.7	0.0001
AS, F	46	1253.19		22	648.8	
AS, AF	40	718.23		20	629.79	
AF	6	534.96	0.0001	2	19.01	0.0001
AS, AF	40	718.23		20	629.79	
AS, SF, AF	30	38.56		10	17.72	
SF	10	679.67	0.0001	10	612.07	0.0001
AS, SF	36	55.04		12	20.1	
AS, SF, AF	30	38.56		10	17.72	
AF	6	16.48	0.0114	2	2.38	0.3052
AS, SF, AF	30	38.56		10	17.72	
ASF	0	0		0	0	
ASF	30	38.56	0.1360	10	17.72	0.0598

Example 3.2 Monocarpic perennial plants

Werner (1975) and Gross (1981) followed the fate (death, survival as a vegetative rosette, or flowering) of individuals of known size and age of the monocarpic perennial plants *Dipsacus sylvestris* and *Verbascum thapsus*, respectively.

The results are shown in Table 3.1. Using the null model AS, F, the effects of size (measured by the SF interaction) and age (measured by the AF interaction) are highly significant in both species. These tests, however, examine the effects of age and size relative to a model containing no other factors. More interesting is the question of whether age (size) provides any additional information, once size (age) has been included. This is tested by evaluating the SF interaction against the model AS, AF, and the AF interaction against the model AS, SF. For *Dipsacus*, the SF interaction is still highly significant after age is included, but the AF interaction is only slightly significant after size is included. For *Verbascum*, the SF interaction maintains its significance

Table 3.2: Results of loglinear analysis of the effects of age and size on reproductive fate of female moose (*Alces alces*) (Caswell 1988).

Model	df	G^2	P
AS, F	28	247.21	
AS, SF	24	234.34	
SF	4	12.87	0.012
AS, F	28	247.21	
AS, AF	20	16.66	
AF	8	230.55	0.0001
AS, AF	20	16.66	
AS, SF, AF	16	12.05	
SF	4	4.61	0.3299
AS, SF	24	234.34	
AS, SF, AF	16	12.05	
AF	8	222.29	0.0001
AS, SF, AF	16	12.05	
ASF	0	0	
ASF	16	12.05	0.7404

when age is included, but the AF interaction is no longer significant when size is included. In both of these species, age loses most or all of its importance once size is accounted for. Size is clearly the more important i-state variable in these species.

Example 3.3 Reproductive output in the moose

A very different pattern appears in data on the reproductive status (nonreproductive, one calf, or twins) of the moose (*Alces alces*) in Norway (Saether and Haagenrud 1983). Females were classified into three weight classes and five age classes. Both the AF and SF interactions are significant when tested against the null model AS, F (Table 3.2), but the SF interaction loses its significance completely when tested against the model AS, AF. Age is thus much more important than body size in determining reproductive output in this species.

Example 3.4 Colony growth and mortality in reef corals

Hughes and Connell (1987) report the effects of age and size on colony growth and survival of three genera of corals (*Acropora, Porites, and*

Table 3.3: Loglinear analysis of age and size effects on colony growth and mortality of three genera of corals (data of Hughes and Connell 1987) (Caswell 1988).

	Acropora			Porites			Pocillopora		
Model	df	G^2	P	df	G^2	P	df	G^2	P
AS, F	15	104.7		15	43.47		15	25.99	
AS, SF	9	34.03		9	10.82		9	8.72	
SF	6	70.67	0.0001	6	32.65	0.0001	6	17.27	0.0083
AS, F	15	104.7		15	43.47		15	25.99	
AS, AF	12	73.5		12	32.98		12	20.44	
AF	3	31.2	0.0001	3	10.49	0.0148	3	5.55	0.1358
AS, AF	12	73.5		12	32.98		12	20.44	
AS, SF, AF	6	14.86		6	1.3		6	2.31	
SF	6	58.64	0.0001	6	31.68	0.0001	6	18.13	0.0059
AS, SF	9	34.03		9	10.82		9	8.72	
AS, SF, AF	6	14.86		6	1.3		6	2.31	
AF	3	19.17	0.0003	3	9.52	0.0231	3	6.41	0.0934
AS, SF, AF	6	14.86		6	1.3		6	2.31	
ASF	0	0		0	0		0	0	
ASF	6	14.86	0.0214	6	1.3	0.9717	6	2.31	0.8893

Pocillopora) in Australia. Colonies were assigned to two age classes (< 4.5 yr and > 4.5 yr) and three size classes, and their growth and survival were followed from 1970 to 1971. Colonies were assigned to one of four fate categories: negative growth, 0–100% growth, > 100% growth, and death.

For *Porites* and *Pocillopora*, size is clearly a better i-state variable than age (Table 3.3). For *Acropora* both size and age effects are significant, and each remains so even after the other has been included in the model.

Hughes and Connell (1987) also investigated the effects of size and age on mortality, without considering growth. The results of this loglinear analysis (Table 3.4) are quite different. Mortality of *Acropora* and *Porites* is highly dependent on size, but almost totally unaffected by age, whereas both age and size have significant effects on the mortality of *Pocillopora*.

Table 3.4: Loglinear analysis of age and size effects on colony mortality in three genera of corals (data of Hughes and Connell 1987) (Caswell 1988).

Model	*Acropora* df	G^2	P	*Porites* df	G^2	P	*Pocillopora* df	G^2	P
AS, F	5	41.69		5	20		5	18.54	
AS, SF	3	1.25		3	3.61		3	7.47	
SF	2	40.44	0.0001	2	16.39	0.0003	2	11.07	0.0039
AS, F	5	41.69		5	20		5	18.54	
AS, AF	4	40.98		4	18.76		4	12.94	
AF	1	0.71	0.3977	1	1.24	0.2664	1	5.6	0.018
AS, AF	4	40.98		4	18.76		4	12.94	
AS, SF, AF	2	0.37		2	1.15		2	0.63	
SF	2	40.61	0.0001	2	17.61	0.0001	2	12.31	0.0021
AS, SF	3	1.25		3	3.61		3	7.47	
AS, SF, AF	2	0.37		2	1.15		2	0.63	
AF	1	0.88	0.347	1	2.46	0.1165	1	6.84	0.0089
AS, SF, AF	2	0.37		2	1.15		2	0.63	
ASF	0	0		0	0		0	0	
ASF	2	0.37	0.8312	2	1.15	0.563	2	0.63	0.7301

Example 3.5 Shoot demography in *Rhododendron maximum*

McGraw (1989) examined the demography of individual shoots of this clonal shrub. Shoots were aged by counting leaf scars, and measured by estimating leaf area. Individual shoots were assigned to one of four fates: death, branching, flowering, and survival without branching or flowering. Both age and size have highly significant effects on demographic fate (Table 3.5).

3.3.3 Quantifying the Relative Importance of State Variables

The preceding examples show that the significance of size and age varies among species, and that in some cases both size and age have significant effects on demographic fate. To measure the relative importance of potential state variables, especially when more than one have significant effects, we need a way to quantify the contributions of the different variables to the determination of individual fate. To do so we use Goodman and Kruskal's (1954) association coefficient τ, one of several measures of association for

Table 3.5: Loglinear analysis of the effects of shoot age and size on fate of ramets of *Rhododendron maximum* (data of McGraw 1989) (Caswell 1988).

Model	df	G^2	P
AS, F	24	404.47	
AS, SF	18	270.59	
SF	6	133.88	0.0001
AS, F	24	404.47	
AS, AF	18	153.34	
AF	6	251.13	0.0001
AS, AF	18	153.34	
AS, SF, AF	12	23.11	
SF	6	130.23	0.0001
AS, SF	18	270.59	
AS, SF, AF	12	23.11	
AF	6	247.48	0.0001
AS, SF, AF	12	23.11	
ASF	0	0	
ASF	12	23.11	0.0268

cross–classified data (Liebetrau 1983).

Consider a two-way table with age classes A_i as rows and fates F_j as columns. Select an individual at random and attempt to predict its fate. There will be a certain proportion of incorrect answers, depending on the marginal distribution of individuals among fates. Now choose an individual and attempt to predict its fate, given a knowledge of its age. The proportion of incorrect answers will decline; the value of age as an i-state variable can be measured by the proportional decrease in the frequency of incorrect predictions. Goodman and Kruskal (1954) defined the index τ_{AF} to measure this reduction in incorrect predictions by

$$\tau_{AF} = \frac{\sum_i \sum_j \frac{m_{ij}^2}{m_{i.}} - \sum_j \frac{m_{.j}^2}{m_{..}}}{m_{..} - \sum_j \frac{m_{.j}^2}{m_{..}}} \tag{3.9}$$

where m_{ij} is the count in cell (i,j), $m_{i.}$ and $m_{.j}$ are the marginal totals of row i and column j, and $m_{..}$ is the total number of cases in the table. Perfect association ($\tau_{AF} = 1$) implies that knowledge of A totally determines the value of F; $\tau_{AF} = 0$ implies that the two variables are statistically independent. This index is not in general symmetrical; $\tau_{AF} \neq \tau_{FA}$.

To compare two potential i-state variables in a three-way table requires the corresponding formulas for multiple and partial associations (analogous to multiple and partial correlation coefficients), which were developed by Gray and Williams (1975). Consider the three-way table with variables age (A), size (S), and fate (F). The multiple association τ_{ASF} measures the extent to which fate is determined by knowledge of *both* age and size. It can be calculated from (3.9) by creating a new variable X whose values consist of all combinations of the values of A and S, and then calculating τ_{XF}.

The partial associations $\tau_{AF|S}$ and $\tau_{SF|A}$ measure the importance of age when size is taken into account and the importance of size when age is taken into account. They are obtained from the simple and multiple associations by the relation

$$\tau_{AF|S} = \frac{\tau_{ASF} - \tau_{AS}}{1 - \tau_{AS}} \tag{3.10}$$

(Gray and Williams 1975), where τ_{AS} is the simple association calculated for the marginal table relating age and size. The formula for $\tau_{SF|A}$ is analogous.

The definition of τ as the proportional decrease in incorrect predictions of fate given information on size or age is clearly related to the criteria for state variables. Light and Margolin (1971) and Anderson and Landis (1980) have also shown that the simple, partial, and multiple τ values measure the proportion of variance explained by the independent variables, exactly as do simple, partial, and multiple R^2 values in regression analysis.

Table 3.6 gives the simple, multiple, and partial associations among age, size, and fate for the examples described in the preceding section, as well as for two of Alm's (1959) experiments (his numbers F3B and F3C) on age, size, and maturity in the trout (*Salmo trutta*). Alm's data were analyzed twice, once with fate categories mature and immature, and once with fate categories mature males, mature females, and immatures. These results show that the relative importance of age and size within a given species can vary depending on conditions.

Comparison of $\tau_{SF|A}$ and $\tau_{AF|S}$ shows that size is a more important state variable than age in all cases except for reproduction in the moose, the ramet demography of *Rhododendron*, and one experiment on maturity in trout. For the other species, size is up to 35 times more important than age, even though age may have statistically significant effects.

Figure 3.1 plots the relative importance of size and age, measured by the ratio $(\tau_{SF|A})/(\tau_{AF|S})$. The values vary smoothly from one extreme to the other among these data sets.

Table 3.6: Simple, multiple, and partial associations among fate, age, and size for the examples considered in Section 3.3.2 (Caswell 1988).

Name	τ_{AF}	τ_{SF}	τ_{ASF}	$\tau_{SF|A}$	$\tau_{AF|S}$	$\dfrac{\tau_{SF|A}}{\tau_{AF|S}}$
Dipsacus sylvestris	0.139	0.390	0.396	0.298	0.010	30.346
Verbascum thapsus	0.013	0.482	0.489	0.482	0.014	35.688
Rhododendron	0.374	0.146	0.424	0.080	0.326	0.245
Alces alces	0.140	0.009	0.147	0.008	0.139	0.058
Porites growth and mortality	0.036	0.151	0.190	0.160	0.046	3.478
Pocillopora growth and mortality	0.026	0.080	0.117	0.093	0.040	2.323
Acropora growth and mortality	0.044	0.109	0.145	0.106	0.040	2.615
Porites mortality	0.014	0.188	0.219	0.208	0.038	5.446
Pocillopora mortality	0.067	0.137	0.212	0.155	0.087	1.788
Acropora mortality	0.003	0.163	0.170	0.168	0.008	20.029
Salmo trutta F3B sex and maturity	0.353	0.361	0.472	0.184	0.174	1.059
Salmo trutta F3C sex and maturity	0.239	0.421	0.483	0.321	0.107	2.994
Salmo trutta F3B maturity	0.552	0.535	0.647	0.212	0.241	0.880
Salmo trutta F3C maturity	0.366	0.624	0.675	0.487	0.136	3.593

3.3.4 Incomplete Data

These analyses require the complete contingency table, in which individuals are jointly classified by all of the variables being evaluated. Far too often, such data are presented as marginal two-way tables, relating fate to each potential state variable separately. Of the examples considered above, only Saether and Haagenrud (1983) reported their data in the form of a complete multiway table.

Such incomplete data lose much of their value. No analysis based on marginal two-way tables can evaluate three-way or higher order interaction effects (e.g., the *ASF* interaction). Using only marginal data it is also impossible to evaluate the importance of one variable after another has been included. In the preceding examples, one would be restricted to the first two tests in Tables 3.1–3.5, and to the first two columns of Table 3.6. Since the importance of age and size can depend on whether size or age has already been included in the model, this is a severe limitation. Still worse, estimates of the association between state and fate from marginal tables can be severely biased [this is known as Simpson's paradox (Simpson 1951); see Cohen (1986) for a demographic application]. Suppose that only marginal

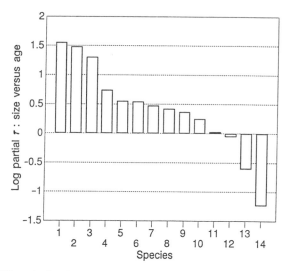

Figure 3.1: The relative importance of size and age in determining demographic fate, as measured by $\log_{10}(\tau_{SF|A}/\tau_{AF|S})$; values greater than 0 indicate that size is more important than age and vice versa. Data sources: 1 *Verbascum thapsus*; 2 *Dipsacus sylvestris*; 3 *Acropora* mortality; 4 *Porites* mortality; 5 *Salmo trutta* F3C maturity; 6 *Porites* growth and mortality; 7 *Salmo trutta* F3C sex and maturity; 8 *Acropora* growth and mortality; 9 *Pocillopora* growth and mortality; 10 *Pocillopora* mortality; 11 *Salmo trutta* F3B sex and maturity; 12 *Salmo trutta* F3B maturity; 13 *Rhododendron maximum*; 14 *Alces alces* reproduction. From Caswell (1988).

age × fate and size × fate tables are available. It is possible for the marginal size × fate table to show mortality increasing with size, even though mortality *decreases* with size within *every* age class! An analysis based on the marginal tables in this case would draw exactly the wrong conclusion about the relation between size and fate.

3.3.5 Sample Size

The conclusion that G^2 follows a χ^2 distribution is an asymptotic result that requires that the expected numbers in all cells are large. Small sample sizes naturally lead to small expected frequencies. In demographic tables, some transitions may be quite rare,[5] so that even with large total sample sizes, some expected values may be small. This can lead to difficulties in interpreting the analyses, but recent results (Fingleton 1984, p. 120) have been lowering the minimum acceptable expected frequencies. Haberman (1977),

---

[5]Transitions which are actually impossible should be indicated as "structural zeros;" they do not contribute to problems with small expected frequencies.

for example, finds that the change in G^2 between two models approximates the χ^2 distribution, even in sparse tables. Larntz (1978) reports that when expected frequencies are small, use of G^2 leads to too many rejections of the null hypothesis, which suggests that care should be taken in interpreting marginally significant G^2 values. Fingleton (1984) suggests that a table is dangerously sparse if more than 20% of the cells have expected frequencies less than one.

Tables with too many small expected frequencies for comfort can be collapsed by reducing the number of categories (e.g., Moloney 1988).

Chapter 4

Stage-Classified
Matrix Models

In this chapter, we investigate matrix models for stage-classified life cycles like those examined in Chapter 3. Instead of grouping individuals into age classes, these models classify them into stages based on the structure of the life cycle.

We begin by deriving the projection matrix from a simple graphical description of the life cycle, and then consider its analysis in exhaustive, if not exhausting, detail. Age-classified models are a special case of stage-classified models, so this material provides the analytical extension of the simulation results of Chapter 2. Finally, we consider several approaches to parameter estimation.

4.1 The Life Cycle Graph

The life cycle can be described, and the corresponding projection matrix derived, from a graphical description of the life cycle. This *life cycle graph* (e.g., Figure 4.1) is constructed as follows.

1. Choose a *projection interval*, defining the time step in the model. The structure of the graph and the resulting matrix depends on whether the time interval $(t, t + 1)$ represents a day, a week, a year, etc.

2. Define a *node* for each stage in the life cycle; number the nodes from 1 through s. The order of the numbering is irrelevant, but it is usually helpful for interpretation to assign the number 1 to a stage representing "newborn" individuals. The symbol n_i will be used interchangeably (and hopefully without creating ambiguity) to denote both node i and the abundance of individuals in stage i.

45

3. Put a directed line or *arc* from node n_i to node n_j if an individual in stage i at time t can contribute individuals (by development or reproduction) to stage j at time $t+1$. (Graphs that include transitions that take more than one interval will be introduced in Chapter 5.)

   A *path* from n_i to n_j is a sequence of arcs, traversed in the direction of the arrows, beginning at n_i and ending at n_j, and passing through no node more than once. A *loop* is a path from a node to itself. The length of a path or a loop is the number of arcs it contains. A *self-loop* is a loop of length 1, connecting a node directly to itself; it indicates that individuals in that stage at t can contribute to that stage at $t+1$.

4. Label each arc by a coefficient; the coefficient a_{ij} on the arc from n_j to n_i gives the number of individuals in stage i at time $t+1$ per individual in stage j at time t. Thus

$$n_i(t+1) = \sum_{j=1}^{s} a_{ij} n_j(t)$$

   These coefficients may be transition probabilities or reproductive outputs.

Figure 4.1 shows three examples. The first is an age-classified life cycle in which the age interval and projection interval are identical. Individuals survive, with probability P_i, to become one time unit older, and reproduce, at a rate F_i, producing new individuals in age class 1. The second is a size-classified life cycle. An individual in size class i may survive and grow to size class $i+1$ with probability G_i, or may survive and remain in size class i with probability P_i. Reproduction produces new individuals in the smallest size class. As drawn, this graph asserts that it is impossible for an individual to shrink, or to grow two or more size classes in a single time interval.

The third graph shows a hypothetical life cycle incorporating two modes of reproduction. Stage n_5 produces new n_1 individuals at a rate F_1, whereas stage n_4 produces new n_3 individuals at a rate F_2. Since the individuals produced by the second reproductive mode are equivalent to newborn individuals of the first mode that have developed to n_3, the first mode might represent sexual reproduction by seed and the second, clonal reproduction by budding or rhizome production.

4.2   The Matrix Model

The life cycle graph is more than a handy pictorial description of the life cycle. It is isomorphic to the population projection matrix **A** in the equation

$$\mathbf{n}(t+1) = \mathbf{A}\mathbf{n}(t)$$

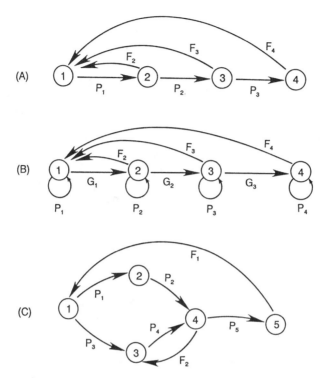

Figure 4.1: Three life cycle graphs. (A) An age-classified life cycle. (B) A size-classified life cycle in which individuals can grow no more than a single size class in the interval $(t, t + 1)$. (C) A hypothetical life cycle including both sexual and vegetative reproduction. From Caswell (1982a).

where $\mathbf{n}(t)$ is now a vector of *stage* abundances. The rule for generating the matrix is simple: a_{ij} is the coefficient on the arc from n_j to n_i in the life cycle graph.

The projection matrices corresponding to the three graphs in Figure 4.1 are

$$\mathbf{A}_a = \begin{pmatrix} 0 & F_2 & F_3 & F_4 \\ P_1 & 0 & 0 & 0 \\ 0 & P_2 & 0 & 0 \\ 0 & 0 & P_3 & 0 \end{pmatrix}$$

$$\mathbf{A}_b = \begin{pmatrix} P_1 & F_2 & F_3 & F_4 \\ G_1 & P_2 & 0 & 0 \\ 0 & G_2 & P_3 & 0 \\ 0 & 0 & G_3 & P_4 \end{pmatrix}$$

and

$$\mathbf{A}_c = \begin{pmatrix} 0 & 0 & 0 & 0 & F_1 \\ P_1 & 0 & 0 & 0 & 0 \\ P_3 & 0 & 0 & F_2 & 0 \\ 0 & P_2 & P_4 & 0 & 0 \\ 0 & 0 & 0 & P_5 & 0 \end{pmatrix}$$

The age-classified graph (Figure 4.1A) yields a Leslie matrix, as we would expect. The matrix $\mathbf{A}_b$ resulting from the size-classified graph (Figure 4.1B) is similar, but includes positive elements on the diagonal, corresponding to individuals remaining in the same size class. This model is widely applicable to size- or stage-classified populations [e.g., trees (Usher 1966, Hartshorn 1975, Enright and Ogden 1979, Pinero et al. 1984, Burns and Ogden 1985), corals (Hughes 1984, Hughes and Jackson 1985), sea turtles (Crouse et al. 1987, copepods (Caswell and Twombly (1989), and fish (Warner and Hughes 1988)]. Following Caswell (1988), I will refer to it as the *standard size-classified model*.

Note that the projection interval affects the structure of the matrix. Changing the projection interval might make possible transitions that are now excluded from the life cycle (e.g., with a longer interval, growth from size class i to $i + 2$ might be possible in Figure 4.1B).

The use of graphs in the analysis of linear equation systems was pioneered by Mason (1953, 1956, Mason and Zimmermann 1960) and Coates (1959) in the study of electrical networks. For reviews, see Chen (1976), Huggins and Entwisle (1968), and Cvetkovik et al. (1979). The life cycle graph as defined here is known technically as the Coates graph of the matrix $\mathbf{A}$; its use in demographic analysis is due to Lewis (1972, 1976), Hubbell and Werner (1979), and Caswell (1982a,b).

The careful construction of a life cycle graph forces an explicit consideration of the transitions taking place during the projection interval. This helps avoid errors in the construction of projection matrices, as shown in the following example, where the error is my own.

Example 4.1 Teasel

Werner and Caswell (1977) presented stage-classified models for eight populations of teasel (*Dipsacus sylvestris*), a monocarpic perennial plant, using a projection interval of 1 year. The life cycle was classified into seven stages:

n_1 Seeds
n_2 Dormant seeds, year 1
n_3 Dormant seeds, year 2
n_4 Small rosettes
n_5 Medium rosettes
n_6 Large rosettes
n_7 Flowering plants

The projection matrix for one of the populations (Field A) was

$$
\mathbf{A}_1 = \left(
\begin{array}{c|cccccc}
0 & 0 & 0 & 0 & 0 & 0 & 431.0 \\
\hline
0.749 & 0 & 0 & 0 & 0 & 0 & 0 \\
0 & 0.966 & 0 & 0 & 0 & 0 & 0 \\
0.008 & 0.013 & 0.010 & 0.125 & 0 & 0 & 0 \\
0.070 & 0.007 & 0 & 0.125 & 0.238 & 0 & 0 \\
0.002 & 0.001 & 0 & 0.036 & 0.245 & 0.167 & 0 \\
0 & 0 & 0 & 0 & 0.023 & 0.750 & 0
\end{array}
\right) \qquad (4.1)
$$

where the first row and column, corresponding to the seed stage, are indicated.

The life cycle graph corresponding to $\mathbf{A}_1$ is shown in Figure 4.2. It is apparent from this graph that the description of reproduction in $\mathbf{A}_1$ is fundamentally flawed. Figure 4.2 shows flowering plants in year t producing seeds in year $t + 1$, some of which germinate to produce vegetative rosettes in year $t + 2$. In reality, flowering plants in year t produce seeds that may germinate to produce rosettes in year $t + 1$. Thus, the projection matrix $\mathbf{A}_1$ has introduced an artifactual delay of 1 year in the process of reproduction.

A corrected life cycle graph is shown in Figure 4.3. The "seeds" category has disappeared; flowering plants produce dormant seeds, small rosettes, medium rosettes, and large rosettes directly. The corresponding population projection matrix is

$$
\mathbf{A}_2 = \left(
\begin{array}{cccccc}
0 & 0 & 0 & 0 & 0 & 322.38 \\
0.966 & 0 & 0 & 0 & 0 & 0 \\
0.013 & 0.010 & 0.125 & 0 & 0 & 3.448 \\
0.007 & 0 & 0.125 & 0.238 & 0 & 30.170 \\
0.008 & 0 & 0 & 0.245 & 0.167 & 0.862 \\
0 & 0 & 0 & 0.023 & 0.750 & 0
\end{array}
\right) \qquad (4.2)
$$

Notice that the entries in $\mathbf{A}_2$ correspond, except for the last column, to the entries in the lower right block of $\mathbf{A}_1$. The entries in the last column are the contributions of the flowering plants to the other stages.

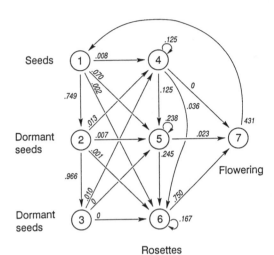

Figure 4.2: The life cycle graph derived from the projection matrix for *Dipsacus sylvestris*, Field A, in Werner and Caswell 1977. Stages: $n_1 =$ seeds, $n_2 =$ first year dormant seeds, $n_3 =$ second year dormant seeds, $n_4 =$ small rosettes, $n_5 =$ medium rosettes, $n_6 =$ large rosettes, and $n_7 =$ flowering plants.

These entries are given by the products of the coefficients for the two steps required for those contributions in Figure 4.2. That is,

$$a_{i6}^{(2)} = a_{17}^{(1)} a_{i+1,1}^{(1)} \qquad (4.3)$$

where $a_{ij}^{(1)}$ and $a_{ij}^{(2)}$ refer to the entries of $\mathbf{A}_1$ and $\mathbf{A}_2$.

The population dynamic consequences of the differences between $\mathbf{A}_1$ and $\mathbf{A}_2$ are appreciable. The eventual rate of population increase (see Section 4.3) calculated from $\mathbf{A}_1$ is $\lambda_1 = 1.797$, whereas $\mathbf{A}_2$ gives a rate of increase $\lambda_1 = 2.322$.

Example 4.2 Multiregional or age-size models

The numbering of the stages in the life cycle determines the appearance (but does not influence the mathematical properties) of $\mathbf{A}$. Different choices may be preferable for different situations. As an example, consider the life cycle graph of Figure 4.4A, which shows a population with three age classes in each of two geographical regions. The nodes of the graph are numbered so that stages n_1–n_3 correspond to the first region and stages n_4–n_6 correspond to the second region.

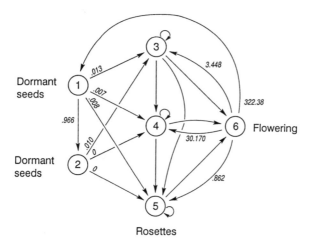

Figure 4.3: The corrected life cycle graph for *Dipsacus sylvestris*, Field A, in Werner and Caswell 1977. Stages: n_1 = first year dormant seeds, n_2 = second year dormant seeds, n_3 = small rosettes, n_4 = medium rosettes, n_5 = large rosettes, and n_6 = flowering plants.

The population vector can be written as

$$
\mathbf{n} = \left(\begin{array}{c} n_1 \\ n_2 \\ \hline n_3 \\ n_4 \\ n_5 \\ n_6 \end{array} \right) \tag{4.4}
$$

and the corresponding projection matrix is

$$
\mathbf{A} = \left(\begin{array}{ccc|ccc}
0 & a_{12} & a_{13} & 0 & 0 & 0 \\
a_{21} & 0 & 0 & a_{24} & 0 & 0 \\
0 & a_{32} & 0 & 0 & a_{35} & 0 \\
\hline
0 & 0 & 0 & 0 & a_{45} & a_{46} \\
a_{51} & 0 & 0 & a_{54} & 0 & 0 \\
0 & a_{62} & 0 & 0 & a_{65} & 0
\end{array} \right) \tag{4.5}
$$

$$
= \left(\begin{array}{c|c} \mathbf{A}_1 & \mathbf{M}_{2 \to i} \\ \hline \mathbf{M}_{1 \to 2} & \mathbf{A}_2 \end{array} \right) \tag{4.6}
$$

The submatrices $\mathbf{A}_1$ and $\mathbf{A}_2$ are Leslie matrices describing the dynamics of age classes within the two regions, whereas $\mathbf{M}_{2 \to 1}$ and $\mathbf{M}_{1 \to 2}$ describe migration between the two regions.

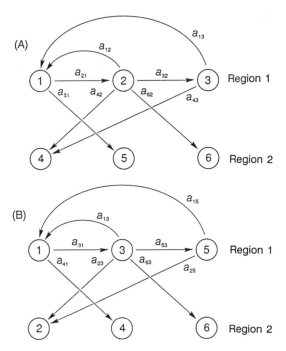

Figure 4.4: Two versions of a multiregional life cycle with three age classes and two regions. (A) Ages grouped within regions. (B) Regions grouped within age classes. Only transitions beginning in Region 1 are drawn; Region 2 is symmetrical.

Rogers (1966, 1968) introduced this model to describe multiregional human demography.[1] However, the same life cyle may be described as in Figure 4.4b, where now age classes have been lumped together, regardless of their location. The population vector is

$$\mathbf{n} = \begin{pmatrix} n_1 \\ n_2 \\ n_3 \\ n_4 \\ n_5 \\ n_6 \end{pmatrix} \tag{4.7}$$

---

[1]The model as given here ignores the possibility that offspring of individuals in one region at t could appear in the other region at $t+1$. This would produce positive entries in the first row of the migration submatrices $\mathbf{M}_{1\to2}$ and $\mathbf{M}_{2\to1}$.

and the projection matrix

$$
\mathbf{A} = \left(\begin{array}{cc|cc|cc}
0 & 0 & a_{13} & a_{14} & a_{15} & a_{16} \\
0 & 0 & a_{23} & a_{24} & a_{25} & a_{26} \\
\hline
a_{31} & a_{32} & 0 & 0 & 0 & 0 \\
a_{41} & a_{42} & 0 & 0 & 0 & 0 \\
\hline
0 & 0 & a_{53} & a_{54} & 0 & 0 \\
0 & 0 & a_{63} & a_{64} & 0 & 0
\end{array}\right)
\tag{4.8}
$$

$$
= \left(\begin{array}{c|c|c}
0 & \mathbf{F}_2 & \mathbf{F}_3 \\
\hline
\mathbf{P}_1 & 0 & 0 \\
\hline
0 & \mathbf{P}_2 & 0
\end{array}\right)
\tag{4.9}
$$

This projection matrix has the age-classified form, but its entries are submatrices, the entries of which combine information on survival, reproduction, and migration. The estimation of these parameters will be considered in Section 4.8.3. Rogers (1985), Schoen (1988), and others have studied this model extensively for use in multiregional human demography. Interesting ecological applications are due to Fahrig (Fahrig et al. 1983, Fahrig and Merriam 1985, Lefkovitch and Fahrig 1985), who studied the effects of demographic stochasticity and migration on extinction in the mouse *Peromyscus leucopus*, Davis (1984), who developed models based on both age and stage for the copepod *Pseudocalanus* sp., with movement generated by the oceanic circulation on Georges Bank, and Horvitz and Schemske (1986), who studied the herbaceous perennial *Calathea ovandensis*, with regions defined as patches in different successional states and transitions between patches generated by a stochastic succession model.

Law (1983) independently introduced a matrix of the same form to describe populations classified by age and size, rather than age and region. Law made the reasonable assumption that all individuals are born in the smallest size class, which requires that the nonzero elements of the fertility submatrices $\mathbf{F}_i$ be restricted to the first row.

We have arrived once again at a matrix projection model for population dynamics, $\mathbf{n}(t+1) = \mathbf{A}\mathbf{n}(t)$, where $\mathbf{A}$ is no longer limited to the age-classified Leslie matrix form. As with the age-classified model in Chapter 2, numerical projection by repeated matrix multiplication is still the simplest form of analysis. However, it is limited to the analysis of specific initial conditions. We would prefer to draw more general and widely applicable conclusions. To do so, we turn in the next sections to analytical approaches based on the methods of matrix algebra.

4.3   Solution of the Projection Equation

We begin by finding a solution to the projection equation

$$\mathbf{n}(t+1) = \mathbf{A}\mathbf{n}(t) \tag{4.10}$$

given an initial population $\mathbf{n}(0)$. We begin by writing $\mathbf{n}(0)$ as a linear combination of the right eigenvectors $\mathbf{w}_i$ of $\mathbf{A}$:

$$\mathbf{n}(0) = c_1\mathbf{w}_1 + c_2\mathbf{w}_2 + \cdots + c_s\mathbf{w}_s \tag{4.11}$$

for some set of coefficients c_i. The linear independence of the eigenvectors[2] of a matrix guarantees that we can write any $\mathbf{n}(0)$ in this form (see Appendix A for eigenvalues and eigenvectors). The coefficients c_i depend on the initial vector $\mathbf{n}(0)$. Equation (4.11) can be rewritten

$$\mathbf{n}(0) = \mathbf{W}\mathbf{c}$$

where $\mathbf{W}$ is a matrix whose columns are the eigenvectors $\mathbf{w}_i$, and $\mathbf{c}$ is a vector whose elements are the c_i. Thus

$$\mathbf{c} = \mathbf{W}^{-1}\mathbf{n}(0) \tag{4.12}$$

Now multiply $\mathbf{n}(0)$ by $\mathbf{A}$ to obtain $\mathbf{n}(1)$:

$$\begin{aligned}
\mathbf{n}(1) &= \mathbf{A}\mathbf{n}(0) \\
&= \sum_i c_i\mathbf{A}\mathbf{w}_i \\
&= \sum_i c_i\lambda_i\mathbf{w}_i
\end{aligned}$$

where λ_i is the eigenvalue corresponding to $\mathbf{w}_i$. If we multiply by $\mathbf{A}$ again, we get

$$\begin{aligned}
\mathbf{n}(2) &= \mathbf{A}\mathbf{n}(1) \\
&= \sum_i c_i\lambda_i\mathbf{A}\mathbf{w}_i \\
&= \sum_i c_i\lambda_i^2\mathbf{w}_i
\end{aligned}$$

It should not be hard to convince yourself that continuing this process yields the solution

$$\mathbf{n}(t) = \sum_i c_i\lambda_i^t\mathbf{w}_i \tag{4.13}$$

---

[2]I assume throughout this book that the eigenvalues of the projection matrix are distinct; this guarantees the linear independence of the eigenvectors.

Compare this to the *scalar* difference equation

$$n(t+1) = an(t)$$

the solution of which is

$$n(t) = n(0)a^t$$

In the case of an s-dimensional matrix, the solution is not a single exponential, but a weighted sum of s exponentials, the weights determined by the initial conditions.

The long-term behavior of $\mathbf{n}(t)$, given by (4.13), depends on the eigenvalues λ_i as they are raised to higher and higher powers. If λ_i is real, then

- if $\lambda_i > 1$, then λ_i^t increases exponentially,

- if $\lambda_i = 1$, then $\lambda_i^t = 1$,

- if $0 < \lambda_i < 1$, then λ_i^t decreases exponentially,

- if $-1 < \lambda_i < 0$, then λ_i^t exhibits damped oscillations,

- if $\lambda_i = -1$, then λ_i^t exhibits undamped oscillations, and

- if $\lambda_i < -1$, then λ_i^t exhibits diverging oscillations.

When λ_i is a complex number, $\lambda_i = a + bi$, we can write it in polar coordinates

$$\lambda_i = |\lambda_i|(\cos\theta + i\sin\theta)$$

where $|\lambda_i| = \sqrt{a^2 + b^2}$ and $\theta = \tan^{-1}(b/a)$ is the angle formed by λ_i in the complex plane. Raising λ_i to the tth power yields

$$\lambda_i^t = |\lambda_i|^t(\cos\theta t + i\sin\theta t) \tag{4.14}$$

Thus, as a complex eigenvalue is raised to higher and higher powers, its magnitude $|\lambda_i|$ increases or decreases exponentially, depending on whether $|\lambda_i|$ is greater or less than 1. Its angle in the complex plane increases by θ each time step, completing an oscillation with a period of $2\pi/\theta$.

Thus (4.13) decomposes the growth of a stage-classified population into a set of exponential contributions, one for each eigenvalue. If $|\lambda_i| < 1$, its contribution decays, smoothly if $\lambda_i > 0$, with damped oscillations if $\lambda_i < 0$ or complex. If $|\lambda_i| > 1$, its contribution to population growth grows exponentially, smoothly if $\lambda_i > 0$, with oscillations if $\lambda_i < 0$ or complex. Knowledge of the set of eigenvalues of the projection matrix (referred to as the *eigenvalue spectrum* of the matrix) thus reveals a great deal about the resulting population dynamics. Much of this information is independent of the particular initial population, since initial conditions affect only the coefficients c_i, and not the eigenvalues or eigenvectors.

Example 4.3 An age-classified population

Keyfitz and Flieger (1971) give an age-classified matrix, with 5-year age classes, for the United States population in 1966. The entries are

i	F_i	P_i
1	0	0.99670
2	0.00102	0.99837
3	0.08515	0.99780
4	0.30574	0.99672
5	0.40002	0.99607
6	0.28061	0.99472
7	0.15260	0.99240
8	0.06420	0.98867
9	0.01483	0.98274
10	0.00089	

The eigenvalues of this matrix (in decreasing order of absolute magnitude), their magnitudes, and the angle θ defined in the complex plane by each are

λ_i	$|\lambda_i|$	θ
1.0498	1.0498	0.0000
$0.3112 + 0.7442i$	0.8067	1.1747
$0.3112 - 0.7442i$	0.8067	-1.1747
$-0.3939 + 0.3658i$	0.5375	-0.7484
$-0.3939 - 0.3658i$	0.5375	0.7484
$0.0115 + 0.5221i$	0.5223	1.5487
$0.0115 - 0.5221i$	0.5223	-1.5487
$-0.4112 + 0.1204i$	0.4284	-0.2849
$-0.4112 - 0.1204i$	0.4284	0.2849
-0.0852	0.0852	0.0000

Figure 4.5 shows this spectrum plotted in the complex plane. (The computation of eigenvalues and eigenvectors is discussed in Section 4.7.)

The eigenvalues λ_i correspond to the roots r_i of Lotka's equation (2.35). A comparison of the two solutions ($\mathbf{n}(t) = \sum c_i \lambda_i^t$ and $B(t) = \sum Q_i \exp(r_i t)$) shows that $\lambda = \exp(r)$, and $r = \ln \lambda$. However, when λ_i is complex, this mapping from λ to r is not one-to-one (Keyfitz 1968).

Let $\lambda = a + bi$ and let $r = x + yi$. Then $x = \ln \sqrt{a^2 + b^2}$ and $y = \tan^{-1}(b/a)$. The set of λ with $|\lambda| < 1$ thus map into the set of r with $x < 0$,

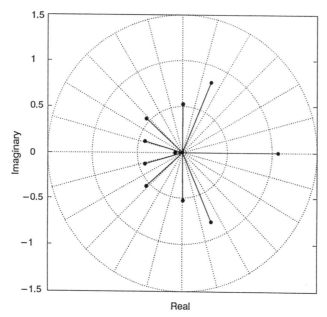

Figure 4.5: The eigenvalue spectrum for the projection matrix for the United States population in 1966, plotted in the complex plane.

and vice versa. However, if $\exp(x + yi) = \lambda$, so also does $\exp(x + yi + 2\pi m)$, for $m = 0, \pm 1, \pm 2, \ldots$. Thus the set of r_i corresponding to λ_i is repeated in an infinite set of strips of width 2π along the imaginary axis.

4.4 Asymptotic Behavior and the Strong Ergodic Theorem

The long-term dynamics of population growth are determined by the asymptotic properties of $\sum c_i \lambda_i^t$ as $t \to \infty$. Thus, the study of asymptotic dynamics relies heavily on the properties of the eigenvalues of the projection matrix.

One of the most important aspects of asymptotic behavior is ergodicity. A population is said to be ergodic if its eventual behavior is independent of its initial state (Cohen 1979c). Demographic ergodic theorems will appear repeatedly throughout the following chapters.

4.4.1 The Perron-Frobenius Theorem

A matrix will be said to be *nonnegative* if all its elements are greater than or equal to zero, and *positive* if all its elements are strictly greater than zero. We can safely assume that a population projection matrix is nonnegative, because negative entries imply the possibility of negative organisms. But, as we have seen, they are not usually positive.

A set of results known collectively as the Perron-Frobenius theorem describes the properties of the eigenvalues of nonnegative matrices. Two additional properties of the matrix are important for this theorem: irreducibility and primitivity.

Irreducibility

A nonnegative matrix, and its associated life cycle graph, is *irreducible* if its life cycle graph is strongly connected, i.e., if there is a path in the graph from every node to every other node (Rosenblatt 1957). A reducible life cycle graph contains at least one stage that cannot contribute, by any developmental path, to some other stage or stages.

Any reducible matrix can be rearranged, by interchanging rows and columns into a normal form:

$$\mathbf{A} = \left(\begin{array}{c|c} \mathbf{B} & \mathbf{0} \\ \hline \mathbf{C} & \mathbf{D} \end{array} \right) \tag{4.15}$$

where the square submatrix $\mathbf{B}$ is either irreducible or can itself be divided to eventually yield a series of irreducible diagonal blocks (Gantmacher 1959).

Most life cycle graphs are irreducible. One exception (Figure 4.6a) to this generality occurs in age-classified life cycles with postreproductive age classes, which cannot contribute to any younger age class. Another exception might arise in spatially structured populations with one-way dispersal patterns. Figure 4.6b shows an example; newborn individuals in habitat 1 may migrate to habitat 2, but individuals in habitat 2 make no contribution to any stage in habitat 1.

Primitivity

A nonnegative matrix $\mathbf{A}$ is *primitive* if it becomes positive when raised to sufficiently high powers, i.e., if $\mathbf{A}^k$ is strictly positive for some $k > 0$. Any primitive matrix is irreducible.

Primitivity can be evaluated from the life cycle graph; a graph is primitive if it is irreducible and the greatest common divisor of the lengths of its loops is 1 (Rosenblatt 1957). An imprimitive matrix is said to be *cyclic*, and to have an *index of imprimitivity d* equal to the greatest common divisor of the loop lengths in the life cycle graph.

It follows that a sufficient condition for primitivity of an irreducible age-classified model is the existence of any two adjacent age classes with positive fertility (Sykes 1969, Demetrius 1971). For irreducible stage-classified models, a sufficient condition for primitivity is the presence of at least one positive diagonal element.

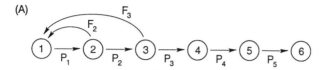

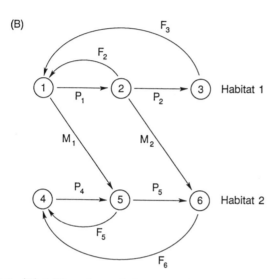

Figure 4.6: (A) A life cycle graph for an age-classified population including postreproductive age classes. The resulting matrix is reducible, because postreproductive age classes cannot contribute to any younger age class. (B) A hypothetical reducible life cycle graph for a spatially structured population with one-way migration. The resulting matrix is reducible because individuals in habitat 2 make no contribution to any stage in habitat 1.

In practice, most population projection matrices are primitive. The only significant exceptions are age-classified matrices with a single reproductive age class (e.g., Figure 2.6), which might be appropriate for semelparous species such as monocarpic perennial bamboos (Janzen 1976), periodical cicadas, or Pacific salmon. The life cycle graph for such an organism (Figure 4.7) contains only one loop of length d, where d is the age of reproduction. Imprimitive matrices also arise in models of annual plants (Section 5.8) and in certain formulations of population growth in periodic environments (Gourley and Lawrence 1977; see Section 8.2.2).

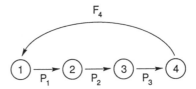

Figure 4.7: An imprimitive life cycle graph for an age-classified population with one fixed age at reproduction. There is only one loop in the graph, with a length equal to the age at reproduction.

Evaluating Irreducibility and Primitivity Numerically

It is easy to evaluate irreducibility and primitivity of small matrices directly from the life cycle graph, but large matrices can be difficult. Horn and Johnson (1985, pp. 507–520) summarize several theorems that provide numerical methods to evaluate irreducibility and primitivity. Suppose that $\mathbf{A}$ is a nonnegative $s \times s$ matrix. Then

- $\mathbf{A}$ is irreducible if and only if $(\mathbf{I} + \mathbf{A})^{s-1}$ is positive.

- Let c denote the length of the shortest loop in the life cycle graph of $\mathbf{A}$. Then $\mathbf{A}$ is primitive if and only if $\mathbf{A}^{s+c(s-2)}$ is positive. Since the exponent increases with c, this result can be applied using the length of *any* loop in the life cycle graph.

- $\mathbf{A}$ is primitive if and only if $\mathbf{A}^{s^2-3s+2}$ is positive.

Thus, for example, a 20×20 matrix can be checked for irreducibility by seeing if $(\mathbf{I} + \mathbf{A})^{19}$ is positive. If the graph of $\mathbf{A}$ contains a loop of length 4, $\mathbf{A}$ is primitive if and only if $\mathbf{A}^{92}$ is positive. Without knowing the lengths of any loops, the primitivity of $\mathbf{A}$ can be checked by seeing if $\mathbf{A}^{342}$ is positive. The calculation of powers in these results is made easier by repeated squaring of the matrix, i.e., calculating $\mathbf{A}^2$, $\mathbf{A}^4$, $\mathbf{A}^8$, etc. The primitivity of a 20×20 matrix can be evaluated by calculating $\mathbf{A}^{512}$ using only 9 matrix multiplications.

The Perron-Frobenius Theorem

The Perron-Frobenius theorem[3] describes the properties of the eigenvalues of a nonnegative matrix $\mathbf{A}$ as follows:

1. If $\mathbf{A}$ is positive, or nonnegative and primitive, then there exists a real eigenvalue $\lambda_1 > 0$ which is a simple root of the characteristic equation. This eigenvalue is strictly greater than the magnitude of any other

---

[3]For proofs see Gantmacher (1959), Seneta (1981), and Horn and Johnson (1985).

eigenvalue, $\lambda_1 > |\lambda_i|$ for $i \neq 1$. The right and left eigenvectors $\mathbf{w}_1$ and $\mathbf{v}_1$ corresponding to λ_1 are real and strictly positive. The eigenvalue λ_1 may not be the only real positive eigenvalue, but if there are others, they do not have nonnegative eigenvectors.

2. If $\mathbf{A}$ is irreducible but imprimitive (cyclic) with index of imprimitivity d, then there exists a real eigenvalue $\lambda_1 > 0$ which is a simple root of the characteristic equation, and which has associated right and left eigenvectors $\mathbf{w}_1 > 0$ and $\mathbf{v}_1 > 0$. The eigenvalues λ_i satisfy $\lambda_1 \geq |\lambda_i|$ for $i \neq 1$, but there are $d - 1$ complex eigenvalues equal in magnitude to λ_1, whose values are given by $\lambda_1 \exp(2k\pi i/d)$, $k = 1, 2, \ldots, d - 1$.

3. If $\mathbf{A}$ is reducible, there exists a real eigenvalue $\lambda_1 \geq 0$ with corresponding right and left eigenvectors $\mathbf{w}_1 \geq 0$ and $\mathbf{v}_1 \geq 0$. This eigenvalue $\lambda_1 \geq |\lambda_i|$ for all $i \neq 1$.

The eigenvalue λ_1 is called the *dominant eigenvalue* of $\mathbf{A}$.

4.4.2 Population Growth Rate and the Stable Stage Distribution

The value of the Perron-Frobenius theorem is that the dominant eigenvalue λ_1 completely determines the ergodic properties of population growth. Consider $\mathbf{n}(t)$ from (4.13):

$$\mathbf{n}(t) = c_1 \lambda_1^t \mathbf{w}_1 + c_2 \lambda_2^t \mathbf{w}_2 + c_3 \lambda_3^t \mathbf{w}_3 + \cdots$$

where the eigenvalues are numbered in order of decreasing magnitude. If λ_1 is strictly greater in magnitude than all the other eigenvalues, it will eventually dominate all the other terms in (4.13). Regardless of the initial population, the other exponential terms will eventually become negligible and the population will grow at a rate given by λ_1 and with a structure proportional to $\mathbf{w}_1$. Dividing both sides by λ_1^t yields

$$\frac{\mathbf{n}(t)}{\lambda_1^t} = c_1 \mathbf{w}_1 + c_2 \left(\frac{\lambda_2}{\lambda_1}\right)^t + c_3 \left(\frac{\lambda_3}{\lambda_1}\right)^t + \cdots \tag{4.16}$$

If $\lambda_1 > |\lambda_2|$ (as must be the case for a primitive matrix), then

$$\lim_{t \to \infty} \frac{\mathbf{n}(t)}{\lambda_1^t} = c_1 \mathbf{w}_1 \tag{4.17}$$

This result is known as the strong ergodic theorem (Cohen 1979c); it shows that if $\mathbf{A}$ is primitive the long-term dynamics of the population are described by the population growth rate λ_1 and the stable population structure $\mathbf{w}_1$. The growth rate λ_1 is related to the intrinsic rate of increase r obtained from Lotka's equation: $\lambda_1 = e^r$ or $r = \ln \lambda_1$.

The stable population structure (the stable age distribution in the age-classified case, the stable stage distribution in general) is given by $\mathbf{w}_1$. Since eigenvectors are determined only up to a scalar constant, $\mathbf{w}_1$ can be scaled as desired, for example so that its elements sum to 1 and represent proportions, or so that they sum to 100 and represent percentages.

Example 4.4 An age-classified model

The eigenvector $\mathbf{w}_1$ corresponding to $\lambda_1 = 1.0498$ for the United States population in 1966 (Example 4.3) is

$$
\mathbf{w}_1 = \begin{pmatrix} 0.1169 \\ 0.1110 \\ 0.1056 \\ 0.1003 \\ 0.0953 \\ 0.0904 \\ 0.0857 \\ 0.0810 \\ 0.0763 \\ 0.0714 \end{pmatrix} \tag{4.18}
$$

Here the entries of $\mathbf{w}_1$ are scaled so that they sum to 1, thus giving the proportions in the different age classes.

Formulas for the stable stage distribution can be derived from the life cycle graph (see Chapter 6). However, the formula for $\mathbf{w}_1$ in the special case of an age-classified matrix is well known. Let $\mathbf{Aw} = \lambda\mathbf{w}$, where $\mathbf{A}$ is a Leslie matrix. The second through sth rows of the matrix produce the relations

$$
\begin{aligned}
P_1 w_1 &= \lambda w_2 \\
P_2 w_2 &= \lambda w_3 \\
P_3 w_3 &= \lambda w_4 \\
&\ \vdots \\
P_{s-1} w_{s-1} &= \lambda w_s
\end{aligned}
$$

Since the eigenvector $\mathbf{w}$ can be scaled at will, let $w_1 = 1$. Then it follows that

$$
\begin{aligned}
w_1 &= 1 \\
w_2 &= P_1 \lambda^{-1} \\
w_3 &= P_1 P_2 \lambda^{-2} \\
&\ \vdots \\
w_s &= P_1 P_2 \cdots P_{s-1} \lambda^{-s+1}
\end{aligned} \tag{4.19}
$$

4.4.3 Asymptotic Behavior of Imprimitive Matrices

An irreducible but imprimitive matrix **A** has d eigenvalues with the same absolute magnitude, where d is the index of imprimitivity. One of these eigenvalues (λ_1) is real and positive; the others are negative or complex, forming angles in the complex plane of $\theta = 2\pi/d$, $4\pi/d, \ldots, (d-1)2\pi/d$. The common magnitude of this set of d eigenvalues is strictly greater than the magnitude of any of the remaining eigenvalues, so as $t \to \infty$ only the d leading eigenvalues have any influence on population dynamics.

Cull and Vogt (1973, 1974, 1976) and Svirezhev and Logofet (1983) discuss this case in detail. Because of the complex eigenvalues, the stage distribution does not converge, but instead oscillates with a period d, as does the total population size. Suppose for the sake of example that $d = 3$, and consider (4.16). The eigenvalues λ_2 and λ_3 are now complex, and $|\lambda_2| = |\lambda_3| = \lambda_1$. Using (4.14) for λ_i^t, the limit (4.17) is now

$$\lim_{t\to\infty} \frac{\mathbf{n}(t)}{\lambda_1^t} = c_1\mathbf{w}_1 + c_2(\cos\theta t + i\sin\theta t)\mathbf{w}_2 + c_3(\cos\theta t - i\sin\theta t)\mathbf{w}_3 \quad (4.20)$$

where $\theta = 2\pi/3$. Since $\mathbf{w}_2$ and $\mathbf{w}_3$ and c_2 and c_3 are complex conjugates, the imaginary parts of (4.20) cancel out, so that $\mathbf{n}(t)$ is real, as it should be.

From (4.20) it follows that $\mathbf{w}_1$ is still a stable stage distribution in the sense that, if $\mathbf{n}(0)$ is proportional to $\mathbf{w}_1$, so that $c_1 = c_2 = 0$, the population will remain at that structure for all time. However, $\mathbf{w}_1$ is *not* stable in the sense that an initial population not proportional to $\mathbf{w}_1$ will converge to it. Instead, the limit in (4.20) is periodic, with period d. (See the numerical example in Figure 2.6, where $d = 3$.)

Cull and Vogt (1973) show that the average population vector, where the average is taken over the period of the oscillation, converges to $\mathbf{w}_1$ and grows at a rate λ_1:

$$\lim_{t\to\infty} \frac{1}{d} \sum_{j=1}^{d} \frac{\mathbf{n}(t+j)}{\lambda_1^{t+j}} = c_1\mathbf{w}_1 \quad (4.21)$$

The oscillatory asymptotic dynamics of imprimitive matrices makes intuitive sense in the context of the life cycle graph. The existence of an index of imprimitivity $d > 1$ means that there is an inherent cyclicity in the life cycle; all loops are multiples of some common loop length. This cyclicity is reflected in the dynamics of the population. Consider two consecutive stages, n_1 and n_2, and suppose that they lie on two loops, one of length x and the other of length y. It is possible to get from n_1 to n_2 in 1 step, in $x+1$ steps, in $y+1$ steps, in $2x+1$ steps, in $2y+1$ steps, in $x+y+1$ steps, or, in general, in $ax+by+1$ steps, for $a, b = 0, 1, 2, \ldots$. Suppose x and y share a common divisor $d > 1$, so that $y = dy'$ and $x = dx'$, where x' and

y' are relatively prime. Then the possible number of steps in the transition from n_1 to n_2 is

$$ax + by + 1 = d(ax' + bx') + 1$$

Changes in a or b change this expression only by integral multiples of d steps. On the other hand, if x and y share no common divisor, then $d = 1$ and the number of steps between n_1 and n_2 can be adjusted as finely as you like.

4.4.4   Asymptotic Behavior of Reducible Matrices

There are two options in the analysis of a reducible life cycle graph. Consider the matrix in normal form (4.15). Let S_1 and S_2 denote the sets of stages in the submatrix $\mathbf{B}$ and $\mathbf{D}$. The stages in S_1 communicate with each other, and may (if $\mathbf{C}$ is nonzero) contribute to S_2, but the stages in S_2 can make no contribution to those in S_1. Thus the dynamics of S_1 are independent of the dynamics of S_2, and the irreducible matrix $\mathbf{B}$ can be analyzed by itself.

> ### Example 4.5 Populations with postreproductive age classes
>
> The life cycle graph for a population including postreproductive age classes (Figure 4.6a) can be put into normal form as
>
> $$\left(\begin{array}{c|c} \mathbf{B} & \mathbf{0} \\ \hline \mathbf{C} & \mathbf{D} \end{array}\right) = \left(\begin{array}{ccc|cc} 0 & F_2 & F_3 & 0 & 0 \\ P_1 & 0 & 0 & 0 & 0 \\ 0 & P_2 & 0 & 0 & 0 \\ \hline 0 & 0 & P_3 & 0 & 0 \\ 0 & 0 & 0 & P_4 & 0 \end{array}\right) \tag{4.22}$$
>
> Here $S_1 = \{n_1, n_2, n_3\}$ and $S_2 = \{n_4, n_5\}$. The irreducible submatrix $\mathbf{B}$ is the population projection matrix for the reproductive age classes. The submatrix $\mathbf{D}$ contains the survival probabilities of the postreproductive age classes. The 10×10 matrix for the United States population in Example 4.3 is based on 5-year age classes; it actually represents the submatrix $\mathbf{B}$, but the vital rates of postreproductive females (over 50 years old) have no impact on the eigenvalues.

A second option is to analyze the entire matrix $\mathbf{A}$, including all the submatrices. The ergodic properties of the population are now complicated by questions of initial conditions. The rearrangement of $\mathbf{A}$ into normal form decomposes the state space into a set of invariant subspaces (Gantmacher 1959), given in the case of (4.15) by S_2 and $S_1 + S_2$. Any initial population in one of these subspaces will remain in that subspace. This means the asymptotic dynamics are sensitive to initial conditions (e.g., an initial population in S_2, composed strictly of postreproductive individuals, is never going to produce individuals in S_1).

Let λ_1 be the dominant eigenvalue of $\mathbf{A}$ and $\mathbf{w}$ its associated eigenvector. Gantmacher (1959, Theorem 6 of Chapter 13) shows that $\mathbf{w}_1$ is strictly positive if and only if λ_1 is also an eigenvalue of the submatrix $\mathbf{B}$, but not of $\mathbf{D}$. In this case, analysis of $\mathbf{B}$ alone yields the same eventual growth rate as the analysis of the entire matrix $\mathbf{A}$, and the eventual stable population has individuals in every stage. However, if λ_1 is an eigenvalue of $\mathbf{D}$ rather than of $\mathbf{B}$, then the stable population has zero entries for stages corresponding to $\mathbf{B}$.

Example 4.6 A geographically subdivided population

The matrix corresponding to the geographically subdivided population in Figure 4.6 is

$$
\left(\begin{array}{c|c} \mathbf{B} & \mathbf{0} \\ \hline \mathbf{C} & \mathbf{D} \end{array}\right) = \left(\begin{array}{ccc|ccc} 0 & F_2 & F_3 & 0 & 0 & 0 \\ P_1 & 0 & 0 & 0 & 0 & 0 \\ 0 & P_2 & 0 & 0 & 0 & 0 \\ \hline 0 & 0 & 0 & 0 & F_5 & F_6 \\ M_1 & 0 & 0 & P_4 & 0 & 0 \\ 0 & M_2 & 0 & 0 & P_5 & 0 \end{array}\right) \tag{4.23}
$$

The invariant coordinate subspaces are $S_2 = \{4,5,6\}$ and $S_1 + S_2 = \{1,2,3,4,5,6\}$. An initial population in S_2 (i.e., consisting only of individuals in habitat 2) will remain in S_2. An initial population consisting of individuals in both habitats may continue to include individuals in both habitats, provided that reproduction in habitat 1 is sufficient to prevent that subpopulation from dying out.

Set all the survival probabilities in (4.23) to 0.5, and the migration probabilities M_1 and M_2 to 0.2. Let $F_2 = 1$ and $F_3 = 2$. The relation between the eigenvalues of $\mathbf{B}$ and $\mathbf{D}$ now depends on the fertilities F_5 and F_6 in habitat 2. When $F_5 = 1.5$ and $F_6 = 3$, the dominant eigenvalue of $\mathbf{A}$ is 1.1777, but the dominant eigenvalue of $\mathbf{B}$ is only 1.000. The stable stage distribution $\mathbf{w}_1$ of $\mathbf{A}$ is

$$
\mathbf{w}_1 = \left(\begin{array}{c} 0 \\ 0 \\ 0 \\ \hline 1.000 \\ 0.425 \\ 0.180 \end{array}\right)
$$

The population in habitat 2 has a higher rate of growth, and eventually dominates the stage distribution. However, when $F_5 = 0.9$ and

$F_6 = 1.9$ the dominant eigenvalue of $\mathbf{A}$ is 1.000, whereas the dominant eigenvalue of $\mathbf{D}$ is only 0.9695. The stable stage distribution is then

$$\mathbf{w}_1 = \begin{pmatrix} 0.203 \\ 0.101 \\ 0.051 \\ \hline 1.000 \\ 0.541 \\ 0.270 \end{pmatrix}$$

and the stable population includes individuals in both habitats.

4.5   Reproductive Value

We turn now to the important but confusing (and often confused) concept of reproductive value. Fisher (1930) introduced the idea:

> We may ask, not only about the newly born, but about persons of any chosen age, what is the present value of their future offspring; and if the present value is calculated at the rate determined as before, the question has the definite meaning — To what extent will persons of this age, on the average, contribute to the ancestry of future generations? The question is one of some interest, since the direct action of Natural Selection must be proportional to this contribution.

The rate Fisher mentions is the intrinsic rate of increase, $r = \ln \lambda_1$, which he had equated with the compound interest rate of an investment. He goes on to say that the present value of the future offspring of a person of age x is "easily seen to be given by the equation"

$$\frac{v(x)}{v(0)} = \frac{e^{rx}}{l(x)} \int_x^\infty e^{-ra} l(a) m(a) \, da \qquad (4.24)$$

With all due respect to R.A. Fisher, I have yet to meet anyone who finds this equation "easily seen." Fisher's claim that the action of natural selection is proportional to $v(x)$ also requires great care in interpretation (Chapter 6).

The amount of future reproduction, the probablity of surviving to realize it, and the time required for the offspring to be produced all enter into the reproductive value of an age-class. Typical reproductive values calculated from (4.24) are low at birth, increase to a peak near the age of first reproduction, and then decline. The low value at birth reflects the probability that a newborn individual will die before reproducing and the delay before reaching reproductive age. This delay is important because, in an increasing population, the value of delayed offspring is "diluted" by the larger population size when they are produced. Reproductive value eventually declines with age as reproductive rates decline and mortality rates increase. For postreproductive individuals, $v(x) = 0$.

The stage-specific reproductive value is given by the left eigenvector $\mathbf{v}_1$ corresponding to λ_1, i.e., by the vector $\mathbf{v}_1$ satisfying

$$\mathbf{v}_1^* \mathbf{A} = \lambda_1 \mathbf{v}_1^* \tag{4.25}$$

We have already noted that the coefficients c_i in the solution (4.13) can be written as

$$\mathbf{c} = \mathbf{W}^{-1} \mathbf{n}(0)$$

where $\mathbf{W}$ is a matrix whose columns are the right eigenvectors $\mathbf{w}_i$. The population eventually grows as $\mathbf{n}(t) = c_1 \lambda_1^t \mathbf{w}_1$. The rate of growth λ_1 is independent of initial conditions, but different choices of $\mathbf{n}(0)$ will change the value of c_1, and thus affect population size at any time t (e.g., Figure 2.5).

Let $\mathbf{\Lambda}$ denote the matrix with the λ_i on the diagonal and zeroes elsewhere. Then $\mathbf{AW} = \mathbf{W\Lambda}$, $\mathbf{\Lambda} = \mathbf{W}^{-1}\mathbf{AW}$, and $\mathbf{W}^{-1}\mathbf{A} = \mathbf{\Lambda W}^{-1}$. This implies that the rows of $\mathbf{W}^{-1}$ are the left eigenvectors[4] $\mathbf{v}_i$ of $\mathbf{A}$. Write $\mathbf{V}$ for $\mathbf{W}^{-1}$. Then

$$\mathbf{c} = \mathbf{V}\mathbf{n}(0) \tag{4.26}$$

Thus c_1 is the scalar product of the first row of $\mathbf{V}$ and $\mathbf{n}(0)$; that is, $c_1 = \langle \mathbf{v}_1, \mathbf{n}(0) \rangle$. This is a weighted combination of the abundance of the different stages in the initial population, the weights being the the elements of $\mathbf{v}_1$.

What do these weights mean? Consider several populations with identical life cycles, starting out with different initial conditions. Asymptotically, they will all grow at the same rate λ_1, but their relative sizes at any time will be proportional to c_1, and will thus reflect the initial population vector. If the initial population is concentrated in stages with large entries in $\mathbf{v}_1$ (i.e., high reproductive value), the eventual population will be larger at any time than if the initial population is concentrated in stages with low reproductive value. Thus "reproductive value" measures the value of an individual as a seed for future population growth.

---

[4] More accurately, they are the complex conjugates of the left eigenvectors; see Appendix A. Since we are interested here in $\mathbf{v}_1$, which is real, the distinction makes no difference.

Example 4.7 An age-classified population

The reproductive value vector $\mathbf{v}_1$ for the United States population (Example 4.3) is

$$\mathbf{v}_1 = \begin{pmatrix} 1.0000 \\ 1.0532 \\ 1.1064 \\ 1.0787 \\ 0.8293 \\ 0.4724 \\ 0.2165 \\ 0.0752 \\ 0.0149 \\ 0.0008 \end{pmatrix} \tag{4.27}$$

Note the increase in v_i from birth to a maximum in age class 3 (ages $10 \leq x \leq 15$), and its subsequent decline.

As with the stable age distribution (4.19), the formula for the reproductive value of age-classified populations can be written down directly from the matrix equations $\mathbf{v}^* \mathbf{A} = \lambda \mathbf{v}^*$. Letting $v_1 = 1$, we obtain

$$\begin{aligned} v_1 &= 1 \\ v_2 &= F_2 \lambda^{-1} + P_2 F_3 \lambda^{-2} + P_2 P_3 F_4 \lambda^{-3} \\ &\quad + \cdots + P_2 P_3 \cdots P_{s-1} F_s \lambda^{-s+1} \\ &\vdots \\ v_s &= F_s \lambda^{-1} \end{aligned}$$

or in general

$$v_i = \sum_{j=i}^{s} \left(\prod_{h=i}^{j-1} P_h \right) F_j \lambda^{-j+1} \tag{4.28}$$

Equation (4.28) is a discrete version of Fisher's formula (4.24).

4.6   Transient Behavior and Convergence

The dominant eigenvalue of $\mathbf{A}$ gives the asymptotic population growth rate that would result if the present environmental conditions were maintained indefinitely. That is, of course, unlikely to happen, and it is of some interest to derive measures of the short-term or *transient behavior* of the population. The simplest approach is numerical projection, which shows exactly what happens to the population from any specific initial condition.

Example 4.8 Transient dynamics of teasel

Caswell and Werner's (1978) study of eight populations of teasel (*Dipsacus sylvestris*) addressed the question of whether the asymptotic properties of the populations, as revealed by λ_1, $\mathbf{w}_1$, and $\mathbf{v}_1$, provided accurate short-term information about the relative performance of the populations. Since teasel is a weedy species inhabiting early successional old-fields, it is unlikely that environmental conditions will remain constant long enough for the asymptotic properties of the population to be revealed.

For each population, an initial population of 100 seeds was projected for 10 years. Two measures of performance were calculated: cumulative seed production and rosette cover. Because teasel is restricted to early successional habitats, its regional success may depend on the cumulative production of seeds by local populations during the relatively short time that they persist. On the other hand, dense stands of teasel rosettes can monopolize space and prevent invasion by later successional species. Thus local persistence might depend on the development of a large area of rosette cover.

The results of the calculation are shown in Figure 4.8. (Note that this figure is based on the size-classified matrices suffering from the error described in Example 4.1.) The different fields varied considerably in both measures. Rosette cover fluctuated significantly during the first few years following colonization, which might be important in determining colonization success.

A more general approach to transient behavior is to use the solution (4.13) to study the rate of convergence to the stable population structure, and the oscillations produced by the subdominant eigenvalues during convergence (e.g., Lefkovitch 1971, Usher 1976, Horst 1977, Longstaff 1984, Rago and Goodyear 1987).

4.6.1 The Damping Ratio and Convergence

The eventual rate of convergence to the stable stage distribution is governed by the eigenvalue(s) of the second largest absolute magnitude. From (4.16) it is clear that, all other things being equal, convergence will be more rapid the larger λ_1 is in relation to the other eigenvalues. This leads to the definition of the *damping ratio*

$$\rho = \lambda_1/|\lambda_2| \tag{4.29}$$

From (4.16) it follows that as $t \to \infty$,

$$\left(\frac{\mathbf{n}(t)}{\lambda^t} - c_1\mathbf{w}_1\right) \to c_2\rho^{-t}\mathbf{w}_2$$

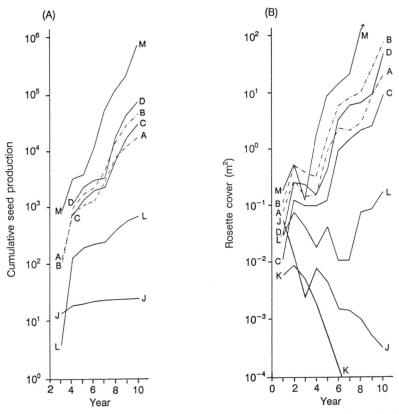

Figure 4.8: Transient analysis by projection for teasel (*Dipsacus sylvestris*). (A) The cumulative production of seeds following input of an initial cohort of 100 seeds. (B) Rosette area following an initial cohort of 100 seeds. From Caswell and Werner (1978).

Thus,

$$\lim_{t\to\infty} \left\| \frac{\mathbf{n}(t)}{\lambda_1^t} - c_1 \mathbf{w}_1 \right\| \leq k\rho^{-t}$$

$$= ke^{-t\ln\rho} \qquad (4.30)$$

for some constant k. That is, convergence to the stable structure is asymptotically exponential, at a rate at least as fast as $\ln\rho$. Convergence could be faster; for example, an initial population for which $c_2 = 0$ would converge at a rate at least as fast as $\ln(\lambda_1/|\lambda_3|)$.

The time t_x required for the contribution of λ_1 to become x times as great as that of λ_2 can be estimated by

$$\left(\frac{\lambda_1}{|\lambda_2|}\right)^{t_x} = x \tag{4.31}$$

from which

$$t_x = \ln(x)/\ln(\rho) \tag{4.32}$$

For a method which considers all the subdominant eigenvalues, see Horst (1977) and Rago and Goodyear (1987).

Entropy and Convergence

Demetrius (e.g., 1974a,b, 1983, 1985) introduced a quantity he calls population entropy H, which is related to the rate of convergence. The derivation of H is based on deep connections between the dynamics of the age structure in a matrix population model and the dynamics of the probability distribution of "genealogies," i.e., of pathways that an individual, its ancestors, and its descendents may take through the life cycle graph (Tuljapurkar 1982c).

The population entropy for an age-classified model is defined in terms of the discrete net fertility function

$$\phi_i = P_1 P_2 \cdots P_{i-1} F_i \tag{4.33}$$

Since, for the age-classified model, the characteristic equation is

$$\sum_i \phi_i \lambda^{-i} = 1 \tag{4.34}$$

the quantity $\phi_i \lambda^{-i}$ can be treated as a probability distribution, and one can calculate the entropy

$$H = -\sum_i \phi_i \lambda^{-i} \ln(\phi_i \lambda^{-i}) \tag{4.35}$$

Demetrius actually uses

$$H = -\frac{1}{T} \sum_i \phi_i \lambda^{-i} \ln(\phi_i \lambda^{-i}) \tag{4.36}$$

where $T = \sum_i i \phi_i \lambda^{-i}$ is a measure of mean generation length.

In this context, H can be thought of as measuring the extent to which reproduction is spread out through the life cycle. For a semelparous life cycle, $H = 0$, while H is maximized by spreading expected reproduction out evenly over the life cycle.

Tuljapurkar (1982c) has shown that H gives a lower bound on the rate of convergence to the stable age distribution. As Tuljapurkar notes, there must be some relation between ρ and H, but what it is is not known.

When applied to iteroparous but imprimitive life cycles (e.g., an age-classified matrix with $F_i > 0$ for $i = 2, 4, 6, \ldots$), which do not converge to a stable age distribution but have positive entropy, H measures the rate at which the age distribution converges to the d-dimensional subspace of the state space within which the oscillating population structure must lie (S.D. Tuljapurkar, personal communication).

Factors Influencing the Damping Ratio

The factors determining ρ in age-classified populations have been studied by Coale (1972) for humans and Taylor (1979) for insects. Both studies used Lotka's continuous time model for the birth series $B(t)$, and measured the damping ratio by $r_1 - u_2$ where u_2 is the real part of the second root of Lotka's equation, $r_2 = u + vi$; this measure is equivalent to $\ln \rho$.

Human Populations   Coale's (1972) calculations are based on the net fertility function $\phi(x) = l(x)m(x)$, which gives the age-specific expected reproductive output of a newborn individual. He assumed that $\phi(x)$ is approximately symmetrical, with mean μ_1 (μ_1 is a measure of mean generation time; see Section 5.6.2). He measured the extent to which reproduction is concentrated near μ_1 by F, defined as the proportion of $\phi(x)$ concentrated in the range $3\mu_1/4 \le x \le 5\mu_1/4$, and measured the asymmetry of $\phi(x)$ by V, the ratio of the median to the mean. Based on calculations of r_1 and r_2 for 47 human life tables, he concludes that $r_1 - u_2$ is negatively correlated with both F and V (partial correlations -0.917 and -0.970, respectively). Thus, populations in which reproduction is spread out symmetrically over a wide range of ages should converge to the stable age distribution more rapidly than those with tightly restricted ages at reproduction, or skewed distributions of age at reproduction.

Insect Populations   Taylor (1979) carried out an extensive investigation of $r_1 - u_2$ in insect populations. He used an age-classified analysis after converting calendar time to units of "degree-days," to compensate for the temperature dependence of development rate in insects. He calculated t_{20} [Equation 4.32], the time required for contribution of the second root to decline to 5% of that of the dominant root, as his measure of the time required for convergence to the stable age distribution.

Based on statistical models of the $l(x)$ and $m(x)$ functions, Taylor concluded that the time to convergence was most strongly affected by the age at first reproduction (earlier reproduction leads to more rapid convergence) and the variance in $m(x)$ (greater variance leads to more rapid convergence). The time to convergence was nearly independent of survivorship and the amount of reproduction.

Taylor also calculated t_{20} from data for 36 populations of 30 species of insects and mites. He found values of t_{20} ranging from 280 degree-days (for the aphid *Myzus persicae*) to 115,120 degree-days (for each of two species of moths). Typical figures for the duration of a growing season are on the order of 1000–3000 degree-days, which would allow 40–70% of the populations Taylor examined to converge to within 5% of their stable age distributions.

Of course, this conclusion assumes constant vital rates during the course of the growing season. As Taylor notes, variation in the vital rates would slow down the process of convergence.

Taylor concludes that "the greater part of insect species existing in seasonal environments never experience, or spend a small proportion of their time in, a stable age distribution" (Taylor 1979, p. 527). This conclusion may be too strong. There is nothing magical about a 5% contribution of the second root as representing convergence. If a 10% threshold is used instead, 55–75% of the populations would have time to converge in a typical growing season. A 20% threshold would allow 65–80% of the populations to converge.

Carey (1983) provides some additional insight into the process of convergence. He collected information on the age distribution (lumped into egg, immature and mature classes) of a tetranychid mite on cotton plants throughout a growing season [mites were among the most rapidly converging species in Taylor's (1979) tabulation]. He compared these distributions with the stable age distribution calculated on the basis of laboratory life table experiments. The laboratory data predicted stable age distributions for increasing, stationary, and declining populations differing only in their fertilities. He found that age distributions of the increasing, stationary, and declining phases of the field population tended to converge to the predicted stable values. This indicates that even if populations do not reach a constant stable age distribution, the patterns of convergence to and deviation from that distribution may provide useful biological information.

Multiregional and Age-Size Models In the context of multiregional or age-size classified models (Example 4.2), one can ask whether the age distribution converges more or less rapidly than the size or region distribution (Liaw 1980, Law and Edley 1988). The answer seems to depend on the details of the model.

Liaw (1980) examined a multiregional model for the human population of Canada, and found that the age distribution converged more rapidly than the region distribution. He interpreted this in terms of the magnitudes of the subdominant eigenvalues of the matrix. Keyfitz (1980) likened the phenomenon to the convergence of temperature in a set of interconnected rooms; the higher rate of mixing homogenizes temperature within each room before the temperature differences between rooms can decay. This interpretation depends, of course, on the fact that migration between regions is generally small.

Law and Edley (1988) draw the opposite conclusion for age-size matrices. They conclude that the size distribution should converge more rapidly than the age distribution. This is partly a function of their assumption that all births take place in the smallest size class. Since all individuals are born at the same size, each cohort proceeds through the life cycle graph with the same distribution of size-at-age. Thus, once the individuals in the initial population have died out, the size distribution no longer changes. This will not be true in a multistate model in which individuals may be born into more than one size class, region, etc.

Stage-Classified Models   The factors influencing ρ in stage-classified models are not well studied. Among the teasel populations in Werner and Caswell (1977), there is a significant negative correlation between ρ and λ_1; more rapidly growing populations tend to converge more slowly to the stable stage distribution (Caswell 1986). It is not clear whether this pattern is general; it does not seem to hold for Taylor's (1979) insect populations.

4.6.2   The Period of Oscillation

When complex eigenvalues are raised to powers, they produce oscillations in the stage distribution, the period of which is given by

$$\mathcal{P}_i = \frac{2\pi}{\theta_i} \tag{4.37}$$

$$= \frac{2\pi}{\tan^{-1}\left(\frac{\Im(\lambda_i)}{\Re(\lambda_i)}\right)} \tag{4.38}$$

where θ_i is the angle formed by λ_i in the complex plane and $\Re(\lambda_i)$ and $\Im(\lambda_i)$ are the real and imaginary parts of λ_i, respectively.

The most important and longest lasting of these oscillatory components is, of course, that associated with λ_2. In age-classified models, $\mathcal{P}_2$ is approximately equal to the mean age of childbearing in the stable population (Lotka 1945, Coale 1972). Thus we would expect that perturbations to the stable age distribution would be followed by damped oscillations with a period about equal to the generation time of the population.

The period $\mathcal{P}_2$ cannot be identified with the mean age of reproduction for complex life cycles, but it still measures the period of the oscillations contributed by the most important subdominant eigenvalue. Resonance between these oscillations and environmental fluctuations is an important factor in the dynamics of populations in periodic environments (Nisbet and Gurney 1982, Tuljapurkar 1985; see Section 8.2.3).

Among the teasel populations of Werner and Caswell (1977), there is a significant negative correlation between P_2 and λ_1; more rapidly growing populations are characterized by shorter period oscillations. This could reflect an association of shorter generation times with higher population growth rates, but its generality is unknown.

4.6.3   Measuring the Distance to the Stable Stage Distribution

To discuss convergence to the stable stage distribution, we need a measure of distance from one stage distribution to another. Three main choices are available; we will discuss two here and defer consideration of the third (the Hilbert projective pseudometric) to Chapter 8.

We wish to measure the distance between $n(t)$ and the stable population w. Without loss of generality, w can be scaled so that $\sum_i w_i = 1$, and we can transform $n(t)$ into $x(t) = n(t)/\sum n_i(t)$, so that both vectors describe the proportions of the population in the different stages.

Keyfitz's Δ

Keyfitz (1968, p. 47) proposed a measure which is equivalent to

$$\Delta(\mathbf{n}, \mathbf{w}) = \frac{1}{2} \sum_i |x_i - w_i| \qquad (4.39)$$

which is a standard measure of the distance between probability vectors. Its maximum value is 1 and its minimum is 0 when the vectors are identical.

Cohen's Cumulative Distance

Keyfitz's Δ measures the distance between n and w independent of the path by which n would actually converge to w. Cohen (1979d) proposed two indices which measure the distance between the two vectors along the pathway by which convergence takes place. We know from (4.17) that $n(t)/\lambda^t$ will converge to $c_1 w_1$. Cohen's indices are obtained by accumulating the differences between $n(t)/\lambda^t$ and $c_1 w_1$:

$$\mathbf{s}[\mathbf{A}, \mathbf{n}(0), t] = \sum_{i=0}^{t} \left(\frac{\mathbf{n}(i)}{\lambda^i} - c_1 \mathbf{w}_1 \right) \qquad (4.40)$$

$$\mathbf{r}[\mathbf{A}, \mathbf{n}(0), t] = \sum_{i=0}^{t} \left| \frac{\mathbf{n}(i)}{\lambda^i} - c_1 \mathbf{w}_1 \right| \qquad (4.41)$$

The vector $s(t)$ accumulates the difference between $n(t)/\lambda^t$ and $c_1 w_1$, whereas $r(t)$ accumulates the absolute value of those differences.

As a measure of the cumulative distance between an initial population $n(0)$ and its eventual limiting distribution, Cohen proposes calculating the limit as $t \to \infty$ of $s(t)$ and $r(t)$, and then adding the absolute values of the elements of the vectors.

$$D_1 = \sum_i \lim_{t \to \infty} |s_i[A, n(0), t]| \qquad (4.42)$$

$$D_2 = \sum_i \lim_{t \to \infty} |r_i[A, n(0), t]| \qquad (4.43)$$

Cohen actually proposes scaling these indices by multiplying by a constant (50 in his example) to make their magnitude comparable to that of Δ, but this does not seem necessary.

Cohen goes on to find an analytical expression for the limit in (4.42). Let $B = wv'$, and let $Z = (I + B - A/\lambda)^{-1}$. Then

$$\lim_{t \to \infty} s[A, n(0), t] = (Z - B)n(0) \qquad (4.44)$$

The limit in D_2, however, must be calculated numerically. When $n(0) = w$, $c_1 = 1$ and $D_1 = D_2 = 0$. There is no well-defined upper bound for either distance.

Example 4.9 Calculation of D_1 and D_2

Consider the matrix

$$A = \begin{pmatrix} 0.4271 & 0.8498 & 0.1273 \\ 0.9924 & 0 & 0 \\ 0 & 0.9826 & 0 \end{pmatrix} \qquad (4.45)$$

(for the 1965 U.S. population with 15-year age intervals, not that it matters here). The stable age distribution and reproductive value are

$$w_1 = \begin{pmatrix} 0.4020 \\ 0.3299 \\ 0.2681 \end{pmatrix} \qquad v_1 = \begin{pmatrix} 1.4487 \\ 1.1419 \\ 0.1525 \end{pmatrix} \qquad (4.46)$$

and the observed age distribution is

$$n(0) = \begin{pmatrix} 0.4304 \\ 0.3056 \\ 0.2640 \end{pmatrix} \qquad (4.47)$$

Thus $c_1 = v_1' n(0) = 1.0127$.

The cumulative deviation vectors $s[A, n(0), t]$ and $r[A, n(0), t]$, for $t = 0, \ldots, 10$ are

t	$r[A, n(0), t]$			$s[A, n(0), t]$		
0	0.0232	0.0285	0.0075	0.0232	−0.0285	−0.0075
1	0.0358	0.0476	0.0306	0.0106	−0.0094	−0.0306
2	0.0424	0.0579	0.0461	0.0172	−0.0198	−0.0151
3	0.0457	0.0633	0.0545	0.0138	−0.0144	−0.0235
4	0.0474	0.0660	0.0589	0.0155	−0.0171	−0.0192
5	0.0483	0.0674	0.0611	0.0147	−0.0157	−0.0214
6	0.0487	0.0681	0.0622	0.0151	−0.0165	−0.0203
7	0.0489	0.0685	0.0628	0.0149	−0.0161	−0.0209
8	0.0490	0.0686	0.0631	0.0150	−0.0163	−0.0206
9	0.0491	0.0687	0.0633	0.0149	−0.0162	−0.0207
10	0.0491	0.0688	0.0633	0.0150	−0.0162	−0.0206
11	0.0491	0.0688	0.0634	0.0150	−0.0162	−0.0207
12	0.0491	0.0688	0.0634	0.0150	−0.0162	−0.0207
13	0.0492	0.0688	0.0634	0.0150	−0.0162	−0.0207
14	0.0492	0.0688	0.0634	0.0150	−0.0162	−0.0207
15	0.0492	0.0688	0.0634	0.0150	−0.0162	−0.0207

By $t = 10$, both $r(\cdot)$ and $s(\cdot)$ have converged to four decimal places. The distance indices are $D_1 = 0.0518$ and $D_2 = 0.1814$.

Unlike Δ, D_1 and D_2 are functions not only of $n(0)$, but also of the projection matrix A, which determines the pathway by which $n(t)$ will converge.

Example 4.10 Effects of the projection matrix

Consider the following three age-classified projection matrices:

$$A_1 = \begin{pmatrix} 0.3063 & 0.6094 & 0.0913 \\ 0.9924 & 0 & 0 \\ 0 & 0.9826 & 0 \end{pmatrix}$$

$$A_2 = \begin{pmatrix} 0 & 0.8784 & 0.1316 \\ 0.9924 & 0 & 0 \\ 0 & 0.9826 & 0 \end{pmatrix}$$

$$A_3 = \begin{pmatrix} 0 & 0.0641 & 0.9603 \\ 0.9924 & 0 & 0 \\ 0 & 0.9826 & 0 \end{pmatrix}$$

These matrices all have the same dominant eigenvalue ($\lambda_1 = 1$) and the same stable age distribution:

$$w = \begin{pmatrix} 0.3370 \\ 0.3344 \\ 0.3286 \end{pmatrix} \qquad (4.48)$$

but A_2 and A_3 have reproduction concentrated in the last two and the last age class, respectively.

Suppose that all three populations begin with the common initial vector (4.47). The distance between $n(0)$ and w as measured by Δ is $\Delta = 0.093$, regardless of which projection matrix is used. However, the values of D_1 and D_2 vary dramatically depending on the pattern of reproduction:

Matrix	D_1	D_2
A_1	0.1995	0.6058
A_2	0.1652	1.5646
A_3	0.1066	5.6866

When measured by D_1, the cumulative distance from $n(0)$ to w_1 decreases as reproduction is concentrated in a single age class. When measured by D_2, the cumulative distance increases as reproduction is concentrated. This reflects the increasing oscillations in the age distribution as reproduction is concentrated. Since $s[A, n(0), t]$ accumulates positive and negative deviations from the stable distribution, oscillations tend to cancel each other out. On the other hand, $r[A, n(0), t]$ accumulates the absolute value of the deviations, and the oscillations are reflected in larger values of D_2.

4.7   Computation of Eigenvalues and Eigenvectors

The use of matrix population models eventually requires the numerical calculation of eigenvalues and eigenvectors. This is not an easy problem (see Wilkinson 1965 for a thorough treatment). In fact, Press et al. (1986), in their compilation of numerical methods, describe it as "one of the few subjects covered in this book for which we do *not* recommend that you avoid canned routines" (see Wilkinson and Renisch (1971) if you really want to try it yourself). Fortunately, canned routines are widely available; most academic computer installations will have EISPACK (a public domain set of FORTRAN subroutines) or the IMSL[5] or NAG[6] libraries, which include routines for the calculation of eigenvalues and eigenvectors.

The IMSL and NAG libraries are also available for microcomputers, but more useful in this domain are two powerful, interactive matrix algebra programs: MATLAB[7] and GAUSS,[8] which make the analysis of matrix models

---

[5]IMSL Inc., 7500 Bellaire Blvd., Houston TX 77036.
[6]NAG Central Office, 7 Banbury Rd., Oxford OX2 6NN, England.
[7]The MathWorks, Inc., 21 Eliot St., South Natick MA 01760.
[8]Aptech Systems, P.O. Box 6487, Kent WA 98064.

as simple as the use of a calculator. Most of the examples in this book were computed with MATLAB, which I highly recommend.

4.7.1 The Power Method

Even without eigenanalysis software, it is easy to calculate the dominant eigenvalue and its eigenvectors of a primitive matrix by raising the matrix to higher and higher powers.

Begin with an arbitrary positive vector $\mathbf{x}(0)$ and multiply it repeatedly by $\mathbf{A}$ to generate $\mathbf{x}(t) = \mathbf{A}^t \mathbf{x}(0)$. By the Perron-Frobenius theorem, $\mathbf{x}(t)$ will eventually converge to a vector proportional to $\mathbf{w}_1$, and the ratio of the entries of $\mathbf{x}(t+1)$ and $\mathbf{x}(t)$ will converge to λ_1.

The rate of convergence depends on λ_2, about which you ordinarily have no information. It is easy, however, to display the values of $x_i(t+1)/x_i(t)$ and watch the convergence yourself. When the ratio is constant to enough decimal places to satisfy you, you can quit. Usually 100 iterations are more than sufficient. Overflow and underflow problems can be avoided by rescaling $\mathbf{x}(t)$ at each time by dividing by the sum of its entries.

To calculate the left eigenvector $\mathbf{v}_1$, take advantage of the fact that the left eigenvectors of $\mathbf{A}$ are the right eigenvectors of the transposed matrix, $\mathbf{A}'$. Apply the same algorithm to $\mathbf{A}'$ and you will get $\mathbf{v}_1$ and another estimate of λ_1, which should be the same as the estimate obtained from $\mathbf{A}$.

An equivalent method, which gives both eigenvectors at the same time, is to simply calculate $\mathbf{A}^t$ for large values of t. If $\mathbf{A}$ is primitive,

$$\lim_{t \to \infty} \frac{\mathbf{A}^t}{\lambda_1^t} = \mathbf{w}_1 \mathbf{v}_1' \qquad (4.49)$$

where $\mathbf{w}_1 \mathbf{v}_1'$ is a matrix whose *columns* are all proportional to $\mathbf{w}_1$ and whose *rows* are all proportional to $\mathbf{v}_1$. The eigenvalue λ_1 can be calculated by multiplying $\mathbf{AB}$ and taking the ratio of any entry to the corresponding entry of $\mathbf{B}$. As in the previous method, overflow problems can be avoided by dividing all entries in $\mathbf{A}^t$ by some constant and continuing the process.

Wilkinson (1965, Chapter 9) discusses the extension of the power method to find the subdominant eigenvalues and their eigenvectors.

4.8 Parameter Estimation

The estimation of parameters in stage-classified matrix models depends on the structure of the matrix and the kind of data available. This section considers estimation problems, and some solutions, for a variety of stage-classified models.[9]

---

[9]I assume that a set of stages has been chosen; this may be a significant problem. See Vandermeer (1978) and Moloney (1986) for the problem of choosing size-class widths.

4.8.1   No Holds Barred Estimation

Studies of stage-classified populations often have to rely on a mixture of methods to get estimates – any estimates – of needed parameters. The resulting coefficients may be derived from different experiments, with different sample sizes, conducted at different times. It is hard to justify this approach on formal statistical grounds, but harder to justify the loss of potentially valuable insight by not at least trying.

> **Example 4.11   Teasel populations**
>
> The age and size-classified matrices for teasel (*Dipsacus sylvestris*) in Werner and Caswell (1977; see Example 4.1) were estimated from experimental introduction of teasel into 8 old-fields. A known number of seeds were introduced into 26 plots ($0.25m^2$) in each field, and the fate and size of each resulting plant were recorded for several years.
>
> In calculating transition probabilities among the rosettes and flowering plants, each plot was considered a replicate. The transition probabilities were estimated whenever there were data [i.e., a_{ij} could only be estimated over the interval $(t, t+1)$ if the plot contained at least one individual of stage j in year t]. The matrix elements were calculated as averages of these probabilities, taken over all plots and years. Seed production by flowering plants was estimated from a separate study relating seed number and size of the flowering heads, and seed germination probabilities were estimated from yet another set of observations.
>
> The resulting matrix elements are averages "over both small-scale spatial and short-term temporal variability, and are currently the best estimates we can make for populations of teasel" (Werner and Caswell 1977, p. 1105). They are also a statistical nightmare, being based on different sample sizes, and compounding both types of variability.

4.8.2   Estimation from Transition Frequency Data

The entries in a projection matrix reflect both the transition probabilities for surviving individuals and the production of new individuals by reproduction (sexual or vegetative). If individuals can be identified and followed, the transition probabilities can be measured by recording the state of individuals at time t and then returning to measure their fate at time $t+1$. This yields a transition frequency table **M**, where m_{ij} is the number of transitions observed from state j to fate i. The table will have one more row than column, corresponding to death, which appears as a fate but not a state.[10]

---

[10]Death could be included as a state, but its dynamics are trivial, since a dead organism at t must also be dead at $t+1$.

Maximum likelihood estimates of the transition probabilities are obtained by dividing each column of $\mathbf{M}$ by its sum, so that each column sums to 1 (Anderson and Goodman 1957, Bishop et al. 1975, p. 262). The demographic transition matrix $\mathbf{A}$ (at least, the parts not having to do with reproduction) is then given by

$$\mathbf{A} = \left(\frac{m_{ij}}{\sum_{i=1}^{s+1} m_{ij}} \right) \qquad \text{for } i, j = 1, 2, \ldots s \qquad (4.50)$$

If observations are made repeatedly, at t, $t + 1$, ..., $t + K$, a series of matrices $\mathbf{A}_t$ can be estimated by applying (4.50) to each successive pair of time instants. An estimate of $\mathbf{A}$ over the entire interval $(t, t + K)$ is obtained by summing the frequency tables over time and applying (4.50). See Section 7.1 for the statistical analysis of such data.

Example 4.12 Size dynamics of bryozoan colonies

Harvell et al. (1989) studied the dynamics of colonies of the bryozoan *Membranipora membranacea* at low and high densities on artificial substrates on the coast of Washington. At two-week intervals from May through September, colonies were counted, measured, and assigned to one of five size classes. The transition frequency table for the high-density treatment, from 12 July to 28 July, was

Fate $(t+1)$	State (t) 1	2	3	4	5
1	13	2	0	0	0
2	5	38	2	0	0
3	0	4	51	4	0
4	0	0	3	18	1
5	0	0	0	3	8
Death	4	1	1	0	0

The corresponding transition probability matrix is

$$\mathbf{A} = \begin{pmatrix} 0.591 & 0.044 & 0 & 0 & 0 \\ 0.227 & 0.844 & 0.035 & 0 & 0 \\ 0 & 0.089 & 0.895 & 0.160 & 0 \\ 0 & 0 & 0.053 & 0.720 & 0.111 \\ 0 & 0 & 0 & 0.120 & 0.889 \end{pmatrix} \qquad (4.51)$$

Note that the sixth row of the transition frequency table, corresponding to death, does not appear in the transition probability matrix.

4.8.3 Multiregional or Age-Size Models

The parameters in the multiregional age-classified model (4.9) can be estimated by taking advantage of the Leslie-like structure of the matrix to develop matrix analogues of the formulas used in Chapter 2 to parameterize the Leslie matrix from the life table. These calculations are summarized briefly here, following Rogers (1985); for details see Nour and Suchindran (1984) and especially Schoen (1988). They are equally applicable to the age-size models of Law (1983, Law and Edley 1988).

We begin by defining multiregional survivorship and maternity functions:

$$\mathbf{l}(x) \;=\; \left(\begin{array}{cc} l_{1\to1}(x) & l_{2\to1}(x) \\ l_{1\to2}(x) & l_{2\to2}(x) \end{array} \right) \tag{4.52}$$

$$\mathbf{m}(x) \;=\; \left(\begin{array}{cc} m_1(x) & 0 \\ 0 & m_2(x) \end{array} \right) \tag{4.53}$$

where, e.g., $l_{1\to2}(x)$ is the probability that an individual born in region 1 is alive and in region 2 at age x, and $m_1(x)$ is the expected offspring production of an individual in region 1 at age x.

The multiregional survivorship function $\mathbf{l}(x)$ integrates mortality and migration information. It can be estimated from age-specific mortality and migration rates as follows (Rogers 1985). Define

$$\mathbf{M}(x) = \left(\begin{array}{cc} M_{1\to d}(x) + M_{1\to2}(x) & -M_{2\to1}(x) \\ -M_{1\to2}(x) & M_{2\to d}(x) + M_{2\to1}(x) \end{array} \right) \tag{4.54}$$

where, e.g., $M_{1\to2}$ is the migration rate from region 1 to 2 and $M_{1\to d}$ is the mortality rate of individuals in region 1. Then a matrix $\mathbf{p}(x)$ can be defined

$$\mathbf{p}(x) = \left(\mathbf{I} + \frac{1}{2}\mathbf{M}(x) \right)^{-1} \left(\mathbf{I} - \frac{1}{2}\mathbf{M}(x) \right) \tag{4.55}$$

where the entries $p_{ij}(x)$ of $\mathbf{p}(x)$ give the probability that an individual aged x in region j will be alive and in region i at age $x + 1$.

The survivorship function is then calculated as

$$\mathbf{l}(0) \;=\; \mathbf{I} \tag{4.56}$$

$$\mathbf{l}(x + 1) \;=\; \mathbf{p}(x)\mathbf{l}(x) \qquad \text{for } x \geq 1 \tag{4.57}$$

In terms of this life table, the submatrices $\mathbf{P}_i$ and $\mathbf{F}_i$, specifying the survival/migration and birth/migration behavior of age class i, are given by

$$\mathbf{P}_i \;=\; [\mathbf{l}(x - 1) + \mathbf{l}(x)][\mathbf{l}(x) + \mathbf{l}(x + 1)]^{-1} \tag{4.58}$$

$$\mathbf{F}_i \;=\; \left(\frac{\mathbf{l}(0) + \mathbf{l}(1)}{2} \right) (\mathbf{m}(i) + \mathbf{m}(i + 1)\mathbf{P}_i) \tag{4.59}$$

This approach can be used for age-size models (Law 1983) by replacing "regions" by size classes and migration rates by growth rates.

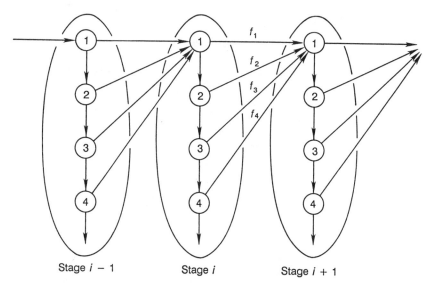

Figure 4.9: A portion of the life cycle graph for three successive stages (e.g., instars) with transition (e.g., molting) probabilities determined by the time spent within the stage (Caswell 1988).

4.8.4 Estimation from Stage Duration Distributions

Some of the parameters in the standard size-classified model (Figure 4.1B) can be estimated from information on the duration of the stages or size classes (Caswell 1988). Consider Figure 4.1B as an approximation to a model (Figure 4.9) in which individuals are classified by age *within* stages (Caswell 1983; for an application to insect populations see Longstaff 1984), with the probability of growing to the next stage depending on the time already spent in the current stage, but independent of the time spent in any previous stage. The problem is to estimate the probabilities P_i and G_i of the size-classified model from information on stage duration and stage-specific survival. This can be done at several degrees of approximation.

The analysis is simplified by introducing two lower-level parameters: the growth probability γ_i for surviving individuals, and the survival probability σ_i (Caswell 1982a, 1983). By simple conditional probability arguments, we can write

$$G_i = \sigma_i \gamma_i \tag{4.60}$$
$$P_i = \sigma_i(1 - \gamma_i) \tag{4.61}$$

The stage duration distribution permits us to estimate γ; combined with information on survival, this can be used to calculate P_i and G_i.

The Geometric Distribution

The simplest approximation supposes that the probability of growing out of stage i is a constant γ_i. Among a cohort of individuals that survives to grow to stage $i + 1$, the stage duration T_i has a zero-truncated geometric distribution

$$P(T_i = k) = \gamma_i(1 - \gamma_i)^{k-1} \qquad k = 1, 2, 3, \ldots,$$

with mean $\bar{T}_i = 1/\gamma_i$. Thus

$$\gamma_i \approx \bar{T}_i^{-1} \tag{4.62}$$

Intuitively, if the average duration of the stage is $\bar{T}_i$, then during each time interval a fraction $\bar{T}_i^{-1}$ of the individuals must grow to the next stage.

Fixed Stage Durations

As a second approximation, suppose that T_i is identical for every individual. The proportion of individuals in stage i that grows to stage $i+1$ at any time now depends on the age distribution within the stage. An approximate constant probability γ_i can be calculated by assuming that the age distribution within the stage has stabilized.

Assume that survival probability is a constant (σ_i) for all ages within stage i. The within-stage stable age distribution[11] is

$$\mathbf{w} = \begin{pmatrix} 1 \\ (\sigma_i/\lambda) \\ (\sigma_i/\lambda)^2 \\ \vdots \\ (\sigma_i/\lambda)^{T_i-1} \end{pmatrix} \tag{4.63}$$

All individuals in the last age class grow, so the proportion growing is

$$\gamma_i = \frac{(\sigma_i/\lambda)^{T_i-1}}{1 + (\sigma_i/\lambda) + (\sigma_i/\lambda)^2 + \cdots + (\sigma_i/\lambda)^{T_i-1}} \tag{4.64}$$

Note that if $\sigma_i/\lambda = 1$, this expression reduces to (4.62).

If $\sigma_i/\lambda < 1$, the series in the denominator of (4.64) is

$$\sum_{j=0}^{T_i-1} \left(\frac{\sigma_i}{\lambda}\right)^j = \frac{(\sigma_i/\lambda)^{T_i} - 1}{(\sigma_i/\lambda) - 1} \tag{4.65}$$

so that

$$\gamma_i = \frac{(\sigma_i/\lambda)^{T_i} - (\sigma_i/\lambda)^{T_i-1}}{(\sigma_i/\lambda)^{T_i} - 1} \tag{4.66}$$

---

[11]The theory needed to derive this will be presented in Chapter 5.

This formula is useful when the "stages" are really groups of age classes. If a stage consists of individuals aged $k, k+1, \ldots, k+T$, then during $(t, t+1)$ all the oldest individuals will graduate to the next stage, and all younger individuals will move up one age class. This model is, in a sense, not "stage classified" at all, since demography is still determined by age, but it is useful when only relatively crude estimates of the survival are available over broad age ranges.

Example 4.13 Loggerhead sea turtle demography

Stage-classified demographic parameters for the loggerhead sea turtle *Caretta caretta* were estimated by Crouse et al. (1987) using the approach of (4.66). Seven stages were defined (hatchlings, small juveniles, large juveniles, subadults, novice breeders, first-year remigrants, and mature breeders). Estimates of survival probabilities and stage durations were obtained from data collected over 20 years on Little Cumberland Island, Georgia.

Equation (4.66), with $\lambda = 1$, was used to estimate the γ_i. Combined with the survival probabilities σ_i, this allowed estimation of the P_i and G_i. The data and the calculated parameters are as follows:

Stage	σ_i	T_i	γ_i	P_i	G_i
1	0.6747	1	1.0000	0.0000	0.6747
2	0.7857	7	0.0618	0.7371	0.0486
3	0.6758	8	0.0218	0.6611	0.0147
4	0.7425	6	0.0698	0.6907	0.0518
5	0.8091	1	1.0000	0.0000	0.8091
6	0.8091	1	1.0000	0.0000	0.8091
7	0.8091	31	0.0003	0.8088	0.0003

In this case, the approximation $\lambda = 1$ used in estimating the parameters is not far off, since the estimate of λ_1 from the completed matrix is 0.945. An iterative procedure which does not rely on the assumption that $\lambda = 1$ is outlined below.

Variable Stage Durations

A more realistic approximation assumes that stage duration varies among individuals, with mean $\bar{T}_i$ and variance $V(T_i)$. The proportion growing into the next stage at any time depends on the within-stage age distribution. Assuming a stable age distribution it is possible to estimate γ_i from $\bar{T}_i$, $V(T_i)$, and the stage-specific survival probability σ_i (Caswell 1983; what follows here is more complete).

Consider individuals within stage i. Let f_j be the probability that an individual in age class j graduates to the next stage, given that it survives; let g_j be the probability density of age at graduation that would be observed in the absence of mortality, and let h_j be the probability of not having graduated by age j, again in the absence of mortality. The three quantities are related:

$$g_j = f_j \prod_{j=1}^{i-1}(1 - f_j) \qquad g_1 = f_1 \qquad (4.67)$$

$$h_j = \prod_{j=1}^{i}(1 - f_j) \qquad h_0 = 1 \qquad (4.68)$$

$$f_j = g_j/h_{j-1} \qquad (4.69)$$

(If we make an analogy between graduating to the next stage and death, these parameters define a life table, with $h_j = l_x$, $g_j = d_x$, and $f_j = q_x$.)

Let $\mathbf{w}$ denote the stable age distribution within stage i. The proportion graduating is

$$\gamma_i = \frac{\sum_j f_j w_j}{\sum_j w_j} \qquad (4.70)$$

The stable age distribution $\mathbf{w}$ is

$$\mathbf{w} = \begin{pmatrix} 1 \\ (1 - f_1)(\sigma/\lambda) \\ (1 - f_1)(1 - f_2)(\sigma/\lambda)^2 \\ \vdots \\ \prod_{k=1}^{j-1}(1 - f_k)(\sigma/\lambda)^{j-1} \\ \vdots \end{pmatrix} \qquad (4.71)$$

and thus

$$\gamma_i = \frac{\frac{\lambda}{\sigma}\sum_j g_j \left(\frac{\lambda}{\sigma}\right)^{-j}}{\frac{\lambda}{\sigma}\sum_j h_j \left(\frac{\lambda}{\sigma}\right)^{-j}} \qquad (4.72)$$

Let $a = \ln(\lambda/\sigma)$. Then we can rewrite (4.72) as

$$\ln \gamma_i = \ln\left(\sum_{j=1} g_j e^{-aj}\right) - \ln\left(\sum_{j=0} h_j e^{-aj}\right) \qquad (4.73)$$

The first term on the right-hand side of (4.73) is the cumulant generating function[12] of g_j. The second term differs from a cumulant generating function only because h_j is not a probability density function. However, it can be transformed into one by dividing by the sum of the function h. Define $\hat{h}_i = h_j / \sum_j h_j$. Then (4.73) can be rewritten

$$\ln \gamma_i = \ln \left(\sum_j g_j e^{-aj} \right) - \ln \left(\sum_j \hat{h}_j e^{-aj} \right) - \ln \bar{T} \qquad (4.74)$$

where $\bar{T}_i = \sum_j h_j$ is the expected stage duration, analogous to the life expectancy $e_0 = \sum_x l_x$ of classical demography.

Expanding the cumulant generating functions in (4.74) up to terms of second order in a yields

$$\ln \gamma_i \approx -a[\kappa_1(g) - \kappa_1(\hat{h})] + \frac{a^2}{2!}[\kappa_2(g) - \kappa_2(\hat{h})] - \ln \bar{T}_i \qquad (4.75)$$

Keyfitz (1977, p. 131) shows that

$$\begin{aligned} \kappa_1(g) &= \bar{T}_i \\ \kappa_2(g) &= V(T_i) \\ \kappa_1(\hat{h}) &= \frac{V(T_i) + \bar{T}_i^2}{2\bar{T}_i} \end{aligned}$$

where $V(T_i)$ denotes the variance of stage duration. Thus, to first order in a, we can write

$$\ln \gamma_i \approx -a \left(\frac{\bar{T}_i}{2} - \frac{V(T_i)}{2\bar{T}_i} \right) - \ln \bar{T}_i \qquad (4.76)$$

or

$$\gamma_i \approx \left(\frac{1}{\bar{T}_i} \right) \exp \left[-a \left(\frac{\bar{T}_i}{2} - \frac{V(T_i)}{2\bar{T}_i} \right) \right] \qquad (4.77)$$

From (4.77) we again obtain the approximation $\gamma_i \approx \bar{T}_i^{-1}$, when a is sufficiently small. When $a = \ln(\lambda/\sigma_i) > 0$, $\gamma_i \approx \bar{T}_i^{-1}$ overestimates γ_i, because it overestimates the abundance of old individuals within the instar by neglecting the effects of mortality and population growth in shifting the age distribution toward young individuals. The smaller the variance $V(T_i)$ in stage duration, and the larger the average stage duration $\bar{T}_i$, the greater the overestimate of γ_i.

---

[12]The cumulant generating function of a probability density F is $\psi(a) = \ln \int_0^\infty F(z)e^{-az} \, dz$. The cumulants κ_i are defined by the series expansion $\psi(a) = -a\kappa_1 + \frac{a^2}{2!}\kappa_2 - \frac{a^3}{3!}\kappa_3 + \cdots$. The first cumulant κ_1 equals the mean μ; the second cumulant κ_2 equals the variance σ^2. Relations between the higher cumulants and the moments of F are given in Kendall and Stuart (1958, p. 71).

Iterative Calculation

The alert reader will have noted that Equations (4.66) and (4.77) for γ_i depend on λ. However, λ is an eigenvalue of the very matrix whose entries are being estimated, and cannot be calculated until the estimation is completed!

One solution is to assume that $\lambda \approx 1$, and ignore it, as in Crouse et al. (1987). An iterative approach, however, may improve the estimates. Choose an initial value of λ and calculate the entries in **A**. The eigenvalues of **A** yield a second estimate of λ, with which the parameters can be estimated again. If repeated, this process usually (but not always, based on the few calculations I have done) converges to a matrix **A** whose entries are compatible with its own eigenvalues. It is unclear how much difference this makes in practice. For example, when applied to the data of Crouse et al. (1987) on the loggerhead turtle, it changes the estimate of λ from 0.9450 to 0.9644. The uncertainty in the original survival and growth data is certainly greater than this.

Negative Binomial Stage Durations

The major weakness of the preceding methods is their reliance on the stability of the within-stage age distribution. This section presents a method that approximates the stage duration distribution by a negative binomial distribution (or, in continuous time, a gamma distribution) with specified mean and variance, without assuming that the age distribution is stable. The negative binomial is a flexible distribution, and can approximate many observed stage duration distributions (Blythe et al. 1984).

Consider a series of k identical stages, in each of which the probability of moving to the next stage is γ. The time T required to grow through all k stages is the time required for the kth success in a series of identical Bernoulli trials with probability of success γ; this time has a negative binomial distribution

$$P(T = x) = \binom{x-1}{k-1} \gamma^k (1 - \gamma)^{x-k}$$

with mean and variance

$$\bar{T} = \frac{k}{\gamma} \tag{4.78}$$

$$V(T) = \frac{k(1 - \gamma)}{\gamma^2} \tag{4.79}$$

To produce a life cycle stage i, the duration of which has a negative binomial distribution, we divide the stage into a series of k identical but invisible "pseudostages." These are not ages within the stage; in fact they cannot be identified at all. They appear in the model only to slow down individuals proceeding through the stage so as to produce a distribution of stage durations with a specified mean and variance.

Mortality and fertility are identical for all pseudostages within a stage. Thus each transition within the stage is multiplied by the stage-specific survival probability σ_i, and is given the same stage-specific fertility coefficient F_i.

Given the mean $\bar{T}_i$ and variance $V(T_i)$ of the stage duration, the parameters specifying the pseudostages are obtained from (4.79) and (4.79)

$$\gamma_i = \frac{\bar{T}_i}{V(T_i) + \bar{T}_i} \tag{4.80}$$

$$k_i = \frac{\bar{T}_i^2}{V(T_i) + \bar{T}_i} \tag{4.81}$$

Estimation Methods Compared

Consider the life cycle graph in Figure 4.10, which contains an immature stage (n_2) of variable duration. The parameters P_2 and G_2 are determined by the stage duration; let the other parameters be $G_1 = 0.5$, $F_3 = 10$, $\sigma_2 = 0.75$, and let the mean and variance of stage duration be $\bar{T}_2 = 5$, $V(T_2) = 3$. Applying the four methods outlined above [using iteration to obtain λ for (4.66) and (4.77)] produces the following estimates of γ_2, and the resultant matrices and their dominant eigenvalues:

1. Geometric stage duration distribution: $\gamma_2 = 0.2$, $\lambda = 1.1587$,

$$\mathbf{A} = \begin{pmatrix} 0 & 0 & 10 \\ 0.5 & 0.6 & 0 \\ 0 & 0.15 & 0 \end{pmatrix} \tag{4.82}$$

2. Fixed stage duration: $\gamma_2 = 0.097$, $\lambda = 1.0246$,

$$\mathbf{A} = \begin{pmatrix} 0 & 0 & 10 \\ 0.5 & 0.677 & 0 \\ 0 & 0.073 & 0 \end{pmatrix} \tag{4.83}$$

3. Variable stage duration, stable age distribution: $\gamma_2 = 0.10$, $\lambda = 1.0289$,

$$\mathbf{A} = \begin{pmatrix} 0 & 0 & 10 \\ 0.5 & 0.675 & 0 \\ 0 & 0.075 & 0 \end{pmatrix} \tag{4.84}$$

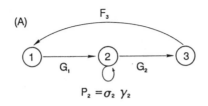

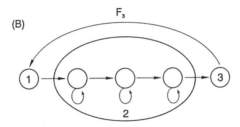

Figure 4.10: A life cycle graph (A) for a population with an immature stage n_2 of variable duration, with the corresponding graph (B) for a model assuming that the duration of n_2 follows a negative binomial distribution. The second stage now contains three identical "pseudostages"; see text for details (Caswell 1988).

4. Negative binomial stage duration distribution: $\gamma_2 = 0.625$, $k = 3$, $\lambda = 1.0548$,

$$
\mathbf{A} = \begin{pmatrix}
0 & 0 & 0 & 0 & 10 \\
0.5 & 0.2813 & 0 & 0 & 0 \\
0 & 0.4688 & 0.2813 & 0 & 0 \\
0 & 0 & 0.4688 & 0.2813 & 0 \\
0 & 0 & 0 & 0.4688 & 0
\end{pmatrix} \tag{4.85}
$$

In this example, the choice of an approximation makes an appreciable difference in the asymptotic behavior of the resulting stage-classified model. It also affects the transient response. Only the negative binomial model actually delays individuals in their progress through n_2; as a result, it converges to its stable structure much more slowly (and more realistically) than the others. Figure 4.11 shows $n_3(t)$ following an initial input of a single individual in n_1. The three models that use a single stage for n_2 all predict the presence of adults by $t = 2$ and converge to the stable stage distribution very rapidly. The negative binomial model, in contrast, exhibits a lag in the appearance of adults and converges much more slowly. This is a direct consequence of the lack of a stable age distribution assumption in this model, and is probably more realistic for many cases.

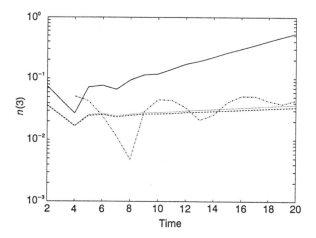

Figure 4.11: The transient dynamics resulting from the four matrices in Equations (4.82)–(4.85). Solid line: geometric distribution, dashed line: fixed stage duration, dotted line: stable age approximation, dot-dash: negative binomial distribution. The abundance of n_3 is plotted, following an input of a single individual in n_1.

4.8.5 Estimation by Regression

Data for mobile organisms, which cannot be tagged and followed individually, are usually obtained as time series of stage distributions, $\mathbf{n}(t)$, $\mathbf{n}(t+1)$,.... An approach to the estimation of stage-classified matrix parameters from such data was introduced by Lefkovitch (1965), using multiple regression (see also Caswell and Twombly 1989).

Consider the the ith row of the matrix projection equation:

$$n_i(t+1) = \sum_j a_{ij} n_j(t) \qquad (4.86)$$

The stage distribution vectors $\mathbf{n}(t)$ and $\mathbf{n}(t+1)$ are known, but the a_{ij} are not. Each pair of vectors $(\mathbf{n}(t)$, $\mathbf{n}(t+1))$ provides another observation, and Lefkovitch showed how to approach the estimation of the a_{ij} by treating them as the unknown coefficients in a multiple regression problem. Lefkovitch applied the method to data on laboratory cultures of the beetle *Lasioderma serricorne* under different conditions. His censuses enumerated eggs, larvae, pupae, and adults.

There are several problems with this method. First, ordinary multiple regression procedures may produce negative estimates for some of the a_{ij}; these are difficult to interpret biologically. Second, one must decide whether to use ordinary regression through the mean, or regression through the origin. The latter is more appropriate, since (4.86) has no constant term, but may produce biased estimates (Lefkovitch 1965). Finally, the method requires long time series. If the life cycle includes s stages, a minimum of $s + 1$ censuses is required to estimate the s^2 coefficients. Since the procedure provides only a single estimate of each of the a_{ij}, the time series must be obtained during a period when the environment is as nearly constant as possible.

Lefkovitch (1965) discusses these problems at length. He copes with negative coefficients by setting them equal to zero and evaluating the resulting change in λ_1; if it is negligible, he concludes that the negative coefficient is not biologically important. He also uses this procedure to evaluate the importance of coefficients that are positive but not significantly different from zero.

It is also possible to use constrained optimization methods to find a best fit set of a_{ij} subject to the restriction that $a_{ij} \geq 0$. One can also restrict some of the a_{ij} to zero based on a priori information about the impossibility of certain transitions in the life cycle. Caswell and Twombly (1989), for example, apply an essentially identical method to estimating the parameters in the standard size-classified matrix (Figure 4.1B), in which only the first row, diagonal, and subdiagonal elements were allowed to be positive.

4.8.6   Fertilities in Stage-Classified Models

Given estimates of the reproductive output of each stage of the life cycle, it is possible in principle to estimate stage-specific fertilities following the same approach as used in the age-classified case (Chapter 2). Although I have never seen them used, I present here birth-flow and birth-pulse formulas for the standard size-classified model.

Birth-Flow Populations

As with the age-classified case, the derivation begins with $B_{(t,t+1)}$ the number of births occurring in the interval $(t, t + 1)$. Assuming that there is some average value m_i for offspring production for individuals in size class i, we can write

$$B_{(t,t+1)} \approx \sum_i m_i \left(\frac{n_i(t) + n_i(t+1)}{2} \right) \tag{4.87}$$

However, $n_i(t+1) = P_i n_i(t) + G_{i-1} n_{i-1}(t)$. Substituting this into (4.87) and collecting terms yields

$$B_{(t,t+1)} \approx \sum_i n_i(t) \left(\frac{(1 + P_i)m_i + G_i m_{i+1}}{2} \right) \tag{4.88}$$

Thus

$$F_i = l(0.5) \left(\frac{(1 + P_i)m_i + G_i m_{i+1}}{2} \right) \tag{4.89}$$

where $l(0.5)$ is the probability of a newborn individual surviving to age $1/2$, at which time it will be counted in $n_1(t+1)$. Estimating $l(0.5)$ is complicated by the fact that this is a size-classified life cycle, and age-specific survival information is not available. However, we do have an estimate of the survival probability of an individual in size class 1: $\sigma_1 = P_1 + G_1$. Assuming that mortality occurs at a constant rate throughout the time interval, we obtain

$$l(0.5) = (\sigma_1)^{1/2} = (P_1 + G_1)^{1/2} \tag{4.90}$$

Equation (4.89) should be compared to (2.22) for the age-classified case. When $P_i = 0$, the formulas are identical.

Birth-Pulse Populations

Size-classified birth-pulse populations differ from age-classified birth-pulse populations. In the age-classified case, both births and aging (birthdays) occur discontinuously in time; thus both reproduction and the age distribution at any time are discontinuous. In the size-classified case, births may continue to occur discontinuously, at a specific season of the year, but growth, and thus the size distribution, is continuous.

As in the age-classified case, let p denote the proportion of the projection interval between the pulse of reproduction and the census. All the births in $(t, t+1)$ occur at $t + 1 - p$, and

$$B(t + 1 - p) = \sum_i n_i(t)(m_i \xi_1 + m_{i+1} \xi_2) \tag{4.91}$$

where ξ_1 is the probability that an individual in size class i at t will be alive and still in size class i at $t+1-p$ and ξ_2 is the probability that an individual in size class i at t will be alive and in size class $i + 1$ at $t + 1 - p$. Assuming that mortality and growth occur at constant rates during $(t, t+1)$,

$$\begin{aligned} \xi_1 &= \sigma_i^{1-p}(1 - \gamma_i^{1-p}) & (4.92) \\ &= (P_i + G_i)^{1-p} - G_i^{1-p} & (4.93) \\ \xi_2 &= \sigma_i^{1-p}\gamma_i^{1-p} & (4.94) \\ &= G_i^{1-p} & (4.95) \end{aligned}$$

Multiplying by $l(p) = \sigma_1^p$, the probability of survival from birth to age p yields

$$F_i = \sigma_1^p \sigma_i^{1-p}\left(m_i(1 - \gamma_i^{1-p}) + m_{i+1}\gamma_i^{1-p}\right) \tag{4.96}$$

Anonymous Reproduction

The measurement of fertility is frequently complicated by the difficulty of tracing offspring to parents. Approximate estimates of the F_i can be obtained from the total production of new offspring $n_1(t + 1)$ and some measured or assumed values of the relative reproductive output of the stages. Huenneke and Marks (1987), for example, constructed size-classified matrices describing the dynamics of stems of red alder (*Alnus incans*), in which new stems are produced at the base of a clump, and cannot be associated with any "parent" stem within the clump. They assumed that the contribution of a parent stem to $n_1(t+1)$ was proportional to its diameter. Dividing $n_1(t + 1)$ by the sum of the diameters of all the stems at time t gives an estimate of a "per-diameter" contribution to reproduction. Multiplying this contribution by the mean diameter of size class i gives an estimate of F_i.

4.9 Assumptions Revisited

All the analyses in this chapter, as in Chapter 2, apply to linear, time-invariant projection models. The criticism that the real world is neither linear nor time-invariant applies to stage-classified models just as it does to age-classified models. The distinction between forecasting of future population dynamics and projecting the hypothetical consequences of present environmental conditions remains the appropriate response to this criticism.

Age-classified models do, however, make an assumption that is not required of stage-classified models: the assumption that the age distribution is a satisfactory state variable. With the methods of this chapter, it is possible to construct and analyze models that reflect, as accurately as possible, the actual biological factors determining the vital rates.

The criticism is sometimes made that stage-classified models require the additional assumption of a stable age distribution *within* stages. This assumption is not necessary. The age distribution within stages is, like any other variable not included in the model, assumed to be irrelevant. This corresponds to the assumption in age-classified models that the size distribution within age classes is irrelevant.

Chapter 5

Analysis of
the Life Cycle Graph

The life cycle graph is more than a handy way of deriving the projection matrix. All of the analyses in Chapter 4 can actually be carried out directly from the graph. In this chapter, we use the life cycle graph to derive simple algebraic formulas for the characteristic equation and the right and left eigenvectors of an arbitrary stage-classified projection matrix. Although numerical computations give the eigenvalues and eigenvectors for specific life cycles, life cycle graph analysis yields general formulas which permit exploration of the general consequences of the *structure* of the life cycle, without requiring specific numerical values for the coefficients.

The life cycle graph represents a system of linear difference equations. The analyses in this chapter rely on a transformation of these equations (the z-transform; Section 5.1) into the complex frequency domain. The advantage of this transformation is that it allows dynamic problems to be solved with algebraic methods. One could go much further with this approach. Transform methods can be used to develop a complete theory of linear systems analysis (e.g., Schwarz and Friedland 1965). Thus the entire demographic machinery developed in this book from matrix models could be replaced with a completely parallel development in the frequency domain (see Lewis 1977, Hubbell and Werner 1979, and the remarkable paper of Thompson 1931).

5.1 The z-Transform

The z-transform of a discrete function is the analogue of the Laplace transform for continuous functions, and is equivalent to the probability generating function (e.g., Feller 1968, p. 264) in discrete probability theory.

Consider a discrete time function $f(t)$, $t = 0, 1, 2, 3, \ldots$; we assume that $f(t) = 0$ for $t < 0$. Let z be a complex variable. The z-transform of $f(t)$ is denoted by $F(z)$, and is defined as

$$Z[f(t)] = F(z) = \sum_{i=0}^{\infty} f(i)z^{-i} \tag{5.1}$$

The series in (5.1) converges for $|z|$ greater than some critical value.

The z-transform is a mapping from a discrete time function $f(t)$ to a power series $F(z)$ in the complex variable z^{-1}. Given the function $f(t)$, $F(z)$ can be calculated by (5.1). Given $F(z)$, the time function can be recovered by any of several inversion methods (e.g., Schwarz and Friedland 1965), or directly by picking out the coefficients of z^{-t} and equating those with $f(t)$.

We will rely on two important properties of the z-transform:

- Linearity: the z-transform is a linear transformation, so that

$$Z[c_1 f_1(t) + c_2 f_2(t)] = c_1 F_1(z) + c_2 F_2(z) \tag{5.2}$$

  for any constants c_1 and c_2 and any functions $f_1(t)$ and $f_2(t)$ for which the z-transforms exist.

- The shifting property: Let $f(t)$ be a function with transform $F(z)$, where $f(t) = 0$ for $t < 0$. Consider a second function $g(t)$, which is $f(t)$ shifted by k time steps, i.e., $g(t) = f(t - k)$. The z-transform of $g(t)$ is

$$
\begin{aligned}
G(z) &= z^{-0} f(-k) + \cdots + z^{-k} f(0) \\
&\quad + z^{-(k+1)} f(1) + z^{-(k+2)} f(2) + \cdots \tag{5.3} \\
&= z^{-k} F(z) \tag{5.4}
\end{aligned}
$$

  In particular, if $g(t) = f(t + 1)$, then $G(z) = zF(z) - zf(0)$.

5.1.1 z-Transform Solution of Difference Equations

The use of the z-transform in solving difference equations relies on the linearity and shifting properties. Consider the scalar difference equation

$$x(t + 1) = ax(t) \tag{5.5}$$

with initial conditions $x(0)$. Taking the z-transform of both sides yields

$$zX(z) - zx(0) = aX(z) \tag{5.6}$$

from which

$$
\begin{aligned}
X(z) &= \frac{x(0)}{1 - az^{-1}} \tag{5.7} \\
&= x(0)\left(1 + az^{-1} + a^2 z^{-2} + \cdots\right) \tag{5.8}
\end{aligned}
$$

The time-domain solution $x(t)$ is found by picking out the coefficients of z^{-t}, $t = 0, 1, 2, \ldots$ in (5.8), and yields the familiar solution $x(t) = x(0)a^t$.

The matrix case proceeds in exactly the same way. If

$$\mathbf{n}(t + 1) = \mathbf{A}\mathbf{n}(t) \tag{5.9}$$

then

$$\mathbf{N}(z) = \mathbf{n}(0)\left(\mathbf{I} - z^{-1}\mathbf{A}\right)^{-1} \tag{5.10}$$

The matrix $(\mathbf{I} - z^{-1}\mathbf{A})^{-1}$ is called the *transfer function* of the system; it maps the initial vector into the transformed population vector time series.

5.1.2 The z-Transformed Life Cycle Graph

Each arc in the life cycle graph represents an expression of the form

$$n_i(t + 1) = a_{ij}n_j(t)$$

Taking the z-transform of this expression yields

$$N_i(z) = a_{ij}z^{-1}N_j(z) + n_i(0)$$

Thus we define the *z-transformed life cycle graph* as the graph obtained by replacing each coefficient a_{ij} in the life cycle graph by $a_{ij}z^{-1}$. Well, actually not quite. We actually define the z-transformed life cycle graph as obtained by replacing each coefficient a_{ij} by $a_{ij}\lambda^{-1}$.

Why, you ask, does z^{-1} suddenly get replaced by λ^{-1}? The symbol z is customary in the engineering literature, and reflects the name of the transform. However, in our applications the complex variable in the transform will be equated with the eigenvalues of the projection matrix, for which λ is the customary symbol. Rather than try to change either tradition, I will call it the z-transform and use λ as the variable.

5.2 Reduction of the Life Cycle Graph

The z-transformed life cycle graph represents an algebraic set of equations in the transformed variables $N_i(z)$. Thus it can be analyzed using the "signal-flow graph" methods of Mason (1953, 1956, Mason and Zimmermann 1960) and Coates (1959) (see Chen 1976 for a review). These methods permit certain reductions of the life cycle graph; the reduced graph retains all the dynamic properties of the original. Figure 5.1 shows the most important of these.

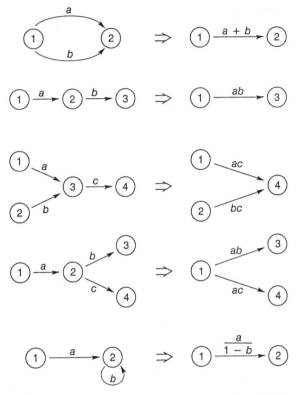

Figure 5.1: Some permissible reductions of the z-transformed life cycle graph. In each case, the reduced graph on the right is equivalent to the unreduced graph on the left. These reductions are *not* permissible in the original graph.

Note that these reductions are not permissible in the original, untransformed life cycle graph. For example, in the time domain, the second graph in Figure 5.1 asserts that

$$n_2(t+1) = an_1(t)$$
$$n_3(t+1) = bn_2(t)$$

Reducing the untransformed graph would yield $n_3(t+1) = P_1 P_2 n_1(t)$, which is *not* equivalent to the original system. The z-transformed system, however, is

$$N_2(z) = P_1 \lambda^{-1} N_1(z)$$
$$N_3(z) = P_2 \lambda^{-1} N_2(z)$$

from which it follows that $N_3(z) = ab\lambda^{-2} N_1(z)$, as indicated by the reduced graph.

The last reduction in Figure 5.1 is particularly important. A self-loop with coefficient $b\lambda^{-1}$ is equivalent to dividing each *incoming* arc by $1 - b\lambda^{-1}$. The terms in the geometric series generated by this division

$$\frac{a\lambda^{-1}}{1 - b\lambda^{-1}} = a\lambda^{-1} + ab\lambda^{-2} + ab^2\lambda^{-3} + \cdots \tag{5.11}$$

represent the probability of an individual moving directly from n_1 to n_2 with probability a, moving from n_1 to n_2 and then staying at n_2 with probability b, moving from n_1 to n_2 and then staying there for two time steps with probability b^2, etc.

> **Example 5.1 Reduction of the age-classified life cycle**
>
> Figure 5.2 shows the reduction of an age-classified life cycle graph. The first reduction combines the two steps from n_1 to n_3 into a single transition. The second reduction has combined the two pathways from n_3 back to n_1 (one directly by reproduction, the other by survival to n_4 followed by reproduction) into a single pathway. The final step has combined the pathways from n_1 to n_3 and from n_3 back to n_1 into a single loop. This reduced graph summarizes the dynamics of the population in terms of the z-transform of $n_1(t)$.

5.2.1 Multistep Transitions

The coefficient λ^{-1} on each arc of the z-transformed life cycle graph can be interpreted as indicating the time (one projection interval) required for the transition. Note that as the graph in Figure 5.2 is reduced, the powers of λ^{-1} appearing on the arcs continue to show the time required for the transitions. This makes it possible to construct life cycle graphs directly that include transitions requiring more than a single projection interval; these transitions are labeled with $a_{ij}\lambda^{-\alpha}$, where α is the time required for the transition. Examples will be shown in Sections 5.7 and 5.8.

5.3 The Characteristic Equation

We begin our demographic application of these methods by deriving the characteristic equation of a matrix **A** from its life cycle graph (Hubbell and Werner 1979). We will need the following terminology.

path transmission T_{ij}: The product of the coefficients on the arcs in the path from n_i to n_j.

loop transmission $L^{(i)}$: The product of the coefficients on the arcs in the ith loop in the graph.

disjoint: Two paths are disjoint if they share no nodes.

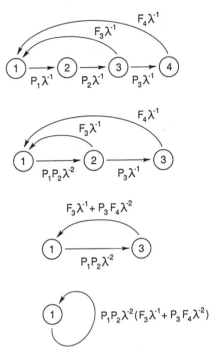

Figure 5.2: Reduction of an age-classified life cycle graph (top) to its simplest form (bottom).

5.3.1   Mason's Determinant Formula

Mason (1956) derived a formula for the determinant of a graph corresponding to a matrix:

$$\det = 1 - \sum_i L^{(i)} + \sum_{i,j}^* L^{(i)} L^{(j)} - \sum_{i,j,k}^* L^{(i)} L^{(j)} L^{(k)} + \cdots \qquad (5.12)$$

where the summations marked with asterisks are taken over products of all pairs, triplets, etc. of mutually *disjoint* loops.

5.3.2   The Characteristic Equation

The characteristic equation of the matrix **A** corresponding to a life cycle graph is obtained by setting the determinant of the z-transformed graph equal to zero:

$$1 - \sum_i L^{(i)} + \sum_{i,j}^* L^{(i)} L^{(j)} - \sum_{i,j,k}^* L^{(i)} L^{(j)} L^{(k)} + \cdots = 0 \qquad (5.13)$$

where the first summation is taken over all the loops in the graph, and the summations marked with asterisks are taken over products of all pairs, triplets, etc. of *disjoint* loops. It is frequently the case, even in complex life cycles, that all loops must pass through a single stage ("newborn" individuals of some sort); in this case the characteristic equation simplifies to

$$\sum_i L^{(i)} = 1 \qquad (5.14)$$

Example 5.2 Age-classified models

We apply (5.14) to the unreduced life cycle graph in Figure 5.2. There are two loops in the graph, with transmissions

$$
\begin{aligned}
L^{(1)} &= P_1 P_2 F_3 \lambda^{-3} \\
L^{(2)} &= P_1 P_2 P_3 F_4 \lambda^{-4}
\end{aligned}
$$

These loops are not disjoint, since they both pass through nodes n_1, n_2, and n_3. The characteristic equation is thus

$$P_1 P_2 F_3 \lambda^{-3} + P_1 P_2 P_3 F_4 \lambda^{-4} = 1 \qquad (5.15)$$

Note that the characteristic equation is invariant under the process of graph reduction. The reduced form of the life cycle graph in Figure 5.2 has only a single loop, with transmission

$$L = P_1 P_2 \lambda^{-2} (F_3 \lambda^{-1} + P_3 F_4 \lambda^{-2})$$

Setting this expression equal to 1 produces the same characteristic equation as the unreduced graph.

In general, applying this method to an age-classified life cycle produces the characteristic equation

$$
\begin{aligned}
1 &= F_1 \lambda^{-1} + P_1 F_2 \lambda^{-2} + P_1 P_2 F_3 \lambda^{-3} + \cdots \\
&= \sum_{i=1}^{s} F_i \lambda^{-i} \left(\prod_{j=1}^{i-1} P_j \right)
\end{aligned}
\qquad (5.16)
$$

Making the crude approximations $F_i = l(1)m(i)$ and $P_i = l(i+1)/l(i)$, and setting $\lambda = e^r$, (5.16) can be seen to be a discrete version of Lotka's integral equation for r. Several authors have addressed the construction of a discrete version of Lotka's equation (e.g., Goodman 1982, Murray and Garding 1984); my opinion is that the appropriate discrete version is the characteristic equation of the Leslie matrix corresponding to the life table. The details of that correspondence depend, as we have seen in Chapter 2, on assumptions about the timing of reproduction.

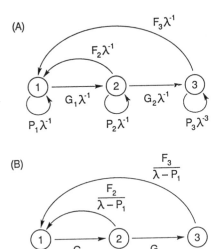

Figure 5.3: The standard size-classified life cycle graph before (A) and after (B) its reduction by absorption of self-loops.

Example 5.3 Size-classified models

Consider the standard size-classified graph in Figure 5.3. There are five loops in the unreduced graph, with transmissions

$$
\begin{aligned}
L^{(1)} &= P_1 \lambda^{-1} \\
L^{(2)} &= P_2 \lambda^{-1} \\
L^{(3)} &= P_3 \lambda^{-1} \\
L^{(4)} &= G_1 F_2 \lambda^{-2} \\
L^{(5)} &= G_1 G_2 F_3 \lambda^{-3}
\end{aligned}
$$

There are four disjoint pairs of loops: $[L^{(1)} L^{(2)}]$, $[L^{(1)} L^{(3)}]$, $[L^{(2)} L^{(3)}]$, and $[L^{(3)} L^{(4)}]$, and one disjoint triplet of loops: $[L^{(1)} L^{(2)} L^{(3)}]$. From (5.13) we obtain the fairly messy characteristic equation:

$$
\begin{aligned}
1 = \; & P_1 \lambda^{-1} + P_2 \lambda^{-1} + P_3 \lambda^{-1} + G_1 F_2 \lambda^{-2} + G_1 G_2 F_3 \lambda^{-3} \\
& - P_1 P_2 \lambda^{-2} - P_1 P_3 \lambda^{-2} - P_2 P_3 \lambda^{-2} - P_3 G_1 F_2 \lambda^{-3} \\
& + P_1 P_2 P_3 \lambda^{-3}
\end{aligned}
\tag{5.17}
$$

The characteristic equation is greatly simplified by reducing self-loops before doing the calculation, because self-loops are always disjoint with each other. The reduced graph in Figure 5.3 contains only two loops:

$$L^{(1)} = \frac{G_1 F_2}{(\lambda - P_1)(\lambda - P_2)}$$

$$L^{(2)} = \frac{G_1 G_2 F_3}{(\lambda - P_1)(\lambda - P_2)(\lambda - P_3)}$$

which are not disjoint. Equation (5.14) yields the characteristic equation:

$$1 = \frac{G_1 F_2}{(\lambda - P_1)(\lambda - P_2)} + \frac{G_1 G_2 F_3}{(\lambda - P_1)(\lambda - P_2)(\lambda - P_3)} \tag{5.18}$$

It takes only a little algebra to show that (5.17) and (5.18) yield the same solutions. Note that if $P_i = 0$, $i = 1, 2, \ldots$, the size-classified life cycle reduces to an age-classified life cycle, and the characteristic equation formula (5.18) reduces to the age-classified formula (5.16).

5.3.3 Derivation

Hubbell and Werner (1979) provided only a brief derivation of the characteristic equation formulas; a more detailed discussion is found in Caswell (1982a). There are two ways of associating a directed graph with a set of linear equations, one called a signal-flow graph (Mason 1953, 1956) and the other a flow graph (Coates 1959). Following Chen (1976), I will refer to these as the Mason graph and Coates graph, respectively, of the system of equations. There are formulas for the calculation of determinants and the solution of equations for both types of graph.

The life cycle graph as defined in this book is the Coates graph of the matrix $\mathbf{A}$, but the characteristic equation (5.13) is obtained by setting the formula for the determinant of the *Mason graph* equal to zero. Why does applying Mason's formula to the z-transformed Coates's graph, and then setting the result to zero, produce the characteristic equation of $\mathbf{A}$?

The Mason and Coates graphs are related by

$$G_C(\mathbf{A}) = G_M(\mathbf{A} - \mathbf{I}) \tag{5.19}$$

where G_C and G_M denote the Coates and Mason graphs, respectively. The Coates graph of the z-transformed matrix is $G_C(z^{-1}\mathbf{A}) = G_M(z^{-1}\mathbf{A} - \mathbf{I})$. Applying Mason's determinant formula to this graph yields

$$\det(z^{-1}\mathbf{A} - \mathbf{I}) = z^{-s} \det(\mathbf{A} - z\mathbf{I}) \tag{5.20}$$

where s is the dimension of the matrix $\mathbf{A}$. Setting this determinant to zero gives the characteristic equation of $\mathbf{A}$.

5.4   The Stable Stage Distribution

The formulas for the right and left eigenvectors of $\mathbf{A}$ were derived by Caswell (1982a). Begin by defining the following transmissions:

$T_{1x}^{(i)}$: the transmission of the ith path from n_1 to n_x.

$L^{(j)}(n_1)$: the transmission of the jth loop which is disjoint with n_1.

$L^{(j)}(T_{1x}^{(i)})$: the transmission of the jth loop which is disjoint with the ith path from n_1 to n_x.

The elements of the right eigenvector $\mathbf{w}$ are given by

$$w_1 = 1 - \sum_j L^{(j)}(n_1) + \sum_{j,k}^* L^{(j)}(n_1)L^{(k)}(n_1) - \cdots \qquad (5.21)$$

and, for $x > 1$,

$$w_x = \sum_i T_{1x}^{(i)}\left(1 - \sum_j L^{(j)}(T_{1x}^{(i)}) + \sum_{j,k}^* L^{(j)}(T_{1x}^{(i)})L^{(k)}(T_{1x}^{(k)}) - \cdots\right) \qquad (5.22)$$

As with the characteristic equation, the summations marked with asterisks are taken over all pairs, triplets, etc. of mutually disjoint loops.

If all loops in the graph pass through n_1, the formula simplifies considerably:

$$w_1 = 1 \qquad (5.23)$$
$$w_x = \sum_i T_{1x}^{(i)} \quad \text{for } x > 1 \qquad (5.24)$$

Although most attention focuses on the eigenvector $\mathbf{w}_1$ corresponding to the dominant eigenvalue λ_1, formulas (5.22) and (5.24) apply equally to any of the eigenvectors, as long as the appropriate eigenvalue is substituted for λ in the z-transformed graph.

Example 5.4 Age-classified model

The age-classified model in Figure 5.2 has four age classes. There are no loops disjoint with n_1, nor are there any loops disjoint with any of the paths from n_1 to any n_x. Thus the stable age distribution (cf. Section 4.4.2) is given by

$$w_1 = 1$$
$$w_2 = P_1\lambda^{-1}$$
$$w_3 = P_1 P_2\lambda^{-2}$$
$$w_4 = P_1 P_2 P_3\lambda^{-3}$$

An element w_x of the eigenvector $\mathbf{w}_1$ can also be written in terms of the elements corresponding to the stages that contribute individuals directly to n_x:

$$w_x = \sum_j a_{xj} \lambda^{-1} w_j \tag{5.25}$$

In the age-classified case, $w_x = P_{x-1} \lambda^{-1} w_{x-1}$. This implies that the stable age distribution is a monotonically nonincreasing function of age in any population for which $\lambda_1 \geq 1$. A peak in an observed age distribution must therefore represent a transient effect.

Example 5.5 Size-classified models

The calculation of $\mathbf{w}$ is greatly simplified if self-loops are absorbed before the calculation, since they are disjoint with each other and (except for a self-loop on n_1) with n_1. When the self-loops are absorbed in the standard size-classified model (Figure 5.3), the stable size distribution is given by

$$w_1 = 1 \tag{5.26}$$

$$w_2 = \frac{G_1}{(\lambda - P_2)} \tag{5.27}$$

$$w_3 = \frac{G_1 G_2}{(\lambda - P_2)(\lambda - P_3)} \tag{5.28}$$

or, in iterative form

$$w_j = \frac{G_{j-1}}{(\lambda - P_j)} w_{j-1} \tag{5.29}$$

Unlike the stable age distribution, which is a strictly decreasing function of age (as long as $\lambda_1 > 1$), the stable size distribution may increase or decrease with size. The condition for $w_j > w_{j-1}$ is that $G_{j-1} > \lambda - P_j$. Thus, if the growth rate into stage j is large, and the probability of growing out of stage j is small, individuals may pile up in stage j, producing a peak in the stable size distribution. Size distributions of organisms with plastic growth patterns (e.g., fish, trees) often contain such peaks; they may be a property of the stable size distribution or a transient result of an earlier disturbance of the size distribution.

5.4.1 Derivation

The derivation of (5.22) also relies on the connection between $G_C(\mathbf{A})$ and $G_M(\mathbf{A} - \mathbf{I})$, as well as on some facts about the characteristic equation (Caswell 1982a). Let $\mathbf{B} = (\mathbf{A} - \lambda\mathbf{I})$ denote the characteristic matrix of

A (i.e., the matrix whose determinant, set equal to zero, provides the characteristic equation). Let B_{ix} denote the (i, x) cofactor of **B**, that is, the determinant of the matrix obtained by deleting row i and column x from **B**. Chiang (1968) shows that the right eigenvector **w** satisfies $w_x = B_{ix}$ for any i.

Without loss of generality, let $i = 1$. The cofactor B_{1x} is the determinant of the matrix formed by replacing the first row and the xth column of **B** with zeroes, and placing a 1 in the $(1, x)$ position. This corresponds to absorbing all self-loops in the life cycle graph, removing all arcs leaving n_x and entering n_1, adding an arc with coefficient 1 from n_x to n_1, and adding self-loops with coefficient 1 to n_1 and n_x.

As a result of these manipulations, all loops passing through n_1 or n_x have been broken, except those passing from n_1 to n_x and back again, the ith of which has a loop transmission equal to $T_{1x}^{(i)}$. There are two self-loops of strength 1 (or one of strength 2, when $x = 1$). Any remaining loops in the graph are disjoint with all the $T_{1x}^{(i)}$ and with the unit self-loops.

The cofactor B_{1x} is the determinant of this modified graph; application of Mason's determinant formula (5.12) gives the result (5.22).

5.5   Reproductive Value

The left eigenvector **v** is obtained by noting that the left eigenvectors of a matrix **A** are the right eigenvectors of the transposed matrix **A**'. Transposing the matrix simply changes the direction of the arrows in the life cycle graph. To express the formula for **v** in terms of the original, untransposed matrix, it is convenient to define

$\tilde{T}_{x1}^{(i)}$: the *transposed transmission* of the ith path from n_x to n_1. The transposed transmission differs from the ordinary transmission only in that self-loops are reduced by dividing all *outgoing*, rather than all incoming, arcs by $(1 - \text{self-loop})$.

In terms of the transposed transmission, the left eigenvector **v** is given by

$$v_1 = 1 - \sum_j L^{(j)}(n_1) + \sum_{i,j}^* L^{(j)}(n_1)L^{(k)}(n_1) - \cdots \qquad (5.30)$$

and, for $x > 1$,

$$v_x = \sum_i \tilde{T}_{x1}^{(i)} \left(1 - \sum_j L^{(j)}(\tilde{T}_{x1}^{(i)}) + \sum_{i,j}^* L^{(j)}(\tilde{T}_{x1}^{(i)})L^{(k)}(\tilde{T}_{x1}^{(i)}) - \cdots \right) \qquad (5.31)$$

If all loops path through n_1, then there are no loops disjoint with any of the pathways from n_x to n_1, and the formulas reduce to

$$v_1 = 1 \tag{5.32}$$

$$v_x = \sum_i \tilde{T}_{x1}^{(i)} \qquad \text{for } x > 1 \tag{5.33}$$

In this case, there is also a recursive formula for the elements of **v**. Let F_x denote the coefficient on the path (if any) leading directly from n_x to n_1. Then

$$v_x = \frac{F_x}{\lambda - a_{xx}} + \sum_j a_{xj} \lambda^{-1} v_j \tag{5.34}$$

That is, the reproductive value of stage x can be partitioned into two components: present reproduction and the contributions of the reproductive values of future stages, weighted by the probabilities of transition to those stages (a_{jx}) and the time required for the transition (λ^{-1}). Williams (1966) first introduced this decomposition in the age-classified case, referring to the two components as "current reproduction" and "residual reproductive value." Equation (5.34) generalizes this idea to complex life cycles.

Example 5.6 Age-classified model

The age-classified life cycle in Figure 5.2 has no disjoint loops, so (5.33) can be used to write down the reproductive values:

$$
\begin{aligned}
v_1 &= 1 \\
v_2 &= P_2 F_3 \lambda^{-2} + P_2 P_3 F_4 \lambda^{-3} \\
v_3 &= F_3 \lambda^{-1} + P_3 F_4 \lambda^{-2} \\
v_4 &= F_4 \lambda^{-1}
\end{aligned}
$$

[cf. (4.28)]. This is a discrete version of Fisher's (1930) continuous-time formula for reproductive value. As with the characteristic equation, there has been some debate about the appropriate discrete formula for reproductive value (Goodman 1982). My opinion is that, just as the characteristic equation of the projection matrix is the appropriate discrete analogue of Lotka's equation for r, so the eigenvector of the projection matrix is the appropriate discrete analogue of Fisher's formula.

Example 5.7 Size-classified models

The standard size-classified model (Figure 5.3) is much more easily analyzed after the self-loops have been absorbed, in which case application of (5.33) yields

$$v_1 = 1$$

$$v_2 = \frac{F_2}{(\lambda - P_2)} + \frac{G_2 F_2 \lambda^{-1}}{(\lambda - P_2)(\lambda - P_3)}$$

$$v_3 = \frac{F_3}{(\lambda - P_3)}$$

5.5.1   A Second Interpretation of Reproductive Value

The identification of v_1 with reproductive value was introduced in Section 4.5 through its effect on asymptotic population size as a function of initial conditions. The formula (5.33) provides a second, more intuitively appealing interpretation of the left eigenvector as a measure of reproductive value. The reproductive value of a stage is obtained by summing all the contributions of that stage back to n_1 (newborn individuals, however defined). The contributions are measured by path transmissions, which take into account probabilities of survival along each path, reproductive output at each stage to which the individuals of the stage under consideration may move, and the time required for the contributions to be made.

The more complex formula (5.31) does the same thing when the life cycle contains disjoint reproductive loops. In that case, however, the value of a reproductive contribution along one pathway is weighted by the processes occurring in the disjoint loops.

5.5.2   A Note on Eigenvectors of Reducible Matrices

In most demographic applications, there is a stage that is naturally labeled "n_1," usually corresponding to newborn individuals. If the matrix $\mathbf{A}$ is irreducible, then *any* stage may be chosen as n_1 and the formula applied directly.

If $\mathbf{A}$ is reducible, some additional care is required, because the formulas for w_i and v_i are scaled relative to w_1 and v_1. In a reducible matrix, w_i and/or v_i may equal 0 for some i; it is impossible to calculate the other entries of $\mathbf{w}$ and $\mathbf{v}$ relative to these values.

Suppose $\mathbf{A}$ is written in the normal form

$$\mathbf{A} = \begin{pmatrix} \mathbf{B} & \mathbf{0} \\ \mathbf{C} & \mathbf{D} \end{pmatrix} \qquad (5.35)$$

(see Section 4.4). Denote the set of stages in the irreducible submatrix $\mathbf{B}$ by S_1, and the remaining stages by S_2. The stages in S_1 can contribute individuals to the stages in S_2, but not vice versa. Let λ_1 denote the dominant eigenvalue of $\mathbf{A}$. If λ_1 is also an eigenvalue of $\mathbf{B}$, then n_1 should be chosen as one of the stages in S_1. This will produce a nonnegative vector $\mathbf{w}_1$

with strictly positive entries corresponding to the stages in S_1, and positive entries for those stages in S_2 to which there exists a path from n_1. The reproductive value vector $\mathbf{v}_1$ will have positive entries for all the stages in S_1, and zero entries for the stages in S_2, since they can make no contribution to n_1. This reflects the fact that an initial population composed of individuals in S_2 never contributes to any of the stages in S_1.

If λ_1 is an eigenvalue of $\mathbf{D}$ and not of $\mathbf{B}$, then n_1 should be chosen from S_2, since both $\mathbf{w}_1$ and $\mathbf{v}_1$ have zero entries corresponding to the stages in S_1. These restrictions are easily generalized to cases in which the canonical matrix has multiple irreducible diagonal blocks (Gantmacher 1959).

5.6 Net Reproductive Rate and Generation Times

Life cycle graph analysis permits us to generalize to stage-classified life cycles two important concepts of classical demography: the net reproductive rate (R_0) and mean generation time (Caswell 1988).

5.6.1 Net Reproductive Rate in Age-Classified Models

The net reproductive rate is the expected number of offspring by which a newborn individual will be replaced by the end of its life. In the continuous age-classified model, it is given by

$$R_0 = \int_0^\infty l(x)m(x)\,dx \tag{5.36}$$

The discrete equivalent is

$$R_0 = F_1 + P_1 F_2 + P_1 P_2 F_3 + \cdots \tag{5.37}$$

$$= \sum_i F_i \prod_{j=1}^{i-1} P_j \tag{5.38}$$

The cases $R_0 < 1$, $R_0 = 1$, and $R_0 > 1$ correspond to $\lambda_1 < 1$, $\lambda_1 = 1$, and $\lambda_1 > 1$, respectively.

5.6.2 Generation Time in Age-Classified Models

There are several measures of the mean length of a generation in age-classified models (Coale 1972):

1. The time T required for the population to increase by a factor of R_0. T satisfies $\lambda_1^T = R_0$, from which

$$T = \ln R_0 / \ln \lambda_1 \tag{5.39}$$

$$= \ln R_0 / r \tag{5.40}$$

2. The mean age of the parents of the offspring produced by a cohort, which is given by the mean of the net fertility schedule $\phi(x) = l(x)m(x)$

$$\mu_1 = \frac{\int_0^\infty a l(a) m(a)\, da}{\int_0^\infty l(a) m(a)\, da} \tag{5.41}$$

or, in discrete time

$$\mu_1 = \frac{\sum_i i F_i \prod_{j=1}^{i-1} P_j}{\sum_i F_i \prod_{j=1}^{i-1} P_j} \tag{5.42}$$

3. The mean age of the parents of the offspring produced by a population at the stable age distribution:

$$\bar{A} = \frac{\int_0^\infty a e^{-ra} l(a) m(a)\, da}{\int_0^\infty e^{-ra} l(a) m(a)\, da} \tag{5.43}$$

or, in discrete time

$$\bar{A} = \frac{\sum_i i \lambda^{-i} F_i \prod_{j=1}^{i-1} P_j}{\sum_i \lambda^{-i} F_i \prod_{j=1}^{i-1} P_j} \tag{5.44}$$

The denominator in both of these equations is the characteristic equation, and is thus equal to 1.

Note that μ_1 can be obtained from (5.44) by setting $\lambda = 1$. Thus, for a stationary population, μ_1 is equivalent to $\bar{A}$.

In human populations the three measures are very similar, with $T \approx (\mu_1 + \bar{A})/2$ (Coale 1972). In species with higher mortality rates and/or rates of increase farther from 1 the differences among these indices of generation time are likely to be greater.

5.6.3   Age-Classified Statistics from Stage-Classified Models

At first glance, the calculation of net reproductive rate and generation times for stage-classified models seems impossible. These statistics are inherently connected with the *age* of reproducing individuals, and stage-classified models in general contain no information on age. A stage will usually contain individuals of many different ages, and individuals of a given age will generally occupy many different stages. However, z-transform methods permit the calculation of these statistics in many cases.

Let us assume that the life cycle graph contains, or can be reduced to contain, no disjoint loops.[1] Self-loops are thus permitted, since they can be

---

[1]Thus there is at least one stage through which all individuals must pass. This corresponds to the assumption that "all individuals are born identical" used by Metz and Diekmann (1986, Chapter IV) in their discussion of related issues in continuous time.

absorbed in the calculation of transmissions, and in particular the standard size-classified model satisfies this assumption.

The characteristic equation for a life cycle satisfying this assumption is

$$1 = \sum_i L^{(i)} \tag{5.45}$$

where $L^{(i)}$ is the ith loop transmission in the z-transformed life cycle graph. Each arc in the z-transformed graph, with the self-loops absorbed, has a transmission of the form

$$\frac{a_{ij}\lambda^{-1}}{1 - a_{ii}\lambda^{-1}} = a_{ij}(\lambda^{-1} + a_{ii}\lambda^{-2} + a_{ii}^2\lambda^{-3} + \cdots) \tag{5.46}$$

Each loop transmission $L^{(i)}$ is a product of terms of this form. Combining terms containing like powers of λ^{-1}, we can thus rewrite the characteristic equation (5.45) as

$$1 = \sum_{i=1}^{\infty} k_i\lambda^{-i} \tag{5.47}$$

where k_i measures the contribution of pathways of length i.

Rewriting (5.45) in the form (5.47) translates the stage-classified model into an age-classified model by including *all* of the possible age-specific trajectories, each weighted by its probability, that an individual might follow as it develops through the stages of the life cycle. The series in (5.47) is known to converge, since it is equal to the characteristic equation (5.45).

Once the connection between the two versions of the characteristic equation [Equations (5.45) and (5.47)] is recognized, the net reproductive rate R_0 can be calculated by direct analogy with the age-classified case as

$$R_0 = \sum_i L^{(i)}\Bigg|_{\lambda=1} \tag{5.48}$$

The generation time indices T, μ_1, and $\bar{A}$ are also easily calculated. T is calculated from R_0 and λ, using (5.39) and (5.48). The mean age of reproduction in the stable population ($\bar{A}$) is calculated by noting that

$$\sum_i ik_i\lambda^{-i} = -\lambda^{-1}\sum_i \frac{\partial(k_i\lambda^{-i})}{\partial\lambda} \tag{5.49}$$

Thus

$$\bar{A} = -\lambda^{-1}\sum_i \frac{\partial L^{(i)}}{\partial\lambda}\Bigg|_{\lambda=\lambda_1} \tag{5.50}$$

The mean of the net fertility function (μ_1) is obtained by evaluating this partial derivative at $\lambda = 1$, and dividing by R_0:

$$\mu_1 = \frac{-\lambda^{-1} \sum_i \frac{\partial L^{(i)}}{\partial \lambda}\Big|_{\lambda=1}}{\sum_i L^{(i)}\big|_{\lambda=1}} \tag{5.51}$$

Example 5.8 Size-classified modular organisms

The basic size-classified model is a suitable first approximation for the genet demography of modular organisms, in which individuals are classified by the number of modules they have accumulated (Caswell 1985). If mortality of an individual requires the simultaneous mortality of most or all its modules, large individuals may be nearly immortal. Indeed, some of the oldest known living organisms are large clones of vegetatively reproducing shrubs and ferns (Cook 1983).

Potts (1983, 1984) has raised an interesting question concerning the generation times of clonal organisms in the context of the evolutionary dynamics of Indo-Pacific reef corals. About half of these reefs lie on continental shelves that have been subject to high-frequency sea level fluctuations since the Pliocene-Quaternary glaciations. He estimates that any given bathymetric level in this region has remained in the depth zone of active coral growth for an average of only 3200 years. He suggests that if large clones of corals were nearly immortal, only a few generations could be completed in this period. These species would thus never have a chance to reach evolutionary equilibrium.

To evaluate this hypothesis adequately would require size-classified demographic data on the appropriate corals, which is not available. However, size-classified matrices are available for tree populations. Trees are also long-lived modular organisms, and the survival probabilities of large individuals are quite high. Generation times from these matrices may tell us something about Potts's hypothesis.

Consider the standard size-classified matrix, characterized by the fertilities F_i in the first row, and the survival and growth probabilities P_i and G_i on the diagonal and subdiagonal. To calculate generation times, we need to obtain the derivatives of the characteristic equation. Define

$$U_i = \frac{F_i}{\lambda - P_1} \tag{5.52}$$

$$W_i = \frac{G_{i-1}}{\lambda - P_i} \tag{5.53}$$

and use these quantities to calculate

$$V_1 = 1 \tag{5.54}$$
$$V_i = V_{i-1}W_i \quad \text{for } i > 1 \tag{5.55}$$

The loop transmissions $L^{(i)}$ are then given by

$$L^{(i)} = V_i U_i \tag{5.56}$$

The generation times $\bar{A}$ and μ_1 are obtained by applying (5.50) and (5.51) to this expression for the loop transmissions. Letting primes denote differentiation with respect to λ,

$$V_1' = 0 \tag{5.57}$$
$$V_i' = W_i V_{i-1}' - \frac{V_i}{\lambda - P_i} \tag{5.58}$$
$$L^{(i)\prime} = V_i' U_i - \frac{L_i}{\lambda - P_1} \tag{5.59}$$

The results of applying this analysis to matrices for the mangrove *Avicennia marina* (Burns and Ogden 1985), the tropical tree *Pentaclethra macroloba* (Hartshorn 1975), and six populations of tropical palm *Astrocaryum mexicanum* (Pinero et al. 1984) are shown in the following table:

Species	R_0	λ	T	$\bar{A}$	μ_1
Avicennia marina	∞	1.227	∞	8.05	∞
Pentaclethra macroloba	1.2	1.002	112.9	110.84	115
Astrocaryum mexicanum	8.0	1.004	495.1	287.30	1107
A. mexicanum 2	17.3	1.011	251.3	115.22	1017
A. mexicanum 3	81.3	1.019	229.3	100.30	1179
A. mexicanum 4	0.5	0.993	650.6	—	93
A. mexicanum 5	1433.0	1.040	185.6	82.36	1137
A. mexicanum 6	281.6	1.023	251.3	98.59	2471

It is apparent that generation times for these long-lived size-classified populations can indeed be very long, although not as astronomical as Potts (1983, 1984) suggested for corals. The crucial factor, of course, is that the average generation time reflects the structure of the entire population, not just the extreme age of the oldest large individuals.

R_0, T, and μ_1 are all extremely sensitive to the diagonal elements of **A** when those elements are close to 1, because of terms of the form $\lambda - P_i$, evaluated at $\lambda = 1$, in the denominator. In many studies, estimates of P_i for the largest size classes are very crude; sample sizes for such large individuals are usually small, and mortality rates may be too small to

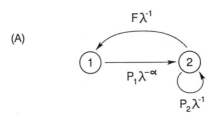

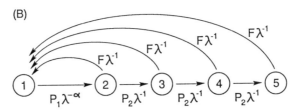

Figure 5.4: Two partial life cycle graphs. (A) A two-stage life cycle, defined by the age at maturity α, the probability P_1 of surviving to maturity, the adult survival probability P_2, and the adult fertility F. (B) A life cycle defined as in (A), but with an additional parameter giving the age at last reproduction, $\omega = 5$.

detect. The mean age in the stable population $(\bar{A})$ is much less sensitive to changes in the P_i and is probably the preferred measure of generation time in such cases. However, for chronically disturbed situations such as that considered by Potts, the cohort generation time μ_1 may be the more relevant index. In such cases, its value and interpretation will depend heavily on estimation of the survival probability of large clones.

5.7   Partial Life Cycle Analysis

Accumulating the data necessary to completely specify a life cycle graph is not easy. It is often useful to be able to derive the demographic consequences of partial life cycle information. Perhaps the simplest possible life cycle graph is that of Figure 5.4A; it is specified by the age at maturity α, the probability P_1 of surviving to maturity, the adult survival probability P_2, and the adult fertility F.

The characteristic equation of this life cycle is

$$1 = \frac{P_1 F \lambda^{-\alpha}}{\lambda - P_2} \tag{5.60}$$

Rearranging the equation and multiplying both sides by λ^α yields

$$\lambda^{\alpha+1} - P_2\lambda^\alpha - P_1F = 0 \tag{5.61}$$

The eigenvectors are

$$w_1 = 1 \tag{5.62}$$
$$w_2 = P_1\lambda^{-\alpha} \tag{5.63}$$
$$v_1 = 1 \tag{5.64}$$
$$v_2 = \frac{F}{\lambda - P_2} \tag{5.65}$$

Cole (1954) studied a slight modification of this model, in which reproduction is assumed to terminate at some age ω. The life cycle graph is shown in Figure 5.4B for $\omega = 5$. The characteristic equation is

$$
\begin{aligned}
1 &= P_1\lambda^{-\alpha}F + P_1P_2\lambda^{-(\alpha+1)}F + P_1P_2^2\lambda^{-(\alpha+2)}F \\
&\quad + \cdots + P_1P_2^{\omega-\alpha}\lambda^{-\omega}F \\
&= P_1F\lambda^{-\alpha}\left(\sum_{j=0}^{\omega-\alpha}\left(\frac{P_2}{\lambda}\right)^j\right)
\end{aligned}
\tag{5.66}
$$

The summation in (5.66) can be rewritten using (4.65) to yield

$$1 = P_1F\lambda^{-\alpha}\left(\frac{\left(\frac{P_2}{\lambda}\right)^{\omega-\alpha}-1}{\left(\frac{P_2}{\lambda}\right)-1}\right) \tag{5.67}$$

which simplifies to

$$1 = -P_1P_2^{\omega-\alpha}F\lambda^{-\omega} + P_1F\lambda^{-\alpha} + P_2\lambda^{-1} \tag{5.68}$$

These partial life cycle descriptions can be used when age at maturity, adult fertility, and juvenile and adult survival can be (even approximately) estimated. Hennemann (1983), Hayssen (1984), and Robinson and Redford (1986), for example, have used this approach to relate λ to the body size, metabolic rate, and diet of mammals using information on α, litter size, and ω from the literature. Lande (1988) used the life cycle graph of Figure 5.4A to determine the most important factors determining the success of the endangered spotted owl (see Example 7.4). Sibley and Calow (1982, 1983, 1984, 1986) have made extensive use of these models in theoretical studies of life history evolution.

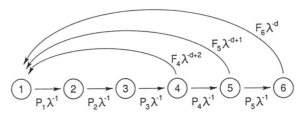

Figure 5.5: A life cycle graph for an annual plant, modeled loosely after *Phlox drummondii* (Leverich and Levin 1979).

5.8   Annual Organisms

The demographic analysis of annual organisms is complicated by the imposition of the annual cycle on top of the timing of mortality and reproduction within the year. One example is Leverich and Levin's (1979) study of the winter annual *Phlox drummondii*. This plant flowers from March through May, producing seeds that remain dormant until December, at which time they germinate and begin vegetative growth. Leverich and Levin collected age-specific survivorship and seed production information, and used standard age-classified theory to calculate r, R_0, reproductive value, etc. Unfortunately, the demographic model they used is inappropriate, since it assumes that offspring begin their own lives immediately, rather than after a period of dormancy. Their analysis predicts that a population starting from a cohort of germinating seeds will eventually reach a stable age distribution with all ages present at all times of the year. This clearly doesn't happen.

An appropriate life cycle graph, which takes the annual cycle into account, is shown in Figure 5.5. The nodes n_1–n_6 represent age-classes of plants; in the case of *P. drummondii* these could be monthly age classes, from December through May. The exponents on the fertility coefficients denote the time required for seeds to reach n_1; this includes the time d from the end of the reproductive season to germination ($d = 7$ months, from May to December, for *P. drummondii*), plus any extra time required by reproduction earlier in the season. The fertility coefficients F_i, of course, include not only seed production by n_i, but also survival of those seeds to germination. The characteristic equation is

$$1 = \lambda^{(-d+5)} \left(P_1 P_2 P_3 F_4 + P_1 P_2 P_3 P_4 F_5 + P_1 P_2 P_3 P_4 P_5 F_6 \right) \qquad (5.69)$$

The stable age distribution and the reproductive value are

$$w_1 = 1 \qquad\qquad v_1 = 1$$
$$w_2 = P_1\lambda^{-1} \qquad\qquad v_2 = \lambda^{-(d+4)}P_2P_3\left(F_4 + P_4F_5 + F_4P_5F_6\right)$$
$$w_3 = P_1P_2\lambda^{-2} \qquad\qquad v_3 = \lambda^{-(d+3)}P_3\left(F_4 + P_4F_5 + P_4P_5F_6\right)$$
$$w_4 = P_1P_2P_3\lambda^{-3} \qquad\qquad v_4 = \lambda^{-(d+2)}\left(F_4 + P_4F_5 + P_4P_5F_6\right)$$
$$w_5 = P_1P_2P_3P_4\lambda^{-4} \qquad\qquad v_5 = \lambda^{-(d+1)}\left(F_5 + P_5F_6\right)$$
$$w_6 = P_1P_2P_3P_4P_5\lambda^{-5} \qquad\qquad v_6 = \lambda^{-d}\left(F_6\right)$$

The graph is primitive; all loops are of length $d + 5$ (12 months for *P. drummondii*). We know from Section 4.4.3 that the age distribution does not converge, but oscillates with a period of 12 months. A running average of the population over this period eventually grows at a rate given by the maximum solution to (5.69), with a structure proportional to **w**. Note that models for annuals using a projection interval of a year (e.g., Schmidt and Lawlor 1983, Schmidt and Levin 1985) have rather different properties; their primitivity, for example, depends on the presence of a seed bank.

Chapter 6

Sensitivity Analysis and Evolutionary Demography

Chapter 4 presented a series of demographic indices that can be calculated from a projection matrix: the asymptotic population growth rate, the stable stage distribution, the reproductive value, the damping ratio, and the period of oscillation of the subdominant eigenvalues. Each of these quantities is an implicit function of the entries in the matrix. An important part of the analysis of the matrix is investigating how the results would vary in response to changes in the matrix. Such changes, of course, represent changes in the life cycle, and may be of interest in several different contexts:

- Measuring "how important" a given vital rate is to population growth. Although population growth is an integrative function of *all* the life cycle coefficients, some organisms seem to "rely on" survival much more than on reproduction, and vice versa. One can ask for a quantitative measure of the contribution of different coefficients to population growth; this is provided in Section 6.1.7.

- Evaluating the effects of errors in estimation. Since λ is a function of the a_{ij}, errors in estimating the a_{ij} result in errors in λ. The most important errors will be those in the coefficients to which λ is most sensitive. Information on the sensitivity of λ to changes in the a_{ij} can thus be used to design sampling procedures that maximize the precision of the estimates of the most critical coefficients.

- Quantifying the effects of environmental perturbations. The responses of the vital rates to environmental factors are diverse. Some factors affect survival but not reproduction, others growth but not survival, etc., and the responses generally differ among stages. The asymptotic growth rate λ_1 (or $r = \ln \lambda_1$) is frequently used as an integrative measure of the population-level consequences of the effects of the environment on the vital rates (Andrewartha and Birch 1954). Such studies, called *life table response experiments* (Caswell 1989a), can be analyzed in terms of the sensitivity of λ_1 to changes in the a_{ij} (Section 6.1.9).

- Evaluating alternative management strategies. Management strategies to protect endangered species or to control pest species can be evaluated by their impact on λ (e.g., Menges 1988, Lande 1988). Knowing how λ responds to the changes in the vital rates produced by alternative strategies may help choose the most appropriate strategy in a given situation (e.g., Crouse et al. 1987).

- Predicting the intensity of natural selection. The vital rates are part of the phenotype, and are subject to genetic variation. Genetic changes in the a_{ij} will produce changes in the demographic indices. Since fitness is a basically demographic notion (a measure of the relative rate at which a genotype propagates itself into future generations), the connection between life cycle perturbations and population growth rate λ provides a measure of the effect of genetic changes on fitness. Natural selection is predicted to favor traits that produce increases in fitness, so sensitivity analysis can predict trait combinations that should be favored by selection. This provides the basis for life history theory; the framework for this theory is presented in Section 6.4.

This chapter will explore sensitivity analyses that answer each of these kinds of questions.

6.1 Eigenvalue Sensitivity

Because of the importance of the eigenvalues of the projection matrix $\mathbf{A}$, we turn first to the sensitivity of the eigenvalues (especially λ_1) to changes in the matrix elements a_{ij}. These results, which play a fundamental role in life history theory, can be generalized to give the sensitivity of λ to other variables as well.

6.1.1 Perturbation of Matrix Elements

The problem at hand is to calculate the sensitivity of λ_1 to small changes in the matrix elements a_{ij}. The simplest approach is to change each of the a_{ij}, perhaps by a constant percentage, and numerically calculate λ_1 (e.g., Sarukhan and Gadgil 1974, Hartshorn 1975, Enright and Ogden 1979, Bierzychudek 1982, Burns and Ogden 1985, Crouse et al. 1987), but this approach can be used only if numerical values for $\mathbf{A}$ are available; it provides no insight into sensitivity independently of those values. Accordingly, we turn instead to analytical methods for evaluating eigenvalue sensitivity.

The eigenvalues are a function of the a_{ij}; that functional dependence is expressed implicitly in the characteristic equation

$$\det(\mathbf{A} - \lambda \mathbf{I}) = 0$$

When the form of the characteristic equation is known *a priori*, implicit differentiation can be used to find $\partial \lambda / \partial a_{ij}$ (Hamilton 1966, Demetrius 1969, Emlen 1970, Goodman 1971, Keyfitz 1971a, Mertz 1971). We will use this approach in Section 6.1.10, but it is limited to cases in which the characteristic equation is known, and of sufficiently simple form that implicit differentiation yields a simple solution.

A simple and general approach to eigenvalue sensitivity, applicable to matrices of any structure, was introduced by Caswell (1978). The formula dates back at least to Jacobi (1846), and has been rederived many times (e.g., Faddeev 1959, Faddeev and Faddeeva 1963, Desoer 1967). For a complete and rigorous discussion, see Kato (1982). Cohen (1978, p. 186) provides an alternative approach to eigenvalue sensitivity.

We begin with the equations defining the eigenvalues and the right and left eigenvectors:

$$\mathbf{A}\mathbf{w}_i \;=\; \lambda_i \mathbf{w}_i \tag{6.1}$$

$$\mathbf{v}_i' \mathbf{A} \;=\; \lambda_i \mathbf{v}_i' \tag{6.2}$$

For the moment, we suppress the subscript i; the following formulas apply to any of the eigenvalues and their corresponding right and left eigenvectors. Taking the differential of both sides of (6.1) yields

$$\mathbf{A}(d\mathbf{w}) + (d\mathbf{A})\mathbf{w} = \lambda(d\mathbf{w}) + (d\lambda)\mathbf{w} \tag{6.3}$$

where the matrix differential $d\mathbf{A} = (da_{ij})$. Form the scalar product of both sides with the left eigenvector $\mathbf{v}$

$$\langle \mathbf{A}(d\mathbf{w}), \mathbf{v} \rangle + \langle (d\mathbf{A})\mathbf{w}, \mathbf{v} \rangle = \lambda \langle (d\mathbf{w}), \mathbf{v} \rangle + \langle (d\lambda)\mathbf{w}, \mathbf{v} \rangle \tag{6.4}$$

Expanding the scalar products and canceling terms leaves

$$d\lambda = \frac{\langle (d\mathbf{A})\mathbf{w}, \mathbf{v} \rangle}{\langle \mathbf{w}, \mathbf{v} \rangle} \tag{6.5}$$

This gives the net effect on λ of changes in all the entries of $\mathbf{A}$.

Now suppose that only one element, a_{ij}, is subject to change, while all the others are held constant. Then $d\mathbf{A}$ contains only one nonzero entry, da_{ij}, in row i and column j. In this case (6.5) reduces to

$$d\lambda = \frac{v_i w_j \, da_{ij}}{\langle \mathbf{w}, \mathbf{v} \rangle} \tag{6.6}$$

Dividing both sides by da_{ij}, and rewriting the differentials as partial derivatives (since all but one of the variables of which λ is a function are being held constant), we get the final formula[1]

$$\frac{\partial \lambda}{\partial a_{ij}} = \frac{v_i w_j}{\langle \mathbf{w}, \mathbf{v} \rangle} \tag{6.8}$$

That is, the sensitivity of λ to changes in a_{ij} is proportional to the product of the ith element of the reproductive value vector and the jth element of the stable stage distribution. The scalar product term in the denominator is independent of i and j, and can be ignored when considering the relative sensitivities of λ to different elements in the same matrix. Or, the eigenvectors may be scaled so that $\langle \mathbf{w}, \mathbf{v} \rangle = 1$, so that the term can be ignored.

Thus the eigenvectors $\mathbf{w}_1$ and $\mathbf{v}_1$ not only provide their own demographic information about the population (stable stage distribution and reproductive value), they also provide complete information about the sensitivity of the asymptotic population growth rate to changes in the elements of the matrix.

Example 6.1 Age-classified sensitivities

Figure 6.1 shows the sensitivity of λ_1 to changes in age-specific fertilities F_i and survival probabilities P_i for three populations (a flour beetle, a vole, and humans). Fertility sensitivities fall off nearly exponentially with age; survival sensitivities are larger than fertility sensitivities at the beginning of the life cycle, but eventually decline more rapidly and cross the fertility sensitivity curves. The sensitivity of λ_1 to changes in the vital rates may vary by as much as 8 orders of magnitude.

6.1.2 Sensitivity and Age

The relationship of eigenvalue sensitivity to age (Figure 6.1) in age-classified models plays an important part in the theory of senescence (Medawar 1952, Williams 1957, Hamilton 1966, Rose 1984b, Gleeson 1984). The eigenvectors $\mathbf{w}$ and $\mathbf{v}$ for age-classified populations are

$$w_1 = 1 \tag{6.9}$$
$$w_i = P_1 P_2 \cdots P_{i-1} \lambda^{-i+1} \qquad \text{for } i > 1 \tag{6.10}$$

---

[1]Actually, we need to be a little more careful. If λ is complex, then (6.8) becomes

$$\frac{\partial \lambda}{\partial a_{ij}} = \frac{\bar{v}_i w_j}{\langle \mathbf{w}, \mathbf{v} \rangle} \tag{6.7}$$

where $\bar{v}_i$ is the complex conjugate of v_i. This distinction is important in calculating sensitivities of the subdominant eigenvalues, and in calculating eigenvector sensitivities.

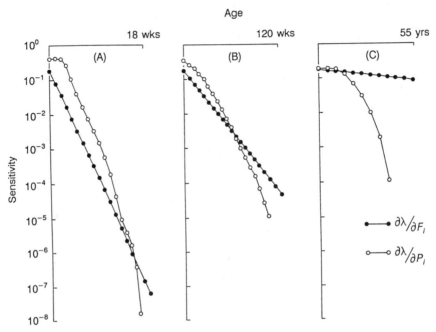

Figure 6.1: The sensitivity of the dominant eigenvalue λ to changes in age-specific fertility F_i and survival probability P_i for (A) a laboratory population of the flour beetle *Calandra oryzae* (Birch 1948), (B) a laboratory population of the vole *Microtus orcadensis* (Leslie et al. 1955), and (C) the human population of the United States in 1965 (Keyfitz and Flieger 1968). From Caswell (1978).

and

$$v_1 = 1 \tag{6.11}$$
$$v_i = F_i\lambda^{-1} + P_iv_{i+1} \qquad \text{for } i > 1 \tag{6.12}$$

Certain inequalities follow from these formulas (Demetrius 1969, Caswell 1978, 1982c). Consider the sensitivity of λ to changes in fertility at successive ages. From (6.8) and (6.10) it follows that

$$\frac{\partial\lambda/\partial F_j}{\partial\lambda/\partial F_{j+1}} = \frac{w_j}{w_{j+1}} \tag{6.13}$$

$$= \frac{\lambda}{P_j} \tag{6.14}$$

Thus the sensitivity of λ to fertility changes is a strictly decreasing function of age as long as $\lambda > 1$. If the P_j are constant, then the decrease will be exponential, as is approximately true in Figure 6.1. Other things being equal, the sensitivity of λ to changes in fertility decreases with age more rapidly the greater the value of λ. In a decreasing population, however, the sensitivity will actually increase from age j to $j + 1$ if $\lambda < P_j$.

The ratio of the sensitivity of λ to changes in survival at successive ages is

$$\frac{\partial\lambda/\partial P_j}{\partial\lambda/\partial P_{j+1}} = \frac{w_j v_{j+1}}{w_{j+1} v_{j+2}} \tag{6.15}$$

$$= \frac{\lambda}{P_j}\left(\frac{F_{j+1}\lambda^{-1} + P_{j+1}v_{j+2}}{v_{j+2}}\right) \tag{6.16}$$

$$= \lambda\frac{P_{j+1}}{P_j} + \frac{F_{j+1}}{P_j v_{j+2}} \tag{6.17}$$

$$\geq \frac{P_{j+1}}{P_j} \quad \text{if } \lambda \geq 1 \tag{6.18}$$

Thus the sensitivity of λ to age-specific survival changes is monotonically decreasing as long as $\lambda \geq 1$ and $P_{j+1} \geq P_j$.

We can also ask how the relative importance of fertility and survival changes varies with age, by examining

$$\frac{\partial\lambda/\partial P_j}{\partial\lambda/\partial F_j} = \frac{v_{j+1}w_j}{v_1 w_j} \tag{6.19}$$

$$= \frac{v_{j+1}}{v_1} \tag{6.20}$$

Thus λ is more sensitive to a change in survival than the same change in fertility as long as $v_{j+1} > v_1$. This condition is satisfied at least up to the age of first reproduction, and we note that in Figure 6.1 $\partial\lambda/\partial P_j > \partial\lambda/\partial F_j$ for young ages; the inequality is eventually reversed for older ages.

6.1.3 Sensitivities in Size-Classified Models

The patterns of sensitivity in the standard size-classified model can be quite different from those exhibited by age-classified populations because, unlike the stable age distribution, the stable size distribution is not monotonically non-increasing, even when $\lambda_1 > 1$. Instead, there may be peaks in the stable size distribution (as is commonly observed in fish and tree size distributions). Combined with the shape of the reproductive value distribution, these peaks can generate sensitivity curves that either increase or decrease with size.

Figures 6.2, 6.3, and 6.4 show the sensitivities of λ_1 to changes in F_i (fertility), G_i (the probability of surviving and growing to the next size class), and P_i (the probability of surviving and staying in the same size class), for populations of five species of trees.[2] The patterns are diverse, but it is clear that what happens at large sizes may, unlike what happens at old ages in age-classified populations, be quite important to population growth.

6.1.4 Sensitivity to Multistep Transitions

We saw in Section 5.2.1 how to include in the life cycle graph transitions that require more than a single projection interval. The coefficients on these transitions, unlike those on single-step transitions, are not elements of the projection matrix $\mathbf{A}$, and their sensitivity analysis requires a modification of the basic formula (Caswell 1985).

Figure 6.5 shows a section of a life cycle graph including α stages, from n_1 to $n_{\alpha+1}$, and the reduction of this section to a single transition requiring α time steps. The coefficient P gives the probability of surviving over the α time steps, where $P = \delta_1 \delta_2 \cdots \delta_\alpha$. The problem is to evaluate $\partial \lambda / \partial P$.

The perturbation of the survival coefficient P can be generated by a perturbation in any of the single-step survival probabilities δ_i. Without loss of generality, we assume that δ_1 is changed. Then

$$\frac{\partial \lambda}{\partial P} = \left(\frac{1}{\delta_2 \delta_3 \cdots \delta_\alpha} \right) \frac{\partial \lambda}{\partial \delta_1}$$

$$= \left(\frac{1}{\delta_2 \delta_3 \cdots \delta_\alpha} \right) \left(\frac{v_2 w_1}{\langle \mathbf{w}, \mathbf{v} \rangle} \right) \tag{6.21}$$

However, v_2 can be rewritten as

$$v_2 = \delta_2 \delta_3 \cdots \delta_\alpha \lambda^{-\alpha+1} v_{\alpha+1} \tag{6.22}$$

Thus

$$\frac{\partial \lambda}{\partial P} = \lambda^{-\alpha+1} \frac{w_1 v_{\alpha+1}}{\langle \mathbf{w}, \mathbf{v} \rangle} \tag{6.23}$$

If $\alpha = 1$, this reduces to the basic formula for the sensitivity of λ to a change in a_{ij}, as it should.

One final note: the scalar product in the denominator of (6.21) refers to the *original*, unreduced life cycle graph. However, for (6.23) we would like to

---

[2]These data come from (A) Burns and Ogden's (1985) study of a population of the mangrove *Avicennia marina* in New Zealand, (B) Pinero et al.'s (1984) study of six populations of the palm *Astrocarym mexicanum* in Mexico, Enright and Ogden's (1979) study of (C) three stands, each with two fertility estimates, of *Nothofagus fusca* in New Zealand and (D) one population of *Araucaria cunninghami* in New Guinea, and (E) Hartshorn's (1975) study of *Pentaclethra macroloba*, a wet forest canopy tree in Costa Rica. These data are also used in Figures 6.6, 6.7, and 6.10–6.12, which are reprinted from Caswell (1986) by permission of the American Mathematical Society.

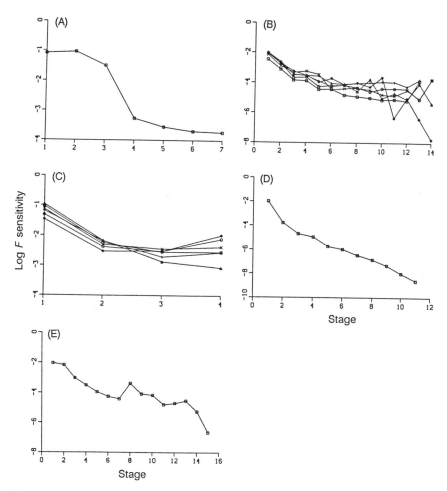

Figure 6.2: The sensitivities of λ to changes in fertility F_i as a function of size class i, for five tree populations. From Caswell (1986).

write $\langle \mathbf{w}, \mathbf{v} \rangle$ directly in terms of the reduced graph, in which $n_2, n_3, \ldots, n_\alpha$ do not appear. We do so by writing

$$w_i = \left(\frac{\lambda^{\alpha-i+1}}{\delta_i \delta_{i+1} \cdots \delta_\alpha} \right) w_{\alpha+1} \qquad (6.24)$$

$$v_i = \delta_i \delta_{i+1} \cdots \delta_\alpha \lambda^{-\alpha+i-1} v_{\alpha+1} \qquad (6.25)$$

for $2 \le i \le \alpha$. Thus

$$w_i v_i = w_{\alpha+1} v_{\alpha+1} \qquad \text{for } 2 \le i \le \alpha \qquad (6.26)$$

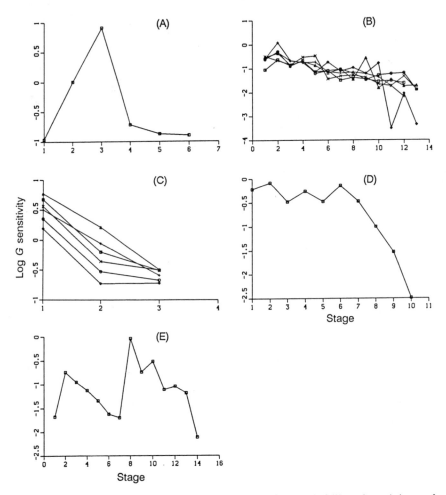

Figure 6.3: The sensitivities of λ to changes in G_i (the probability of surviving and growing to the next size class) as a function of size class i, for five tree populations. From Caswell (1986).

and in terms of the *reduced* life cycle graph

$$\langle \mathbf{w}, \mathbf{v} \rangle = w_1 v_1 + \alpha w_{\alpha+1} v_{\alpha+1} + \cdots \qquad (6.27)$$

6.1.5   Sensitivity to Lower Level Parameters

Equation (6.8) gives the sensitivity of λ to changes in a single a_{ij}. In many cases of interest, however, the a_{ij} are functions of some lower level variable, and simple chain rule differentiation provides the sensitivity of λ to these

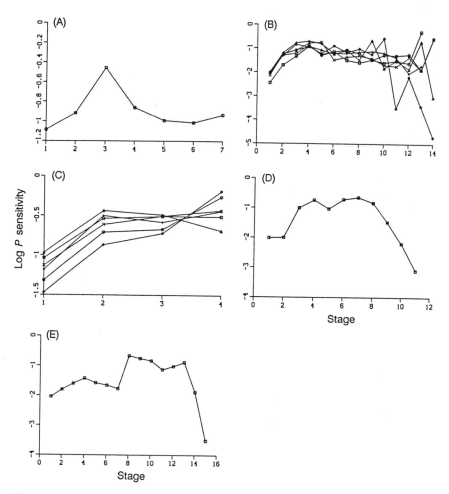

Figure 6.4: The sensitivities of λ to changes in P_i (the probability of surviving and remaining in the same size class) as a function of size class i, for five tree populations. From Caswell (1986).

variables. Suppose the a_{ij} are functions of x; then

$$\frac{\partial \lambda}{\partial x} = \sum_{i,j} \frac{\partial \lambda}{\partial a_{ij}} \frac{\partial a_{ij}}{\partial x} \tag{6.28}$$

This result can be used to analyze cases in which a single trait effects more than one vital rate (Templeton 1980). McGraw and Antonovics (1983), for example, use it to evaluate the sensitivity of λ to changes in the parameters of a growth model, in a study of the shoot demography of *Dryas octopetala*.

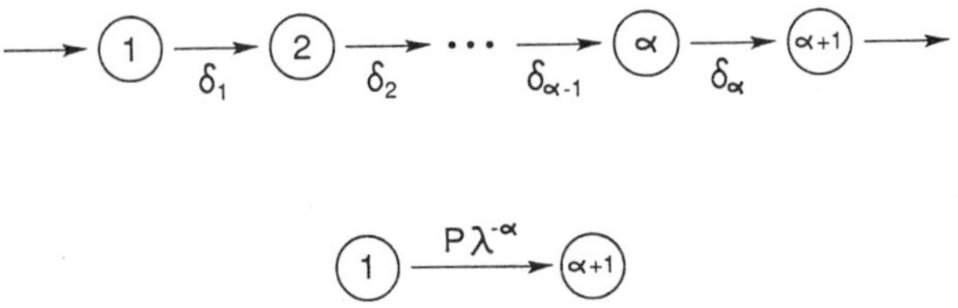

Figure 6.5: The lower graph segment is a reduction of the upper segment, where the δ_i are survival probabilities, whose product is equal to P. From Caswell (1985).

Example 6.2 Survival and growth sensitivity in size-classified populations

The standard size-classified model is parameterized in terms of F_i, G_i (the probability that an individual in size class i survives and grows into class $i + 1$), and P_i (the probability that an individual in class i survives and remains in the same class). The G_i and P_i can be rewritten as functions of the survival probability of size class i (σ_i) and the growth probability for a surviving individual of size class i (γ_i):

$$G_i = \sigma_i \gamma_i \tag{6.29}$$

$$P_i = \sigma_i(1 - \gamma_i) \tag{6.30}$$

From (6.28)

$$\frac{\partial \lambda}{\partial \sigma_i} = \frac{\partial \lambda}{\partial G_i}\frac{\partial G_i}{\partial \sigma_i} + \frac{\partial \lambda}{\partial P_i}\frac{\partial P_i}{\partial \sigma_i} \tag{6.31}$$

$$= \frac{w_i(v_i + \gamma_i \Delta v_i)}{\langle \mathbf{w}, \mathbf{v}\rangle} \tag{6.32}$$

where $\Delta v_i = v_{i+1} - v_i$ is the change in reproductive value from size class i to $i + 1$. Similarly,

$$\frac{\partial \lambda}{\partial \gamma_i} = \frac{\partial \lambda}{\partial G_i}\frac{\partial G_i}{\partial \gamma_i} + \frac{\partial \lambda}{\partial P_i}\frac{\partial P_i}{\partial \gamma_i} \tag{6.33}$$

$$= \frac{w_i(\sigma_i \Delta v_i)}{\langle \mathbf{w}, \mathbf{v}\rangle} \tag{6.34}$$

The sensitivity to growth rate changes (6.34) is negative if $v_{i+1} < v_i$. That is, λ is reduced by increasing the growth rate from n_i to n_{i+1} if stage $i + 1$ has a lower reproductive value than stage i.

Figures 6.6 and 6.7 show the sensitivities of λ to the survival and growth probabilities for the five tree species examined in Figures 6.2 – 6.4.

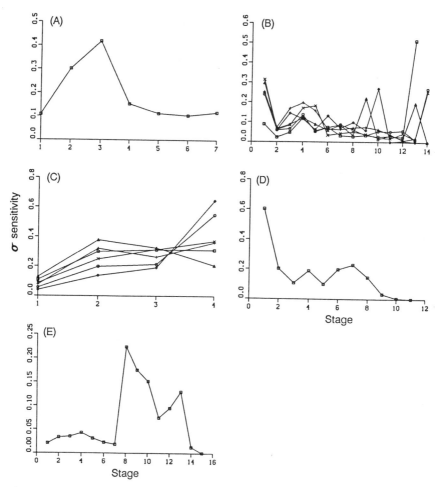

Figure 6.6: The sensitivities of λ to changes in the survival probability σ_i as a function of size class i, for five tree populations. From Caswell (1986).

6.1.6 An Overall Eigenvalue Sensitivity Index

The sensitivity of λ to all the a_{ij} can be integrated into an overall index S that measures the sensitivity of λ to changes in the the entire life cycle (Caswell 1978). Taking norms of both sides of (6.5), assuming the eigenvectors have been scaled so that $\langle \mathbf{w}, \mathbf{v} \rangle = 1$, yields

$$
\begin{aligned}
|d\lambda| &= \|\mathbf{v}'d\mathbf{A}\mathbf{w}\| \\
&\leq \|\mathbf{v}'\|\,\|d\mathbf{A}\|\,\|\mathbf{w}\| \\
&= S\|d\mathbf{A}\|
\end{aligned}
$$

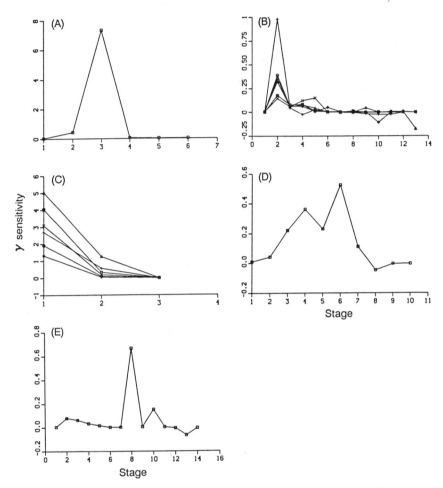

Figure 6.7: The sensitivities of λ to changes in the growth probability γ_i as a function of size class i, for five tree populations. From Caswell (1986).

where $\|\mathbf{x}\| = \sqrt{\sum x_i^2}$ is the Euclidean norm of the vector $\mathbf{x}$, $\|d\mathbf{A}\|$ is the corresponding matrix norm[3] of $d\mathbf{A}$, and

$$S = \|\mathbf{v}'\| \, \|\mathbf{w}\| = \sqrt{\sum_{i,j} \left(\frac{\partial \lambda}{\partial a_{ij}} \right)} \tag{6.35}$$

---

[3]The spectral norm; see Horn and Johnson (1985, p. 295). Caswell (1978) used the Euclidean norm of $d\mathbf{A}$, which is not strictly correct. However, the conclusion that S provides a bound on the magnitude of $|d\lambda|$ is correct.

is the sensitivity index. It gives an upper bound on the magnitude of the change in λ produced by a perturbation of $\mathbf{A}$ of a given magnitude.

Another way to think of S is to suppose that the a_{ij} are independent random variables with a common variance σ_a^2. Then, to a first approximation,

$$\sigma_\lambda^2 \approx \sum_{i,j} \left(\frac{\partial \lambda}{\partial a_{ij}} \right)^2 \sigma_a^2 \tag{6.36}$$

so that

$$S \approx \frac{\sigma_\lambda}{\sigma_a} \tag{6.37}$$

is the approximate standard deviation in λ resulting from a unit standard deviation in the a_{ij}. Thus S measures the amplification of variance in the vital rates into variance in λ.

S can be modified by excluding from the summation in (6.35) those matrix entries that are known *a priori* not to vary. For example, only the first row and subdiagonal of a Leslie matrix can be nonzero; it makes no sense to include in S the contributions from the sensitivity of λ to other entries in the matrix, since they are restricted to be zero.

Example 6.3 Tropical trees

The overall sensitivity index S has not been calculated often enough to know what significance to attach to particular values. As an example of both inter- and intra-specific comparison, consider the size-classified models of the tropical trees *Pentaclethra macroloba* (Hartshorn 1975) and *Astrocaryum mexicanum* (Pinero et al. 1984). These populations were close to equilibrium, as indicated by values of λ close to 1. Overall sensitivity indices calculated from these data are

Species	λ	S_{total}	$S_{\text{restricted}}$
P. macroloba	1.0017	105.4091	1.0677
A. mexicanum	1.0042	32.5757	0.6551
A. mexicanum	1.0114	36.6515	0.7292
A. mexicanum	1.0194	42.7363	0.7488
A. mexicanum	0.9933	19.5321	1.3466
A. mexicanum	1.0399	22.7738	0.8847
A. mexicanum	1.0227	27.0772	0.7638

where S_{total} is calculated over the entire matrix, and $S_{\text{restricted}}$ is calculated by summing only over the first row, diagonal, and subdiagonal.

In general, the overall sensitivity of the *Pentaclethra* population is about five times greater than that of the *Astrocaryum* populations as

measured by S_{total}. However, when attention is restricted to matrix
elements in which changes could conceivably occur, all the populations
are much more comparable. Certainly the value for *Pentaclethra* falls
within the range of variation among populations of *Astrocaryum*.

6.1.7 Elasticity

Transition probabilities (which may not exceed 1) and fertilities (which are
under no such restriction) are measured on different scales; this can make
comparison of their sensitivities difficult. If, for example, $\partial\lambda/\partial F_i < \partial\lambda/\partial P_i$,
then a given change in F_i will have much less effect on λ than the same
change in P_i. However, if F_i is much greater than P_i, the "given change"
in the two parameters will represent a much greater *proportional* change in
P_i than in F_i. We would like to have a measure of the sensitivity of λ to
proportional changes in the matrix coefficients. Caswell et al. (1984) and de
Kroon et al. (1986) introduced a simple analytical approach to this problem,
using the economist's concept of "elasticity" as a measure of proportional
sensitivity.

The elasticity of λ with respect to a_{ij} is defined as

$$e_{ij} \;=\; \frac{a_{ij}}{\lambda}\frac{\partial\lambda}{\partial a_{ij}} \tag{6.38}$$

$$=\; \frac{\partial\log\lambda}{\partial\log a_{ij}} \tag{6.39}$$

It gives the proportional change in λ resulting from a proportional change
in a_{ij}.

Example 6.4 Fertility elasticity in teasel

Consider the teasel population from Field A of Werner and Caswell
(1977). The sensitivity of λ to changes in the fertility of flowering
plants is $\partial\lambda/\partial a_{17} = 0.001$. By contrast, the sensitivities of λ to changes
in growth and survival transitions among small, medium, and large
rosettes range from 0.01 to 1.28. This suggests that growth and survival are from 10 to 1000 times as important as is fertility. However,
the fertility term $a_{77} = 431$ is three orders of magnitude larger than
the possible values for the transition probabilities. Calculation of the
elasticities of λ with respect to these coefficients yields $e_{77} = 0.249$,
which is the largest elasticity in the entire matrix. From the perspective of proportional sensitivity, fertility is the most, rather than one of
the least important coefficients in the life cycle.

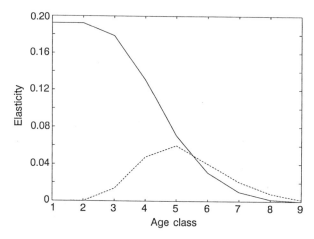

Figure 6.8: The elasticities of λ with respect to changes in age-specific survival probability P_i (solid line) and fertility F_i (dashed line) for the population of the United States, 1965.

Example 6.5 Age-classified elasticities

As in Section 6.1.2, we can examine the variation in elasticity with age. The ratio of successive fertility elasticities is

$$\frac{e_{1j}}{e_{1,j+1}} = \left(\frac{F_j}{F_{j+1}}\right)\left(\frac{\lambda}{P_j}\right) \tag{6.40}$$

This is not restricted to be greater than one, so fertility elasticities may increase or decrease with age. The survival elasticities, on the other hand, are monotonically nonincreasing, as long as $\lambda \geq 1$. The ratio of successive survival elasticities is

$$\frac{e_{j+1,j}}{e_{j+2,j+1}} = \frac{P_{j+1}}{P_j}\frac{\partial\lambda/\partial P_j}{\partial\lambda/\partial P_{j+1}} \tag{6.41}$$

$$= \lambda + \frac{F_{i+1}}{P_{i+1}v_{i+2}} \tag{6.42}$$

[cf. Equation (6.17)].

As an example, the elasticity of λ with respect to age-specific survival and fertility is shown in Figure 6.8 for the population of the United States in 1966.

Elasticity and Contributions to λ

The elasticities of λ with respect to the a_{ij} also provide an estimate of the "contribution" of each of the a_{ij} to λ. The "contribution" must be interpreted carefully, since λ is, of course, a function of *all* the a_{ij}, and the importance of each will depend on the values of the others.

First, de Kroon et al. (1986) show that

$$\sum_{i,j} e_{ij} \;=\; \frac{1}{\lambda} \sum_{i,j} \frac{a_{ij} v_i w_j}{\langle \mathbf{w}, \mathbf{v} \rangle} \tag{6.43}$$

$$= \; \frac{1}{\lambda} \left(\sum_i v_i \sum_j \frac{a_{ij} w_j}{\langle \mathbf{w}, \mathbf{v} \rangle} \right) \tag{6.44}$$

$$= \; \frac{1}{\lambda} \left(\sum_i \frac{\lambda v_i w_i}{\langle \mathbf{w}, \mathbf{v} \rangle} \right) \tag{6.45}$$

$$= \; 1 \tag{6.46}$$

The elasticities thus sum to 1, and each represents a proportional contribution to the total elasticity of the life cycle. Multiplying both sides of (6.46) by λ yields

$$\lambda \;=\; \sum_{i,j} \lambda e_{ij} \tag{6.47}$$

$$= \; \sum_{i,j} a_{ij} s_{ij} \tag{6.48}$$

where $s_{ij} = \partial \lambda / \partial a_{ij}$. Thus, each e_{ij} gives the proportional contribution of its corresponding a_{ij} to λ. Moreover, this decomposition of λ is the only expression of the form

$$\lambda = \sum_{i,j} a_{ij} b_{ij}$$

where the contributions b_{ij} can be written as the product of one term that is a function only of i and another that is a function only of j (Caswell 1986).

The e_{ij} thus provide valuable information about the extent to which population growth depends on survival, growth, and reproduction at different stages in the life cycle.

Example 6.6 Important pathways in the teasel life cycle

Figure 6.9 shows the contributions of the pathways in the teasel life cycle of Figure 4.3 to λ. These contributions are the elasticities, expressed as percentages. Only five pathways, shown by heavy arrows, contribute more than 5% to λ. To a good approximation (73% of λ), the growth rate of teasel can be described in terms of only three

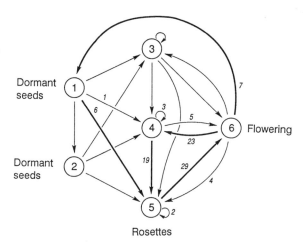

Figure 6.9: The contributions, expressed as percentages, of the pathways in the teasel life cycle (Figure 4.3) to λ. Only contributions of more than 1% are shown. Heavy arrows indicate those pathways contributing 5% or more of λ.

transitions: flowering plants $\to$ medium rosettes $\to$ large rosettes $\to$ flowering plants. Adding the pathway flowering plants $\to$ dormant seeds $\to$ large rosettes adds an additional 13% of λ.

Example 6.7 Important pathways in size-classified tree life cycles

Teasel is a short-lived herbaceous plant. It is interesting to compare the patterns shown in Figure 6.9 with those exhibited by more long-lived species. Figures 6.10 – 6.12 show the elasticities of λ with respect to P_i, G_i, and F_i (in the standard size-classified model) for five tree species. The elasticities for P_i are consistently larger than those for G_i or F_i. These tree populations thus seem to rely less on growth and reproduction, and more on their ability to survive and remain in the same size class, than is true for teasel. This provides quantitative support for what would probably be the subjective assessment by most ecologists of the relative importance of these factors in trees and herbaceous plants.

Lower Level Elasticities

It is possible to calculate the elasticity of λ to a lower level variable x, as

$$\frac{x}{\lambda}\frac{\partial\lambda}{\partial x} = \frac{x}{\lambda}\sum_{i,j}\frac{\partial\lambda}{\partial a_{ij}}\frac{\partial a_{ij}}{\partial x} \tag{6.49}$$

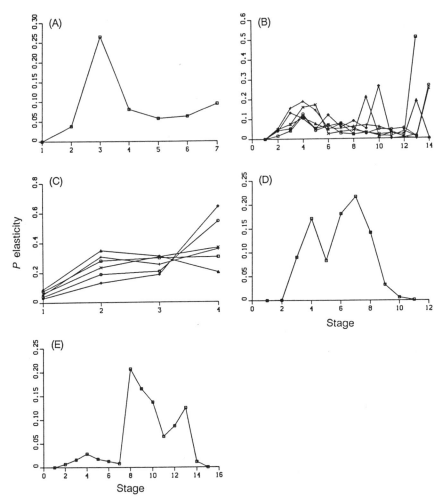

Figure 6.10: The elasticities of λ with respect to P_i as a function of size class i, for five tree populations. From Caswell (1986).

Such an elasticity gives the proportional change in λ resulting from a proportional change in x, but does *not* satisfy (6.46) or (6.48). Thus these elasticities do not sum to 1, nor do they give the contribution of the various variables to λ.

6.1.8 A Third Interpretation of Reproductive Value

Our first interpretation of the left eigenvector $\mathbf{v}_1$ as a measure of reproductive value was in terms of the effects of initial population structure on asymptotic

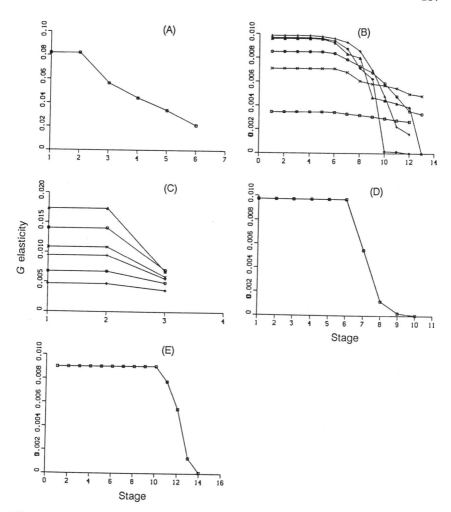

Figure 6.11: The elasticities of λ with respect to G_i as a function of size class i, for five tree populations. From Caswell (1986).

population size (Section 4.5). The second was based on the graph-theoretic formulas for v_i in terms of the transmission of the paths from n_i back to n_1 (Section 5.5).

The sensitivity formula (6.8) provides a third justification for defining reproductive value as the left eigenvector $\mathbf{v}_1$ of the population projection matrix. Consider a stage j that can contribute individuals to two other stages, 1 and 2 (Figure 6.13). Increases in either a_{1j} or a_{2j} will increase λ, and a reasonable measure of the "value" of stages 1 and 2 is the relative

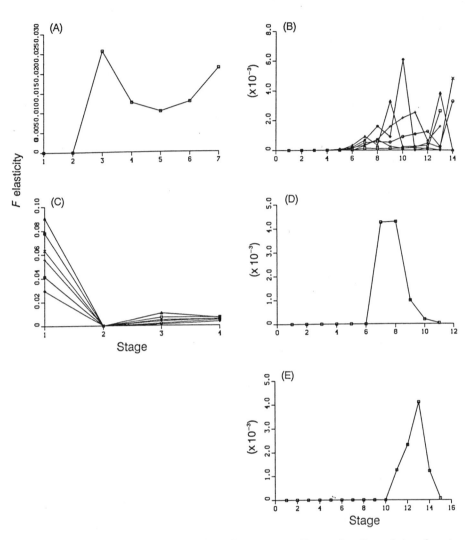

Figure 6.12: The elasticities of λ with respect to F_i as a function of size class i, for five tree populations. From Caswell (1986).

sensitivity of λ to changes in a_{1j} and a_{2j}:

$$\frac{\partial\lambda/\partial a_{1j}}{\partial\lambda/\partial a_{2j}} = \frac{v_1 w_j}{v_2 w_j}$$

$$= \frac{v_1}{v_2} \tag{6.50}$$

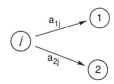

Figure 6.13: A portion of a life cycle graph showing a stage j which can contribute to two other stages, n_1 and n_2.

That is, the relative sensitivity of λ to changes in a_{1j} and a_{2j} is given by the relative magnitudes of v_1 and v_2. An individual in stage j, confronted with the choice of contributing to stage 1 or stage 2 and desiring to increase λ, should contribute to the stage with the higher value of v_i — that is, to the more valuable stage.

6.1.9 Decomposing Treatment Effects in Life Table Response Experiments

Life table response experiments (LTREs) are experiments in which the "life table," or more generally the collective vital rates of the organism, appears as the response variable in an experimental design (Caswell 1989a). LTREs are designed to evaluate population-level responses to environmental factors. Examples include Birch's (1953) study of the effects of temperature, moisture, and food on three species of flour beetles, and numerous studies of chronic exposure to toxic substances [e.g., Marshall 1962 (gamma radiation); Hummon and Hummon 1975 (DDT); Winner and Farrell 1976 (copper); Daniels and Allan 1981 (Dieldrin); Allan and Daniels 1982 (Kepone); Fitzmayer et al. 1982 (Simazine); Gentile et al. 1982 (heavy metals); Walton et al. 1982 (pH)].

The asymptotic growth rate λ (or r) is frequently used to summarize the results of LTREs because it combines information on survival and fertility throughout the life cycle in a biologically meaningful way.

In this section, we present a way to *decompose* the effect of a treatment factor on λ into *contributions* from the different vital rates. I will use superscripts in parentheses to denote treatments and subscripts to denote matrix elements. Thus $\mathbf{A}^{(i)}$ is the projection matrix obtained under treatment i, $\lambda^{(i)}$ is its dominant eigenvalue, and $a_{kl}^{(i)}$ the (k, l) entry of $\mathbf{A}^{(i)}$. Means are denoted by replacing a superscript by a dot, e.g.,

$$\mathbf{A}^{(i\cdot)} = \frac{1}{m} \sum_{j}^{m} \mathbf{A}^{(ij)} \tag{6.51}$$

where m is the number of levels of the second treatment.

One-Way Designs

Consider n levels of a single treatment factor (e.g., exposure to a toxicant), yielding projection matrices and growth rates $\mathbf{A}^{(i)}$ and $\lambda^{(i)}$, $i = 1, \ldots, n$. By analogy to the analysis of variance, we write a linear model

$$\lambda^{(i)} = \lambda^{(\cdot)} + \alpha^{(i)} \tag{6.52}$$

where $\alpha^{(i)}$ is the effect of the ith level of the treatment, measured as a deviation from the growth rate generated by the average projection matrix. This yields the estimates of $\alpha^{(i)}$:

$$\hat{\alpha}^{(i)} = \lambda^{(i)} - \lambda^{(\cdot)} \tag{6.53}$$

The effect $\alpha^{(i)}$ measures the effect of treatment i on λ; it reflects all the differences in survival and fertility between the treatment matrix and the mean matrix. We wish to decompose $\alpha^{(i)}$ into the contributions due to the differences in each matrix element. This decomposition is provided by the first-order approximation of $\hat{\alpha}^i$:

$$\tilde{\alpha}^i = \sum_{k,l} \left(a_{kl}^{(i)} - a_{kl}^{(\cdot)} \right) \left. \frac{\partial \lambda}{\partial a_{kl}} \right|_{\frac{1}{2}(\mathbf{A}^{(i)} + \mathbf{A}^{(\cdot)})} \tag{6.54}$$

The terms in this summation are the contributions of the differences in each matrix element a_{kl} to the overall treatment effect; each term is a difference in a matrix element weighted by the sensitivity of λ to that element. The sensitivity is evaluated at a matrix "midway" between the two matrices being compared.

The approximations satisfy

$$\sum \tilde{\alpha}^{(i)} \approx 0 \tag{6.55}$$

The summation will differ from zero to the extent that λ is a nonlinear function of the a_{kl}. The accuracy of the approximation can be checked by calculating a predicted value of $\lambda^{(i)}$,

$$\tilde{\lambda}^{(i)} = \lambda^{(\cdot)} + \tilde{\alpha}^{(i)} \tag{6.56}$$

and comparing this with the actual value of $\lambda^{(i)}$.

Example 6.8 Larval development mode in *Streblospio benedicti*

Levin et al. (1987) studied the demographic consequences of larval development mode in the polychaete *Streblospio benedicti*. Two genetic strains of this species exist, one of which produces nonfeeding lecithotrophic larvae and one of which produces feeding planktotrophic larvae. The lecithotrophic strain produces many fewer offspring, but they are larger, supplied with yolk, and survive better.

Levin et al. (1987) measured life tables for *S. benedicti* in the laboratory and calculated projection matrices $\mathbf{A}^{(l)}$ for lecithotrophs and $\mathbf{A}^{(p)}$ for planktotrophs, with corresponding rates of increase $\lambda^{(l)} = 1.319$ and $\lambda^{(p)} = 1.205$. Since this LTRE examines the effect of an internal genetic factor rather than an external environmental factor, the interpretation of λ as a measure of fitness (Section 6.4) is particularly relevant. The effect of larval development mode on fitness is an integrated result of differences in age-specific survival and fertility; which of those differences are most important?

The upper panels of Figure 6.14 plot the differences between the strains in age-specific fertility and survival probability, measured relative to the mean $\mathbf{A}^{(\cdot)} = (\mathbf{A}^{(l)} + \mathbf{A}^{(p)})/2$. There is a huge lecithotrophic fertility disadvantage between 20 and 30 weeks of age, a lecithotrophic survival advantage between 0 and 10 weeks of age, and a lecithotrophic survival disadvantage between 30 and 40 weeks of age.

The contributions of these differences to $\tilde{\alpha}^{(l)}$ and $\tilde{\alpha}^{(p)}$, calculated from (6.54), are shown in the lower panels of Figure 6.14. The large fertility differences between 20 and 30 weeks of age make almost no contribution to the difference in λ. Indeed, all but a very small proportion of the effect on λ is contributed by fertility and survival effects occurring before 15 weeks of age.

Note that the curves for $\tilde{\alpha}^{(l)}$ and $\tilde{\alpha}^{(p)}$ are nearly complements of each other, as implied by (6.55). The predicted values, $\tilde{\lambda}^{(l)} = 1.335$ and $\tilde{\lambda}^{(p)} = 1.203$ are quite accurate.

Factorial Designs

LTREs may be extended to arbitrarily complex factorial designs, which permit the examination of interactions between factors. Examples include Birch's (1953) study cited above, Stiven's (1962) study of temperature and food effects in three species of *Hydra*, the study of Birch et al. (1963) on temperature and genetic strain in *Drosophila serrata*, King's (1967) examination of the effects of food type, food level, and clone age on the rotifer *Euchlanis dilatata*, George's (1985) study of temperature and salinity effects in the copepod *Eurytemora herdmani*, and the study by Rao and Sarma (1986) on the effects of DDT exposure and food level on the rotifer *Brachionus patulus*. Most of these studies report significant interaction effects, emphasizing the importance of examining combinations of treatment factors.

Consider two cross-classified treatments (the extension to higher order designs is straightforward), with $\mathbf{A}^{(ij)}$ the projection matrix resulting from

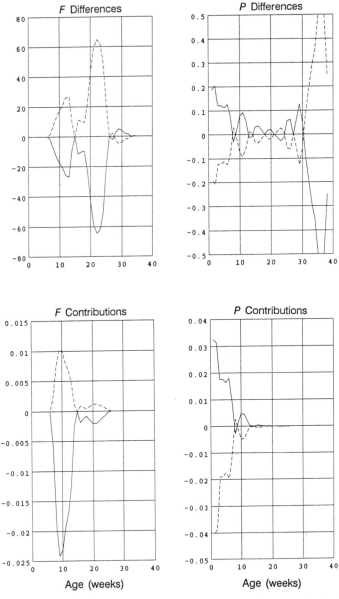

Figure 6.14: Analysis of the LTRE of Levin et al. (1987) comparing lecithotrophic (solid lines) and planktotrophic (dashed lines) strains of the polychaete *Streblospio benedicti*. Upper panels: Effects of genetic strain on age-specific fertility (left) and survival (right), measured relative to the mean. Lower panels: The contributions of these age-specific effects to $\tilde{\alpha}$, the main effect of genetic strain.

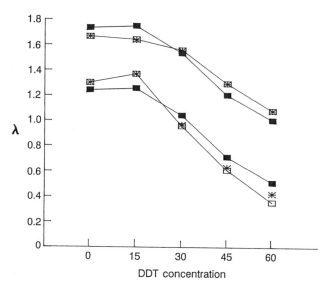

Figure 6.15: Population growth rate λ as a function of DDT concentration (abscissa) and food level (lower lines: low food; upper lines: high food) for the rotifer *Brachionus patulus* (Rao and Sarma 1986). Open squares: observed values, asterisks: values predicted from the linear approximation including the interaction terms, solid squares: values from the additive model, ignoring interaction effects.

treatment combination (ij). The model for such an experiment is

$$\lambda^{(ij)} = \lambda^{(\cdot\cdot)} + \alpha^{(i)} + \beta^{(j)} + (\alpha\beta)^{(ij)} \tag{6.57}$$

where $\alpha^{(i)}$ and $\beta^{(j)}$ are the main effects of the ith level of treatment 1 and the jth level of treatment 2, and $(\alpha\beta)^{(ij)}$ is the interaction effect. Estimates of the treatment effects are given by

$$\hat{\alpha}^{(i)} = \lambda^{(i\cdot)} - \lambda^{(\cdot\cdot)} \tag{6.58}$$

$$\hat{\beta}^{(j)} = \lambda^{(\cdot j)} - \lambda^{(\cdot\cdot)} \tag{6.59}$$

$$\widehat{(\alpha\beta)}^{(ij)} = \lambda^{(ij)} - \hat{\alpha}^{(i)} - \hat{\beta}^{(j)} - \lambda^{(\cdot\cdot)} \tag{6.60}$$

These effects can be decomposed into contributions from each matrix element, by calculating

$$\tilde{\alpha}^{(i)} = \sum_{k,l} \left(a_{kl}^{(i\cdot)} - a_{kl}^{(\cdot\cdot)} \right) \left. \frac{\partial \lambda}{\partial a_{kl}} \right|_{\frac{1}{2}(\mathbf{A}^{(i\cdot)} + \mathbf{A}^{(\cdot\cdot)})} \tag{6.61}$$

$$\tilde{\beta}^{(j)} = \sum_{k,l} \left(a_{kl}^{(\cdot j)} - a_{kl}^{(\cdot\cdot)} \right) \left. \frac{\partial \lambda}{\partial a_{kl}} \right|_{\frac{1}{2}(\mathbf{A}^{(\cdot j)} + \mathbf{A}^{(\cdot\cdot)})} \tag{6.62}$$

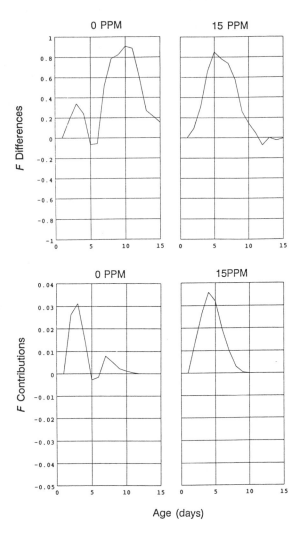

$$\widetilde{(\alpha\beta)}^{(ij)} \;=\; \sum_{k,l} \left(a_{kl}^{(ij)} - a_{kl}^{(\cdot\cdot)} \right) \left. \frac{\partial \lambda}{\partial a_{kl}} \right|_{\frac{1}{2}(\mathbf{A}^{(ij)} + \mathbf{A}^{(\cdot\cdot)})} \;-\; \tilde{\alpha}^{(i)} - \tilde{\beta}^{(j)} \quad (6.63)$$

Each of these equations approximates an observed change in λ as a linear function of the changes in the entries of the matrix; the slope of the linear approximation is evaluated at the midpoint of the two matrices being compared.

Each term in the interaction effect $\widetilde{(\alpha\beta)}^{(ij)}$ is the difference between the actual contribution of a_{kl} to $\lambda^{(ij)}$ and the difference predicted on the basis of an additive model (i.e., the corresponding term in $\tilde{\alpha}^{(i)} + \tilde{\beta}^{(j)}$). A positive

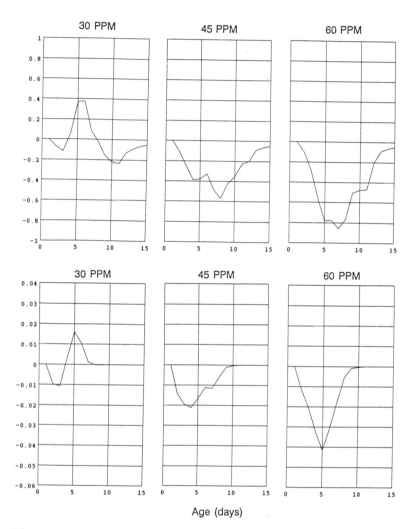

Figure 6.16: Decomposition of the fertility contributions to $\tilde{\alpha}^{(i)}$, $i = 1, \ldots, 5$, the main effects of DDT concentration. Upper panels: Effects of the treatment levels on age-specific fertility, measured relative to the mean. Lower panels: Contributions of those effects to $\tilde{\alpha}^{(i)}$. Data of Rao and Sarma (1986).

contribution to $\widetilde{(\alpha\beta)}^{(ij)}$ thus indicates that the interaction has increased $\lambda^{(ij)}$ above the value predicted by the additive model.

Example 6.9 Food and DDT toxicity in a rotifer

Rao and Sarma (1986) exposed the rotifer *Brachionus patulus* to five levels (0, 15, 30, 45, and 60 ppm) of DDT and two levels (1×10^6 and

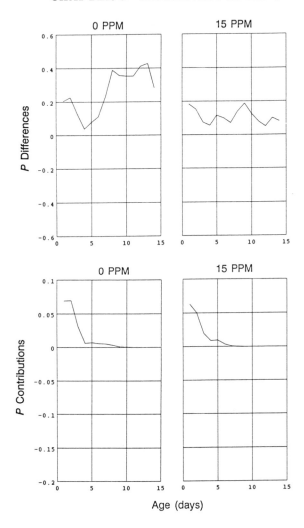

3×10^6 *Chlorella* cells ml^{-1}) of food. The effects of the treatments on
λ calculated from their data are shown in Figure 6.15. There was a
clear positive effect of high food, and a negative effect of DDT concentration. In Rao and Sarma's (1986) analysis of variance, there was also
a significant Food $\times$ DDT interaction, with the growth rate reduction
due to DDT being more severe at low than at high food levels.

Let $\alpha^{(i)}$ denote the effect of the ith DDT treatment and $\beta^{(j)}$ denote
the effect of the jth food treatment. The effects of DDT on fertility,
and the contributions of those effects to $\tilde{\alpha}^{(i)}$, $i = 1, \ldots, 5$, are shown
in Figure 6.16. Fertility declines as DDT concentration increases, first

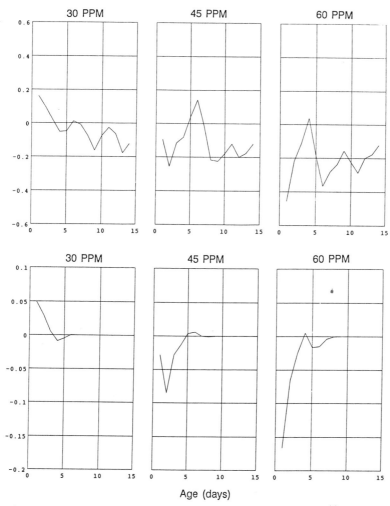

Age (days)

Figure 6.17: Decomposition of the survival contributions to $\tilde{\alpha}^{(i)}$, $i = 1, \ldots, 5$, the main effects of DDT concentration. Upper panels: Effects of the treatment levels on age-specific survival probability, measured relative to the mean. Lower panels: Contributions of these effects to $\tilde{\alpha}^{(i)}$. Data of Rao and Sarma (1986).

at older ages (10–15 days), then at progressively younger ages.

The lower panels in Figure 6.16 show the contributions of these fertility differences to $\tilde{\alpha}^{(i)}$. Fertility differences after age 10 have essentially no impact on λ, and most of the fertility-mediated impact of DDT on λ occurs in the first 7–8 days of life.

Figure 6.17 shows the corresponding analysis for survival effects. Increasing DDT concentrations reduce survival probability, first at later ages and then, at the two highest concentrations, at younger ages. The contributions of these effects to $\tilde{\alpha}^{(i)}$, however, are limited to the first 5–7 days of life. The large effects of DDT on survival of individuals from 7 to 15 days of age make a negligible contribution to differences in λ.

The main effects of food level are shown in Figure 6.18. High food levels increase fertility, especially from 3 to 9 days of age. The contributions of these effects to $\tilde{\beta}^{(j)}$ are limited to the first 7 days of life. The effect of food on survival is greatest at later ages (7–15 days), but these effects make no contribution to population growth rate.

The contributions of survival effects to the interaction terms $\widetilde{(\alpha\beta)}^{(ij)}$ are shown in Figure 6.19. As with the main effects, contributions beyond age 7 days are negligible. At low DDT concentrations, the interaction terms for low food (solid lines) are positive (the terms for high food are complementary, since the sum of the low and high food interaction effects is approximately zero), indicating that the low food treatment does better than would be expected from an additive model. At higher DDT concentrations, the effects reverse, and the low food treatment does much worse than would be expected on an additive model. Thus, low food levels exacerbate, whereas high food levels counteract, the survival effects of DDT toxicity.

The contributions of fertility differences to the interaction terms are much smaller than the corresponding survival contributions (compare the scales of Figures 6.19 and 6.20), and are more difficult to interpret. There is some tendency for the interaction effects to be opposite in sign for contributions due to early (0–5 days) and later (5–10 days) fertility. At early ages, low food levels *counteract* the effect of DDT concentration (cf. the interaction plots for 0 and 60 ppm). At later ages, the effect is reversed. The mechanism for this switch is unknown.

The accuracy of the linear approximations is shown in Figure 6.15, which compares the observed values of λ with those predicted by the estimated model including the interaction terms and those predicted by the additive model without the interaction. The observed and estimated values are extremely close. The deviation of the additive model predictions from the observed values shows the nature of the interaction; at low food levels λ declines with DDT concentration faster than predicted by the additive model, whereas at high food levels λ declines more slowly than predicted by the additive model.

The results of this analysis can be summarized as follows:

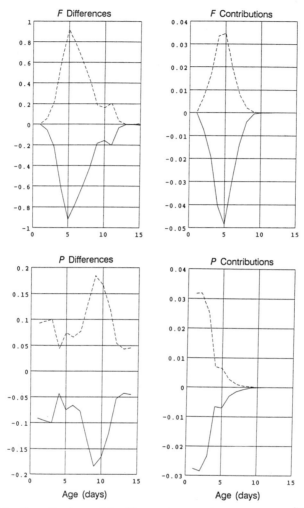

Figure 6.18: Contributions of fertility and survival differences to $\tilde{\beta}^{(j)}$, $j = 1, 2$, the main effects of food level. Solid line: low food; dashed line: high food. Upper panels: Effects of food on fertility (left) and contributions of those effects to $\tilde{\beta}^{(j)}$ (right). Lower panels: Effects of food on survival probability (left) and contributions of those effects to $\tilde{\beta}^{(j)}$ (right). Data of Rao and Sarma (1986).

1. Increasing DDT concentration reduces population growth rate by reducing fertility during the first 10 days of life and survival probability during the first 5–7 days of life. DDT has sizable effects on later survival and fertility, but these effects have negligible impact on λ.

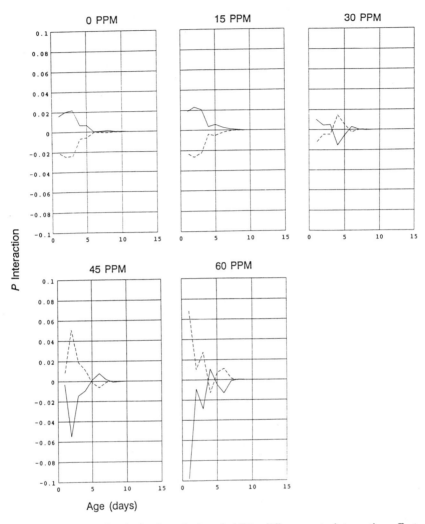

Figure 6.19: Contributions of survival probability differences to interaction effects $(\alpha\beta)^{(ij)}$. Solid lines: low food, dashed lines: high food. Data of Rao and Sarma (1986).

2. Low food levels reduce population growth rate by reducing fertility and survival during the first 7 days of life. Large effects of food level on survival between ages 7 and 15 days have negligible impact on λ.

3. The interaction effect between food level and DDT concentration is mediated mainly through survival effects during the first 7 days

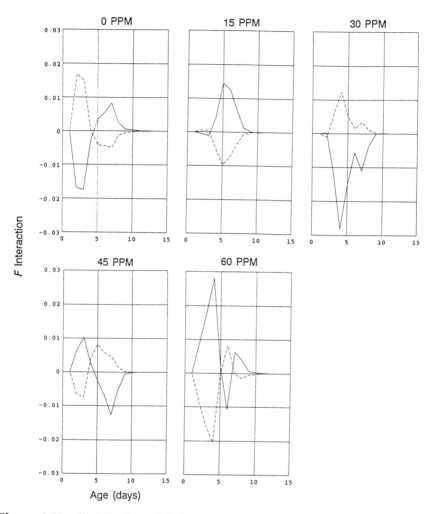

Figure 6.20: Contributions of fertility differences to interaction effects $(\alpha\beta)^{(ij)}$. Solid lines: low food, dashed lines: high food. Data of Rao and Sarma (1986).

of the life cycle. Low food levels exacerbate the survival effects of DDT toxicity; high food levels counteract it.

6.1.10 Sensitivity to Changes in Development Rate

The rate of increase is sensitive not only to changes in the a_{ij}, but also to changes in the timing of events in the life cycle. The effects of changes in development rate have been examined by Lewontin (1965), Mertz (1971),

Caswell and Hastings (1980), Caswell (1982c), Hoogendyk and Estabrook (1984), and Ebert (1985) among others. Here I will present one method specific to age-classified models, and a second that is applicable to a large class of stage-classified models.

Changes in the Moments of the Net Maternity Schedule

The net maternity function in the age-classified model is

$$\phi_i = F_i \prod_{j=1}^{i-1} P_j \tag{6.64}$$

The net reproductive rate is $R_0 = \sum_i \phi_i$, and the characteristic equation can be written

$$1 = \sum_{i=1}^{\infty} \lambda^{-i} \phi_i \tag{6.65}$$

Define $f_i = \phi_i/R_0$, which gives the net maternity function rescaled as a probability density function. The characteristic equation can be rewritten

$$1 = R_0 \sum_{i=1}^{\infty} \lambda^{-i} f_i \tag{6.66}$$

Now imagine a change in development rate that simply shifts the net maternity function earlier or later. The effect of this shift can be examined by calculating $\partial \lambda / \partial \mu$, where μ is the mean of the distribution f_i.

To obtain this sensitivity, we take logs of both sides of (6.66) to obtain

$$- \ln R_0 = \ln \sum_{i=1}^{\infty} \lambda^{-i} f_i \tag{6.67}$$

The summation on the right hand side is the cumulant generating function (Kendall and Stuart 1958) of f (we have encountered cumulant generating functions in Section 4.8.4). Expanding the summation gives (Lotka 1945)

$$\ln R_0 = r\mu - r^2 \frac{\sigma^2}{2!} + r^3 \frac{\kappa_3}{3!} - \cdots \tag{6.68}$$

where $r = \ln \lambda_1$, μ and σ^2 are the mean and variance of the net maternity function, and κ_i, $i \geq 3$ are the higher cumulants of f.

The series (6.68) can be truncated after the second term if f is approximately normal (in which case $\kappa_i = 0$ for $i \geq 3$), or if r is small, or both. Implicit differentiation of (6.68) with respect to μ yields

$$\frac{\partial r}{\partial \mu} = \frac{-r}{\mu - r\sigma^2} \tag{6.69}$$

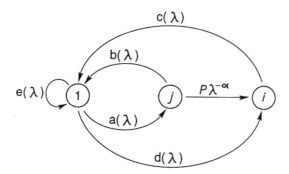

Figure 6.21: A life cycle graph for evaluating the sensitivity of λ to changes in α, the time required for the transition from stage j to stage i.

(Keyfitz 1977). It is also easy to calculate the sensitivity of r to the variance in reproductive age as

$$\frac{\partial r}{\partial \sigma^2} = \frac{r^2}{2(\mu - r\sigma^2)} \tag{6.70}$$

Since $\mu - r\sigma^2$ is usually positive, (6.69) suggests that increasing the mean age of reproduction will decrease r (and thus λ_1), whereas spreading reproduction out over a greater range will increase r.

Changes in Time Required for Life Cycle Transitions

Equations (6.69) and (6.70) are limited to age-classified populations. Since the time required for a transition appears explicitly in the z-transformed life cycle graph it is possible to evaluate the sensitivity of λ to changes in development rate between any two stages in a complex life cycle (Caswell 1986; the version here is more complete).

Consider the life cycle graph in Figure 6.21. We wish to evaluate $\partial\lambda/\partial\alpha$, where α is the time required for the transition between stage j and stage i. The probability of surviving this transition is P. The coefficients on the other arcs in this figure represent transmissions, as follows:

- $a(\lambda)$ for all paths between n_1 and n_j,

- $b(\lambda)$ for all paths between n_j and n_1,

- $c(\lambda)$ for all paths between n_i and n_1,

- $d(\lambda)$ for all paths from n_1 to n_i which do not pass through n_j, and

- $e(\lambda)$ all loops involving neither n_i nor n_j.

We assume that there are no disjoint loops in the graph. The following method can be extended to life cycles containing such loops, but the results are more complicated.

The characteristic equation is

$$1 = a(\lambda)c(\lambda)P\lambda^{-\alpha} + G(\lambda) \tag{6.71}$$

$$= \mathcal{F}(\lambda) \tag{6.72}$$

where $G(\lambda) = a(\lambda)b(\lambda) + c(\lambda)d(\lambda) + e(\lambda)$. Differentiating $\mathcal{F}$ implicitly with respect to α gives

$$\frac{\partial\lambda}{\partial\alpha} = \frac{-\partial\mathcal{F}/\partial\alpha}{\partial\mathcal{F}/\partial\lambda} \tag{6.73}$$

The numerator of (6.73) depends on whether P is constant or depends on α. We consider these two cases separately.

Case 1: Constant P   In this case,

$$\frac{\partial\mathcal{F}}{\partial\alpha} = -a(\lambda)c(\lambda)P\lambda^{-\alpha}\ln(\lambda)$$

$$= -\ln\lambda[1 - G(\lambda)] \tag{6.74}$$

We calculate $\partial\mathcal{F}/\partial\lambda$ by rewriting the characteristic equation as

$$1 = \mathcal{F}(\lambda) = \sum_{i=1}^{\infty} k_i\lambda^{-i} \tag{6.75}$$

from which

$$\frac{\partial\mathcal{F}}{\partial\lambda} = -\lambda^{-1}\sum_{i=1}^{\infty} ik_i\lambda^{-i}$$

$$= -\lambda^{-1}\bar{A} \tag{6.76}$$

where $\bar{A}$ is the mean age of the parents in the stable population (see Section 5.6.2). Thus, from (6.73)

$$\frac{\partial\lambda}{\partial\alpha} = \frac{-\lambda\ln(\lambda)[1 - G(\lambda)]}{\bar{A}} \tag{6.77}$$

From this, it follows immediately that $\partial\lambda/\partial\alpha < 0$ whenever $\lambda > 1$; slowing development anywhere in the life cycle of an increasing population reduces λ. The sensitivity of λ to changes in development rate is inversely proportional to generation time.

Case 2: $P = e^{-\mu\alpha}$ The probability of surviving from one stage to another is unlikely to be independent of the time required for the transition. If the survival probability P represents the results of exposure for α time units to a mortality rate μ, then $P = \exp(-\mu\alpha)$, and the numerator of (6.73) becomes

$$-\frac{\partial \mathcal{F}}{\partial \alpha} = (\ln \lambda + \mu)[1 - G(\lambda)] \tag{6.78}$$

The denominator, $\partial f/\partial \lambda$ is still given by (6.76). Thus

$$\frac{\partial \lambda}{\partial \alpha} = \frac{-\lambda(\ln \lambda + \mu)[1 - G(\lambda)]}{\bar{A}} \tag{6.79}$$

Comparing this with (6.77), it is apparent that making survival probability dependent on development rate makes it even more difficult for an increase in α to increase λ.

Sensitivity analysis can be applied to other quantities besides λ_1, including the other eigenvalues, indices of transient behavior derived from those eigenvalues, and the eigenvectors can all be subjected to similar analyses. The following sections will derive some of these sensitivities and provide a few examples of their use. None of them has yet been applied extensively enough to be sure of the implications of the patterns that may appear.

Note that calculation of these sensitivities involves the complete eigenvalue spectrum of the projection matrix. Since some of these eigenvalues are almost always complex, one must be careful in using the appropriate complex scalar product in connection with the appropriate definition of the left eigenvectors. See Appendix A for details.

6.2   Transient Sensitivities

The damping ratio ρ and the period $\mathcal{P}$ of oscillation are functions of the subdominant eigenvalues of **A** (Section 4.6). The sensitivity of ρ and $\mathcal{P}$ to changes in the matrix elements can be calculated using the basic formula (6.7).

6.2.1   Damping Ratio Sensitivity

The damping ratio is $\rho = \lambda_1/|\lambda_2|$. Let $\lambda_2 = x \pm iy$. Then the sensitivity of ρ is

$$\frac{\partial \rho}{\partial a_{ij}} = \frac{1}{|\lambda_2|} \left[\frac{\partial \lambda_1}{\partial a_{ij}} - \frac{\rho}{|\lambda_2|} \left(x\frac{\partial x}{\partial a_{ij}} + y\frac{\partial y}{\partial a_{ij}} \right) \right] \tag{6.80}$$

where $\partial x/\partial a_{ij}$ and $\partial y/\partial a_{ij}$ are the real and imaginary parts of $\partial \lambda_2/\partial a_{ij}$ (Caswell 1986).

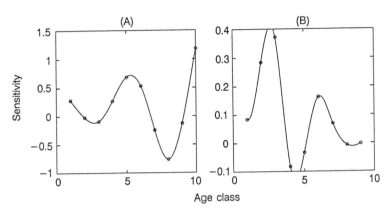

Figure 6.22: The sensitivity of the damping ratio ρ to changes in age-specific fertility F_i (A) and age-specific survival probability P_i (B), for the population of the United States.

Example 6.10 An age-classified example

Figure 6.22 shows the sensitivity of the damping ratio to changes in age-specific fertility and survival probability for the U.S. population in 1966 (Example 4.3). Increasing F_i in the middle of the life cycle (age classes 4–6) increases ρ, whereas increasing F_i early or late in the life cycle tends to decrease ρ (Figure 6.22A). This agrees with the results of Coale (1972), who found that ρ was positively correlated with the concentration of reproduction in the middle of the life cycle (Section 4.6.1). The sensitivity of ρ to survival changes (Figure 6.22B) has the complementary pattern; ρ declines when P_4 or P_5 increase, and increases with increases in P_i early or late in life.

6.2.2 Period Sensitivity

The period of the oscillations generated by λ_2 is $2\pi/\theta$, where θ is the angle formed by λ_2 in the complex plane. The sensitivity of $\mathcal{P}$ (Caswell 1986) is

$$\frac{\partial \mathcal{P}}{\partial a_{ij}} = \frac{-2\pi}{\theta^2 |\lambda_2|^2} \left(x \frac{\partial y}{\partial a_{ij}} - y \frac{\partial x}{\partial a_{ij}} \right) \tag{6.81}$$

Example 6.11 An age-classified example

Figure 6.23 shows the sensitivity of $\mathcal{P}$ to changes in age-specific fertility and survival, using the same data as Example 6.10. The period of

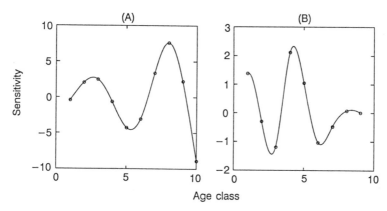

Figure 6.23: The sensitivity of the period of oscillation $\mathcal{P}$ to changes in age-specific fertility F_i (A) and age-specific survival probability P_i (B), for the population of the United States.

oscillation is increased by increases in F_i early or late in the life cycle (Figure 6.23A), whereas increases in F_i in the middle of the life cycle reduce $\mathcal{P}$. Again, survival changes have the complementary effect (Figure 6.23B).

6.3 Eigenvector Sensitivities

The eigenvector sensitivities provide information on how the stable stage distribution and the reproductive value schedule change in response to changes in **A**. The following derivation was used in Caswell (1980); it follows the approach of Faddeev and Faddeeva (1963) and Desoer (1967).

We denote the eigenvalues, right eigenvectors, and left eigenvectors of **A** by λ_i, $\mathbf{w}_i$, and $\mathbf{v}_i$, respectively. We assume that the eigenvalues are distinct, and that the eigenvectors have been scaled so that $\langle \mathbf{w}_i, \mathbf{v}_i \rangle = 1$; we will also use the fact that $\langle \mathbf{w}_i, \mathbf{v}_j \rangle = 0$ for $i \neq j$.

As in the derivation of the eigenvalue sensitivities, we begin with

$$\mathbf{A}\mathbf{w}_i = \lambda_i \mathbf{w}_i \tag{6.82}$$

Taking the differential of both sides yields

$$(d\mathbf{A})\mathbf{w}_i + \mathbf{A}(d\mathbf{w}_i) = (d\lambda_i)\mathbf{w}_i + \lambda_i(d\mathbf{w}_i) \tag{6.83}$$

If we consider $d\lambda_i$ as known, (6.83) is a linear equation in the eigenvector sensitivity $d\mathbf{w}_i$:

$$(\mathbf{A} - \lambda_i\mathbf{I})d\mathbf{w}_i = (d\lambda_i\mathbf{I} - d\mathbf{A})\mathbf{w}_i \qquad (6.84)$$

Since $(\mathbf{A} - \lambda_i\mathbf{I})$ is singular, (6.84) cannot be solved directly for $d\mathbf{w}_i$. However, we can write any solution as a linear combination of the eigenvectors $\mathbf{w}_j$:

$$d\mathbf{w}_i = \sum_{j=1}^{s} k_{ij}\mathbf{w}_j \qquad (6.85)$$

for some as yet unknown coefficients k_{ij}. Note that the value of k_{ii} is irrelevant, since when (6.85) is substituted in (6.84), $k_{ii}(\mathbf{A} - \lambda_i\mathbf{I})\mathbf{w}_i = 0$, regardless of the value of k_{ii}. In what follows, we will set $k_{ii} = 0$.

Leaving this expression for $d\mathbf{w}_i$ aside for the moment, form the scalar product of both sides of (6.83) with $\mathbf{v}_j$, for $j \neq i$:

$$\langle(d\mathbf{A})\mathbf{w}_i, \mathbf{v}_j\rangle + \langle\mathbf{A}d\mathbf{w}_i, \mathbf{v}_j\rangle = d\lambda_i\langle\mathbf{w}_i, \mathbf{v}_j\rangle + \lambda_i\langle d\mathbf{w}_i, \mathbf{v}_j\rangle \qquad (6.86)$$

The second term on the left-hand side of (6.86) simplifies to $\lambda_j\langle d\mathbf{w}_i, \mathbf{v}_j\rangle$, and the first term on the right-hand side is zero if $i \neq j$. Simplifying yields

$$\langle d\mathbf{w}_i, \mathbf{v}_j\rangle = \frac{\langle(d\mathbf{A})\mathbf{w}_i, \mathbf{v}_j\rangle}{\lambda_i - \lambda_j} \qquad (6.87)$$

Now, substitute (6.85) for $d\mathbf{w}_i$ into (6.87):

$$\sum_{m\neq i} k_{im}\langle\mathbf{w}_m, \mathbf{v}_j\rangle = \frac{\langle(d\mathbf{A})\mathbf{w}_i, \mathbf{v}_j\rangle}{\lambda_i - \lambda_j} \qquad (6.88)$$

Since $\langle\mathbf{w}_m, \mathbf{v}_j\rangle = 0$ for $j \neq m$, and equals 1 for $j = m$, (6.88) simplifies to an expression for k_{ij}:

$$k_{ij} = \frac{\langle(d\mathbf{A})\mathbf{w}_i, \mathbf{v}_j\rangle}{\lambda_i - \lambda_j} \qquad (6.89)$$

When (6.89) is substituted into (6.85), we obtain the desired expression for the sensitivity of the right eigenvector $\mathbf{w}_i$:

$$d\mathbf{w}_i = \sum_{j\neq i}^{s} \frac{\langle(d\mathbf{A})\mathbf{w}_i, \mathbf{v}_j\rangle}{\lambda_i - \lambda_j}\mathbf{w}_j \qquad (6.90)$$

The corresponding expression for the sensitivity of the left eigenvector $\mathbf{v}_i$ follows from noting that the left eigenvectors of $\mathbf{A}$ are the right eigenvectors of $\mathbf{A}'$, so that

$$d\mathbf{v}_i = \sum_{j\neq i}^{s} \frac{\langle(d\mathbf{A}')\mathbf{v}_i, \mathbf{w}_j\rangle}{\lambda_i - \lambda_j}\mathbf{v}_j \qquad (6.91)$$

Equations (6.90) and (6.91) give the perturbations $d\mathbf{w}_i$ and $d\mathbf{v}_i$ resulting from the perturbation $d\mathbf{A}$ in the matrix $\mathbf{A}$. As with the eigenvalue sensitivities, these expressions can be simplified if only a single entry, say a_{kl} in the matrix is perturbed. Using superscripts to distinguish the eigenvectors and subscripts to denote their elements (e.g., $w_l^{(i)}$ is the lth element of $\mathbf{w}_i$), the resulting expressions are

$$\frac{\partial \mathbf{w}_i}{\partial a_{kl}} = \sum_{j \neq i}^s \frac{w_l^{(i)} \bar{v}_k^{(j)}}{\lambda_i - \lambda_j} \mathbf{w}_j$$

$$= w_l^{(i)} \sum_{j \neq i}^s \frac{\bar{v}_k^{(j)}}{\lambda_i - \lambda_j} \mathbf{w}_j \tag{6.92}$$

$$\frac{\partial \mathbf{v}_i}{\partial a_{kl}} = v_k^{(i)} \sum_{j \neq i}^s \frac{\bar{w}_l^{(j)}}{\lambda_i - \lambda_j} \mathbf{v}_j \tag{6.93}$$

Sensitivities of Scaled Eigenvectors

The stable stage distribution and reproductive value are customarily scaled so that $\sum w_i = 1$ (or perhaps 100, in which case the entries are interpreted as percentages) and $v_1 = 1$. The sensitivities of these scaled eigenvectors can be calculated using (6.92) and (6.93).

Let $\|\mathbf{w}\| = \sum_i |w_i|$ and suppose the scaled stable stage distribution is given by $\mathbf{w}/\|\mathbf{w}\|$. Its sensitivity is then given by

$$\frac{\partial \frac{\mathbf{w}}{\|\mathbf{w}\|}}{\partial a_{kl}} = \frac{\frac{\partial \mathbf{w}}{\partial a_{kl}} \|\mathbf{w}\| - \mathbf{w} \sum_i \frac{\partial w_i}{\partial a_{kl}}}{\|\mathbf{w}\|^2} \tag{6.94}$$

If the eigenvector whose sensitivity is being evaluated is already scaled so that $\|\mathbf{w}\| = 1$, this simplifies to

$$\frac{\partial \frac{\mathbf{w}}{\|\mathbf{w}\|}}{\partial a_{kl}} = \frac{\partial \mathbf{w}}{\partial a_{kl}} - \mathbf{w} \sum_i \frac{\partial w_i}{\partial a_{kl}} \tag{6.95}$$

where $\partial \mathbf{w}/\partial a_{kl}$ is given by (6.92).

Similarly, if the scaled reproductive value vector is defined as $\mathbf{v}/v_1$, and if the vector whose sensitivity is being evaluated is already scaled so that $v_1 = 1$, the sensitivity of the scaled reproductive value vector is

$$\frac{\partial \frac{\mathbf{v}}{v_1}}{\partial a_{kl}} = \frac{\partial \mathbf{v}}{\partial a_{kl}} - \mathbf{v} \frac{\partial v_1}{\partial a_{kl}} \tag{6.96}$$

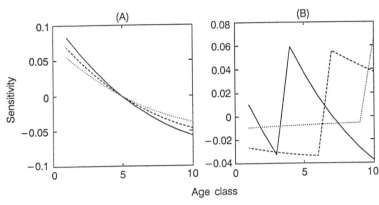

Figure 6.24: (A) The sensitivity of the stable age distribution **w** to changes in age-specific fertility F_i for the population of the United States. Solid line: F_3; dashed line: F_6; dotted line: F_9. (B) The sensitivity of **w** to changes in age-specific survival probabilities P_i for the population of the United States. Solid line: P_3; dashed line: P_6; dotted line: P_9. The vector **w** is scaled so that $\sum w_i = 1$.

Example 6.12 An age-classified population

Applying this analysis to the stable age distribution for the population of the United States as of 1966 (a 10×19 matrix with 5-year age classes) yields the results shown in Figures 6.24A and 6.24B. An increase in fertility at any age increases the proportion of the population in age classes younger than that age and decreases the proportion in the older age classes. This reflects the increase in λ_1 resulting from the increase in fertility, since fertilities affect the stable age distribution only through λ_1. Changes in fertility at younger ages have a greater effect on the stable age distribution than changes at later ages.

The effect of changes in survival is more complex. An increase in P_i will clearly increase the representation of age-class $i + 1$ in the stable age distribution. Since the age distribution is constrained to sum to 1, this implies a decrease in the representation of some other classes. Results are shown for changes in P_3, P_6, and P_9 in Figure 6.24B.

Figure 6.25A shows the sensitivity of the scaled reproductive value to changes in fertility. Increasing F_i increases the reproductive value of all age classes up to and including i. The effect then drops, and eventually asymptotically approaches zero at later ages. Changes in survival probability have qualitatively similar patterns (Figure 6.25B). Thus, increasing survival probability or fertility at a given age increases relative reproductive value at earlier ages, and decreases it at later ages.

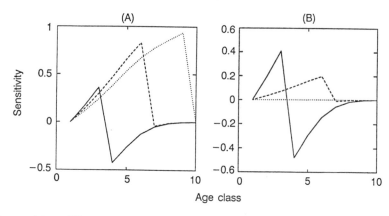

Figure 6.25: (A) The sensitivity of the reproductive value **v** to changes in age-specific fertilities F_i for the population of the United States. Solid line: F_3; dashed line: F_6; dotted line: F_9. (B) The sensitivity of **v** to changes in age-specific survival probabilities P_i for the population of the United States. Solid line: P_3; dashed line: P_6; dotted line: P_9. The vector **v** is scaled so that $v_1 = 1$.

6.4 Fitness, λ, and Evolutionary Demography

The connection between demography and evolution follows from the recognition that, if the life cycle is the unit of description of the organism, it is a part of the phenotype. As such, the life cycle is as much (or as little) subject to adaptive explanation as is the anatomy, physiology, or behavior of the organism.

This connection was clearly recognized by Fisher (1930), in his oft-quoted statement

> It would be instructive to know not only by what physiological mechanism a just apportionment is made between the nutriment devoted to the gonads and that devoted to the rest of the parental organism, but also what circumstances in the life-history and the environment would render profitable the diversion of a greater or lesser share of the available resources towards reproduction.

The real beginnings of evolutionary demography, however, can be traced to three seminal papers: Lack (1947, see also 1954) on clutch size, Medawar (1952) on senescence, and Cole (1954) on semelparity and iteroparity. Each of these authors explicitly adopted the view that the life cycle was subject to evolutionary explanation.

> The thesis advanced here is that the reproductive rate of animals, like other characters, is a product of natural selection, hence

that each species lays that number of eggs which results in the maximum number of surviving offspring. (Lack 1954, p. 154)

In this paper it will be regarded as axiomatic that the reproductive potentials of existing species are related to their requirements for survival; that any life history features affecting reproductive potential are subject to natural selection; and that such features observed in existing species should be considered adaptations, just as purely morphological or behavioral patterns are commonly so considered. (Cole 1954, p. 114)

Each of these papers began with an apparent paradox. Lack (1947) asked why, when reproduction was so obviously a part of fitness, birds did not lay as many eggs as physiologically possible. Medawar (1952) asked why, when survival was so obviously a part of fitness, senescence should be such a conspicuous characteristic of the life cycle of most organisms. Cole (1954) asked why, when reproduction was so obviously a part of fitness, semelparity (i.e., reproducing only once) should be so widespread. In each case, the resolution of the paradox turned on the recognition of interaction between different parts of the life cycle (egg production and juvenile survival, early and late survival, early and later reproduction); this concern with interaction is fundamental to evolutionary demography.

Evolutionary demography rests on two theoretical bases: a theory of selection explaining how differences in fitness result in genotypic and phenotypic changes, and a theory relating fitness to the demographic properties of the life cycle.

The action of selection is described by an enormous literature on population and quantitative genetics. Most of that literature, however, ignores the internal structure of the population. Important exceptions are the important work of Charlesworth (1980 and earlier) and especially of Lande (1982a,b), which will be examined in detail below.

The connection between demography and fitness was first made by Fisher (1930), who defined the "Malthusian parameter" m (the solution of Lotka's integral equation) for a genotype as a measure of the fitness of that genotype, since " m measures fitness to survive by the objective fact of representation in future generations" (Fisher 1930, p. 34). That is, fitness is a measure of the rate at which a genotype is able to propagate itself into future generations; that rate is measured, all other things being equal, by m (or $\lambda = e^m$) for that genotype.

Unfortunately, coupling genetics and demography produces complications that require simplifying assumptions — both genetic and demographic. These assumptions permit the use of eigenvalue sensitivity analyses in an evolutionary context, but the effects of relaxing them are still not well understood.

6.4.1 The Secondary Theorem of Natural Selection

We begin with the so-called "Secondary Theorem of Natural Selection" (Robertson 1968).[4] In its simplest form, it asserts that the rate of change under selection in the mean value of a quantitative trait is proportional to the genetic covariance between that trait and fitness (for derivations, see Price 1970, 1972, Emlen 1970).

Consider the standard population genetics model for a single locus with n alleles, with frequencies p_i and fitnesses W_i. The rate of change, per generation, in the gene frequency p_i is

$$\Delta p_i = p_i \left(\frac{W_i - \overline{W}}{\overline{W}} \right) \tag{6.97}$$

where $\overline{W} = \sum_i p_i W_i$ is the mean fitness.

Now consider a metric trait, with z_i the average value of that trait among carriers of allele i. The mean phenotype $\bar{z} = \sum_i p_i z_i$. Assuming that epistasis, pleiotropy, and linkage are unimportant, and that selection is slow enough that z_i can be considered approximately constant, then

$$
\begin{aligned}
\Delta \bar{z} &= \sum_i z_i \Delta p_i \\
&= \sum_i \frac{z_i p_i (W_i - \overline{W})}{\overline{W}} \\
&= \frac{\sum_i p_i z_i W_i - \overline{W} \sum_i p_i z_i}{\overline{W}} \\
&= \frac{\text{Cov}(z, W)}{\overline{W}}
\end{aligned}
\tag{6.98}
$$

where $\text{Cov}(z, W)$ denotes the genetic covariance between the trait z and fitness. This is the Secondary Theorem of Natural Selection.[5]

As noted by Price (1970) and Emlen (1970), (6.98) can be rewritten by noting that $\text{Cov}(z, W) = b\sigma_z^2$, where b is the slope of the linear regression relating W to z, and σ_z^2 is the genetic variance in z. Thus

$$\Delta \bar{z} = \frac{1}{\overline{W}} \frac{\partial W}{\partial z} \sigma_z^2 \tag{6.99}$$

---

[4]This theorem is, in my opinion, even more important than Fisher's more well-known Fundamental Theorem, which can actually be derived from the Secondary Theorem as a special case. Fisher, however, got to name his theorem first.

[5]The Fundamental Theorem follows when the trait z is identified with fitness itself: the rate of change in mean fitness is then seen to be proportional to the genetic variance in fitness.

where $\partial W/\partial z$ is the slope of the regression of fitness on the phenotypic value z.

Emlen (1970) referred to the partial derivative term in (6.99) as the *selective pressure* on the trait z. Since the genetic variance term is always positive, the direction of selection is determined by the sign of the selective pressure.

Much of evolutionary ecology is devoted to deriving, hypothesizing, or outright guessing of the patterns of selective pressure on various traits in various circumstances.

> Therefore, at any step in constructing hypotheses about evolution through natural selection — for example, about why human canines do not protrude, why deer antlers are annually shed and renewed, why parrots mimic, why dolphins play — one can ... consider whether the slope [i.e., the selective pressure] really would be appreciably non-zero under the assumptions of the theory. If there is no slope, then there is no frequency change (except by sampling drift) and the hypothesis is probably wrong. (Price 1970)

The contribution of the genetic variance term is often taken for granted, either by assuming that there is always enough genetic variance for selection to operate, or that the genetic variation in all traits is roughly the same. It is now being realized how mistaken this attitude can be, particularly with regard to demographic traits (e.g., Istock 1983, Dingle and Hegmann 1982, Loeschke 1987) . In Section 6.4.2, we will see that the patterns of genetic covariance among traits are even more important, when the action of selection on multiple, correlated traits is considered.

6.4.2   Lande's Generalization of the Secondary Theorem

Several extensions are required before the Secondary Theorem can be applied directly to evolutionary demographic analysis:

- the model must be expanded to include age or stage structure and overlapping generations,

- the definition of fitness must be related to the demogaphic parameters of the different types in the population, and

- account must be taken of multiple, correlated traits, since interactions between demographic traits are fundamental to evolutionary demography.

These extensions (except for the extension to size- or stage-classified life cycles) are provided in two important papers by Lande (1982a,b). Because of its importance the derivation will be presented in detail here. Before embarking on the derivation, however, the result may be stated simply. Consider a vector $\mathbf{z}$ of phenotypic traits, with mean $\bar{z}$, and additive genetic variance-covariance matrix $\mathbf{G}$. Then

$$\Delta \bar{z} = \lambda^{-1} \mathbf{G} \nabla \lambda \tag{6.100}$$

where λ is the dominant eigenvalue of the projection matrix $\mathbf{A}$ for the population evaluated at the average phenotype, and the gradient $\nabla \lambda$ is

$$\nabla \lambda = \begin{pmatrix} \frac{\partial \lambda}{\partial z_1} \\ \frac{\partial \lambda}{\partial z_2} \\ \vdots \\ \frac{\partial \lambda}{\partial z_k} \end{pmatrix} \tag{6.101}$$

The vector $\nabla \lambda$ is known as the *selection gradient*; it is the multivariate analog of the selective pressure in (6.99).

That is, Lande shows that (given genetic and demographic assumptions that will be outlined below), λ is an acceptable measure of the fitness of a life cycle, and that the change in the mean phenotype under selection depends on the selective pressures and on the patterns of genetic variance and covariance.

Quantitative Genetics Background

The simplest quantitative genetic description of selection (e.g., Lerner 1958, Falconer 1981) considers a single trait, with phenotypic value $z = x + e$, where x is the *additive genetic value* or *breeding value* of the individual and e is the *environmental effect*. The phenotypic variance is decomposed into a genetic and an environmental component $\sigma_z^2 = \sigma_g^2 + \sigma_e^2$, and the *heritability* is defined as $h^2 = \sigma_g^2 / \sigma_z^2$. This model assumes that any genotype-environment interactions are negligible, and lumps nonadditive genetic components (e.g., dominance) with the environmental effects.

Suppose that generations are discrete and nonoverlapping. Consider artificial selection imposed on a population by choosing, as parents for the next generation, only those individuals whose phenotypic value z exceeds some threshold. The *selection differential* $s = \bar{z}_s - \bar{z}$ is defined as the difference between the mean $\bar{z}_s$ of the selected individuals and the mean $\bar{z}$ of the population as a whole. The expected change, per generation, in the mean $\bar{z}$ is then

$$\Delta \bar{z} = h^2 s \tag{6.102}$$

Lande's analysis extends this simple calculation in several directions. First, he considers an age-classified population with overlapping generations, so the response to selection must be expressed in calendar time instead of generations. Second, he considers natural selection, rather than artificial truncation selection. The selection differential thus depends on the differences in survival and reproduction among the phenotypes, rather than being imposed artificially. Finally, he considers multiple, interacting traits, so that genetic covariances as well as genetic variance must be taken into account.

Demography

Lande assumes a standard age-classified model [see Lande (1982a) for the continuous time version, and Lande (1982b) for the discrete time version]. Here, however, we assume only that

$$\mathbf{n}(t+1) = \mathbf{A}\mathbf{n}(t) \tag{6.103}$$

where $\mathbf{A}$ is a primitive matrix whose life cycle graph can be reduced to contain no disjoint loops. Thus the characteristic equation of $\mathbf{A}$ can be written

$$1 = \sum L^{(i)}$$

where $L^{(i)}$ is the ith loop transmission in the z-transformed life cycle graph.

Expanding the $L^{(i)}$ and collecting like powers of λ, the characteristic equation can be rewritten

$$1 = \sum_{i=1}^{\infty} W_i \lambda^{-i} \tag{6.104}$$

where W_i is the total transmission of all loops of length i. The quantity $q_i = W_i \lambda^{-i}$ gives the distribution of the ages of the parents of the offspring produced in the stable population. The average age of these parents is

$$\bar{A} = \sum_{i=1}^{\infty} i q_i \tag{6.105}$$

$$= \sum_{i=1}^{\infty} i W_i \lambda^{-i} \tag{6.106}$$

(cf. Section 5.6.3, where these relationships were derived in a different notation.)

Lande (1982a,b) refers to the quantity W_i as the "fitness" of an individual in age-class i. This is confusing, since fitness is better thought of as a property of the entire life cycle. Regardless of what it is called, though, W_i measures the contribution to population growth of reproductive loops of length i.

Phenotype, Genotype, and Environment

Suppose that the multivariate phenotype of an individual is specified by a vector $\mathbf{z}$, which is assumed to be the sum of the additive genetic or breeding value $\mathbf{x}$ and the environmental effect $\mathbf{e}$; $\mathbf{z} = \mathbf{x} + \mathbf{e}$. This expression lumps nonadditive genetic components with environmental effects. It also assumes the absence of genotype-environment interactions, which play an important role in the evolution of phenotypic plasticity (Via and Lande 1985, Via 1987).

The demographic parameters in $\mathbf{A}$ are assumed to be functions of the phenotype $\mathbf{z}$; thus the W_i are also, and the characteristic equation can be written as a function of the phenotype:

$$1 = \sum_{i=1}^{\infty} W_i(\mathbf{z})\lambda^{-i}$$

Lande assumes that the phenotype, breeding value, and environmental effect distributions within the population are (or can be transformed to be) multivariate normal, with means $\bar{\mathbf{z}}$, $\bar{\mathbf{x}}$, and $\bar{\mathbf{e}}$, and variance-covariance matrices $\mathbf{P}$, $\mathbf{G}$, and $\mathbf{E}$, respectively. Thus, the probability density function for $\mathbf{z}$ is

$$p(\mathbf{z}) = \frac{e^{-\frac{1}{2}(\mathbf{z}-\bar{\mathbf{z}})'\mathbf{P}^{-1}(\mathbf{z}-\bar{\mathbf{z}})}}{\sqrt{(2\pi)^k|\mathbf{P}|}} \tag{6.107}$$

with similar expressions for the density functions $g(\mathbf{x})$ and $\xi(\mathbf{e})$.

Since both the genotype and the environment are measured in units of phenotype, it is possible to specify the conditional probability distribution $\xi(\mathbf{z} - \mathbf{x})$, which gives the probability that the environment produces phenotype $\mathbf{z}$ from genotype x, i.e.,

$$\xi(\mathbf{z} - \mathbf{x}) = P(\text{phenotype } \mathbf{z}|\text{genotype } \mathbf{x}) \tag{6.108}$$

The mean of $W_i(\mathbf{z})$, calculated over the phenotype distribution $p(\mathbf{z})$, is

$$\overline{W}_i = \int p(\mathbf{z})W_i(\mathbf{z})\,d\mathbf{z} \tag{6.109}$$

Since $\mathbf{z} = \mathbf{x} + \mathbf{e}$, the environmental effect can be defined as a deviation from the breeding value: $\mathbf{e} = \mathbf{z} - \mathbf{x}$. Then the probability of having a particular phenotype $\mathbf{z}$ is

$$p(\mathbf{z}) = \int g(\mathbf{x})P(\text{phenotype } \mathbf{z}|\text{genotype } \mathbf{x})\,d\mathbf{x} \tag{6.110}$$

$$= \int g(\mathbf{x})\xi(\mathbf{z} - \mathbf{x})\,d\mathbf{x} \tag{6.111}$$

Substituting this expression in (6.109) yields

$$\overline{W}_i \;=\; \int g(\mathbf{x}) \int W_i(\mathbf{z})\xi(\mathbf{z}-\mathbf{x})\,d\mathbf{z}\,d\mathbf{x} \qquad (6.112)$$

$$=\; \int g(\mathbf{x})\tilde{W}_i(\mathbf{x})\,d\mathbf{x} \qquad (6.113)$$

where

$$\widetilde{W}_i(\mathbf{x}) = \int W_i(\mathbf{z})\xi(\mathbf{z}-\mathbf{x})\,d\mathbf{z} \qquad (6.114)$$

Genetics

Because the survival probabilities depend on the phenotype, the phenotype distribution will differ among ages within the population. We focus attention on the phenotype distribution $\mathbf{z}_0$ in newborn individuals. At birth, before the environment has had a chance to exert its influence, the phenotypic and genotypic values are identical:

$$\mathbf{z}_0 = \mathbf{x}_0 \qquad (6.115)$$

However, the genetic composition of newborn individuals is by definition equal to the mean breeding value of their parents; thus

$$\bar{\mathbf{z}}_0(t) = \sum_i q_i\bar{\mathbf{x}}_i(t) \qquad (6.116)$$

The average breeding value of age i individuals is given by

$$\bar{\mathbf{x}}_i(t) = \bar{\mathbf{x}}_0(t-i) + \boldsymbol{\delta}_i \qquad (6.117)$$

where $\boldsymbol{\delta}_i$ is defined as the *genotypic selection differential* at age i (i.e., the difference between the mean breeding value at birth and at age i).

Selection

Now we consider the dynamics of selection. We assume a constant environment. Even so, if selection is very intense, it can change the genetic structure of the population, and thus the vital rates, so rapidly that the population will never have time to converge to its stable structure. We will assume that selection is weak enough that this does not happen. This permits us to use stable population theory to describe the dynamics of the population, and to examine genetic change against this constant background.

Suppose that the mean phenotype at birth has been changing at a constant rate $\Delta\bar{\mathbf{z}}_0$ per unit time. Then

$$\widetilde{\mathbf{z}}_0(t-i) = \bar{\mathbf{z}}_0(t) - i\Delta\bar{\mathbf{z}}_0 \qquad (6.118)$$

Substituting (6.118) into (6.116) and (6.117), we obtain

$$
\begin{aligned}
\bar{\mathbf{z}}_0(t) &= \sum_i q_i[\bar{\mathbf{z}}_0(t) - i\Delta\bar{\mathbf{z}}_0 + \delta_i] \\
&= \bar{\mathbf{z}}_0(t)\sum_i q_i - \Delta\bar{\mathbf{z}}_0\sum_i iq_i + \sum_i q_i\delta_i \\
&= \bar{\mathbf{z}}_0(t) - \bar{A}\Delta\bar{\mathbf{z}}_0 + \sum_i q_i\delta_i \quad (6.119)
\end{aligned}
$$

Thus

$$
\Delta\bar{\mathbf{z}}_0 = \bar{A}^{-1}\sum_i q_i\delta_i \quad (6.120)
$$

The response to selection per unit time is equal to the average genetic selection differential divided by the generation time.

The Selection Differential

We turn now to the genetic selection differential δ_i, which equals the difference between the mean breeding value at age i and at birth. The genotypes at age i represent those that have survived from birth to age i, weighted by their reproductive output; this contribution is given by $\widetilde{W}_i$. The mean breeding value is thus given by

$$
\bar{\mathbf{x}}_i = \int \mathbf{x}_0\, g(\mathbf{x}_0)\frac{\widetilde{W}_i}{\overline{\widetilde{W}}_i}\, d\mathbf{x} \quad (6.121)
$$

and the selection differential by

$$
\delta_i = \int (\mathbf{x}_0 - \bar{\mathbf{x}}_0)g(\mathbf{x}_0)\frac{\widetilde{W}_i}{\overline{\widetilde{W}}_i}\, d\mathbf{x} \quad (6.122)
$$

The selection differential reflects the fact that different phenotypes have different fitnesses; if this were not the case, there would be no within-generation change in the phenotype (or genotype) distributions. The dependence of fitness on phenotype can be quantified by the gradient $\nabla\overline{W}_i$ of $\overline{W}_i$, i.e., by the vector function

$$
\nabla\overline{W}_i = \begin{pmatrix} \frac{\partial\overline{W}_i}{\partial\bar{z}_1} \\ \frac{\partial\overline{W}_i}{\partial\bar{z}_2} \\ \vdots \\ \frac{\partial\overline{W}_i}{\partial\bar{z}_k} \end{pmatrix} \quad (6.123)
$$

Note that the differentiation is carried out at birth, when $\mathbf{x}_0 = \mathbf{z}_0$, so either variable can be used in calculating the gradient.

Applying the gradient operator to both sides of (6.113) yields

$$\nabla \overline{W}_i = \int \widetilde{W}_i(\mathbf{x}_0) \nabla g(\mathbf{x}_0)\, d\mathbf{x} \qquad (6.124)$$

The gradient of the genotype distribution $g(\mathbf{x}_0)$ has a particularly simple form when, as we have assumed, $g(\mathbf{x}_0)$ is multivariate normal (6.113) with variance-covariance matrix $\mathbf{G}$:

$$\nabla g(\mathbf{x}_0) = \mathbf{G}^{-1}(\mathbf{x}_0 - \bar{\mathbf{x}}_0) g(\mathbf{x}_0) \qquad (6.125)$$

Thus

$$\nabla \overline{W}_i \;=\; \mathbf{G}^{-1} \int (\mathbf{x}_0 - \bar{\mathbf{x}}_0) g(\mathbf{x}_0) \widetilde{W}_i\, d\mathbf{x} \qquad (6.126)$$

$$\;=\; \mathbf{G}^{-1} \boldsymbol{\delta}_i \overline{W}_i \qquad (6.127)$$

Substituting this result for $\boldsymbol{\delta}_i$ in (6.120) yields

$$\Delta \bar{\mathbf{z}}_0 = \bar{A}^{-1} \mathbf{G} \sum_i q_i \overline{W}_i^{-1} \nabla \overline{W}_i \qquad (6.128)$$

Remembering that $q_i = \lambda^{-i} \overline{W}_i$, (6.128) simplifies to

$$\Delta \bar{\mathbf{z}}_0 = \bar{A}^{-1} \mathbf{G} \sum_i \lambda^{-i} \nabla \overline{W}_i \qquad (6.129)$$

One last step.[6] As in Section 6.1.10, rewrite the characteristic equation $\sum_i \lambda^{-i} \overline{W}_i = 1$ as $\mathcal{F}[\mathbf{z}, \lambda(\mathbf{z})] = 1$. Implicit differentiation yields

$$\nabla \mathcal{F} + \frac{\partial \mathcal{F}}{\partial \lambda} \nabla \lambda = 0$$

or

$$\nabla \lambda \;=\; \frac{-\nabla \mathcal{F}}{\partial \mathcal{F}/\partial \lambda}$$

$$\;=\; \frac{-\sum_i \lambda^{-i} \nabla \overline{W}_i}{\frac{\partial}{\partial \lambda} \sum_i \lambda^{-i} \overline{W}_i}$$

$$\;=\; \lambda \bar{A}^{-1} \sum_i \lambda^{-i} \nabla \overline{W}_i \qquad (6.130)$$

Substituting this into (6.129) yields Lande's result:

$$\Delta \bar{z}_0 = \lambda^{-1} \mathbf{G} \nabla \lambda \qquad (6.131)$$

---

[6]I don't know what motivated Lande to take this crucial step, but it certainly works.

Comments

Fitness Lande's theorem provides a rigorous quantitative genetic justification for the use of λ as a measure of fitness. The demographic methods in the preceding chapters make it possible to examine in detail the sensitivity of λ to *any* variable that affects the vital rates. We can now legitimately identify this sensitivity with the selection gradient on that variable.[7]

Assumptions Lande's theorem relies on both genetic and demographic assumptions. The first is basically a separation of time scales. It is assumed that the demographic processes reach equilibrium faster than selection (usually phrased as assuming that selection is "weak"). The second is the additivity assumption which rules out the importance of genotype-environment interactions, dominance, and epistasis. Finally, there is an implicit assumption that fitness is neither frequency- nor density-dependent. These genetic assumptions are common in evolutionary theory, but the consequences of violating them are not well understood.

The main demographic assumption is that the environment is constant, which rules out abiotic stochastic variation and density-dependent effects. We will examine evolution in stochastic environments (Section 8.4.7) and in density-dependent models (Section 9.4) in subsequent chapters, but the theory for these more realistic cases is not as well developed as that discussed in this chapter.

Natural populations are certainly not always, and probably not often, at their stable stage distribution. A heuristic justification for the use of stable population theory can be made as follows. The actual population growth rate is given by λ_1 only if the population is at its stable stage distribution; otherwise, the growth rate is $\sum_i c_i \lambda_i$, where the c_i depend on the deviation from the stable structure. Thus, although λ_1 may not measure the actual rate of growth, it is always positively *correlated* with the rate of growth. The strength of the correlation is greater the closer the population is to its stable stage distribution. If fitness is equated with the growth rate, then for nonstable populations λ_1 is a character positively correlated with fitness, and thus will increase under selection. This informal argument needs to be supported by a formal quantitative genetic analysis.

---

[7]Other definitions of fitness have been proposed (e.g., Cooper 1984). Demetrius (1974a,b, 1983, 1985 and elsewhere) has proposed that selection be analyzed in terms of population entropy (Section 4.6.1). This theory is demographically sophisticated, but lacks a firm genetic basis at this time.

6.4.3   Pleiotropy, Correlation, and Constraints

Lande's theorem emphasizes the importance of genetic correlations between traits. Consider a particular trait z_1. From (6.131),

$$\Delta \bar{z}_1 = \lambda^{-1} \left(\frac{\partial \lambda}{\partial z_1} g_{11} + \sum_{j \neq 1} \frac{\partial \lambda}{\partial z_j} g_{1j} \right) \qquad (6.132)$$

where the g_{ij} are elements of the genetic covariance matrix $\mathbf{G}$. If z_1 is highly correlated with other traits with conflicting selective pressures, $\Delta \bar{z}_1$ may show little or no relation to the selection gradient on z_1 alone. This phenomenon (so-called "genetic slippage") has long been known in livestock selection (Dickerson 1955), but is also probably extremely important in natural selection.

> ### Example 6.13 Natural selection in *Gammarus lawrencianus*
>
> Doyle and Hunte (1981) report an interesting experiment on the adaptation of the amphipod *Gammarus lawrencianus* to laboratory culture conditions. Individuals were collected from the field, and raised in the laboratory for approximately 26 generations. Their demography was measured, and compared with measurements (under identical laboratory conditions) of individuals from the field. There was no intentional artificial selection applied to the experimental population, so changes in the demographic parameters should represent the results of natural selection for adaptation to a novel environment.
>
> Figure 6.26 shows the relation between the selective pressures $\partial \lambda / \partial P_i$ and $\partial \lambda / \partial F_i$ calculated from Doyle and Hunte's data and the observed responses ΔP_i and ΔF_i. In the absence of genetic correlation effects, the simplest prediction would be that the observed changes would be directly proportional to the selective pressures. This is clearly not the case.
>
> Doyle and Hunte's data do not include genetic correlations between the age-specific survival and fertility parameters. They did document significant negative phenotypic correlations between development rate and fertility, and negative genetic correlations between life span and individual growth rate.
>
> This example makes it clear that the practice within life history theory (of which I am as guilty as anyone) of basing predictions strictly on the patterns of selective pressure cannot be rigorously justified, and that improving our understanding of the genetic covariance structure of demographic traits is an important priority.

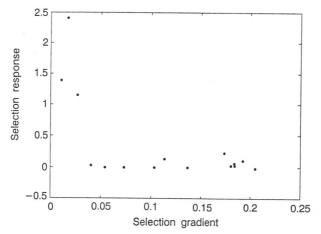

Figure 6.26: Observed phenotypic change versus selective presure on age-specific survival probability and fertility for *Gammarus lawrencianus* over 26 generations of adaptation to laboratory culture. Data from Doyle and Hunte (1981).

Predictions based on hypothesized patterns of covariance among traits form an important part of life history theory. Indeed, the explanations for the patterns of clutch size (Lack 1947), senescence (Medawar 1952), and parity (Cole 1954) with which evolutionary demography began are all based on this idea.

The expression (6.131) for $\Delta \bar{z}$ can be modified by noting that the genetic covariance g_{ij} between z_i and z_j can be written as

$$g_{ij} = \sigma_i^2 \frac{\partial z_i}{\partial z_j} \tag{6.133}$$

where the partial derivative is the slope of the linear regression of z_i on z_j. Thus

$$\Delta \bar{z}_i = \lambda^{-1} \left(\frac{\partial \lambda}{\partial z_i} + \sum_{j \neq i} \frac{\partial \lambda}{\partial z_j} \frac{\partial z_j}{\partial z_i} \right) \sigma_i^2 \tag{6.134}$$

which makes clear how the effect of selection on $\bar{z}_i$ depends on both the direct selective pressure on z_i and on the indirect selective pressure caused by changes in traits related to z_i. This result can be used to predict situations in which increases in one trait will be favored at the expense of another (e.g., Hamilton 1966, Caswell 1978, and Charlesworth 1980 for senescence; Caswell 1985 for alternate modes of reproduction).

The widespread occurrence of negative genetic correlations between fitness components (e.g., Falconer 1981, Antonovics 1976, Rose 1982, Rose and Charlesworth 1981, Rose et al. 1987) provides a framework for the use of optimization theory. Suppose that two traits (e.g., survival and reproduction) both contribute to fitness, but are negatively correlated. The correlation between the two traits defines a constraint function, that any phenotype must satisfy. Constrained optimization theory seeks combinations of the traits that satisfy the constraints and maximize fitness.

One intriguing possibility is that of calculating the shape of the constraint function from knowledge of the sensitivities and the hypothesis of optimization, as shown in the following example.

Example 6.14 Optimal life histories and age-specific costs of reproduction

Consider an age-classified population (Caswell 1982d), and suppose that there are age-specific costs of reproduction, so that

$$\frac{\partial P_i}{\partial F_i} = -c_i \tag{6.135}$$

$$\frac{\partial F_{i+1}}{\partial F_i} = -d_i \tag{6.136}$$

The cost c_i is assessed in terms of survival (a "survival cost") and the cost d_i is a "fertility cost." The constraint surfaces of which c_i and d_i are the slopes need not be linear; the derivatives are simply measured locally at the realized phenotype of the population.

The necessary conditions for maximization of λ are

$$\begin{aligned}
\frac{d\lambda}{dF_i} &= \frac{\partial \lambda}{\partial F_i} + \frac{\partial \lambda}{\partial P_i}\frac{\partial P_i}{\partial F_i} \\
&= \frac{\partial \lambda}{\partial F_i} - c_i\frac{\partial \lambda}{\partial P_i} \\
&= 0
\end{aligned} \tag{6.137}$$

and

$$\begin{aligned}
\frac{d\lambda}{dF_i} &= \frac{\partial \lambda}{\partial F_i} + \frac{\partial \lambda}{\partial F_{i+1}}\frac{\partial F_{i+1}}{\partial F_i} \\
&= \frac{\partial \lambda}{\partial F_i} - d_i\frac{\partial \lambda}{\partial F_{i+1}} \\
&= 0
\end{aligned} \tag{6.138}$$

These conditions imply that

$$\begin{aligned}
c_i &= \frac{\partial \lambda/\partial F_i}{\partial \lambda/\partial P_i} \\
&= \frac{v_1}{v_{i+1}}
\end{aligned} \tag{6.139}$$

$$d_i = \frac{\partial \lambda / \partial F_i}{\partial \lambda / \partial F_{i+1}}$$

$$= \frac{w_i}{w_{i+1}} \tag{6.140}$$

That is, survival costs should vary with age as the inverse of the reproductive value curve, whereas fertility costs should vary as the slope of the stable age distribution.

These predictions have been tested using data from human populations (Caswell 1982d) and from populations of the sedge *Eriophorum vaginatum* (Fetcher 1983). In both cases, the predictions were surprisingly accurate, considering the crudity of the data on costs of reproduction.

In human populations (and, indeed, in most age-classified populations) the stable age distribution is approximately a negative exponential over the reproductive life span (Caswell 1982d), so that the predicted fertility costs (6.140) should be very nearly age-invariant. Reproductive value curves, on the other hand, typically rise to a maximum near the age of first reproduction and then decline; the predicted survival costs (6.139) should thus decline at first, and then increase with age.

To examine these predictions in human populations, Caswell (1982d) used age-specific rates of maternal mortality due to complications of pregnancy as a measure of survival costs. This mortality rate increases dramatically with age after about age 20, independent of the level of medical technology in the country from which the data are obtained.

The inverse reproductive value curve typically has a minimum at age 10–20 and increases thereafter. Rates of stillbirth and neonatal and infant mortality, and the duration of postpartum amenorrhea are measures of fertility costs (Caswell 1982d). In agreement with prediction, these costs are nearly age-invariant in human populations. What age variation there is agrees closely with the deviation from an exponential slope in the stable age distribution in a set of artificial life tables thought to be representative of early human populations.

This analysis can be extended to complex life cycles (Caswell 1984); the general result is that the hypothesis of constrained optimization predicts that the cost of an increase in a_{kl}, assessed in terms of its effect on a_{ij}, must satisfy

$$\frac{\partial a_{ij}}{\partial a_{kl}} = \frac{-v_k w_l}{v_i w_j} \tag{6.141}$$

Collection of data on the correlations among demographic traits, coupled with estimation of a projection matrix, could be used to test these predictions of the optimization hypothesis.

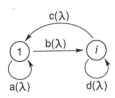

Figure 6.27: A reduced life cycle graph focusing on stage i, with no loops disjoint with both n_1 and n_i.

6.4.4 Fitness and Reproductive Value Maximization

The connection of reproductive value and selection has a long, distinguished, and confused history. When he introduced the concept, Fisher (1930) proposed that the action of selection was "proportional to" reproductive value. Williams (1966) and Hirshfield and Tinkle (1975) used the decomposition of reproductive value into current reproduction and residual reproductive value (5.34) to discuss the evolution of reproductive effort. Schaffer (1974) and Taylor et al. (1974) formalized this notion by proving, for age-classified populations, that "maximizing fitness is equivalent to maximizing reproductive value at every age." A misunderstanding of the statement of Schaffer's theorem led to a debate (Caswell 1980, 1981, Yodzis 1981, Schaffer 1981) and, finally, a generalization of the result to stage-classified populations (Caswell 1982b).

Here we show in just what sense maximization of fitness and maximization of reproductive value are equivalent, for a wide class of stage-classified models. The life cycle graph in Figure 6.27 focuses on stage n_i. The loop $a(\lambda)$ denotes the total transmission of all loops that pass through n_1 but not n_i. Similarly, $d(\lambda)$ denotes all loops that pass through n_i but not n_1. $b(\lambda)$ and $c(\lambda)$ denote all the pathways from n_1 to n_i and vice versa. We assume that there are no loops that are disjoint with both n_1 and n_i.

The reproductive value of stage i is

$$v_i = \frac{\tilde{c}(\lambda)}{1 - \tilde{d}(\lambda)} \tag{6.142}$$

and the characteristic equation can be written

$$
\begin{aligned}
1 &= \tilde{a}(\lambda) + \tilde{b}(\lambda)\tilde{c}(\lambda) + \tilde{d}(\lambda) - \tilde{a}(\lambda)\tilde{d}(\lambda) && (6.143) \\
&= \mathcal{F}(\lambda) && (6.144)
\end{aligned}
$$

(I have written the characteristic equation in terms of transposed loop transmissions (see Section 5.5) to facilitate comparison with v_i; loop transmissions and transposed loop transmissions are identical.)

Suppose that there is some variable x_i (e.g., reproductive effort, clutch size, etc.) that affects the vital rates of stage i, and thus $\tilde{c}(\lambda)$ and $\tilde{d}(\lambda)$. By implicit differentiation,

$$\frac{\partial \lambda}{\partial x_i} = \frac{-\partial \mathcal{F}/\partial x_i}{\partial \mathcal{F}/\partial \lambda} \tag{6.145}$$

Maximization of λ requires that

$$\frac{\partial \mathcal{F}}{\partial x_i} = \tilde{b}(\lambda)\frac{\partial \tilde{c}(\lambda)}{\partial x_i} + \frac{\partial \tilde{d}(\lambda)}{\partial x_i} - \tilde{a}(\lambda)\frac{\partial \tilde{d}(\lambda)}{\partial x_i} = 0 \tag{6.146}$$

whereas maximization of v_i requires that

$$\frac{\partial v_i}{\partial x_i} = \frac{\left(1 - \tilde{d}(\lambda)\right)\frac{\partial \tilde{c}(\lambda)}{\partial x_i} + \tilde{c}(\lambda)\frac{\partial \tilde{d}(\lambda)}{\partial x_i}}{\left(1 - \tilde{d}(\lambda)\right)^2} = 0 \tag{6.147}$$

Comparing (6.146) and (6.147), we see that extrema of λ and v_i coincide if and only if $\partial \tilde{d}(\lambda)/\partial x_i = 0$, i.e., if the variable x_i affects only pathways from n_i back to n_1.

In summary, maximization of fitness is equivalent to maximizing reproductive value at each stage with respect to variables that affect only the reproductive pathways from the stage in question back to n_1, as long as the life cycle graph can be reduced to the form in Figure 6.27.

Chapter 7

Statistical Inference

This chapter presents two approaches to evaluating the statistical significance of differences among matrix models for populations in different habitats, at different times, or subject to different experimental treatments. One approach evaluates the significance of differences between entire transition matrices. A second approach focuses on the dominant eigenvalue λ of the projection matrix. Since λ integrates the effect of the environment on the vital rates into a single statistic it is frequently used as a dependent variable in life table response experiments (Section 6.1.9). I will present two methods for associating confidence intervals with the observed estimates of λ in order to evaluate the significance of intertreatment differences. These two topics by no means exhaust the possibilities for statistical analysis of matrix population models. There is, for example, a large literature on statistical analysis of life table data which could certainly be applied to age-classified matrix models.

7.1 Differences between Transition Matrices

Section 4.8.2 discussed the estimation of the transition probabilities from data on transition frequencies; these transition probabilities describe the fates of individuals in the population exclusive of reproduction.

I assume here that a set of transition matrices $\mathbf{M}$ has been estimated by following the fates over some time interval of individuals of known initial states. The fate categories need not be the same as the initial state categories, but in many cases they will be, or will be the initial state categories with the addition of a category representing death. The transition matrices are estimated under two or more conditions, which may be defined by multiple factors in a cross-classified experimental design.

The problem is to evaluate the significance of the differences among the transition matrices. The analysis utilizes the same loglinear analyses introduced in Section 3.3.2 to evaluate state variables. The null hypotheses and the tests of treatment effects differ slightly, however, because of the structure of the transition data.

7.1.1 One Treatment

Consider a set of transition matrices M_i, where i denotes the level of some treatment. We wish to test whether the transition matrices M_i differ significantly from each other. The null hypothesis is that all the populations are governed by a single transition matrix.

Tests of this null hypothesis were introduced by Anderson and Goodman (1957) in the context of testing the time-homogeneity of Markov chains. In that case, the treatment consists of different times at which transitions are observed. They proposed a likelihood ratio test which is identical to that used in loglinear contingency analysis (see Bishop et al. 1975). This test has since been applied to matrix population models by Bierzychudek (1982) and Cochran (1986), but the loglinear approach can be extended to more complex experimental designs.

Without loss of generality, suppose that the treatment is time. The transition data then form a three-way state (S) × fate (F) × time (T) contingency table. The (ijk) entry of this table is the number of individuals making the transition from state i to fate j at time k.

Suppose that time has no effect. Then the fate of an individual depends only on its initial state, and not on the time. That is, F is independent of T, conditional on S. It is this *conditional* independence that makes the hypothesis testing slightly different from that in Chapter 3, where the tests were concerned with whether fate was dependent on various measures of initial state.

The saturated model for the contingency table is

$$\log m_{ijk} = u + u_{S(i)} + u_{F(j)} + u_{T(k)}$$
$$+ u_{SF(ij)} + u_{ST(ik)} + u_{FT(jk)} + u_{SFT(ijk)}$$

Under the null hypothesis of conditional independence, fate may be affected by state, so we must keep the $u_{SF(ij)}$ term. Similarly, the initial state distribution may differ from one time to another, so we keep the $u_{ST(ik)}$ term. However, once we know the distribution of individuals among the initial states, and the overall state × fate interaction, we should require no additional information to specify the table completely. Thus we test for conditional independence by eliminating the FT and SFT terms from the model and fitting the model SF, ST:

$$\log m_{ijk} = u + u_{S(i)} + u_{F(j)} + u_{T(k)}$$
$$+ u_{SF(ij)} + u_{ST(ik)} \qquad (7.1)$$

Conditional independence models always require that at least one two-way interaction be eliminated from the loglinear model (Bishop et al. 1975); this also requires elimination of all higher order interactions involving that two-way interaction.

Example 7.1 Temporal variation in jack-in-the-pulpit demography

Bierzychudek (1982) measured size-classified projection matrices for two consecutive years (1977–78 and 1978–79) in two populations (Brooktondale and Fall Creek) of jack-in-the-pulpit (*Arisaema triphyllum*), a perennial herbaceaous plant. She used Anderson and Goodman's (1957) method to examine temporal variation in demography at each site, by testing the pair of matrices at each site versus their mean. Since the Anderson-Goodman test is explicitly developed in terms of a Markov chain, she restricted her analysis to size transitions among surviving plants, so that there was no loss from the population. It is possible, however, to test the complete set of transitions, including mortality using loglinear analysis.

The transition frequency tables for the Brooktondale population are given by

1977–78
State

Fate	1	2	3	4	5	6	Total
1	495	91	0	0	1	0	587
2	90	221	13	1	1	1	327
3	1	30	36	6	1	0	74
4	0	6	17	18	5	1	47
5	0	0	4	19	8	5	36
6	0	0	0	1	6	4	11
Dead	361	2	4	0	0	0	367
Total	947	350	74	45	22	11	1449

1978–79

	1	2	3	4	5	6	
1	496	96	3	2	0	0	597
2	91	219	35	15	6	1	367
3	0	9	22	8	11	1	51
4	0	3	11	8	3	0	25
5	0	2	5	12	7	1	27
6	0	0	0	0	7	7	14
Dead	364	12	4	4	2	1	387
Total	951	341	80	49	36	11	1468

Notice that death appears as a fate, but not as a state.

The corresponding transition matrices are

$$
M_1 = \begin{pmatrix}
0.523 & 0.260 & 0 & 0 & 0.045 & 0 \\
0.095 & 0.631 & 0.176 & 0.022 & 0.045 & 0.091 \\
0.001 & 0.086 & 0.486 & 0.133 & 0.045 & 0 \\
0 & 0.017 & 0.230 & 0.400 & 0.227 & 0.091 \\
0 & 0 & 0.054 & 0.422 & 0.364 & 0.455 \\
0 & 0 & 0 & 0.022 & 0.273 & 0.364
\end{pmatrix}
$$

$$
M_2 = \begin{pmatrix}
0.522 & 0.282 & 0.038 & 0.041 & 0 & 0 \\
0.096 & 0.642 & 0.438 & 0.306 & 0.167 & 0.091 \\
0 & 0.026 & 0.275 & 0.163 & 0.306 & 0.091 \\
0 & 0.009 & 0.138 & 0.163 & 0.083 & 0 \\
0 & 0.006 & 0.063 & 0.245 & 0.194 & 0.091 \\
0 & 0 & 0 & 0 & 0.194 & 0.636
\end{pmatrix}
$$

Fitting the model (7.1) to these data (after adding 0.5 to each cell, as suggested by Fingleton 1984) yielded a G^2 value of 79.95 with 36 degrees of freedom; the probability of such a large value by chance alone is $P < .0001$. Thus we conclude that the transition matrix for the Brooktondale population varies significantly between the two years.

The same analysis for the Fall Creek population (the data are not shown here) yields a G^2 value of 42.90, 36 degrees of freedom, $P = 0.1994$. There is thus no evidence for significant temporal variation in the Fall Creek population.

These conclusions are at odds with Bierzychudek's conclusions based on only those individuals that survived throughout both years; she concluded that both populations exhibited significant temporal variation.

This analysis can be extended by decomposing the G^2 value for the conditional independence model into contributions from each initial state. That is, the $S \times F \times T$ table can be decomposed into a set of $F \times T$ tables, one for each initial state. For each of these tables, the null hypothesis is independence of fate and time; the sum of the G^2 values testing this independence hypothesis equals the G^2 value for the test of conditional independence in the entire table.

Example 7.2 Decomposing G^2 for jack-in-the-pulpit

Examination of the columns of the transition matrices M_1 and M_2 in Example 7.1 suggests that the fates of size classes 2, 3, and 4 differ a great deal from year to year, whereas size classes 1, 5, and 6 appear more homogeneous. Decomposing G^2 for the three-way SFT table into values for the two-way FT tables specific to each initial state confirms this:

Brooktondale

State	G^2	P
1	0.53	.9974
2	21.27	.0016
3	17.25	.0084
4	24.53	.0004
5	11.61	.0711
6	4.76	.5725
Sum	79.95	

When this analysis is repeated for the Fall Creek population, the results suggest that there are some small, marginally significant time effects on initial states 2 and 4, which do not show up in the test of the entire transition matrix:

Fall Creek

State	G^2	P
1	2.03	.9168
2	13.21	.0398
3	8.18	.2252
4	13.11	.0414
5	2.51	.8670
6	3.85	.6964
Sum	42.89	

7.1.2   Multiple Treatments

The loglinear analysis of transition matrices extends naturally to designs with multiple treatments. To be specific, let us suppose that transition matrices are measured at several different times at several different locations. The resulting data set can be organized as a four-way state (S) × fate (F) × time (T) × location (L) contingency table.

The Null Hypothesis

The null hypothesis is that the fate of an individual is independent of time and location, conditional on its initial state. In the corresponding loglinear model the FT and FL interactions are set to zero, along with all higher order interactions involving those terms (SFT, SFL, FTL, $SFTL$). The resulting model for the null hypothesis is SF, STL:

$$\begin{aligned}
\log m_{ijkl} = {} & u + u_{S(i)} + u_{F(j)} + u_{T(k)} + u_{L(l)} \\
& + u_{SF(ij)} + u_{ST(ik)} + u_{SL(il)} \\
& + u_{STL(ikl)}
\end{aligned} \tag{7.2}$$

If the null hypothesis SF, STL fails to fit, we conclude that fate is significantly affected by time, location, or both. To test the location effect, we add the time effect and test the model STL, SFT. If it fits, location must be responsible for the lack of fit of SF, STL. Similarly, to test the time effect we examine the model STL, SFL, which includes only the location effect. If it fits, time must be responsible for the lack of fit of SF, STL. If none of the three models fit, then both time and location must have significant effects.

If both time and location are significant, they may or may not interact. If the model STL, SFT, SFL fits the data both time and location affect fate (conditional on state), but the effects are separable. That is, time and location have independent additive effects on the SF interaction. If STL, SFT, SFL fails to fit, then the $SFTL$ interaction is also significant; this implies that the effects of time and location interact.

Example 7.3 Jack-in-the-pulpit: time and location effects

Bierzychudek's complete data set for *Arisaema triphyllum* includes transition matrices for two times at two locations. The results of fitting the sequence of loglinear models to the data are

Model	G^2	df	P
STL, SF	707.44	108	$< .0001$
STL, SFT	627.58	72	$< .0001$
STL, SFL	122.85	72	.0002
STL, SFT, SFL	46.62	36	.2076

The first test implies that time, location, or both are significant. The second test includes the FT interaction; its failure to fit the data implies that location has a significant effect. Similarly, the third test implies that time has a significant effect. The final model includes all terms except $SFTL$; its success implies that the interaction of time and location is *not* significant.

Decomposing G^2 by State

As with the single treatment analysis, the effects of multiple treatments can be examined for each initial state, decomposing the total G^2 value into contributions from each state. However, there are now more models to consider, because the contingency tables for each initial state are now three-way FTL tables. The decompositions corresponding to the four models in Example 7.3 are

$$G^2_{STL,SF} = \sum_S G^2_{TL,F} \tag{7.3}$$

$$G^2_{STL,SFT} = \sum_S G^2_{TL,FT} \tag{7.4}$$

$$G^2_{STL,SFL} = \sum_S G^2_{TL,FL} \tag{7.5}$$

$$G^2_{STL,SFT,SFL} = \sum_S G^2_{TL,FT,FL} \tag{7.6}$$

A high-order contingency table can be decomposed into a large number of lower order tables. Tests of all these tables, specific to initial states, may reveal significant effects on fate that do not appear in the tests of the whole transition matrix structure. Some care must probably be exercised to avoid inflating experiment-wise error rates since, as the number of tests becomes large, some significant results will be expected by chance alone. A conservative approach is to test the entire transition matrix structure and then dissect those effects that appear significant. For example, testing Bierzychudek's data as a four-way contingency table (Example 7.3) shows that both time and location have significant effects. Breaking the table down into the two locations and analyzing the resulting three-way tables (Example 7.1) show that the time effects are significant in the Brooktondale population, but not in the Fall Creek population. Further examination of the Brooktondale data (Example 7.2) shows that the time effect is due mainly to changes in the fate of individuals in states 2, 3, and 4.

Loglinear analysis has also been used by Moloney (1988), in a study of culm demography of the grass *Danthonia sericea*, and by Harvell et al. (1989) in a study of effects of density and time on colony demography in the bryozoan *Membranipora membranacea*. Moloney (1988) tested for effects of location and time on fate within individual size classes, but did not test the entire transition matrices. His study also exemplifies the importance of specifying appropriate null hypotheses for the tests. He reported his results in terms of "marginal" and "partial" associations (see, e.g., Fingleton 1984). The partial association values correspond to tests of the appropriate null hypotheses for conditional independence; the marginal associations do not. Only one of the six initial states yields significant FT effects in the former case, but four out of six do so in the latter case. The marginal associations greatly overestimate the true effects of time in this study.

7.2 Confidence Intervals for λ

We turn now to the estimation of confidence intervals for the dominant eigenvalue λ of a population projection matrix. There is obviously uncertainty about the entries in any projection matrix estimated from real data. Since λ is a function of those matrix entries, there is some uncertainty associated with the estimate of λ. Unfortunately, there seems to be no general formula giving the distribution of λ in terms of the joint distribution of the a_{ij}, or even an expression for the variance of λ as a function of the variance of the a_{ij}. Thus standard statistical theory for significance testing is inapplicable.

Two approaches have been used to circumvent this problem. The first relies on the eigenvalue sensitivity formula (6.8) to develop an approximate expression for the variance in λ (cf. Section 6.1.6), and uses normal distribution theory to translate this variance into a confidence interval. The second approach uses computer-intensive resampling methods (the bootstrap or the jackknife) to develop nonparametric confidence intervals by repeatedly calculating λ for subsets of the total data set.

Each of these approaches has its limitations, but since values of λ in the literature are rarely accompanied by *any* estimate of variance or confidence intervals, no matter how approximate, they deserve to be more widely applied.

7.2.1 Approximate Confidence Intervals

Suppose that the population is described by a projection matrix $\mathbf{A}$ whose elements are independent random variables with means $\bar{a}_{ij}$ and variances $V(a_{ij})$; assume furthermore that the variances are small. Then a first-order approximation to the variance $V(\lambda)$ is

$$V(\lambda) \approx \sum_{i,j} \left(\frac{\partial \lambda}{\partial a_{ij}} \right)^2 V(a_{ij}) \qquad (7.7)$$

Since the sensitivities of λ to changes in the a_{ij} (or in other parameters, such as age at maturity, which may appear in the life cycle graph) can be calculated easily, (7.7) can be evaluated if the variances of the vital rates are known or can be approximated.

Example 7.4 The spotted owl

The habitat of the northern spotted owl (*Strix occidentalis caurina*) in coniferous forests in the Pacific Northwest has been greatly reduced

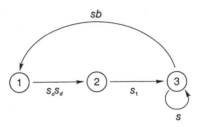

Figure 7.1: Life cycle graph corresponding to Lande's (1988) model for spotted owl demography. The model assumes a birth-pulse population, a postbreeding census, and a projection interval of 1 year.

by logging, and there is considerable controversy over its management. Lande (1988) has used demographic models to examine this issue.

Lande's description of spotted owl demography is equivalent to the life cycle graph of Figure 7.1, assuming a birth-pulse population, post-breeding census, and a projection interval of 1 year. The parameters, using Lande's notation, are s_0 = fledgling survival probability, s_d = probability of successful dispersal, s_1 = subadult survival probability, s = adult survival probability, and b = mean annual clutch size. The characteristic equation is

$$1 = \frac{s_0 s_d s_1 s b \lambda^{-3}}{1 - s\lambda^{-1}} \tag{7.8}$$

which simplifies to

$$\lambda^3(1 - s\lambda^{-1}) = s_0 s_d s_1 s b \tag{7.9}$$

Solution of (7.9) using estimated values of the parameters (see below) yields $\lambda = 0.961$. Is this significantly different from 1?

The sensitivities of λ to the parameters can be easily derived by implicit differentiation of (7.9):

$$\frac{\partial \lambda}{\partial x} = \frac{\lambda}{xT} \quad \text{for } x = s_0, s_d, s_1, b \tag{7.10}$$

$$\frac{\partial \lambda}{\partial s} = \frac{\lambda(T - 2)}{sT} \tag{7.11}$$

where $T = 3 + s/(\lambda - s)$.

To derive the variances of the parameters, Lande notes that s_0, s_d, s_1 and s are survival probabilities with binomial sampling distributions, with variances given by

$$V(x) = \frac{x(1 - x)}{N_x} \quad x = s_0, s_d, s_1, s \tag{7.12}$$

where N_x denotes the sample size on which the estimate of x is based. Based on data from the literature, Lande assumes that the variance in the clutch size is 1.3 times its mean; thus the variance in the mean clutch size b is

$$V(b) = 1.3b/N_b \qquad (7.13)$$

The numerical data and results are as follows:

Parameter	Value	N	Variance	Sensitivity	Contribution
s_0	0.60	135	1.78×10^{-3}	0.030	0.016×10^{-4}
s_d	0.18	44	3.36×10^{-3}	0.102	0.349×10^{-4}
s_1	0.71	7	2.94×10^{-2}	0.026	0.199×10^{-4}
s	0.94	69	7.92×10^{-4}	0.981	7.620×10^{-4}
b	0.24	438	7.12×10^{-4}	0.076	0.041×10^{-4}
				Sum	8.225×10^{-4}

The contributions to $V(\lambda)$ are the terms in the summation (7.7). Their sum is $V(\lambda) \approx 8.225 \times 10^{-4}$. Note that s_1 has by far the largest variance, but that it makes only a small contribution to $V(\lambda)$. Most of $V(\lambda)$ is contributed by variance in adult survival s, to which λ is particularly sensitive.

The standard error of λ is given by the square root of $V(\lambda)$; crude confidence limits of ± 2 standard errors give an interval estimate of the rate of increase as $\lambda = 0.961 \pm 0.058$. Thus Lande concludes that λ is not significantly different from 1, and that the population is in approximate equilibrium.

7.2.2   Resampling Methods

The assumptions of independence of parameters, small variances, and normality of λ are obvious weaknesses. In many cases, the sampling variance in life history parameters may be large, covariances among life history parameters are likely to be the rule rather than the exception, and the distribution of λ, although it will depend on the details of the distributions of the a_{ij}, cannot be assumed to be normal (Rago and Dorazio 1984).

An alternative approach, which escapes some or all of these assumptions, is based on resampling methods (the *jackknife* and *bootstrap*). These methods have been applied to life table data by Lenski and Service (1982) and Meyer et al. (1986, 1987). For general descriptions of the methods, see Efron (1982), Diaconis and Efron (1983), and Efron and Tibshirani (1986).

The jackknife and the bootstrap are both based on the idea of treating the sample as a sort of statistical universe, repeatedly resampling it, and using the samples to estimate means, variances, bias, and confidence intervals for the parameters of interest. These methods are very computation-intensive, thinking nothing of repeating calculations (in our case, computations of eigenvalues) thousands of times. As faster computers become more readily available, this becomes less and less of a concern.

Resampling methods require the specification of a basic unit of data; the resampling is carried out on these units. I will assume that this unit is an individual. In a cohort life table study, for example, the data consist of records on a set of m individuals followed from birth to death, with offspring production recorded as it occurs. The $l(x)$ and $m(x)$ functions are constructed from these individual records, the matrix entries P_i and F_i estimated from the life table, and λ calculated from the matrix. Resampling methods are difficult or impossible to apply to data in which there is no common unit of data (e.g., Lande's analysis of the spotted owl, in which parameters were derived from different studies).

Note that while I will discuss resampling methods in the context of inferences about λ, they can be applied to *any* statistic, so they can be used to make inferences about any of the demographic properties calculated from a projection matrix: eigenvalues, eigenvectors, sensitivities, elasticities, etc.

The Jackknife

Suppose that the data set consists of m individuals. Let $\hat{\lambda}^{(all)}$ denote the dominant eigenvalue of $\mathbf{A}^{(all)}$, the projection matrix based on the entire data set; $\hat{\lambda}^{(all)}$ is an estimate of the (unknown) true λ characteristic of the population from which the individuals were sampled. The jackknife procedure begins by omitting each of the individuals in turn, and calculating an eigenvalue $\hat{\lambda}^{(i)}$, $i = 1, 2, \ldots, m$ based on the remaining $m - 1$ individuals. Denote the mean of these values by

$$\hat{\lambda}^{(\cdot)} = \frac{1}{m} \sum_i \hat{\lambda}^{(i)} \tag{7.14}$$

This quantity can be used to estimate the bias in $\lambda^{(all)}$ as an estimate of the true λ for the population:

$$BIAS = (m - 1)(\hat{\lambda}^{(\cdot)} - \hat{\lambda}^{(all)}) \tag{7.15}$$

(Efron 1982). The bias-corrected jackknife estimate of λ is

$$\begin{aligned} \lambda^J &= \hat{\lambda}^{(all)} - BIAS \\ &= m\hat{\lambda}^{(all)} - (m - 1)\hat{\lambda}^{(\cdot)} \end{aligned} \tag{7.16}$$

The jackknife values $\hat{\lambda}^{(i)}$ also provide estimates of the variance and standard deviation:

$$V(\lambda^J) \;=\; \frac{m-1}{m} \sum_i \left(\hat{\lambda}^{(i)} - \hat{\lambda}^{(\cdot)} \right)^2 \tag{7.17}$$

$$\hat{\sigma}(\lambda^J) \;=\; \sqrt{V(\lambda^J)} \tag{7.18}$$

The standard deviation $\hat{\sigma}(\lambda^J)$ can be used to develop approximate confidence intervals, using either $\lambda^J \pm z_\alpha \hat{\sigma}(\lambda^J)$ or $\lambda^J \pm t_{m-1,\alpha}\hat{\sigma}(\lambda^J)$, where z_α and $t_{m-1,\alpha}$ are the upper $\alpha/2$ percentage points of the normal distribution and the t distribution, respectively.

Example 7.5 Artificial data: jackknife

As an example, consider the following artificial data, simulating an experiment in which age-classified life table data were collected on a cohort of 20 individuals. The data are summarized in the form of a table of reproduction, with "–" indicating the death of the individual (e.g., individual 2 died after producing 1.3 offspring at age 4).

				Individuals					
1	2	3	4	5	6	7	8	9	10
0.00	0.00	0.00	0.00	0.00	0.00	0.00	0.00	0.00	0.00
0.00	0.00	0.00	0.00	0.00	0.00	0.00	–	0.00	0.00
–	0.00	–	0.00	0.00	0.00	0.00	–	0.00	0.00
–	1.30	–	1.59	0.51	2.01	1.35	–	1.12	2.14
–	–	–	1.01	1.37	1.10	–	–	0.51	0.62
–	–	–	2.21	1.31	1.23	–	–	3.07	1.66
–	–	–	1.44	–	1.81	–	–	–	1.77
–	–	–	2.71	–	–	–	–	–	–
–	–	–	2.49	–	–	–	–	–	–
–	–	–	–	–	–	–	–	–	–

11	12	13	14	15	16	17	18	19	20
0.00	0.00	0.00	0.00	0.00	0.00	0.00	0.00	0.00	0.00
0.00	0.00	0.00	0.00	0.00	–	–	0.00	0.00	0.00
0.00	0.00	0.00	–	0.00	–	–	0.00	–	0.00
1.54	0.86	2.35	–	–	–	–	1.51	–	1.04
2.34	1.62	1.51	–	–	–	–	1.50	–	2.10
2.24	1.22	1.97	–	–	–	–	1.10	–	–
1.09	2.07	–	–	–	–	–	–	–	–
2.58	2.17	–	–	–	–	–	–	–	–
0.97	–	–	–	–	–	–	–	–	–
–	–	–	–	–	–	–	–	–	–

The age-classified projection matrix generated from these data had an eigenvalue $\hat{\lambda}^{(\text{all})} = 1.2536$. A series of 20 10 $\times$ 10 projection matrices was generated, each based on 19 of the 20 individuals. The resulting $\hat{\lambda}^{(i)}$ values were

$$
\begin{array}{cccc}
1.2687 & 1.2212 & 1.2393 & 1.2611 \\
1.2644 & 1.2611 & 1.2647 & 1.2374 \\
1.2611 & 1.2486 & 1.2687 & 1.2400 \\
1.2253 & 1.2687 & 1.2492 & 1.2687 \\
1.2549 & 1.2687 & 1.2397 & 1.2536
\end{array}
\tag{7.19}
$$

From these numbers, the bias, the bias-corrected estimate, the variance, and the standard deviation can all be calculated:

$$
\begin{align}
\hat{\lambda}^{(\cdot)} &= 1.2533 \tag{7.20}\\
BIAS &= -0.0073 \tag{7.21}\\
\lambda^{J} &= 1.2609 \tag{7.22}\\
V(\lambda^{J}) &= 0.0041 \tag{7.23}\\
\hat{\sigma}(\lambda^{J}) &= 0.0638 \tag{7.24}
\end{align}
$$

The approximate 95% confidence intervals for λ are then 1.2609 ± 0.1250 (using the normal distribution) and 1.2609 ± 0.1335 (using the t distribution with 19 degrees of freedom).

The Bootstrap

The bootstrap differs from the jackknife in the way the samples are drawn. The original data consist of a sample of size m drawn from some (unknown) distribution; in our case, m individuals, with their associated schedules of survival and reproduction. The nonparametric maximum likelihood estimate of the unknown distribution consists of those m data points, each with probability $1/m$. We draw a "bootstrap sample" from this distribution, by drawing m individuals, *with replacement*, at random from the observed data set. Because the sample is taken with replacement, it is likely that some individuals will not be represented, whereas others will be represented more than once. We repeat the process b times (b is the "bootstrap sample size"), producing a set of bootstrap values $\lambda^{*(i)}$, $i = 1, 2, \ldots, b$.

The bootstrap estimate of the bias of $\hat{\lambda}^{(\text{all})}$ as an estimate of the true population value of λ is

$$
BIAS = \lambda^{*(\cdot)} - \hat{\lambda}^{(\text{all})}
\tag{7.25}
$$

where $\lambda^{*(\cdot)} = \frac{1}{b}\sum_{i=1}^{b} \lambda^{*(i)}$ is the mean of the b bootstrap values. The bias-adjusted bootstrap value of λ is then

$$\lambda^B = \hat{\lambda}^{(\text{all})} - BIAS \tag{7.26}$$
$$= 2\hat{\lambda}^{(\text{all})} - \lambda^{*(\cdot)} \tag{7.27}$$

The bootstrap estimates of the variance and standard deviation of λ are

$$V(\lambda^B) = \frac{1}{b-1}\sum_i^b \left(\lambda^{*(i)} - \lambda^{*(\cdot)}\right)^2 \tag{7.28}$$

$$\hat{\sigma}(\lambda^B) = \sqrt{V(\lambda^B)} \tag{7.29}$$

The bootstrap sample size b influences the accuracy of the estimates (see Figure 7.3), but 1000 is probably sufficient in most cases (see Meyer et al. 1986).

Bootstrap Confidence Intervals

The bootstrap provides several ways to estimate confidence intervals for an estimated parameter. Efron and Tibshirani (1986) discuss these in detail, with examples; here we consider several of the most immediately applicable methods.

Standard Error Methods   The standard error of an estimate is a crude but useful measure of its statistical accuracy. An approximate confidence interval can be constructed by treating the distribution of the estimate as if it were normal, and writing

$$\lambda^B \pm \hat{\sigma}(\lambda^B)z_\alpha \tag{7.30}$$

where z_α is the upper $\alpha/2$ percentage point of the standard normal distribution. As Efron and Tibshirani (1986) state, this estimate is "sometimes good, and sometimes not so good." It can produce very inaccurate results if the distribution of λ is far from normal.

The Percentile Method   The bootstrap calculation provides a genuinely nonparametric way to estimate confidence intervals. The set of bootstrap values $\{\lambda^{(*i)}, i = 1,\ldots,b\}$ provides an estimate of the distribution of λ. From this distribution, one can find the upper and lower confidence limits for any desired significance level.

Let $\widehat{G}$ denote the cumulative frequency distribution of the $\lambda^{*(i)}$, that is

$$\widehat{G}(x) = \text{proportion of } \lambda^{*(i)} \leq x \tag{7.31}$$

The percentile method consists of using the upper and lower tails of this cumulative distribution, so that the confidence interval for λ is

$$\left[\widehat{G}^{-1}(\alpha/2),\ \widehat{G}^{-1}(1 - \alpha/2)\right] \tag{7.32}$$

The Bias-Corrected Percentile Method The accuracy of the estimated confidence intervals can be improved by using a bias-corrected percentile method (see Schenker 1985 and Efron and Tibshirani 1986 for assumptions). This method modifies the endpoints of the confidence interval slightly, as follows. Let Φ denote the cumulative distribution function of the standard normal distribution, and define

$$z_0 = \Phi^{-1}[\widehat{G}(\hat{\lambda}^{(\text{all})})] \tag{7.33}$$

The bias-corrected percentile method then defines the confidence interval as

$$\left[\widehat{G}^{-1}[\Phi(2z_0 - z_\alpha)],\ \widehat{G}^{-1}[\Phi(2z_0 + z_\alpha)]\right] \tag{7.34}$$

Note that if $\hat{\lambda}^{(\text{all})}$ falls at the median of the bootstrap distribution (i.e., is median unbiased), then $\widehat{G}(\hat{\lambda}^{(\text{all})}) = 0.5$, $z_0 = 0$, and the bias-corrected percentile method reduces to the percentile method.

Meyer et al. (1986) examine both real and artificial data in detail, comparing the jackknife and the bootstrap. Here I will present an artificial example that shows the steps in the bootstrap procedure.

Example 7.6 Artificial data: bootstrap

The data set in Example 7.5 was used as the basis for the bootstrap calculations. Two thousand bootstrap samples were drawn, each consisting of 20 individuals selected at random with replacement from the data set. For each sample, an age-classified projection matrix was constructed, and its dominant eigenvalue calculated. The results were

$$\hat{\lambda}^{(\text{all})} = 1.2536 \tag{7.35}$$
$$\lambda^{*(\cdot)} = 1.2473 \tag{7.36}$$
$$BIAS = -0.0063 \tag{7.37}$$
$$\lambda^B = 1.2599 \tag{7.38}$$
$$\hat{\sigma}(\lambda^B) = 0.0649 \tag{7.39}$$

The distribution of $\lambda^{*(i)}$ is shown in Figure 7.2; it is not quite normal, suggesting that normal-based confidence intervals may not be accurate. The 95% confidence intervals calculated using the standard deviation, the percentile method, and the bias-corrected percentile method are

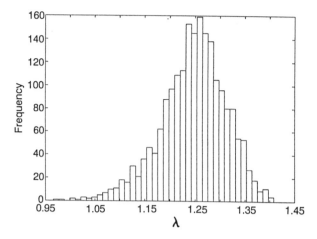

Figure 7.2: The distribution of 2000 bootstrap estimates of λ for the artificial data in Example 7.5.

Method	Lower Limit	Upper Limit
Standard deviation	1.1201	1.3745
Percentile	1.1005	1.3578
Bias-corrected percentile	1.1056	1.3635

In this case, the bias-corrected percentile method is not a great improvement over the percentile method, since $\hat{\lambda}^{(\text{all})}$ is nearly median unbiased $[\widehat{G}(\hat{\lambda}^{(\text{all})}) = 0.5120]$. However, the confidence interval based on the standard deviation is noticeably too wide at the upper end and too narrow on the lower end.

The Bootstrap Sample Size

The accuracy of estimates of standard deviations and confidence intervals depend on the bootstrap sample size b. Sample sizes on the order of 500 to 1000 seem to be widely considered accurate. Figure 7.3 shows the bias-adjusted value λ^B, the standard deviation, and the percentile method confidence intervals as a function of b, for the data of Example 7.6. The estimate of λ^B converges after only a few hundred bootstrap samples, but reliable estimates of the standard deviation and confidence intervals require slightly larger sample sizes.

More important, the accuracy of confidence intervals seems to depend on the *original* sample size m, i.e., in our case, the number of individuals in the original sample (Schenker 1985). If the original sample is too small, the

(A)

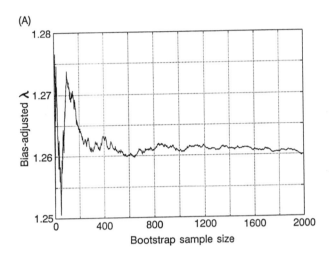

(B)

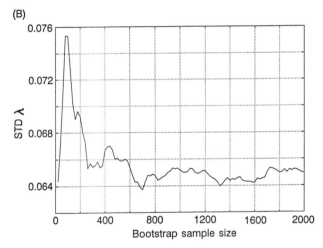

coverage of the confidence intervals is not what it is claimed to be. However the differences in Schenker's case are small, and it is not clear how important the effect may be.

The approaches presented in this chapter are both recent developments in statistics, and I expect that much more will be known about their use in the near future. The jackknife and the bootstrap are particularly powerful tools for statistical inference about λ and other demographic parameters. Although one may quibble about the details and the precise accuracy of the confidence intervals, and although one is probably well advised to treat the results as approximations, in my opinion *any* of the confidence intervals of

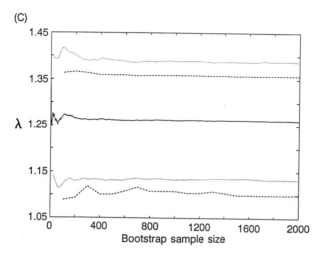

Figure 7.3: The effects of the bootstrap sample size on estimates, using the artificial data of Example 7.6. (A) The bias-adjusted bootstrap estimate λ^B. (B) The bootstrap estimate of the standard deviation $\hat{\sigma}(\lambda^B)$. (C) The bias-adjusted bootstrap estimate λ^B with 95% confidence limits calculated using the standard deviation (dotted lines) and the percentile method (dashed lines).

Examples 7.5 and 7.6 would be a great improvement over the mere reporting of $\lambda = 1.2536$, with no indication of the uncertainty associated with the estimate.

Chapter 8

Time-Varying and Stochastic Models

In this chapter we relax the assumption of time-invariance that has characterized the models analyzed in the preceding chapters. We will retain the assumption of linearity, so the variation to be considered here is due to extrinsic environmental variability, rather than to changes in the density of the population itself, relative to its resources, competitors, or predators. Such density-dependent variability is the subject of Chapter 9.

Much of the theory of time-varying matrix models is relatively new, and the primary literature can be dauntingly technical. As a result, there are as yet relatively few applications of the theory, and, in comparison with the preceding chapters, this chapter may seem relatively short on results with direct application to data analysis. However, the basic ideas follow naturally from the time-invariant theory, and point to possible applications and to unsolved questions.

8.1 The General Format

The general format for a time-varying model is

$$\mathbf{n}(t+1) \quad = \quad \mathbf{A}_t \mathbf{n}(t) \qquad (8.1)$$
$$= \quad \mathbf{A}_t \mathbf{A}_{t-1} \mathbf{A}_{t-2} \cdots \mathbf{A}_0 \mathbf{n}(0) \qquad (8.2)$$

where the sequence of projection matrices $\mathbf{A}_0, \mathbf{A}_1, \ldots$ describes the demographic consequences of a sequence of environments.

A model of this form is actually a three-level description of population dynamics (Cohen 1979c). The first level is a model describing the temporal variation in the environment. At the next level is a sequence of projection matrices generated by the model for the environment. Finally, there is the sequence of stage structure vectors $\mathbf{n}(t)$ generated by the sequence of projection matrices operating on an initial population vector.

The patterns of environmental variability can be classified according to the properties of the sequence of projection matrices:

1. Deterministic environments

   (a) Constant environments: the sequence is constant, with $\mathbf{A}_t = \mathbf{A}$.

   (b) Periodic environments: the sequence is periodic, with $\mathbf{A}_k = \mathbf{A}_{2k} = \mathbf{A}_{3k} = \ldots$ for some period k.

   (c) Aperiodic environments: the sequence is an arbitrary but not periodic sequence of matrices.

2. Stochastic environments: the sequence of projection matrices is generated by a stochastic process operating on some underlying space $\mathcal{A}$ of possible projection matrices. In this chapter, I will assume that the stochastic process is a first-order finite state ergodic Markov chain, but many of the results can be extended to much more general stochastic processes (Cohen 1977a,b, Heyde and Cohen 1985, Tuljapurkar 1986).

   (a) Homogeneous vs. inhomogeneous environments. The environmental Markov chain specifies the probability distribution of environments at time $t + 1$ as a function of the environment at time t. If that probability distribution does not itself change through time, the environment is said to be homogeneous. If the pattern of environmental variability is itself variable over time, the environment is said to be inhomogeneous.

   (b) Independent vs. autocorrelated environments. The autocorrelation pattern, or lack thereof, in a stochastic environment can have a major impact on population dynamics. Assuming that successive environments are independent is often analytically convenient, but should be regarded as a simplifying assumption.

8.1.1   Issues

The issues in the study of variable environments are familiar from the time-invariant case, but environmental variability raises significant new problems. They include

- Ergodicity. The asymptotic structure of a time-invariant model is captured by the dominant eigenvector $\mathbf{w}_1$, and there are powerful results about the convergence of the population to this structure. We will consider analogous theorems about the ergodic properties of time-varying models.

- Measures of population growth rate. The asymptotic growth rate of a time-invariant model is given by the dominant eigenvalue λ_1. In stochastic models, there are several possible measures of asymptotic population growth rate, each with different properties and different interpretations.

- Transient analysis. The rate of convergence to the asymptotic population structure depends, in the time-invariant case, on the damping ratio. In time-varying models, it is also influenced by the nature of the environmental variability, and must be calculated in a slightly different fashion.

- Extinction probability. In time-invariant models, ultimate extinction is either certain ($\lambda_1 < 1$) or impossible ($\lambda_1 \geq 1$). In stochastic models there is a probability of extinction due to the possibility that the population may experience a sequence of particularly bad environmental conditions.

- Evolutionary demography. Variability is an obviously important environmental factor, to which a population might adapt. The question of measuring fitness in a variable environment, and of relating fitness to demographic changes, is more difficult than in the time-invariant case.

8.2 Periodic Environments

Periodic environment models are relevant because of the pronounced seasonal periodicities in many environments. If environmental differences between years are negligible in comparison with differences between seasons, projection models with a time step shorter than the annual cycle naturally appear to vary in a periodic fashion. In this section, we consider three different approaches to studying such systems.

8.2.1 Periodic Matrix Products

Skellam (1966) discussed in detail the dynamics of a periodic environment model in which

$$\mathbf{n}(t+k) \quad = \quad \mathbf{A}_k \mathbf{A}_{k-1} \cdots \mathbf{A}_1 \mathbf{n}(t) \qquad (8.3)$$
$$= \quad \mathbf{B}\mathbf{n}(t) \qquad (8.4)$$

where the matrix $\mathbf{B} = \prod_{j=1}^{k} \mathbf{A}_j$ describes population growth over a single environmental cycle.

The dynamics of the population over k-interval periods are described by the eigenvalues and eigenvectors of $\mathbf{B}$, to which all of the time-invariant theory applies.

Primitivity of Matrix Products

The primitivity of **B** depends on the nature of the $\mathbf{A}_j$ and on the order in which they appear in the product. Necessary and sufficient conditions for the primitivity of a product of two or of an arbitrary number of age-classified Leslie matrices are given by Keller (1980) and G. C. Taylor (1985), respectively.

The conditions for two age-classified matrices are fairly simple. Let S_{A_1} denote the set of age classes with positive fertility in $\mathbf{A}_1$, and similarly for S_{A_2}. If $\mathbf{A}_1$ and $\mathbf{A}_2$ are Leslie matrices and $\mathbf{B} = \mathbf{A}_1\mathbf{A}_2$ is irreducible, then **B** is primitive if and only if

$$\gcd\left\{\frac{(i+j)}{2} | i \in S_{A_1}, j \in S_{A_2}, i + j \text{ even}\right\} = 1 \tag{8.5}$$

That is, form all pairs of ages for which fertility is positive in both matrices and the sum of the ages is even; take the average of these ages. The greatest common divisor of this set of ages must be 1.

The conditions for primitivity of a longer series of Leslie matrices are sufficiently complicated (G. C. Taylor 1985) that it is difficult to draw conclusions from them.

The primitivity of a product of matrices of arbitrary structure can be evaluated in several ways. First, recall that the primitivity of a matrix depends only on the pattern of nonzero entries, not on the actual values of those entries. Thus, one could take a series of matrices $\mathbf{A}_j$ and replace them by their adjacency matrices[1] $\mathbf{C}_j$, actually calculate the product of the $\mathbf{C}_j$, and examine the pattern of positive entries to see if the product is primitive (e.g., using the results in Section 4.4).

An alternative approach utilizes the life cycle graph directly. Suppose that only two matrices are involved, with life cycle graphs G_1 and G_2, and consider the construction of a two-step graph G_{12} corresponding to the product $\mathbf{A}_2\mathbf{A}_1$ (note order of matrix multiplication!). There will be an arc from n_j to n_i in G_{12} if and only if there is an arc from n_j to n_k in G_1 *and* an arc from n_k to n_i in G_2, for some k.

This approach, complicated only by the requirement of keeping track of all possible transitions at each step, can be extended to arbitrarily long sequences of arbitrarily complex matrices. The result is the graph corresponding to the periodic matrix product. The primitivity of this graph, at least when the graph is small, can be evaluated by inspection.

---

[1]The adjacency matrix of **A** contains a 0 where the corresponding entry of **A** is 0 and a 1 where the corresponding entry of **A** is positive.

Eigenvalues and Eigenvectors

Assuming that $\mathbf{B}$ is irreducible and primitive, the dominant eigenvalue λ_1 gives the asymptotic growth rate (per k time steps) of the population observed at times t, $t + k$, etc. However, the sequence of projection matrices in the matrix product $\mathbf{B}$ implies an observation point (e.g., a season of the year) at which the observation is made. The asymptotic growth rate should be independent of the choice of this observation point. All that is required to prove this is to show that, for any two matrices $\mathbf{A}_1$ and $\mathbf{A}_2$, the eigenvalues of $\mathbf{B}_1 = \mathbf{A}_2\mathbf{A}_1$ and $\mathbf{B}_2 = \mathbf{A}_1\mathbf{A}_2$ are identical. The proof (J.E. Cohen, personal communication) is easy. Suppose that $\mathbf{x}$ is an eigenvector of $\mathbf{A}_2\mathbf{A}_1$. Then $\mathbf{A}_2\mathbf{A}_1\mathbf{x} = \lambda\mathbf{x}$. Multiplying both sides by $\mathbf{A}_1$ yields

$$(\mathbf{A}_1\mathbf{A}_2)\mathbf{A}_1\mathbf{x} = \lambda\mathbf{A}_1\mathbf{x} \tag{8.6}$$

so λ is also an eigenvector of $\mathbf{A}_1\mathbf{A}_2$, with eigenvector $\mathbf{A}_1\mathbf{x}$.

Unlike the asymptotic growth rate, the stage distribution of the population depends on the observation point within the environmental cycle. Suppose that, at some time t, the population $\mathbf{n}(t)$ is proportional to the dominant eigenvector $\mathbf{w}$ of the product matrix $\mathbf{B}$. The resulting sequence of population vectors is given by

$$\begin{aligned}
\mathbf{n}(t+1) &= \mathbf{A}_1\mathbf{w} \\
\mathbf{n}(t+2) &= \mathbf{A}_2\mathbf{A}_1\mathbf{w} \\
&\vdots \\
\mathbf{n}(t+k) &= \mathbf{A}_k \cdots \mathbf{A}_1\mathbf{w} \\
&= \lambda\mathbf{w}
\end{aligned}$$

Thus, the population structure $\mathbf{n}(t)$ is asymptotically cyclic, with period k. The vectors $\mathbf{w}$, $\mathbf{A}_1\mathbf{w}$, $\mathbf{A}_2\mathbf{A}_1\mathbf{w}$, ... are the eigenvectors of the matrices $\mathbf{B}_1$, $\mathbf{B}_2$, ...

Note that noncyclic permutations that change the order in which the different environements are encountered do not preserve the population growth rate (e.g., Darwin and Williams 1964 for an example on harvesting of a rabbit population).

8.2.2   Classification by Season of Birth

An alternative model for periodic environments was introduced by Gourley and Lawrence (1977). Rather than focusing on the product matrix $\mathbf{B}$, they developed a life cycle graph using the original projection interval, with individuals classified by age and season of birth. Consider a projection interval of 6 months in a cyclic environment with two seasons ("summer" and "winter"). Classify individuals by both their age and by the season of their birth.

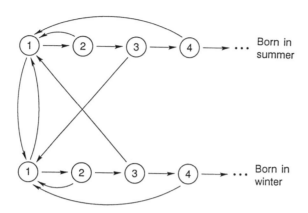

Figure 8.1: A life cycle graph for an age-classified population in a cyclic environment with period 2 ("summer" and "winter"). Individuals are classified by both their age and the season of their birth.

The life cycle graph is shown in Figure 8.1. Individuals born in the summer (upper half of the graph) are 1 unit (6 months) old in the winter, 2 units old the next summer, and so on. Individuals born in the winter (lower half of the graph) are 1 unit old in the summer, 2 units old the next winter, and so on.

The pattern of reproductive paths in the graph follows from the fact that reproduction during the winter (by individuals of any age and origin) produces newborn individuals in the following summer, and vice versa.

This graph is irreducible, but the cycle lengths are 2, 4, 6, 8, ... Thus it is imprimitive with an index of imprimitivity $d = 2$. In general, the index of imprimitivity equals the cycle length of the environment and the population structure oscillates with the same period as that of the environment (Gourley and Lawrence 1977).

8.2.3 Discrete Fourier Analysis

A third approach to periodic environments was introduced by Tuljapurkar (1985); it focuses on the relation between the frequency of the environmental cycle and the amplitude and phase of the oscillations in the population structure.

Tuljapurkar's model is (8.1), where the matrix $\mathbf{A}_t$ is given by

$$\mathbf{A}_t = \mathbf{A} + \mathbf{B}\cos(\omega t) \tag{8.7}$$

and where the period of the environmental oscillation is $k = 2\pi/\omega$. The matrix $\mathbf{A}$ contains the mean values and the matrix $\mathbf{B}$ the amplitudes of the variation in the demographic parameters.

In order to guarantee that $\mathbf{A}_t$ is nonnegative, it is necessary to assume that $|b_{ij}| \leq a_{ij}$. If $|b_{ij}| < a_{ij}$, then the incidence matrix of $\mathbf{A}_t$ is the same as that of $\mathbf{A}$, and $\mathbf{A}_t$ will be irreducible and primitive if $\mathbf{A}$ is.

Tuljapurkar assumes that the periodic variation in the vital rates will produce periodic variation in the population structure, and uses Fourier decomposition to express this periodic variation in terms of the ω and its higher harmonics. This yields expressions for the growth rate and the amplitude and phase of the oscillation of each stage in the population.

The effect of the periodic environment depends on the relation between ω and the frequency of the oscillation of the complex subdominant eigenvalues of the mean matrix $\mathbf{A}$. Recall that $\mathcal{P}_j = 2\pi/\tan^{-1}(a/b)$ is the period of oscillation generated by the complex eigenvalue $\lambda_j = a \pm bi$. Then the strongest response comes when $k \approx \mathcal{P}_j$, especially for $j = 2$ (i.e., the largest subdominant eigenvalue). For age-classified populations, in which $\mathcal{P}_2$ is approximately the length of a generation, this implies that the population is most sensitive to environmental fluctuations with a period of about one generation.

Tuljapurkar finds that the population growth rate is increased by environmental fluctuations of about one generation length, and decreased by oscillations with much shorter or longer periods. Similarly, the magnitude of the oscillations in individual age classes is greatest when the period of the environment matches the period of one of the subdominant eigenvalues.

Tuljapurkar's approach has the great advantage of avoiding the periodic matrix product (8.4). Although that product includes all relevant information about the periodic environment, it is difficult to extract from it information on the effect of particular parts of the life cycle, because each element in the product matrix contains many elements of the matrices that make up the product.

8.3 Deterministic, Aperiodic Environments

We now turn to population growth in environments characterized by arbitrary, deterministic, but aperiodic sequences of projection matrices. Within this context, the most important theoretical problem is that of ergodicity: in what sense can one expect such a pattern of population growth to forget its past. The result is known as the "weak ergodic theorem"; it is also important in developing models for stochastic environments.

8.3.1 Weak Ergodicity

In a constant environment characterized by an irreducible, primitive projection matrix, the population structure converges exponentially from any nonzero initial vector to a distribution proportional to the dominant right eigenvector, and the population grows exponentially at a rate given by the dominant eigenvalue. This result is the strong ergodic theorem of demography; we showed it in Section 4.4.2 by noting that, for such a matrix,

$$\lim_{t \to \infty} \frac{\mathbf{n}(t)}{\lambda_1^t} = c_1 \mathbf{w}_1 \tag{8.8}$$

where $c_1 = \mathbf{v}_1' \mathbf{n}(0)$ is determined by the initial conditions. Since $\mathbf{n}(t) = \mathbf{A}^t \mathbf{n}(0)$ we can rewrite this as

$$\lim_{t \to \infty} \frac{\mathbf{A}^t}{\lambda_1^t} = \mathbf{w}_1 \mathbf{v}_1' \tag{8.9}$$

where the matrix on the right-hand side is of rank 1, with every row proportional to $\mathbf{v}_1$ and every column proportional to $\mathbf{w}_1$.

Convergence of $\mathbf{n}(t)$ to a fixed, stable stage distribution is too much to expect when the environment varies. However, ergodicity also implies that, in the long run, population dynamics become independent of initial conditions. An ergodic population thus "forgets" its past. This interpretation of ergodicity can be applied in variable as well as in constant environments. Consider two different initial populations, $\mathbf{n}(0)$ and $\mathbf{m}(0)$, and suppose that they are subjected to the same time-invariant projection matrix $\mathbf{A}$, so that

$$\begin{aligned} \mathbf{n}(t) &= \mathbf{A}^t \mathbf{n}(0) \\ \mathbf{m}(t) &= \mathbf{A}^t \mathbf{m}(0) \end{aligned} \tag{8.10}$$

If $\mathbf{A}$ is primitive, $\mathbf{n}(t)$ and $\mathbf{m}(t)$ both become proportional to $\mathbf{w}_1$. As this happens, the difference between the *proportional* structures of $\mathbf{n}(t)$ and $\mathbf{m}(t)$ decreases to zero.

This property can be generalized to a variable environment, in which $\mathbf{n}(0)$ and $\mathbf{m}(0)$ experience a sequence of projection matrices:

$$\begin{aligned} \mathbf{n}(t) &= \mathbf{A}_t \mathbf{A}_{t-1} \cdots \mathbf{A}_1 \mathbf{n}(0) \\ \mathbf{m}(t) &= \mathbf{A}_t \mathbf{A}_{t-1} \cdots \mathbf{A}_1 \mathbf{m}(0) \end{aligned} \tag{8.11}$$

The *weak ergodic theorem* of demography establishes conditions under which the distance between $\mathbf{n}(t)$ and $\mathbf{m}(t)$ decays to zero as t increases, even though neither converges to a fixed structure. It was first proved by Lopez (1961); here we will approach it using the so-called contraction properties of multiplication by positive matrices (Furstenberg and Kesten 1960, Hajnal 1976; the

matrix theory is reviewed by Seneta 1981 and the demographic applications
by Cohen 1979c, 1987).

To develop this theory, we need to measure the distance between two
stage-distribution vectors; we will use a measure called the Hilbert projective
pseudometric.

The Hilbert Projective Pseudometric

This metric measures the distance between two nonnegative vectors in a way
that depends only on their proportional composition, independent of their
absolute size. This makes it ideal for our purposes, since we care only about
convergence of the proportional, not the absolute structure. Let $\mathbf{x}$ and $\mathbf{y}$ be
positive vectors. The Hilbert metric distance between $\mathbf{x}$ and $\mathbf{y}$ is

$$d(\mathbf{x},\mathbf{y}) \;=\; \ln\left(\frac{\max_i\left(\frac{x_i}{y_i}\right)}{\min_i\left(\frac{x_i}{y_i}\right)}\right) \tag{8.12}$$

$$= \; \max_{i,j} \ln\left(\frac{x_i y_j}{x_j y_i}\right) \tag{8.13}$$

The Hilbert metric can be defined between vectors containing zero entries
only if the locations of the zeroes coincide; the ratio x_i/y_i is defined to be
zero if $y_i = 0$, and the minimum in the denominator of (8.13) is taken over
all nonzero values of the ratio.

When $\mathbf{x}$ and $\mathbf{y}$ are proportional to each other, the ratio x_i/y_i is constant,
and $d(\mathbf{x},\mathbf{y}) = 0$. In fact, $d()$ has almost all the properties of a true metric:

$$d(\mathbf{x},\mathbf{y}) \;\geq\; 0$$
$$d(\mathbf{x},\mathbf{y}) \;=\; d(\mathbf{y},\mathbf{x})$$
$$d(\mathbf{x},\mathbf{y}) \;\leq\; d(\mathbf{x},\mathbf{z}) + d(\mathbf{z},\mathbf{y})$$

and, in addition, the properties that make it suitable for measuring the
distance between population structures:

$$d(\mathbf{x},\mathbf{y}) \;=\; 0 \qquad \text{iff } \mathbf{x} = a\mathbf{y}$$
$$d(\mathbf{x},\mathbf{y}) \;=\; d(a\mathbf{x},b\mathbf{y}) \qquad \text{for } a,b > 0$$

Contraction Properties of Nonnegative Matrices

The use of the Hilbert metric in studies of ergodicity is based on the fact
that multiplication by a positive matrix is a strict contraction in this metric

(Birkhoff 1957). Suppose that $\mathbf{A}$ is a positive matrix, $\mathbf{x}(t)$ and $\mathbf{y}(t)$ are positive vectors, and $\mathbf{x}(t+1) = \mathbf{A}\mathbf{x}(t)$ and $\mathbf{y}(t+1) = \mathbf{A}\mathbf{y}(t)$. Then

$$
\begin{aligned}
\frac{x_i(t+1)}{y_i(t+1)} &= \frac{\sum_j a_{ij} x_j(t)}{\sum_k a_{ik} y_k(t)} \\
&= \sum_j \left(\frac{a_{ij} y_j(t)}{\sum_k a_{ik} y_k(t)} \right) \frac{x_j(t)}{y_j(t)} \\
&= \sum_j p_{ij} \frac{x_j(t)}{y_j(t)}
\end{aligned}
\tag{8.14}
$$

where $p_{ij} > 0$ and $\sum_j p_{ij} = 1$. That is, $x_i(t+1)/y_i(t+1)$ is a weighted average of the $x_j(t)/y_j(t)$, and thus (e.g., Hardy et al. 1952, p. 14)

$$
\min_j \frac{x_j(t)}{y_j(t)} < \frac{x_i(t+1)}{y_i(t+1)} < \max_j \frac{x_j(t)}{y_j(t)}
\tag{8.15}
$$

unless all the $x_j(t)/y_j(t)$ are equal, in which case the two vectors are already proportional. Thus

$$
d[\mathbf{x}(t+1), \mathbf{y}(t+1)] < d[\mathbf{x}(t), \mathbf{y}(t)]
\tag{8.16}
$$

unless $d[\mathbf{x}(t), \mathbf{y}(t)] = 0$.

Projection matrices are generally nonnegative, but not positive. This weakens the result in (8.15). If we suppose that $\mathbf{A}$ has at least one positive entry in each row [Hajnal (1976) calls such matrices "row allowable"; any irreducible matrix is row allowable], the vectors $\mathbf{x}(t+1)$ and $\mathbf{y}(t+1)$ will be positive if $\mathbf{x}(t)$ and $\mathbf{y}(t)$ are, thus ensuring that the Hilbert metric is defined. However, some of the p_{ij} in (8.14) may equal 0, in which case the strict inequalities in (8.15) must be changed to $\leq$.

The rate at which matrix multiplication contracts the distance between two vectors is quantified by the *contraction coefficient* $0 \leq \tau(\mathbf{A}) \leq 1$ defined by

$$
\tau(\mathbf{A}) = \sup_{\mathbf{x}, \mathbf{y}} \frac{d(\mathbf{A}\mathbf{x}, \mathbf{A}\mathbf{y})}{d(\mathbf{x}, \mathbf{y})}
\tag{8.17}
$$

In terms of this coefficient,

$$
d(\mathbf{A}\mathbf{x}, \mathbf{A}\mathbf{y}) \leq \tau(\mathbf{A}) d(\mathbf{x}, \mathbf{y})
\tag{8.18}
$$

The contraction coefficient $\tau(\mathbf{A})$ can be calculated explicitly in terms of the entries a_{ij} of the matrix, but the formulas are complicated and unenlightening (Seneta 1981, Chapter 3.4). However, several important properties will be useful to us.

- If $\mathbf{A}$ is positive, $\tau(\mathbf{A}) < 1$.

- The contraction coefficient of the product of two matrices is not greater than the product of the contraction coefficients:

$$\tau(\mathbf{A_1A_2}) \leq \tau(\mathbf{A_1})\tau(\mathbf{A_2}) \tag{8.19}$$

- The contraction coefficient $\tau(\mathbf{A}) = 0$ if and only if

$$\mathbf{A} = c\mathbf{w}\mathbf{v}' \tag{8.20}$$

for some constant c and some vectors $\mathbf{w}, \mathbf{v} > 0$. In this case the matrix $\mathbf{A}$ maps any two vectors immediately into proportional vectors.

These results provide an immediate proof of the *strong* ergodic theorem. Recall that a matrix is primitive if there exists some constant k such that $\mathbf{A}^t$ is positive for all $t \geq k$. Thus sufficiently high powers of a primitive matrix are positive; applying Birkhoff's theorem to powers $\mathbf{A}^k$ shows that, as $t \to \infty$, the distance between any two initial vectors decays to zero (Golubitsky et al. 1975).

The Weak Ergodic Theorem

Let $\mathbf{H}_{t,s}$ denote the product of a series of matrices from $\mathbf{A}_s$ to $\mathbf{A}_t$:

$$\mathbf{H}_{t,s} = \mathbf{A}_t\mathbf{A}_{t-1}\cdots\mathbf{A}_s \tag{8.21}$$

The product $\mathbf{H}_{t,s}$ is *weakly ergodic* if and only if

$$\lim_{t\to\infty} \tau(\mathbf{H}_{t,s}) = 0 \qquad \text{for all } s \tag{8.22}$$

which implies that

1. The product $\mathbf{H}_{t,s}$ asymptotically annihilates the Hilbert distance between any two vectors:

$$d(\mathbf{H}_{t,s}\mathbf{x}, \mathbf{H}_{t,s}\mathbf{y}) \to 0 \qquad \text{for all } s \tag{8.23}$$

2. The series of matrix products $\mathbf{H}_{t,s}$ eventually converges to a sequence of rank 1 matrices:
$$\mathbf{H}_{t,s} \to \lambda^{(t)}\mathbf{w}^{(t)}\mathbf{v}^{(t)\prime} \tag{8.24}$$

where $\lambda^{(t)}$ is the dominant eigenvalue of $\mathbf{H}_{t,s}$ and $\mathbf{w}^{(t)}$ and $\mathbf{v}^{(t)}$ are the corresponding eigenvectors.

Thus, if (8.22) is satisfied, the structures of any two initial populations exposed to the sequence of matrices $\mathbf{H}_{t,s}$ will converge. This is weak ergodicity.

Sufficient Conditions for Ergodicity Application of the weak ergodic theorem requires some way to determine whether a sequence of matrices satisfies (8.22). A variety of results that give sufficient conditions for weak ergodicity are known (Hajnal 1976, Seneta 1981, Cohen 1979b,c,e). Some of the more useful are summarized here.

An *ergodic set* of matrices is the analogue of a primitive matrix in the time-invariant case: it is a set of matrices with the property that there exists a $p > 0$ such that any product of length p of matrices drawn from the set (with repetitions allowed) is strictly positive (Hajnal 1976). Any sequence $H_{t,s}$ composed of matrices from an ergodic set is weakly ergodic, and the decline of $\tau(H_{t,s})$ to zero is asymptotically exponential. The proof (Golubitsky et al. 1975) is obtained by breaking the sequence into a product of subsequences of length p:

$$H_{t,0} = \cdots H_{2p,p+1} H_{p,0} \qquad (8.25)$$

Since each of those subsequences is positive (by the definition of an ergodic set), it follows from Birkhoff's theorem that the contraction coefficient of each of them must be strictly less than 1. Since the contraction coefficient $\tau(H_{t,0}) \leq \cdots \tau(H_{2p,p+1})\tau(H_{p,0})$, it follows that $\tau(H_{t,0}) \to 0$.

Examples of ergodic sets include the following:

1. Any single nonnegative, primitive matrix. By definition, for any primitive matrix there exists some p such that $A^t > 0$ for $t \geq p$. Thus the *strong* ergodic theorem follows as a special case of the weak ergodic theorem.

2. Any set of primitive matrices with a common incidence matrix and bounds on the elements, so that, for some finite K,

$$\frac{\max(a_{aij})}{\min^+(a_{ij})} < K$$

where $\min^+(a_{ij})$ is the minimum of the positive entries of A. Such a set describes an environment in which the variability is small enough that no demographic transition that is positive in some environment ever goes to zero in some other environment.

The requirement that the matrices in $H_{t,0}$ be drawn from an ergodic set is sufficient for weak ergodicity, but is far more strict than necessary. For example, Cohen (1979b) has considered the contractive properties of matrices that do not form an ergodic set because some or all of them are reducible. Consider matrices of the form

$$A = \begin{pmatrix} B & 0 \\ C & D \end{pmatrix} \qquad (8.26)$$

where $\mathbf{B}$ is irreducible. Suppose that $\mathbf{H}_{t,0}$ is composed of matrices from a set of these matrices. Cohen shows that $\tau(\mathbf{H}_{t,0}) \rightarrow 0$ if

1. all the matrices $\mathbf{A}$ have the same incidence matrix,

2. the irreducible submatrices $\mathbf{B}$ form an ergodic set,

3. the submatrices $\mathbf{C}$ are row-allowable, and

4. the nonzero elements of $\mathbf{B}$ and $\mathbf{C}$ are bounded away from zero.

In the context of nonhuman populations, these results leave something to be desired, because they rule out the possibility of occasional environments that are so severe that only certain stages can survive and/or reproduce, or in which reproduction is eliminated altogether. Such variation could render some of the matrices in the set imprimitive, or keep them from sharing a common incidence matrix. The effects of such variability, and the consequences to be expected when weak ergodicity does not hold, are not well understood.

Kim and Sykes (1976) report an empirical study of weak ergodicity, examining the properties of matrix products constructed from matrices for human populations in Keyfitz and Flieger (1968, 1971). They found that the convergence of $\tau(\mathbf{H}_{t,0})$ to zero was essentially complete by $t = 30$ (i.e., 150 years, since these matrices use a 5-year projection interval). Based on these matrices, any differences between initial age distributions would be eliminated within 150 years.

8.4 Stochastic Environments

We turn now to the analysis of models in which the sequence of environments that produces the sequence of population projection matrices is stochastic.[2] The results we will summarize are due mainly to Cohen (1976, 1977a,b, 1979a,b,c) and Tuljapurkar (1982a,b, 1986, 1989, Tuljapurkar and Orzack 1980), and trace back to the seminal work on products of random matrices by Furstenberg and Kesten (1960). See Cohen (1987) and Tuljapurkar (1989) for reviews.

---

[2]This chapter will consider only environmental stochasticity. *Demographic stochasticity*, the result of the chance application of vital rates to individuals, has been treated by Pollard (1966, 1973) in the context of human populations. It is most important in small populations, and may have implications for conservation of rare species (Goodman 1987, Menges 1990).

8.4.1 Formulation

We assume that the matrices $\mathbf{A}_t$ are drawn from a finite set $\mathcal{A}$, and that the environmental variation is described by a first-order finite-state Markov chain. Although it is possible to work with much more general stochastic processes (Cohen 1977a,b, Heyde and Cohen 1985), I know of no study that has obtained enough environmental information to specify even this simple a model, so the neglect of more complex environmental models is no great loss.

Let $\mathbf{A}^{(i)}$ denote the ith matrix in $\mathcal{A}$, and let

$$p_{ij}(t) = P(\mathbf{A}_{t+1} = \mathbf{A}^{(i)} | \mathbf{A}_t = \mathbf{A}^{(j)}) \tag{8.27}$$

The column-stochastic matrix $\mathbf{P}(t)$ describes the changes in the environment; if $\mathbf{P}(t)$ is time-invariant, we say that the environment is *homogeneous*; if not, it is *inhomogeneous*. The corresponding ergodic theorems are the *strong stochastic ergodic theorem* and the *weak stochastic ergodic theorem*, respectively. They depend on the set $\mathcal{A}$ and the Markov process specified by $\mathbf{P}(t)$.

8.4.2 Stochastic Ergodic Theorems

The situation in which we are now interested [corresponding to (8.10) and (8.11)] is

$$\begin{aligned} \mathbf{n}(t) &= \mathbf{A}_t \mathbf{A}_{t-1} \cdots \mathbf{A}_1 \mathbf{n}(0) \\ \mathbf{m}(t) &= \mathbf{B}_t \mathbf{B}_{t-1} \cdots \mathbf{B}_1 \mathbf{m}(0) \end{aligned} \tag{8.28}$$

The sequential products $\mathbf{A}_t \mathbf{A}_{t-1} \cdots \mathbf{A}_1$ and $\mathbf{B}_t \mathbf{B}_{t-1} \cdots \mathbf{B}_1$ represent two independent sample paths of the environmental process specified by $\mathbf{P}(t)$. Unlike the deterministic case (8.11), not only is the environment varying through time, but two different initial populations will experience different environmental sequences, because of the stochastic nature of the variation. We are interested in the long-run convergence of $\mathbf{n}(t)$ and $\mathbf{m}(t)$.

The Weak Stochastic Ergodic Theorem

We begin with the weak stochastic ergodic theorem because, as in the deterministic case, the strong stochastic ergodic theorem follows as a special case.

The crux of this problem is the fact that the stage distribution vectors $\mathbf{n}(t)$ and $\mathbf{m}(t)$ are now random variables, whose distribution reflects the environmental stochasticity. The approach (Cohen 1976, 1977a,b) is to combine two different but related results. First, if the environmental Markov chain is ergodic, the probability distribution of environmental states eventually converges to a stationary distribution, and thus forgets its past. Second, once the environmental distribution has converged, if the set of projection matrices $\mathcal{A}$ is ergodic, every sequence of matrices eventually becomes contracting. Combining these two sorts of "forgetting the past" permits one to show that the process as a whole is ergodic.

The Joint Process $[\mathbf{n}(t), \mathbf{A}_t]$ Since the probability distribution of $\mathbf{A}_{t+1}$ depends only on $\mathbf{A}_t$, and $\mathbf{n}(t+1)$ depends only on $\mathbf{A}_{t+1}$ and $\mathbf{n}(t)$, the *joint* process $[\mathbf{n}(t), \mathbf{A}_t]$ is Markovian (Cohen 1976, 1977a,b).

Let A denote any subset of the set $\mathcal{A}$ of transition matrices, and let B denote any measurable set of positive stage distribution vectors, normalized so the total population size is 1. Then Cohen (1977a,b) shows how to calculate the joint probability distribution

$$F_t(A, B) = P[\mathbf{A}_t \in A, \mathbf{n}(t) \in B] \tag{8.29}$$

The calculation, which involves solution of an integral equation, is complicated (Cohen 1977b, Tuljapurkar 1986); the important point for our considerations here is that the distribution exists, and that, under certain conditions, it will permit us to draw conclusions about the convergence of the probability distributions of population structure.

Suppose that the Markov chain on $\mathcal{A}$ is ergodic (i.e., if homogeneous, the transition matrix $\mathbf{P}$ is irreducible and primitive; if inhomogeneous, the sequence $\mathbf{P}(t)$ is weakly ergodic), and the set $\mathcal{A}$ is an ergodic set of projection matrices. Recall the basic setup of (8.28). Then the probability distributions of the joint processes $[\mathbf{A}_t, \mathbf{n}(t)]$ and $[\mathbf{B}_t, \mathbf{m}(t)]$ eventually converge to each other, and become independent of both the initial population and the initial environment (Cohen 1976). That is, for any initial population vectors $\mathbf{n}(0)$ and $\mathbf{m}(0)$, and any initial environments $\mathbf{A}_1, \mathbf{B}_1$, for any $\epsilon > 0$, there exists some time $\hat{t}$ such that for any $t > \hat{t}$

$$|P[\mathbf{A}_t \in A, \mathbf{n}(t) \in N | \mathbf{A}_1, \mathbf{n}(0)]$$
$$-P[\mathbf{B}_t \in A, \mathbf{m}(t) \in N | \mathbf{B}_1, \mathbf{m}(0)]| < \epsilon \tag{8.30}$$

Now let us focus on the population structure vectors $\mathbf{n}(t)$ and $\mathbf{m}(t)$. Their distributions are obtained as marginal distributions from (8.29), by letting $A = \mathcal{A}$. Equation (8.30) implies that, as $t \to \infty$, the probability distributions of $\mathbf{n}(t)$ and $\mathbf{m}(t)$ converge. Since $\mathbf{n}(t)$ and $\mathbf{m}(t)$ converge in distribution, all their moments converge. Applying the Hilbert metric, this leads to the result[3] that

$$\lim_{t \to \infty} d\left(E[\mathbf{n}(t)^b], E[\mathbf{m}(t)^b] \right) = 0 \tag{8.31}$$

---

[3]Cohen (1977b) states this result for the first moment, and shows that in this case the convergence is exponential.

for any integer $b \geq 1$.

This theorem provides the stochastic analogue of the deterministic weak ergodic theorem. In the stochastic case, the population structure at any time is a random variable; the stochastic weak ergodic theorem implies that the random variable forgets its past. The distributions of population structure resulting from any two initial population-environment combinations, each subjected to an independent realization of the stochastic environmental process, eventually converge.

The Strong Stochastic Ergodic Theorem (Cohen 1976)

The strong stochastic ergodic theorem follows as a special case when the environment is described by a homogeneous Markov chain. In this case, if the Markov chain is ergodic (i.e.,if the transition matrix $\mathbf{P}$ is irreducible and primitive) and the set of matrices $\mathcal{A}$ is ergodic, the distribution $F_t(A, B)$ in (8.29) eventually converges to a stationary distribution:

$$F_t(A, B) \rightarrow F(A, B) \tag{8.32}$$

The convergence in distribution of (8.30) still holds, but, as in the deterministic case, not only does the process forget its past, but there is a fixed stationary distribution of structures to which all initial populations converge (Cohen 1976).

Sufficient Conditions for Stochastic Ergodicity

We turn now to sufficient conditions on $\mathcal{A}$ for stochastic ergodicity. The simplest (Cohen 1976, 1977a,b, 1979c) is to assume that the set $\mathcal{A}$ is an ergodic set, so that any product of matrices, along any sample path of the stochastic environment, eventually becomes positive and acts as a contraction in the Hilbert metric. This assumption, combined with the assumption that the environmental stochastic process is ergodic, is sufficient for stochastic ergodicity. The requirement that $\mathcal{A}$ be an ergodic set is doubtless stronger than necessary. For example, the contracting sets of reducible matrices (8.26) studied by Cohen (1979b) probably also produce stochastic ergodicity.

Kingman (1976; see also Cohen 1988) proves an important ergodic result for the special case of independent environments. Suppose that the matrices $\mathbf{A}_i$ are independent random matrices. The population is weakly ergodic with probability 1 if, for some $t \geq 1$,

$$P[\tau(\mathbf{A}_t \mathbf{A}_{t-1} \cdots \mathbf{A}_1) < 1] > 0 \tag{8.33}$$

That is, as long as there is some nonzero probability that a sequence of matrices will be contracting for some t, the population process is ergodic.

This condition would be satisfied if even a single matrix in $\mathcal{A}$ were primitive, a much weaker condition than requiring that $\mathcal{A}$ is an ergodic set.

An Overview of Ergodic Results

The ergodic theorems of demography express, in one form or another, the tendency of population dynamics to become independent of initial conditions. We can summarize the results as follows:

- *The strong ergodic theorem:* in a constant environment, any initial population eventually converges to a stable form.

- *The weak ergodic theorem:* if two initial populations are exposed to the same specific sequence of environments, the difference between the resulting stage distributions decays to zero.

- *The strong stochastic ergodic theorem:* in a time-homogeneous stochastic environment, the probability distribution of the population stage structure eventually converges to a stationary distribution.

- *The weak stochastic ergodic theorem:* in an inhomogeneous stochastic environment, the difference between the probability distributions of stage structure resulting from any two initial populations, exposed to independent sample paths of the stochastic environment, converges to zero.

Each of these theorems requires some restrictions on the nature of the projection matrices describing the environmental sequences. In the deterministic strong ergodic theorem, the matrix must be primitive, which guarantees that sufficiently high powers become positive. In the ergodic theorems for variable environments, the set of matrices describing the environmental variability must meet conditions that guarantee that sufficiently long sequences act as positive matrices. The questions of whether these conditions are usually met by real environmental sequences, and of what would happen if they were not, are still unresolved.

Ergodic theorems are appealing because they hold out the promise of liberation from history. In the absence of some sort of ergodic result, an explanation of population structure at a given time would require an explanation of the structure of the initial population. Initial conditions are usually regarded as accidental rather than interesting; what we want is explanations of the present population structure in terms of the mechanisms governing population dynamics in the present and (hopefully) recent past.

> The weak ergodic theorem makes a science of age structures possible. If in order to explain the current age structure of a population it were necessary to know its prior age structures indefinitely

far into the past, the task would be hopeless. The weak ergodic theorem provides assurance that, regardless of the age structure of a population some years ago, the vital rates since then completely determine the current age structure. (Cohen 1979c, p. 286)

It is important to note that there are alternatives to this view. In fact, whether "accidental" initial conditions are important to the explanation of current population structure is an empirical question that has not been addressed.

8.4.3 Distributional Properties of $N(t)$

In stochastic environments population size[4] $N(t)$ is a random variable. The distributional properties of $N(t)$ provide important insight into the nature of population growth in a stochastic environment.

Consider a large number of replicate populations, each experiencing an independent realization of the stochastic environment. At any time t there will be a distribution of population sizes $N(t)$; the basic result (Furstenberg and Kesten 1960, Tuljapurkar and Orzack 1980) is that this distribution is asymptotically lognormal, with a mean and variance that increase exponentially with time. That is, for large t

$$\ln N(t) \sim \mathcal{N}(t \ln \lambda, t\sigma^2) \tag{8.34}$$

where $\mathcal{N}(a, b)$ denotes the normal distribution with mean a and variance b.

Equation (8.34) implies that the expected log of population size grows at a rate given by $\ln \lambda$:

$$\lim_{t \to \infty} \frac{1}{t} E[\ln N(t)] = \ln \lambda \tag{8.35}$$

We will consider this important growth rate in more detail in Section 8.4.4.

The most important property of the lognormal distribution in this context is its skewness. Suppose that some variable X is lognormally distributed

$$\ln X \sim \mathcal{N}(a, b) \tag{8.36}$$

where a is the mean and b the variance of $\ln X$. Then

$$E(X) = \exp(a + b/2) \tag{8.37}$$

---

[4]The distributional properties discussed here apply equally to any weighted sum of stage abundances, $N(t) = \sum_i c_i n_i(t)$, $c_i \geq 0$ (Heyde and Cohen 1985); this includes the abundance of any single stage or the total abundance of any set of stages, as well as the abundance of the total population, as special cases.

$$V(X) \;=\; E(X)^2 \left(e^{2b} - 1\right) \tag{8.38}$$

$$CV(X) \;=\; \sqrt{e^{2b} - 1} \tag{8.39}$$

$$\text{Median}(X) \;\approx\; \frac{E(X)}{CV(X)} = e^a \tag{8.40}$$

$$\text{Mode}(X) \;=\; e^{a-b} \tag{8.41}$$

From (8.34) we see that the mean and variance of $\ln N(t)$ both increase linearly with time. For large time, then, the coefficient of variation $CV(N)$ grows exponentially at a rate σ^2, whereas the mean $E(N)$ increases more rapidly than $\text{Median}(N)$, which in turn increases more rapidly than $\text{Mode}(N)$. In sum, the distribution becomes more and more skewed. As we will see in the next section, this makes the mean population size $E(N)$ less and less useful as a description of population dynamics as t increases. It also has implications for extinction probability, since the skewness of the distribution toward small population sizes can mean that many realizations of the population may die out (see Section 8.4.6).

8.4.4   Measures of Population Growth Rate

We turn now to the important issue of measuring population growth rates in stochastic environments. In a constant environment, the only logical measure of asymptotic growth rate is λ_1 (or $r = \ln \lambda_1$), since the strong ergodic theorem guarantees that the population will eventually grow at this rate. The strong ergodic theorem shows that if **A** is primitive with a dominant eigenvalue λ_1,

$$\lim_{t \to \infty} \frac{N(t)}{\lambda_1^t} = c \tag{8.42}$$

where the constant c depends on the initial conditions. Equivalently, we can write

$$\lambda_1 = \lim_{t \to \infty} N(t)^{\frac{1}{t}} \tag{8.43}$$

or

$$\ln \lambda_1 = \lim_{t \to \infty} \frac{1}{t} \ln N(t) \tag{8.44}$$

Because of its convenient form as an average of the quantities $\ln N(t)$, we will use the form (8.44).

   In a stochastic environment population growth rate is a random variable. Every sample path of the environmental process may produce a different rate of growth. The goal of the next sections is to incorporate this variability into reasonable measures of population growth rate.

Growth Rates of Scalar Populations

The complications inherent in calculating growth rates in stochastic environments were first emphasized by Lewontin and Cohen (1969). Consider a *scalar* population growing according to

$$N(t+1) = \lambda^{(t)} N(t) \tag{8.45}$$

and suppose that the $\lambda^{(t)}$ are independent random variables. Population size $N(t)$ is thus also a random variable. One approach to measuring growth rate is to consider the expected population size $E[N(t)]$:

$$E[N(t)] = N(0) E \left(\prod_{i=1}^{t} \lambda^{(i)} \right) \tag{8.46}$$

Since the $\lambda^{(i)}$ are independent and identically distributed random variables, the expectation of the product is the product of the expectations, and thus

$$E[N(t)] = N(0) \bar{\lambda}^t \tag{8.47}$$

where $\bar{\lambda} = E(\lambda)$. Then

$$\ln E[N(t)] = t \ln \bar{\lambda} + \ln N(0) \tag{8.48}$$

or

$$\ln \bar{\lambda} = \lim_{t \to \infty} \frac{1}{t} \ln E[N(t)] \tag{8.49}$$

Thus the average population size grows exponentially at a rate equal to the average of the growth rates.

Consider, however, the probability distribution of $N(t)$ or, in particular, the probability $P(K_1 \leq N(t) \leq K_2)$ that $N(t)$ falls into any particular interval. Since the natural logarithm is a monotonic function,

$$P[K_1 \leq N(t) \leq K_2] = P[\ln K_1 \leq \ln N(t) \leq \ln K_2] \tag{8.50}$$

But $\ln N(t) = \ln N(0) + \sum_{i=1}^{t} \ln \lambda^{(i)}$, so (8.50) reduces to

$$P[K_1 \leq N(t) \leq K_2] = P \left(\frac{1}{t} \ln \frac{K_1}{N(0)} \leq \frac{1}{t} \sum_i \ln \lambda^{(i)} \leq \frac{1}{t} \ln \frac{K_2}{N(0)} \right) \tag{8.51}$$

However, by the Central Limit Theorem, the quantity $(1/t) \sum \ln \lambda^{(i)}$ is asymptotically normally distributed with a mean $E(\ln \lambda)$ (i.e., the geometric mean of the $\lambda^{(i)}$) and a variance $V(\ln \lambda)/t$. As $t \to \infty$, then, the variance decays to zero, and

$$\frac{1}{t} \ln N(t) \to E(\ln \lambda) \tag{8.52}$$

in probability.

Here we have two fundamentally different results. The average population size grows at a rate given by the arithmetic mean of the $\lambda^{(i)}$. However, the probability of observing any rate of population growth other than the geometric mean of the $\lambda^{(i)}$ is asymptotically zero. The geometric mean is always less than the arithmetic mean (unless the variance is zero); in fact,

$$E(\ln X) \approx E(X) - \frac{V(X)}{2E(X)} \tag{8.53}$$

Thus the growth rate of average population size overestimates the growth of almost all realizations of the process[5]. It is even possible for the arithmetic mean of the λ_i to exceed 1, so that the average population size grows exponentially to ∞, while the geometric mean is less than 1, so that the probability of extinction grows asymptotically to 1.

These results apply only to scalar populations in random environments. The multiplicative nature of matrix population models produces the same discrepancy between the growth rate of expected population size and the expected growth rate (hinted at by the discussion of the lognormality of $N(t)$ above). However, the noncommutative nature of matrix multiplication makes the situation more complex than simply a difference between an arithmetic and a geometric mean.

Growth Rates of Structured Populations

For matrix models in stochastic environments (assuming that the strong stochastic ergodic theorem holds) we can define two measures of population growth rate:

$$\ln \lambda = \lim_{t \to \infty} \frac{1}{t} E[\ln N(t)] \tag{8.54}$$

$$\ln \mu = \lim_{t \to \infty} \frac{1}{t} \ln E[N(t)] \tag{8.55}$$

These two indices[6] measure growth rate in very different fashions. Imagine a large number of replicate initial populations, each experiencing an independent realization of the stochastic environment. Calculating the asymptotic growth rate $\lim_{t \to \infty}(1/t) \ln N(t)$ for each population and averaging the

---

[5]The situation is analogous to that in Lake Wobegon, Minnesota where, as Garrison Keillor assures us, "all the children are above average." Here, asymptotically, almost all the population sizes are below average.

[6]I am adopting here the notation of Cohen (1979a and elsewhere); Tuljapurkar (1982a,b, Tuljapurkar and Orzack 1980) uses a for $\ln \lambda$. Note that λ here is defined by (8.54); it is not the eigenvalue of a projection matrix.

results produces $\ln \lambda$. Averaging population size at each time t and calculating the growth rate of this average population size produces $\ln \mu$. Thus $\ln \lambda$ is an average of growth rates; $\ln \mu$ is a growth rate of average population size.[7]

The asymptotic lognormality of $N(t)$ implies some additional relationships. Recall that $\ln N(t)$ is asymptotically distributed as $\mathcal{N}(t \ln \lambda, t\sigma^2)$. Then, based on the lognormal distribution, the growth rate of mean population size must be

$$\lim_{t \to \infty} \frac{1}{t} \ln E[N(t)] = \ln \lambda + \frac{\sigma^2}{2} \qquad (8.56)$$

whereas growth rates for the mode and median are

$$\lim_{t \to \infty} \frac{1}{t} \ln \text{Mode}[N(t)] = \ln \lambda - \sigma^2 \qquad (8.57)$$

$$\lim_{t \to \infty} \frac{1}{t} \ln \text{Median}[N(t)] = \ln \lambda \qquad (8.58)$$

Properties of Growth Rate Measures

The properties of $\ln \lambda$ and $\ln \mu$ have been investigated by Cohen (1979a,b) and Tuljapurkar (1982a). We list some of them here.

1. Relative magnitude:

$$\ln \lambda \leq \ln \mu \qquad (8.59)$$

with strict inequality in general. That is, the growth rate of mean population size always exceeds the average growth rate. This is true regardless of the environmental autocorrelation.

2. Most probable growth rate:

Suppose that population size is followed along a single sample path of the stochastic environment. Then

$$\lim_{t \to \infty} \frac{1}{t} \ln N(t) = \lim_{t \to \infty} \frac{1}{t} E[\ln N(t)] \qquad (8.60)$$

with probability 1. That is, eventually all populations except a set of measure zero grow at the rate $\ln \lambda$, although the average population size is increasing more rapidly. A heuristic explanation[8] of this follows from the lognormality of $N(t)$. Equation (8.34) implies that

$$\frac{1}{t} \ln N(t) \sim \mathcal{N}(\ln \lambda, \frac{\sigma^2}{t}) \qquad (8.61)$$

---

[7]See Tuljapurkar (1982a) for derivation of growth rates of the higher moments, in particular the variance, of $N(t)$.

[8]This demonstrates convergence in probability, rather than convergence with probability 1; for the formal proof of the latter, see Furstenberg and Kesten (1960).

Thus $t^{-1} \ln N(t)$ is also normally distributed, but with a variance that decreases to zero as $t \to \infty$.

3. Bounds for $\ln \lambda$:

Let π_i denote the asymptotic probability of environment i, and let $R_{\min}^{(i)}$ and $R_{\max}^{(i)}$ denote the minimum and maximum row sums, respectively, of matrix $\mathbf{A}_i$. Then

$$\sum_i \pi_i R_{\min}^{(i)} \leq \ln \lambda \leq \sum_i \pi_i R_{\max}^{(i)} \qquad (8.62)$$

That is, $\ln \lambda$ is bounded between the average minimum and maximum row sums of the matrices describing the variable environment.

4. Bounds for $\ln \mu$:

Let $C_{\min}^{(i)}$ and $C_{\max}^{(i)}$ denote the minimum and maximum column sums of $\mathbf{A}_i$. Then (Tuljapurkar 1982a)

$$\min_i C_{\min}^{(i)} \leq \ln \mu \leq \max_i C_{\max}^{(i)} \qquad (8.63)$$

5. $\ln \lambda$, $\ln \mu$, and the eigenvalues of the $\mathbf{A}_i$:

By analogy with the results for growth rates of *scalar* populations in variable environments, it is tempting to try to relate $\ln \lambda$ and $\ln \mu$, at least approximately, to the set of eigenvalues $\lambda^{(i)}$ of the matrices $\mathbf{A}_i$ (e.g., Boyce 1977). Cohen (1979a,c), however, has shown that this strategy almost always fails; neither $\ln \lambda$ nor $\ln \mu$ can be approximated by either the arithmetic or geometric mean of the $\lambda^{(i)}$.

Calculation of $\ln \mu$

Cohen (1977a,b, 1979a) and Tuljapurkar (1982a) discuss in detail the calculation of μ in Markovian environments. Suppose that the projection matrices $\mathbf{A}_i$ are s-dimensional, and that there are k environments, so that the column-stochastic transition matrix $\mathbf{P}$ is k-dimensional, and define the $sk \times sk$ block-diagonal matrix

$$\mathbf{F} = \text{diag}(\mathbf{A}_1, \mathbf{A}_2, \cdots, \mathbf{A}_k) \qquad (8.64)$$

Then μ is the dominant eigenvalue $\lambda_1^{(\mathbf{B}_1)}$ of the $sk \times sk$ matrix

$$\mathbf{B}_1 = \mathbf{F}\,(\mathbf{P} \otimes \mathbf{I}) \qquad (8.65)$$

where $\otimes$ denotes the Kronecker product.

In the special case of independent environments, this reduces to the dominant eigenvalue of the average projection matrix:

$$\mu = \lambda_1^{(\bar{A})} \tag{8.66}$$

Tuljapurkar (1982a) explores the effects of environmental autocorrelation on μ; in general, the assumption of independence is *not* innocuous, although in many cases there may be no data available with which to test it.

Tuljapurkar (1982a) also considers the growth rates of the other arithmetic moments of population size. In particular, the variance of $N(t)$ grows at a rate β:

$$\ln \beta = \lim_{t \to \infty} \frac{1}{t} \ln V[N(t)] \tag{8.67}$$

Define the block-diagonal matrix

$$F_2 = \text{diag}\,(A_1 \otimes A_1, A_2 \otimes A_2, \ldots, A_k \otimes A_k) \tag{8.68}$$

then β is the dominant eigenvalue $\lambda^{(B_2)}$ of the $sk^2 \times sk^2$ matrix

$$B_2 = F_2\,[P \otimes (I \otimes I)] \tag{8.69}$$

Calculation of $\ln \lambda$

The analytical calculation of $\ln \lambda$ is difficult. It requires explicit calculation of the stationary joint distribution $F(A, B)$ (8.32) of the environment and the population structure, and then the solution of an integral equation for $\ln \lambda$ from this distribution (Cohen 1977b, Tuljapurkar 1986). The calculation is impractical for even reasonably large matrices (Cohen et al. 1983). There are two feasible approaches to the calculation of $\ln \lambda$, one using numerical calculation (and applicable both to models and to empirical data) and one using perturbation results for small amounts of environmental variability.

Numerical Calculations Numerical methods for the calculation of $\ln \lambda$ are given by Heyde and Cohen (1985) and Cohen (1986). Consider a sequence of population sizes $N(1), N(2), \ldots, N(T)$, and suppose that these data are in fact generated by the asymptotic behavior of a stochastic matrix model satisfying the stochastic strong ergodic theorem. Heyde and Cohen (1985) show that the maximum likelihood estimator $\widehat{\ln \lambda}$ of $\ln \lambda$ is

$$\widehat{\ln \lambda} = \frac{\ln N(T) - \ln N(1)}{T - 1} \tag{8.70}$$

This is familiar as the estimator of the growth rate of an exponentially growing population over T time units. It is also equivalent to calculating a series of one-step estimates of $\ln \lambda$ and averaging them (Cohen et al. 1983), i.e.,

$$\widehat{\ln \lambda}(i) = \ln N(i + 1) - \ln N(i) \tag{8.71}$$

$$\widehat{\ln \lambda} = \frac{1}{T-1} \sum_i \widehat{\ln \lambda}(i) \tag{8.72}$$

Heyde and Cohen (1985) also consider the estimation of the variance parameter σ^2. They suggest the following estimator, which is consistent (i.e., converges in probability to the true value as $T \to \infty$):

$$\hat{\sigma} = \left(\frac{1}{2}\right)\left(\frac{\pi}{2}\right)^{1/2} \left(\frac{1}{\ln(T-1)} \sum_{j=1}^{T-1} j^{-3/2} \left|\ln N(1+j) - \ln N(1) - j\widehat{\ln \lambda}\right| \right.$$

$$\left. + \frac{1}{\ln(T-2)} \sum_{j=1}^{T-2} j^{-3/2} \left|\ln N(2+j) - \ln N(2) - j\widehat{\ln \lambda}\right| \right) \tag{8.73}$$

Note that neither of these results uses the projection matrices $\mathbf{A}_t$ at all; instead they rely on the asymptotic lognormality of $N(t)$. Thus they can be used in two ways. First, given a set of matrices and an environmental transition matrix $\mathbf{P}$ (either measured or hypothesized), one can begin with an arbitrary initial condition and simulate the stochastic process for some time T (after an initial period to allow the transient effects of the initial population to die out) and use the resulting series of population sizes to esimate $\ln \lambda$ using (8.72). The precision of this estimate can be measured by calculating the variance $V[\widehat{\ln \lambda}(i)]$ of the $\widehat{\ln \lambda}(i)$; an approximate 95% confidence interval on $\widehat{\ln \lambda}$ is given by $\widehat{\ln \lambda} \pm (1.96)\sqrt{V[\widehat{\ln \lambda}(i)]/m}$, where m is the number of iterations.

Alternatively, one can apply the method to an empirical time series of population sizes, given only the assumption that they have been generated by an appropriately stationary stochastic environment. Heyde and Cohen (1985) and Cohen (1986) apply this approach to data on the striped bass in the Potomac River and the human population of Sweden.

When $\widehat{\ln \lambda}$ is calculated on the basis of an observed time series of population sizes, the estimate of σ provided by (8.73) can be used to generate a confidence interval for $\ln \lambda$; approximate $100(1 - \alpha)\%$ confidence limits on $\ln \lambda$:

$$\widehat{\ln \lambda} \pm z_{\alpha/2}\hat{\sigma}(T-1)^{-1/2} \tag{8.74}$$

where T is the length of the time series on which the estimate is based.

Example 8.1 Striped bass in the Potomac River

Cohen et al. (1983) and Heyde and Cohen (1985) present a detailed analysis of data on the striped bass (*Morone saxatilis*) in the Potomac

River. They modeled the population using an age-classified, post-reproductive birth-pulse Leslie matrix model. They assumed that only the survival probability $P_1(t)$ from birth to age 1 was subject to environmental variability. In addition, they assume that the $P_1(t)$ were independent random variables with a constant mean.

Parameter estimates were obtained from several sources. Age-specific fertility estimates were calculated from literature values. The survival probabilities of all age classes beyond the first were assumed to be equal, and arbitrarily set equal to 0.4, 0.5, or 0.6 in three different trials. The mean and variance of $P_1(t)$ were estimated from a time-series of data on abundance of fingerlings (i.e., age-class 2 individuals). This calculation required a number of assumptions, which are carefully set out and, as far as possible, justified empirically, in the original paper. The result was a sequence of 13 matrices, each characterized by a different value of $P_1(t)$. There was no statistical evidence for a trend in the values of $P_1(t)$.

Since Cohen et al. (1983) had assumed independence of successive environments, μ could be calculated as the dominant eigenvalue of the average projection matrix, which yielded $\mu = 0.927$, $\ln \mu = -0.076$. Note that in this case, with $k = 13$ environments and $s = 15$ age classes, the matrix $\mathbf{B}_1$ used to estimate μ for autocorrelated environments would be of dimension 195×195 — not impossible to analyze, but certainly unwieldy.

Cohen et al. (1983) also calculated $\ln \lambda$; Heyde and Cohen (1985) subsequently extended that analysis. They began with an arbitrary initial population and multiplied it by a series of 100 independent random matrices chosen from the observed set $\mathbf{A}_1, \ldots, \mathbf{A}_{13}$, to eliminate transient effects. They then repeated this process for another 1000 time steps. Equation (8.70) yielded

$$\widehat{\ln \lambda} = -0.083 \tag{8.75}$$

Note that $\ln \lambda < \ln \mu$, as it should be.

Example 8.2 Jack-in-the-pulpit

Bierzychudek's (1982) study of *Arisaema triphyllum* yielded two size-classified projection matrices at each of two sites. Obviously these two matrices tell something (more, at least than only one matrix would) about environmental variation in the life cycle at the two sites. In the absence of any further information about the environment, a reasonable approach is to hypothesize, as Bierzychudek did, that the two observed matrices occur independently, with probability 1/2, and to evaluate the consequences for population growth.

Given the assumption of an independent environment, μ can be calculated as the dominant eigenvalue of the average projection matrix. The average growth rate $\ln \lambda$ can be calculated numerically, using the Heyde-Cohen estimate. The results, for the two populations Bierzychudek studied, are

	Fall Creek	Brooktondale
$\lambda_1^{(1977-78)}$	1.3176	0.9801
$\lambda_1^{(1978-79)}$	1.2733	0.8473
μ	1.2925	0.9005
$\ln \mu$	0.2566	-0.1049
$\widehat{\ln \lambda}$	0.25669 ± 0.00199	-0.10765 ± 0.00322

The estimates $\widehat{\ln \lambda}$ are based on 3000 iterations, following an initial 1000 iterations to eliminate transient effects. Figure 8.2 shows the convergence of the estimates of $\widehat{\ln \lambda}$ as a function of the number of iterations. Clearly, 3000 iterations are none too many, and if additional accuracy were desired, even more iterations would not be inappropriate.

In this case, the stochastic dynamics of the two populations are quite different. The almost certain fate of the Brooktondale population is extinction, whereas the Fall Creek population is almost certain to grow rapidly.

A Perturbation Approach   In the limit as the environmental variability becomes small, $\ln \lambda$ must approach the log of the dominant eigenvalue of the projection matrix describing the constant environment. Tuljapurkar (1982b) uses this fact to develop a perturbation formula for $\ln \lambda$ when the differences between the $\mathbf{A}_i$ are small. This formula is not only useful for theoretical calculations of $\ln \lambda$, it also reveals some of the qualitative properties of $\ln \lambda$.

Let $\bar{\mathbf{A}}$ denote the average projection matrix and denote its eigenvalues (in decreasing order of magnitude) by $\lambda_1, \ldots, \lambda_s$ and its right and left eigenvectors by $\mathbf{w}_1, \ldots, \mathbf{w}_s$ and $\mathbf{v}_1, \ldots, \mathbf{v}_s$. Note that the eigenvalues of $\bar{\mathbf{A}}$ are not the averages of the eigenvalues of the $\mathbf{A}_i$. Assume without loss of generality that the eigenvectors have been scaled so that $\langle \mathbf{w}_i, \mathbf{v}_i \rangle = 1$ for all i. Define the deviation matrices

$$\mathbf{D}_i = \mathbf{A}_i - \bar{\mathbf{A}} \qquad (8.76)$$

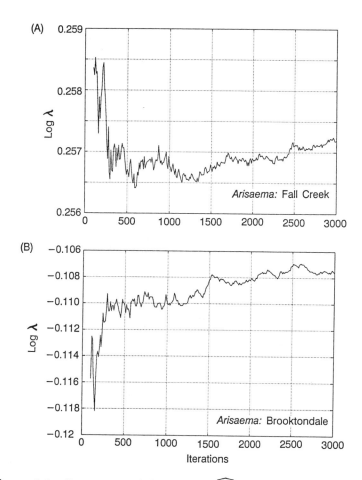

Figure 8.2: Convergence of the estimate $\widehat{\ln \lambda}$ of the stochastic growth rate for the Fall Creek (A) and Brooktondale (B) populations of *Arisaema triphyllum*, as a function of the number of iterations. Data of Bierzychudek (1982).

and the matrices

$$\mathbf{C}_i = E\left(\mathbf{D}_{t+i} \otimes \mathbf{D}_t\right) \tag{8.77}$$

which give the period-i autocovariances of the elements of $\mathbf{A}_i$. In particular, the entries of $\mathbf{C}_0$ are the covariances of the elements of the projection matrices. If the environments are independent, $\mathbf{C}_i = 0$ for $i > 0$.

Now define two matrices (using Tuljapurkar's notation):

$$\tau^2 = \left(\mathbf{v}_1 \otimes \mathbf{v}_1\right)' \mathbf{C}_0 \left(\mathbf{w}_1 \otimes \mathbf{w}_1\right) \tag{8.78}$$

$$\theta = \sum_{j=2}^{s} (\mathbf{v}_1 \otimes \mathbf{v}_j)' \left(\sum_{l=1}^{\infty} \left(\frac{\lambda_j}{\lambda_1} \right)^{l-1} \mathbf{C}_l \right) (\mathbf{w}_j \otimes \mathbf{w}_1) \qquad (8.79)$$

Given all this machinery, Tuljapurkar (1982b) shows that

$$\ln \lambda \approx \ln \lambda_1 - \frac{\tau^2}{2\lambda_1^2} + \frac{\theta}{\lambda_1^2} \qquad (8.80)$$

Let us examine the pieces of this formula. First, note that if successive environments are independent, $\mathbf{C}_l = 0$ for $l \geq 1$, so that $\theta = 0$. Thus in independent environments,

$$\ln \lambda \approx \ln \lambda_1 - \frac{\tau^2}{2\lambda_1^2} \qquad (8.81)$$

Let us take τ apart for the simple case when $s = 2$. In that case

$$\mathbf{C}_0 = E \begin{pmatrix} d_{11}^2 & d_{11}d_{12} & d_{12}d_{11} & d_{12}^2 \\ d_{11}d_{21} & d_{11}d_{22} & d_{12}d_{21} & d_{12}d_{22} \\ d_{21}d_{11} & d_{21}d_{12} & d_{22}d_{11} & d_{22}d_{12} \\ d_{21}^2 & d_{21}d_{22} & d_{22}d_{21} & d_{22}^2 \end{pmatrix} \qquad (8.82)$$

This is simply a matrix of variances and covariances among all the elements of the projection matrix $\mathbf{A}$.

The Kronecker products of the eigenvectors are

$$\mathbf{v}_1 \otimes \mathbf{v}_1 = \begin{pmatrix} (v_1^{(1)})^2 \\ v_1^{(1)} v_2^{(1)} \\ v_2^{(1)} v_1^{(1)} \\ (v_2^{(1)})^2 \end{pmatrix} \qquad (8.83)$$

with a similar expression for $\mathbf{w}_1 \otimes \mathbf{w}_2$.

Recalling that $\partial \lambda_1 / \partial a_{ij} = v_i^{(1)} w_j^{(1)}$ (assuming that the scalar product of the vectors is one), we can put all these pieces together and find that

$$\tau^2 = \sum_{i,j} \left(\frac{\partial \lambda_1}{\partial a_{ij}} \right)^2 V(a_{ij}) + \sum_{i,j \neq k,l} \frac{\partial \lambda_1}{\partial a_{ij}} \frac{\partial \lambda_1}{\partial a_{kl}} \text{Cov}(a_{ij}, a_{kl}) \qquad (8.84)$$

For small deviations around the mean, this is the linear approximation to the variance $V(\lambda_1)$ (Sections 6.1.6 and 7.2.1). Thus we can rewrite the approximation as

$$\ln \lambda \approx \ln \lambda_1 - \frac{V(\ln \lambda_1)}{2\lambda_1} \qquad (8.85)$$

This is similar in appearance to the geometric mean approximation (8.53) that appears in stochastic models for scalar populations. However, there are fundamental differences because $\ln \lambda_1$ is the dominant eigenvalue of the mean matrix, not the mean of the dominant eigenvalues of the $\mathbf{A}_i$ (Tuljapurkar 1989). The qualitative conclusions, though, are quite similar. Factors that increase the variance in λ_1 (increases in variance of the individual matrix elements, positive covariances between matrix elements) reduce $\ln \lambda$. Negative covariances between matrix elements reduce $V(\lambda_1)$ and increase $\ln \lambda$ (cf. Real 1980a,b, Lacey et al. 1983).

The θ term appearing in autocorrelated environments is much more complicated, but closer examination reveals the pieces of which it is made. All of the eigenvalues contribute to this term, and the environmental autocovariance matrices C_l have effects that are weighted by the exponentially decaying terms $(\lambda_j/\lambda_1)^{l-1}$. Thus long-period autocorrelations in the environment become less and less important, at rates determined by the rate of convergence of the hypothetical average population to its stable structure.

8.4.5 Factors Influencing $\ln \lambda$

The expected growth rate $\ln \lambda$ is determined by the set of matrices $\mathcal{A}$ and the stochastic model of the environment. Tuljapurkar and Orzack (1980) examined the dependence of $\ln \lambda$ on the environment in a numerical experiment. They modeled the environment by a two-state Markov chain, characterized by the proportion π_1 of time spent in environment 1 and the autocorrelation ρ. Population dynamics were described by a two-age-class Leslie matrix; environmental variation affected only F_2, which was given by $F_2 = \bar{F}_2 \pm \eta$, depending on the state of the environment. The parameter η measures the standard deviation of the vital rates.

On the basis of their simulations, Tuljapurkar and Orzack (1980) concluded that

1. $\ln \lambda$ depends on π_1 and η, but is almost completely independent of the autocorrelation ρ. [This conclusion may change for matrices larger than 2×2, although the effects of autocorrlation are still small (S.D. Tuljapurkar, personal communication; cf. Section 8.4.7)].

2. Since the first environment has the higher fertility, $\ln \lambda$ increases with π_1; the increase is more dramatic the more variable the vital rates are (i.e., the larger the value of η).

3. As η increases, $\ln \lambda$ may either increase or decrease, depending on π_1. If π_1 is large, so that the environment is frequently in state 1, then $\ln \lambda$ increases with increasing η. But if π_1 is small, so that most time is spent in the poorer environment, $\ln \lambda$ declines with increasing η.

4. Tuljapurkar and Orzack (1980) also found that the lognormal variance parameter σ^2 increased rapidly with ρ and η, and was maximized at intermediate values of π_1.

Additional insight can be derived from the perturbation expansion (8.84). There it is apparent that, in independent environments, $\ln \lambda$ is decreased by increases in the variance of the matrix elements and by positive covariances between matrix elements, and increased by negative covariances.

Since environmental autocorrelation has only small effects on $\ln \lambda$, these conclusions are probably not very sensitive to the assumption of independence. The effects of environmental autocorrelation appear in the term θ (8.80). Tuljapurkar (1982b) shows that positive autocorrelation has a positive, and negative autocorrelation a smaller negative effect on $\ln \lambda$.

8.4.6   Extinction Probability

Extinction is a trivial problem in deterministic models; if $\lambda \geq 1$ the population persists; otherwise it declines exponentially. In stochastic environments, extinction may be a possibility even when some environments are capapble of supporting rapid population growth. Tuljapurkar and Orzack (1980) and Lande and Orzack (1988) have considered this problem.

We know that $\ln N(t)$ is asymptotically distributed as $\mathcal{N}(\ln \lambda, \sigma^2)$; this means that $\ln N(t)$ can be described as a Wiener process, with extinction an absorbing boundary at some defined extinction threshold (e.g., one individual). Lande and Orzack (1988) use the diffusion approximation to this Wiener process to calculate the probability of extinction and the expected time to extinction.

The probability of ultimate extinction, given the initial population size $\ln N(0)$ measured as a deviation from the extinction threshold, is

$$Q[\infty | N(0)] \;=\; 1 \qquad\qquad\qquad \text{for } \ln \lambda \leq 0 \qquad (8.86)$$

$$\;=\; \exp\left(\frac{-2 \ln N(0) \ln \lambda}{\sigma^2}\right) \qquad \text{for } \ln \lambda > 0 \qquad (8.87)$$

Thus $\ln \lambda = 0$ represents a critical value for ultimate extinction, much as the dominant eigenvalue of a time-invariant model. Unlike the time-invariant case, however, there is still a probability of extinction even when expected population growth is positive. This probability is directly proportional to σ^2 and inversely proportional to $\ln \lambda$.

Lande and Orzack (1988) also consider the *conditional* distribution of extinction times. For $\ln \lambda \leq 0$, all sample paths ultimately become extinct. For $\ln \lambda > 0$ some fraction of the sample paths will become extinct; the conditional distribution of extinction times is the distribution of extinction times among those sample paths that do become extinct. Let T denote the conditional extinction time; then

$$E(T) = \frac{\ln N(0)}{|\ln \lambda|} \tag{8.88}$$

$$V(T) = \frac{\sigma^2 \ln N(0)}{|\ln \lambda|^3} \tag{8.89}$$

Note that $E(T)$ depends only on the magnitude, not the sign, of $\ln \lambda$. If $\ln \lambda < 0$, $E(T)$ decreases with $\ln \lambda$. But if $\ln \lambda > 0$, $E(T)$ decreases with increases in $\ln \lambda$, because as $\ln \lambda$ increases the probability of extinction decreases, and the few sample paths that do lead to extinction do so early, before the population has had a chance to increase from $N(0)$.

Rates of Convergence

In time-invariant models, the rate of convergence to the stable stage distribution can be characterized by the damping ratio ρ, given by the ratio of the magnitudes of the dominant and the subdominant eigenvalues of the projection matrix. Tuljapurkar (1986) investigates the corresponding situation in stochastic environments; he shows that the so-called Lyapunov characteristic exponents of the process provide information on the rate of convergence. The calculation of these exponents, except in some special cases, is difficult; see Tuljapurkar (1986) for discussion. In the special case of age-classified matrices, we have the following results. Denote the characteristic exponents by $\ln \rho_i$, $i = 1, 2, \ldots, s$, where the first characteristic exponent $\ln \rho_1$ is equal to $\ln \lambda$. Then

$$\ln \lambda + \ln \rho_2 + \cdots + \ln \rho_s = E \left(\ln P_1 P_2 \cdots P_{s-1} F_s \right) \tag{8.90}$$

In the 2×2 case, this simplifies to

$$\ln \lambda + \ln \rho_2 = E \left(\ln P_1 F_2 \right) \tag{8.91}$$

Once $\ln \lambda$ is calculated, this result can be used to derive $\ln \rho_2$. The difference $\ln \lambda - \ln \rho_2$ measures the rate of convergence (it is the analogue of the log of the damping ratio in the time-invariant case).

8.4.7 Evolutionary Demography

We now have a framework for describing demography in stochastic environments, including ergodic theorems and means to calculate the almost sure asymptotic growth rate $\ln \lambda$. We turn briefly here to the application of this machinery to life history problems, by considering the action of natural selection in stochastic environments. In population models without age structure, geometric mean fitness plays a crucial role in determining the outcome of selection (Haldane and Jayakar 1963, Karlin and Lieberman 1974); it seems reasonable to suppose that $\ln \lambda$ might play a similar role in populations with age or stage structure.

That this is so was demonstrated by Tuljapurkar (1982b). He analyzed a simple one-locus, two-allele selection model, in which each genotype was assigned its own projection matrix, subject to stochastic environmental variation. Let the alleles be denoted A_1 and A_2; Tuljapurkar analyzes selection by assuming that one allele (say, A_1) is fixed, and considering the invasion of A_2. By linearizing the equations for allele frequency, he is able to show that the asymptotic growth rate of the frequency p_2 of the invading allele is

$$\frac{1}{t} \ln p_2(t) \to \ln \lambda^{(A_1 A_2)} - \ln \lambda^{(A_1 A_1)} \tag{8.92}$$

That is, the success or failure of the invasion of A_2 depends on whether $\ln \lambda$ for the heterozygote exceeds that of the homozygote present. Thus $\ln \lambda^{(A_i A_j)}$ is the relevant measure of fitness for genotype $A_i A_j$.

Tuljapurkar (1982b) considers some applications of this result to life history problems. It is, as he notes, rather more subtle than the use of λ_1 as a measure of fitness in the time-invariant case, because $\ln \lambda$ is affected not only by the average vital rates, but by their variances and covariances and by the autocorrelation in the environment. Much remains to be done in this area.

Orzack (1985) has applied these results to the problem of the evolutionary advantages of homeostasis (i.e., insensitivity of some aspect of the phenotype to environmental fluctuations). The evolution of homeostasis (or its converse, phenotypic plasticity) has been addressed by a number of authors (see Bradshaw 1965, Caswell 1983, Schlichting 1986); the usual conclusion has been that homeostasis of the vital rates should be selectively advantageous (Gillespie 1974, 1977).

To approach the problem in age-structured populations, Orzack (1985) used Tuljapurkar's (1982b) results for selection in a one-locus, two-allele system, and examined the way in which $\ln \lambda$ varies with homeostasis. In independent environments, (8.84) shows that increased homeostasis, which reduces $V(a_{ij})$, is favored, although covariances between matrix entries can reduce the extent of this selection. This agrees with the results for the scalar case.

However, in autocorrelated environments the second term of (8.80) must also be taken into account. Orzack found, by extensive numerical investigation, that the frequencies of the different environmental states and the autocorrelation[9] could eliminate the advantage of the homeostatic genotype,

---

[9]Thus, although Tuljapurkar and Orzack (1980) and Tuljapurkar (1982b) report that

and favor decreases in homeostasis. Thus selection on age-structured populations in autocorrelated stochastic environments may differ fundamentally from selection on nonstructured populations in independent environments.

Orzack and Tuljapurkar (1989) have used the response of $\ln \lambda$ to environmental variability to examine the evolutionary advantages of iteroparity.

$\ln \lambda$ is insensitive to autocorrelation, in some cases those small effects can be sufficient to determine the outcome of selection.

Chapter 9

Density-Dependent Models

In this chapter we turn to models in which the vital rates depend on population density. Such models are constructed by writing the matrix elements a_{ij} as functions of density,[1] just as they were written as functions of time in the models in Chapter 8. However, the resulting equations are nonlinear, which renders most of the analyses in the early chapters of this book inapplicable. In particular, solutions of the projection equations can no longer be written in terms of eigenvalues and eigenvectors, so that the long-term behavior of the population can no longer be deduced from the eigenvalues of the projection matrix.

Even the simplest nonlinear, density-dependent models are capable of a tremendous range of complex dynamic behaviors. The mathematical properties of these dynamics are not yet well understood, let alone their biological interpretation. Some of these complexities will be considered in the latter parts of this chapter.

9.1 Formulation

The projection equation for a density-dependent population can be written

$$\mathbf{n}(t+1) = \mathbf{A}_n \mathbf{n}(t) \tag{9.1}$$

where the notation $\mathbf{A}_n$ indicates that the matrix entries $a_{ij}(\mathbf{n})$ depend on the population vector $\mathbf{n}$. Formulating such a model requires a measure of effective density and a functional form expressing the effect of density on the vital rates; these choices strongly influence the resulting dynamics.

---

[1]Density-dependent models for multiple interacting populations are an obvious extension, but one must draw the line somewhere, and they will not be considered in this book.

9.1.1 Measures of Density

Each stage in the life cycle may utilize resources at different rates, and may thus differ in its contribution to "density." In full generality each matrix element a_{ij} would be a function of all the n_i, but it is often easier to use an integrated measure of total density. A reasonable first approximation is a linear combination of stage densities:

$$N(t) = \sum_i c_i n_i(t) \tag{9.2}$$

where c_i measures the contribution of n_i to resource consumption, or whatever interaction is responsible for the density dependence.

In one direction, this can be simplified to the total population size $N(t) = \sum_i n_i(t)$, assuming that each stage makes an equal contribution to density effects. In the other direction, it may be assumed that density effects are mediated by only one or a few stages. For example, in models of fish populations (e.g., DeAngelis et al. 1980, Levin and Goodyear 1980) it is often assumed that only young-of-the-year fish contribute to density effects, in which case $N(t) = n_1(t)$.

Other measures of density are possible. For example, Easterlin (1961) found that human fertility is affected by the initial cohort size of the age group in question. Women born in large cohorts seem to produce fewer children at a given age than women born in small cohorts. Fertility at age i can, on this hypothesis, be written

$$
\begin{aligned}
F_i[\mathbf{n}(t)] &= F_i[n_1(t-i)] \\
&= F_i[c_i n_i(t)]
\end{aligned}
\tag{9.3}
$$

where $c_i = (P_1 P_2 \cdots P_{i-1})^{-1}$. Leslie (1959) considered a similar time-lag effect. Lee (1974), Wachter (1988), and Wachter and Lee (1988) have considered mechanisms that might generate the Easterlin effect, and the question of whether it might be responsible for fluctuations in U.S. birth rates.

9.1.2 Effects of Density

Compensation, Overcompensation, and Depensation

Consider two possible functional forms for a density-dependent coefficient $a_{ij}(N)$:

$$
\begin{aligned}
a_{ij} &= \frac{a_{ij}(0)}{1 + cN} \tag{9.4} \\
a_{ij} &= a_{ij}(0)e^{-cN} \tag{9.5}
\end{aligned}
$$

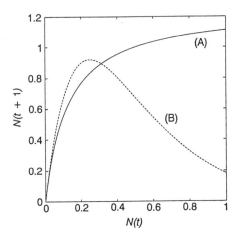

Figure 9.1: Density-dependent functions expressing the production of one stage as a function of the density of another. (A) Compensatory, or Beverton-Holt function. (B) Overcompensatory, or Ricker function.

Both of these functions are nonnegative (unlike, say, a linear decreasing function of N, which becomes negative for sufficiently large N). They both decrease smoothly toward zero from a maximum at $N = 0$. The coefficient c in each case describes the strength of density-dependence.

Now consider the number of n_i individuals produced by the transition a_{ij} as a function of the number of n_j individuals, holding all other stages constant. The corresponding functions are

$$n_i(t+1) \;=\; \frac{a_{ij}(0)n_j(t)}{1 + cn_j(t)} \qquad \text{(compensation)} \qquad (9.6)$$

$$n_i(t+1) \;=\; a_{ij}(0)n_j(t)e^{-cn_j(t)} \qquad \text{(overcompensation)} \qquad (9.7)$$

These functions are plotted in Figure 9.1. Equation (9.6) yields an asymptotic function, a pattern termed *compensation*, and associated with contest competition (Hassell 1978). The curve is also known as the *Beverton-Holt* function. Equation (9.7) produces a peaked curve, a pattern termed *overcompensation*, and associated with scramble competition (Hassell 1978). This function is also known as the *Ricker* curve. As we will see (Examples 9.3 and 9.4), the difference become compensation and overcompensation has important dynamic consequences.

Sometimes a coefficient a_{ij} will exhibit a positive response to density, at least over some range of densities. This is referred to as *depensation*; its importance was emphasized by Allee (1931, 1951), who argued that physiological and demographic processes often possess an optimal density, with the response decreasing at either higher or lower densities. Andrewartha and Birch (1954) and Watt (1960) surveyed a variety of density studies showing this effect.

Depensation can result from behavioral effects on reproduction, if low densities limit reproductive output by reducing the probability of fertilization. The foraging behavior of pollinators can produce the same effect in plant populations (e.g., Silander 1978). Pearl et al. (1927) and Frank et al. (1957) document an Allee effect in survival (of *Drosophila melanogaster* and *Daphnia pulex*, respectively) in the laboratory. Depensation can produce threshold densities such that extinction results if the population falls below that density (Volterra 1938, Odum and Allee 1954; see Beddington 1974 and Longstaff 1977 for examples in matrix models).

Other Functional Forms

Usher (1972) proposed a sigmoid function that can be written as

$$a_{ij}(N) = \frac{1}{1 + \exp(cN + b)} \tag{9.8}$$

By adjusting the parameters c and b, this function may be adjusted from a smooth decrease with increasing N to an almost step-function like response, in which increasing density has little effect until some threshold is passed, at which point a_{ij} suddenly decreases to a lower value, which is again relatively insensitive to further increases in N. Such a function could be used to study "density-vague" population regulation (Strong 1986).

Other authors (Pennycuick et al. 1968, Pennycuick 1969, Beddington 1974, Longstaff 1977) have used a variety of functions, including polynomials, log polynomials, and a complex function developed by Watt (1960). There is in principle no reason why any arbitrary nonnegative function of density may not be used to describe density-dependent transition coefficients.

Example 9.1 Two fishery models

Levin and Goodyear (1980) and DeAngelis et al. (1980) constructed and analyzed models for fish populations. The models differ in the parameterization of the age-specific projection matrix and the form of the density effects assumed.

DeAngelis et al. (1980) assumed a birth-pulse population, with the census immediately following breeding. In this case (see Section 2.3.2), the fertility terms are given by $F_i = P_i m_i$. They assumed that competition occurs only among the first age class, so that P_1 is density-dependent.

The resulting matrix $\mathbf{A}_n$ is

$$\begin{pmatrix} P_1(n_1)m_1 & P_2 m_2 & \cdots & P_{s-1}m_{s-1} & P_s m_s \\ P_1(n_1) & 0 & \cdots & 0 & 0 \\ 0 & P_2 & \cdots & 0 & 0 \\ \vdots & \vdots & \ddots & \vdots & \\ 0 & 0 & \cdots & P_{s-1} & P_s \end{pmatrix} \qquad (9.9)$$

They used a compensatory density effect:

$$P_1(n_1) = \frac{c_1}{1 + c_2 n_1} \qquad (9.10)$$

Levin and Goodyear (1980) also assumed a birth-pulse population, but with the census taken just prior to reproduction, so that $F_i = l(1)m_i$ (see Section 2.3.2). They assumed that competition affects only survival during the first year of life, with the intensity of competition proportional to $N(t) = \sum_i m_i n_i(t)$ (a weighted sum of age classes, with the weights being the reproductive output). Using the overcompensatory Ricker function as a model for density effects, they set $l(1) = \alpha \exp(-\beta N)$, where α is the density-independent survival probability to age 1 [i.e., $l(1)$ evaluated at $N = 0$], and β measures the strength of the density dependence. The resulting matrix $\mathbf{A}_n$ is

$$\begin{pmatrix} \alpha e^{-\beta N}m_1 & \alpha e^{-\beta N}m_2 & \cdots & \alpha e^{-\beta N}m_{s-1} & \alpha e^{-\beta N}m_s \\ P_1 & 0 & \cdots & 0 & 0 \\ 0 & P_2 & \cdots & 0 & 0 \\ \vdots & \vdots & \ddots & \vdots & \vdots \\ 0 & 0 & \cdots & P_{s-1} & P_s \end{pmatrix} \qquad (9.11)$$

These models both assume that competion occurs only among the first year class, during their first year of life. Because of the choice of parameterizations, however, they appear very different. The DeAngelis model has density-dependent parameters only in the first fertility and survival terms, whereas in the Levin-Goodyear model all the fertility terms are density-dependent.

9.1.3 The Liu-Cohen Logistic Matrix Model

Liu and Cohen (1987) have recently presented a general age-classified, density-dependent matrix model which includes many of the models in the literature as special cases. They begin with the continuous time McKendrick-von

Foerster equation

$$\frac{\partial n}{\partial t} + \frac{\partial n}{\partial a} = -\mu(a)n(a,t) \tag{9.12}$$

$$n(0,t) = \int_0^\omega m(a,t)n(a,t)\,da \tag{9.13}$$

They replace the density-independent death rate $\mu(a)$ by a linear density-dependent death rate

$$D(n)(a,t) = \mu(a) + \int_0^\omega \gamma(a,\xi)n(\xi,t)\,d\xi \tag{9.14}$$

and the density-independent fertility by a density-dependent fertility function

$$F(n)(a,t) = m(a)\exp\left(-\int_0^\omega \tilde{\gamma}(a,\xi)n(\xi,t)\,d\xi\right) \tag{9.15}$$

The coefficients $\gamma(a,\xi)$ and $\tilde{\gamma}(a,\xi)$ give the effect of an individual age ξ on the mortality and the fertility, respectively, of an individual aged a. Thus this model includes the full generality of specifying a unique effect of each stage on each other stage.

Liu and Cohen obtain their density-dependent matrix by discretizing (9.12). Let $\mathbf{P}$ denote a matrix with survival probabilities, evaluated at $\mathbf{n} = 0$, on the subdiagonal, and let $\mathbf{F}$ denote a matrix with fertilities, evaluated at $\mathbf{n} = 0$, in the first row. The Leslie matrix for the population at zero density is $\mathbf{A} = \mathbf{P} + \mathbf{F}$. Let the matrix $\mathbf{E}(\mathbf{n})$ be a diagonal matrix with the (i,i) entry given by

$$e_{ii} = \exp\left(-\sum_j \gamma_{ij} n_j\right) \tag{9.16}$$

where γ_{ij} measures the effect of n_j on the survival probability of age-class i. Similarly, let $\tilde{\mathbf{E}}(\mathbf{n})$ be a diagonal matrix with

$$\tilde{e}_{ii} = \exp\left(-\sum_j \tilde{\gamma}_{ij} n_j\right) \tag{9.17}$$

where $\tilde{\gamma}_{ij}$ measures the effect of n_j on ther fertility of age-class i. Given these definitions, the density-dependent projection matrix is

$$\mathbf{A}_n = \mathbf{F}\tilde{\mathbf{E}} + \mathbf{P}\mathbf{E} \tag{9.18}$$

A number of simple special cases can be written down in terms of the basic model (9.18). Suppose that density effects on survival and fertility are the same, and are the same for all age classes, so that $\gamma_{ij} = \tilde{\gamma}_{ij} = \gamma$. Then

$$\mathbf{A}_n = e^{-\gamma N}(\mathbf{F} + \mathbf{P}) \tag{9.19}$$

a model which has been analyzed by Desharnais and Cohen (1986) and Cushing (1989). Leslie (1948) considered a similar model, using a compensatory rather than an overcompensatory density effect. In the notation used here, Leslie's model would be written

$$\mathbf{A}_n = (a + bN)^{-1}(\mathbf{F} + \mathbf{P}) \qquad (9.20)$$

If each age class contributes the same amount to the effect of density, so that $\gamma_{ij} = \gamma_i$ and $\tilde{\gamma}_{ij} = \tilde{\gamma}_i$ for all j, then

$$e_{ii} = e^{-\gamma_i N} \qquad (9.21)$$
$$\tilde{e}_{ii} = e^{-\tilde{\gamma}_i N} \qquad (9.22)$$

Leslie (1959) studied a similar model, again using a compensatory density effect.

Note that, although Liu and Cohen began by assuming a linear increase in mortality with increasing density, their discrete time model has an exponential decrease in survival probability. This arises in the discretization process, because the mortality rate is applied continuously over the interval from t to $t + 1$. It is not clear how a compensatory density effect would arise in the discretization of a continuous age model, but such effects may be incorporated in a discrete model in their own right.

Example 9.2 *Tribolium* population dynamics

Desharnais and Liu (1987) present a detailed analysis of laboratory populations of the flour beetle *Tribolium castaneum* which shows how the Liu-Cohen model can be applied to real data. They use a very large (300 × 300) age-classified matrix, but divide the set of age-classes into sets representing eggs (E), larvae (L), pupae (P), and adults (A). The most important effects of density on the vital rates are (1) fertility is reduced by the density of adults, (2) eggs are cannibalized by larvae and adults, and (3) pupae are cannibalized by adults. Larval and adult survival are independent of density, and adult fertility is independent of the density of immature stages.

Desharnais and Liu estimate the coefficients $\tilde{\gamma}$ and γ from a mixture of data and assumptions. Assuming that fertility is affected by total adult density, independent of age distribution, and that all adult age classes are affected equally, reduces the entries of the matrix $\tilde{\mathbf{E}}$ of (9.18) to

$$\tilde{e}_{ii} = \exp\left(-\tilde{\gamma} \sum_{j \in A} n_j\right) \qquad (9.23)$$

The coefficient $\tilde{\gamma}$ is estimated as the slope of a semilogarithmic plot of fertility versus adult density.

The rate of egg cannibalism by larve increases linearly with larval age, independent of the age of the eggs. Denote the slope of this relationship by C_{EL}. The rate of egg cannibalism by adults is assumed to be constant, denoted by C_{EA}. Then the coefficient γ_{ij} describing density effects on egg survival is

$$\gamma_{ij} = \gamma_{Ej} = \begin{cases} C_{EL}x_j & \text{for } i \in E, \ j \in L \\ C_{EA} & \text{for } i \in E, \ j \in A \end{cases} \tag{9.24}$$

where x_j, the larval age of an individual of calendar age j, is the number of days it has spent as a larva.

Finally, Desharnais and Liu assume a constant rate of cannibalism of pupae by adults, independent of age, and estimate this rate as the slope C_{PA} of the curve relating pupal survival and adult density. The density coefficient is then

$$\gamma_{ij} = \gamma_{Pj} = C_{PA} \quad \text{for } i \in P, j \in A \tag{9.25}$$

Finally, the density-independent fertility and survival terms [the elements of the matrices $\mathbf{F}$ and $\mathbf{P}$ of (9.18)] were estimated, assuming constant mortality within each developmental stage, from laboratory data on isolated individuals.

Although this formulation has made a great many simplifying assumptions, especially concerning age independence of density effects, it has incorporated a great deal of information into the description of density dependence. The results of the model show a remarkable agreement with patterns of fluctuation of laboratory populations.

9.2 Stability

We begin the analysis of density-dependent models by examining their equilibria. We will present the standard local stability analysis for the equilibria, and then go on to consider the dynamics exhibited when an equilibrium is unstable.

9.2.1 Equilibria

An equilibrium population $\hat{n}$ is a vector such that

$$\hat{n} = \mathbf{A}_{\hat{n}}\hat{n} \tag{9.26}$$

In other words, $\hat{n}$ must be an eigenvector of $\mathbf{A}_{\hat{n}}$ corresponding to $\lambda = 1$. The solution of this equation for the equilibrium population $\hat{n}$ depends on the form of the density functions included in $\mathbf{A}_n$. If $\mathbf{A}_n$ depends only on the total density $N = \sum_i n_i$, then (9.26) depends only on a scalar, and a plot of $|\mathbf{A}_n - I|$ vs. N will reveal the values $\hat{N}$ at which the dominant eigenvalue of $\mathbf{A}_n$ is equal to 1. The equilibrium population vector $\hat{\mathbf{n}}$ is then simply the corresponding eigenvector, normalized to sum to $\hat{N}$.

An alternative approach is to write the net reproductive rate R_0 as a function of N

$$R_0(N) = \sum_i F_i(N) \prod_{j=1}^{i-1} P_j(N) \qquad (9.27)$$

Hastings (1978) shows that a positive equilibrium $\hat{N}$ exists if and only if $R_0(\hat{N}) = 1$. Smouse and Weiss (1975) and Liu and Cohen (1987) also provide existence and uniqueness results for age-classified models.

If the density dependence is more complicated than a simple dependence on N, it can be difficult to locate the equilibria. Multiple equilibria are also possible (Beddington 1974, Longstaff 1977).

9.2.2   Local Stability Analysis

As with any nonlinear dynamic system, the existence of an equilibrium does not imply its stability. The local stability analysis of nonlinear matrix models was introduced by Beddington (1974). Suppose that $\hat{\mathbf{n}}$ is an equilibrium population. Define a deviation vector $\boldsymbol{\delta}$

$$\boldsymbol{\delta}(t) = \mathbf{n}(t) - \hat{\mathbf{n}} \qquad (9.28)$$

so that $\mathbf{n}(t) = \boldsymbol{\delta}(t) + \hat{\mathbf{n}}$. Then

$$\boldsymbol{\delta}(t+1) + \hat{\mathbf{n}} = \mathbf{A}_{[\delta(t)+\hat{n}]} \left[\boldsymbol{\delta}(t) + \hat{\mathbf{n}} \right] \qquad (9.29)$$

Expanding $\mathbf{A}_{[\delta(t)+\hat{n}]}$ in a Taylor series around $\hat{\mathbf{n}}$ yields

$$\boldsymbol{\delta}(t+1) + \hat{\mathbf{n}} \approx \left(\mathbf{A}_{\hat{n}} + \sum_i \delta_i \left. \frac{\partial \mathbf{A}}{\partial n_i} \right|_{\hat{n}} \right) \left[\boldsymbol{\delta}(t) + \hat{\mathbf{n}} \right] \qquad (9.30)$$

$$= \mathbf{A}_{\hat{n}} \hat{\mathbf{n}} + \mathbf{A}_{\hat{n}} \boldsymbol{\delta}(t)$$
$$+ \left(\sum_i \delta_i \left. \frac{\partial \mathbf{A}}{\partial n_i} \right|_{\hat{n}} \right) \boldsymbol{\delta}(t) + \left(\sum_i \delta_i \left. \frac{\partial \mathbf{A}}{\partial n_i} \right|_{\hat{n}} \right) \hat{\mathbf{n}} \quad (9.31)$$

The first term on the right-hand side of (9.31) equals $\hat{\mathbf{n}}$, and cancels with the corresponding term on the left-hand side. The third is of order δ_i^2, and can be neglected for sufficiently small $\boldsymbol{\delta}$. Eliminating these terms leaves the linear approximation

$$\boldsymbol{\delta}(t+1) = \mathbf{A}_{\hat{n}} \boldsymbol{\delta}(t) + \left(\sum_i \delta_i \left. \frac{\partial \mathbf{A}}{\partial n_i} \right|_{\hat{n}} \right) \hat{\mathbf{n}} \qquad (9.32)$$

Now define a set of matrices $\mathbf{H}_i$, where $\mathbf{H}_i$ has $\hat{\mathbf{n}}$ in column i, and zeros elsewhere. Then (9.32) can be rewritten

$$\delta(t+1) = \left(\mathbf{A}_{\hat{n}} + \sum_i \left. \frac{\partial \mathbf{A}}{\partial n_i} \right|_{\hat{\mathbf{n}}} \mathbf{H}_i \right) \delta(t) \tag{9.33}$$

$$\equiv \mathbf{B}\delta(t) \tag{9.34}$$

The stability properties of $\hat{\mathbf{n}}$ are determined by the eigenvalues of the linear approximation matrix $\mathbf{B}$. If the maximum eigenvalue of $\mathbf{B}$ is less than 1 in magnitude, the equilibrium point is asymptotically stable; if it is greater than 1, the equilibrium is unstable. A maximum eigenvalue of magnitude exactly 1 implies neutral stability of the linearized system. In this case the linearized system is structurally unstable, and the nonlinear terms cannot be ignored in studying stability.

Note that $\mathbf{B}$ is *not* a population projection matrix. It is not, in general, even nonnegative. Thus its largest eigenvalue need not be real or positive.

Example 9.3 The DeAngelis fishery model

The fish population model (9.9) can be analyzed using this methodology. Remember that competition is assumed to occur only within the first age class, and to affect only P_1. Thus, for this model

$$\mathbf{B} = \mathbf{A}_{\hat{n}} + \left. \frac{\partial \mathbf{A}}{\partial n_1} \right|_{\hat{\mathbf{n}}} \mathbf{H}_1 \tag{9.35}$$

$$= \mathbf{A}_{\hat{n}} + \begin{pmatrix} m_1 \hat{n}_1 \frac{\partial P_1}{\partial n_1} & 0 & \cdots & 0 \\ \hat{n}_1 \frac{\partial P_1}{\partial n_1} & 0 & \cdots & 0 \\ 0 & 0 & \cdots & 0 \\ \vdots & \vdots & \ddots & \vdots \\ 0 & 0 & \cdots & 0 \end{pmatrix} \tag{9.36}$$

$$= \begin{pmatrix} m_1 \left(P_1 + \hat{n}_1 \frac{\partial P_1}{\partial n_1} \right) & P_2 m_2 & \cdots & P_{s-1} m_{s-1} & P_s m_s \\ P_1 + \hat{n}_1 \frac{\partial P_1}{\partial n_1} & 0 & \cdots & 0 & 0 \\ 0 & P_2 & \cdots & 0 & 0 \\ \vdots & \vdots & \ddots & \vdots & \vdots \\ 0 & 0 & \cdots & P_{s-1} & P_s \end{pmatrix}$$

where P_1 and $\partial P_1/\partial n_1$ are understood to be evaluated at $\hat{n}_1$.

The linear approximation matrix $\mathbf{B}$ in this case has the same form as the original age-classified matrix (although we cannot assume that it is nonnegative, because $\partial P_1/\partial n_1$ may be negative). However, we do know the form of the characteristic equation. Define

$$P_1' = \left(P_1 + \hat{n}_1 \frac{\partial P_1}{\partial n_1}\right)\Big|_{\hat{n}} \qquad (9.37)$$

Then the characteristic equation of **B** is

$$
\begin{aligned}
1 &= P_1' m_1 \lambda^{-1} + P_1' P_2 m_2 \lambda^{-2} + P_1' P_2 P_3 m_3 \lambda^{-3} \\
&+ \cdots + \frac{P_1' P_2 \cdots P_s m_s \lambda^{-s}}{1 - P_s \lambda^{-1}}
\end{aligned} \qquad (9.38)
$$

The characteristic equation for the projection matrix $\mathbf{A}_n$ at equilibrium has exactly the same form, but with P_1' replaced by P_1; by definition this equation has a maximal solution of $\lambda = 1$. If $0 < P_1' < P_1$, then the real root of (9.38) will be less than 1, and the equilibrium will be stable.

DeAngelis et al. (1980) use the Beverton-Hold function, so that

$$P_1 = \frac{c_1}{a + c_2 n_1} \qquad (9.39)$$

Then, at equilibrium

$$
\begin{aligned}
P_1' &= \frac{c_1}{1 + c_2 \hat{n}_1} - \frac{\hat{n}_1 c_1 c_2}{(1 + c_2 \hat{n}_1)^2} \\
&= \frac{P_1}{1 + c_2 \hat{n}_1}
\end{aligned} \qquad (9.40)
$$

Thus $0 < P_1' < P_1$, and the equilibrium is always stable.

Overcompensation can change the stability results. Suppose that, instead of (9.39),

$$P_1(n_1) = \alpha e^{-\beta n_1}$$

In this case,

$$P_1' = \alpha e^{-\beta \hat{n}_1}(1 - \hat{n}_1 \beta) \qquad (9.41)$$

the sign of which depends on the value of $\hat{n}_1$.

At equilibrium,

$$
\begin{aligned}
P_1 &= (F_1 + P_2 F_2 + P_2 P_3 F_3 + \cdots)^{-1} \qquad (9.42) \\
&\equiv 1/R \qquad (9.43)
\end{aligned}
$$

where R is a measure of the net reproductive rate (close to, but not quite exactly the familiar R_0, because of the birth-pulse form of the matrix). Thus

$$\alpha R e^{-\beta \hat{n}_1} = 1 \qquad (9.44)$$

so that $\hat{n}_1 = \ln(\alpha R)/\beta$. Thus, the expression for P_1' simplifies to

$$P_1' = R^{-1}\left[1 - \ln(\alpha R)\right] \tag{9.45}$$

Note that $\ln(\alpha R) > 0$ if $\hat{n}_1 > 0$. Thus the equilibrium is stable as long as $\ln(\alpha R) < 1$. However, if $\ln(\alpha R) > 1$, $P_1' < 0$, the matrix $\mathbf{B}$ is no longer nonnegative, and the dominant root of the characteristic equation need no longer be real. The dynamic consequences of this will be explored in the next example, in the context of the overcompensatory Levin-Goodyear model, which uses this competition function.

Example 9.4 The Levin-Goodyear model

Versions of this model were analyzed by Levin and Goodyear (1980) and Levin (1981) in a study of the striped bass (*Morone saxitalis*). The matrix $\mathbf{A}_n$ is an age-classified matrix with density-independent survival terms P_i, and density-dependent fertilities $F_i = \alpha \exp(-\beta N)m_i$, where $N = \sum_i n_i m_i$.

The equilibrium population is found by noting that

$$
\begin{aligned}
N(t) &= \sum_i m_i n_i(t) \\
&= \sum_i m_i n_1(t - i + 1) \prod_{j=1}^{i-1} P_j \\
&= \sum_i m_i \alpha N(t-i) e^{-\beta N(t-i)} \prod_{j=1}^{i-1} P_j
\end{aligned} \tag{9.46}
$$

At equilibrium, $N(t) = N(t - i) = \hat{N}$, for all i, so that

$$\hat{N} = \hat{N} e^{-\beta \hat{N}} \sum_i \alpha m_i \prod_{j=1}^{i-1} P_j \tag{9.47}$$

The summation term in this expression is just the net reproductive rate, evaluated at $N = 0$. Defining this as R_0^*, we finally obtain

$$\hat{N} = \frac{\ln R_0^*}{\beta} \tag{9.48}$$

From this equilibrium value of $\hat{N}$ the rest of the population can be determined:

$$
\begin{aligned}
\hat{n}_1 &= \alpha \hat{N} e^{-\beta \hat{N}} \\
\hat{n}_i &= \hat{n}_1 \prod_{j=1}^{i-1} P_j \qquad \text{for } i > 1
\end{aligned} \tag{9.49}
$$

Levin (1981) presents the stability analysis of a two-age-class version of this model. The projection matrix is

$$\mathbf{A}_n = \begin{pmatrix} F_1(\mathbf{n}) & F_2(\mathbf{n}) \\ P_1 & 0 \end{pmatrix} \tag{9.50}$$

where

$$F_1(\mathbf{n}) = m_1 \alpha e^{-\beta N} \tag{9.51}$$
$$F_2(\mathbf{n}) = m_2 \alpha e^{-\beta N} \tag{9.52}$$

The linear approximation matrix $\mathbf{B}$, calculated following (9.34), turns out (after some tedious algebra) to be

$$\mathbf{B} = \begin{pmatrix} m_1 Q & m_2 Q \\ P_1 & 0 \end{pmatrix} \tag{9.53}$$

where

$$Q = \left(\frac{1 - \ln R_0^*}{m_1 + P_1 m_2} \right)$$

The stability of the equilibrium depends on whether the eigenvalues of $\mathbf{B}$ are within the unit circle. Necessary and sufficient conditions for this are given by the Schur-Cohn criteria (see May 1974 for a simple version, Jury 1964 for a detailed discussion). For the two-dimensional case under consideration here, the characteristic equation is a quadratic $\lambda^2 + a\lambda + b = 0$; its roots lie within the unit circle if and only if

$$2 > 1 + b > |a| \tag{9.54}$$

Applying (9.54) to $\mathbf{B}$ gives the conditions for stability as

$$2 > (1 - P_1 m_2 Q) > -m_1 Q \tag{9.55}$$

A considerable further amount of algebra reduces this to the following two inequalities

$$\ln R_0^* < \frac{m_1}{P_1 m_2} + 2 \tag{9.56}$$

and, if $P_1 < m_1/m_2$,

$$\ln R_0^* < \frac{2m_1}{m_1 - P_1 m_2} \tag{9.57}$$

Figure 9.2 shows the region of parameter space satisfying (9.56) and (9.57). Increases in R_0^* are always destabilizing. The cusp in the stability region implies that increases in P_1 are stabilizing up to a point, and then destabilizing. See Levin and Goodyear (1980) and Levin (1981) for the effects of age at maturity and the dispersion of reproduction on stability in this model.

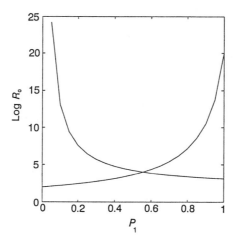

Figure 9.2: The stability region for the simple two age-class model of Equation (9.50). The equilibrium is stable if R_0^* and P_1 fall in the region under the two curves.

9.2.3 An Ergodic Theorem

Desharnais and Cohen (1986) and Cushing (1989) have proved an ergodic theorem for the stage structure of simple density-dependent models, like (9.19) and (9.20), in which density affects all the vital rates equally. Suppose that the matrix $\mathbf{A}_n$ is written

$$\mathbf{A}_n = h(\mathbf{n})\mathbf{A} \tag{9.58}$$

where $\mathbf{A}$ is a (density-independent) irreducible, primitive nonnegative matrix, and the scalar function $h(\mathbf{n})$ expresses the density dependence. If $h(\mathbf{n})$ is defined so that $h(0) = 1$, then $\mathbf{A}$ becomes the population matrix in the limiting case of low densities.

Let $\mathbf{w}$ denote the dominant right eigenvector of $\mathbf{A}$, normalized so that $\|\mathbf{w}\| = \sum_i w_i = 1$. In the density-independent case, the strong ergodic theorem guarantees that the population stage distribution $\mathbf{x}(t) = \mathbf{n}(t)/\|\mathbf{n}(t)\|$ converges to $\mathbf{w}$. Cushing shows that this is also true in the density-dependent case, regardless of the form of $h(\mathbf{n})$.

Note that $\mathbf{n}(t) = \mathbf{x}(t)\|\mathbf{n}(t)\|$. Thus the projection equation

$$\mathbf{n}(t+1) = h(\mathbf{n})\mathbf{A}\mathbf{n}(t) \tag{9.59}$$

can be rewritten

$$\mathbf{n}(t+1) = h(\mathbf{n})\|\mathbf{n}(t)\|\mathbf{A}\mathbf{x}(t) \tag{9.60}$$

Taking norms of both sides yields

$$\|\mathbf{n}(t+1)\| = h[\mathbf{n}(t)]\|\mathbf{n}(t)\|\,\|\mathbf{A}\mathbf{x}(t)\| \tag{9.61}$$

Dividing both sides of (9.60) by (9.61) yields

$$x(t+1) = \frac{\mathbf{A}x(t)}{\|\mathbf{A}x(t)\|} \tag{9.62}$$

If $\mathbf{A}$ is primitive, the matrices $\mathbf{A}/\|\mathbf{A}x(t)\|$ form an ergodic set as long as $x(0) \neq 0$, and thus the stage distribution vector $x(t+1)$ converges to $\mathbf{w}$ by the weak ergodic theorem (Section 8.3.1).

Although the stage structure converges, the dynamics of total population size $N(t) = \|\mathbf{n}(t)\|$ may be much more complex. $N(t)$ satisfies the non-autonomous scalar difference equation

$$N(t+1) = \|\mathbf{A}x(t)\| h[x(t)N(t)]N(t) \tag{9.63}$$

As $t \to \infty$ and $x(t) \to \mathbf{w}$, this converges to an autonomous but nonlinear difference equation

$$N(t+1) = \lambda h[\mathbf{w}N(t)]N(t) \tag{9.64}$$

The ergodicity of population structure does *not* guarantee the stability of population size. Cushing shows that, depending on the function $h(\mathbf{n})$, $N(t)$ may converge to a stable equilibrium, converge to a stable limit cycle, or even fluctuate chaotically, whereas population structure converges to its stable value.

9.3   Instability and Bifurcation

In this section, we consider the dynamics following the instability of an equilibrium $\hat{\mathbf{n}}$. If $\hat{\mathbf{n}}$ is unstable, nearby solutions do not converge to $\hat{\mathbf{n}}$. They must go somewhere; the question is where.

The dynamics of unstable systems are characterized by a series of qualitative changes ("bifurcations") in solutions as some parameter is varied. The possibilities include fixed points, cycles, quasiperiodic fluctuations (combinations of two or more incommensurate frequencies), and chaos. Multiple attractors can, and often do exist. When multiple attractors are present, the boundaries between their basins of attraction can be extremely complex.

The reader is referred to Guckenheimer and Holmes (1983), Berge et al. (1984), Cvitanovic (1984), Schuster (1984), Devaney (1986), Holden (1986), and Thompson and Stewart (1986) for general discussions of chaos, and to Gleick (1987) for a popular account. Chaos is characterized by

- Sensitive dependence on initial conditions. The trajectories originating from two initial states diverge exponentially, no matter how close the initial states. The rates of divergence are given by the Lyapunov exponents (one for each dimension of the state space); chaotic systems are characterized by the presence of at least one positive Lyapunov exponent.

- Broad band power spectra. The power spectrum of a periodic solution consists of isolated peaks corresponding to the periodic frequency and perhaps some of its harmonics. The power spectrum of a quasiperiodic solution contains peaks corresponding to the two incommensurate frequencies comprising the solution, plus their sums and differences. The power spectrum of a chaotic solution, in contrast, contains broad, "noisy" regions, representing apparently noisy dynamics over a broad frequency range.

- Fractal dimension. Chaotic attractors typically possess non-integer dimension. Close examination of their structure reveals complex, scale-invariant geometric patterns.

The bifurcation patterns and the nature of chaotic dynamics in one-dimensional maps are now well understood (Collett and Eckmann 1980). Higher dimensional maps, such as nonlinear matrix population models, have more possibilities open to them, and their mathematics is much less certain. The next sections will survey some of these dynamics. A complete treatment is impossible here; my goal is simply to outline the *kinds* of dynamics that are possible, the transitions between them, and the parameters that determine these transitions.

9.3.1 Bifurcations in One-Dimensional Maps

The bifurcation patterns of one-dimensional maps have been discussed in the context of population models by May (1974, 1976) and May and Oster (1976); their mathematics is reviewed by Collett and Eckmann (1980) and Devaney (1986). Consider a model

$$N(t+1) = F[\mu, N(t)] \tag{9.65}$$

where μ is a parameter and $F(\mu, N)$ is a nonlinear function, as shown in Figure 9.3. The linear approximation to (9.65) in the neighborhood of the equilibrium $\hat{N}$ is

$$\delta(t+1) = F'[\mu, \delta(t)] \tag{9.66}$$

where $F' = \partial F/\partial N$. The equilibrium $\hat{N}$ is stable if and only if $|F'| < 1$.

Suppose that $\hat{N}$ is stable for $\mu < \mu_1$, but unstable for $\mu > \mu_1$. If $F'(\mu_1, N) = -1$, the unstable $\hat{N}$ is replaced by a stable orbit of period 2 (a "pitchfork" bifurcation). If μ is increased further, a second bifurcation may appear at μ_2, in which the period-2 solution becomes unstable and is replaced by a period-4 solution. This period-doubling sequence continues, the width of the stability intervals for each period decreasing geometrically

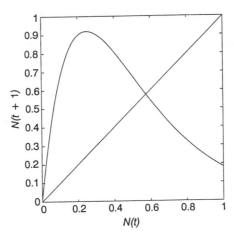

Figure 9.3: A one-dimensional nonlinear map, relating $N(t+1)$ and $N(t)$.

$[(\mu_i - \mu_{i-1})/(\mu_{i+1} - \mu_i) \rightarrow 4.6692]$ until a critical value μ_c is reached, beyond which solutions become chaotic. Further increases in μ yield a complicated succession of chaotic intervals and windows of stable periodic solutions. Those stable periodic solutions can result from "tangent" bifurcations through $F' = 1$, which create new stable solutions that are not multiples of previous periodic solutions.

This period-doubling route to chaos has been extensively studied; most of its properties are universal to very wide classes of one-dimensional maps. In contrast, the bifurcation patterns in higher dimensional maps are less well understood, but there are clearly defined routes to chaotic behavior that apply in these models.

9.3.2   The Hopf Bifurcation in Multidimensional Maps

Bifurcations in one-dimensional maps can occur only when the "eigenvalue" of the linear approximation — which, being one-dimensional, is just $F'(\mu, \hat{N})$ — passes through $+1$ or -1. In matrix models, there is the additional possibility that a pair of eigenvalues can pass through the unit circle as complex conjugates. The results are described in the Hopf bifurcation theorem for maps (Ruelle and Takens 1971; see Marsden and McCracken 1976 for a review, Wan 1978 and Iooss 1979 for gory details, and Guckenheimer et al. 1977 for an ecological application).

The outcome of a Hopf bifurcation is destabilization of the equilibrium and the simultaneous appearance of a stable *invariant circle*: a closed, continuous curve around which the state of the population hops. Motion on this invariant circle is not periodic; if it were, the attractor would be a finite set of points rather than a continuous curve.

The Hopf bifurcation theorem for maps[2] defines conditions sufficient for the creation of such an attractor. Consider a model

$$\mathbf{n}(t+1) = \mathbf{A}_n\mathbf{n}(t) \tag{9.67}$$
$$\equiv \Phi[\mu, \mathbf{n}(t)] \tag{9.68}$$

with a linear approximation [e.g., (9.34)] at the equilibrium $\hat{\mathbf{n}}$ given by the matrix $\mathbf{B}$ with a dominant eigenvalue $\lambda_1^{(\mathbf{B})}$. Suppose that

1. For $\mu < \mu_1$, $|\lambda_1^{(\mathbf{B})}| < 1$.

2. For $\mu = \mu_1$, there are two complex conjugate eigenvalues $\lambda_1^{(\mathbf{B})} = \bar{\lambda}_2^{(\mathbf{B})}$, with $|\lambda_1^{(\mathbf{B})}| = |\lambda_2^{(\mathbf{B})}| = 1$. The other eigenvalues are all strictly less than 1 in magnitude.

3. The magnitude of the dominant eigenvalue is increasing at $\mu = \mu_1$, i.e.

$$\frac{d}{d\mu}\left(|\lambda_1^{(\mathbf{B})}|\right) > 0 \tag{9.69}$$

4. The dominant eigenvalue at μ_1 is not one of the first four roots of unity:

$$\left(\lambda_1^{(\mathbf{B})}\Big|_{\mu_1}\right)^q \neq 1 \qquad \text{for } q = 1, 2, 3, 4 \tag{9.70}$$

Then either $\Phi(\mu, \mathbf{n})$ will have an attracting invariant circle for $\mu > \mu_1$ (a forward Hopf bifurcation or a repelling invariant circle for $\mu < \mu_1$ (a backward Hopf bifurcation). The distinction between the forward and backward bifurcations depends on a technical and computationally difficult stability condition (see Wan 1978 for computational details). If the condition is not satisfied, the stable equilibrium disappears, but is not replaced with any attractor (Lanford 1973); it does not seem necessary to worry about this condition in practice.

If the bifurcation takes place through one of the first four roots of unity, the dynamics can be complex (Iooss 1979). The most likely outcome seems

---

[2]There is a fly in the mathematical ointment concerning this theorem. Ruelle and Takens (1971) proved the theorem for diffeomorphisms (continuous, *invertible* maps). Most matrix population models are not invertible, particularly if they include overcompensatory density functions. Guckenheimer et al. (1977) point out that this makes the applicability of the theorem to their model questionable. Wan (1978), however, applies the theorem to their model, calling it a diffeomorphism even though it clearly is not. Aronson et al. (1982) justify their application of the theorem by the *local* invertibility of the map in the neighborhood of the equilibrium. If this is generally valid, it would apply to most matrix population models.

to be a periodic orbit; a bifurcation through one of the cube roots of unity (e.g., Guckenheimer et al. 1977) produces a solution of period three, etc. Except in special cases, bifurcations through these particular values of λ are unlikely to be structurally stable.

The usual outcome of a Hopf bifurcation is an attracting invariant circle. The dynamics on this attractor are characterized by the presence of two incommensurate frequencies. These frequencies appear in time series as one oscillation modulated by another (Levin and Goodyear 1980, Caswell and Weeks 1986; see Example 9.5 and Chapter 10). The frequency spectrum of quasiperiodic trajectories contains peaks corresponding to the two frequencies, as well as peaks corresponding to their sums and differences.

Example 9.5 A simple two age-class model

As an example, consider a simple model with

$$\mathbf{A}_n = \left(\begin{array}{cc} b_1 \exp(-0.1N) & b_2 \exp(-0.1N) \\ 0.9 & 0 \end{array} \right) \qquad (9.71)$$

where $N = n_1 + n_2$. The simple fishery model (9.50) of Levin (1981) has this form. Guckenheimer et al. (1977) also analyzed a special case of this model with $b_1 = b_2$. The coefficients b_i are the bifurcation parameters in this model. For this example, we let $b_1 = \mu$ and $b_2 = 2\mu$, and use μ as the bifurcation parameter.

Figure 9.4 shows the magnitude of the dominant eigenvalue of the linear approximation as a function of the bifurcation parameter μ. The equilibrium is stable until $\mu = \mu_1 \approx 11.458$, at which point the two eigenvalues are $-0.7341 \pm 0.6790i$. These eigenvalues are not simple roots of unity, so we expect a Hopf bifurcation to an invariant circle at μ_1.

Figure 9.5 shows the invariant circle and an example of the dynamics on this attractor, for $\mu = 12$. The plot of $n_1(t)$ shows the modulation characteristic of quasiperiodic motion. Figure 9.6 shows the power spectrum for $n_1(t)$. It contains prominent peaks at frequencies $\omega_1 = 0.3784$ and $\omega_2 = 0.2437$ (corresponding to periods 2.64 and 4.10, respectively), and a peak at $\omega = \omega_1 - \omega_2 = 0.1348$.

Levin and Goodyear (1980) investigate such dynamics in detail in the context of the age-classified fishery model (9.11).

9.3.3   From Quasiperiodicity to Chaos

The Hopf bifurcation theorem is a local result; it describes the attractor that appears as the eigenvalues of the linearized map cross the unit circle. What happens beyond is complex.

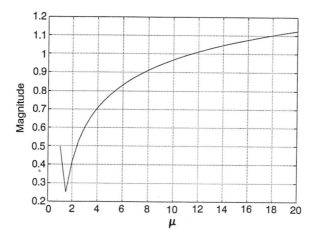

Figure 9.4: The magnitude of the dominant eigenvalue of the linear approximation to the density-dependent model (9.71), evaluated at the equilibrium point, as a function of the bifurcation parameter μ.

Much of what is known about quasiperiodic dynamics is the result of study of maps of the circle (just as quadratic maps of the interval serve as universal models for the period-doubling cascade to chaos). Consider an invariant circle, as in Figure 9.5. The state of the system on this circle can be described by its angle θ relative to some point in the interior defined as the center, and its dynamics are defined by a map giving $\theta(t+1)$ as a function of $\theta(t)$ (e.g., Schuster 1984).

A map on the circle can be characterized by its *winding number*

$$\eta = \lim_{t \to \infty} \frac{\theta(t)}{2\pi t} \tag{9.72}$$

If the winding number is irrational, the orbit of the map covers the circle densely; this corresponds to quasiperiodic motion, containing two incommensurate frequencies. A rational winding number, say $\eta = p/q$ for some integers p and q, corresponds to a periodic orbit of the circle map.

The winding number on the invariant circle immediately following the Hopf bifurcation at $\mu = \mu_1$ is irrational. As the bifurcation parameter increases beyond μ_1, the winding number eventually becomes rational over some interval of μ; this is referred to as *frequency locking*, and appears as a collapse of the invariant circle to a periodic orbit.

Further increases in μ following frequency locking can yield a sequence of period-doubling bifurcations or a return to quasiperiodicity. Eventually, for μ large enough, chaos arrives. There are four ways (at least) to leave your

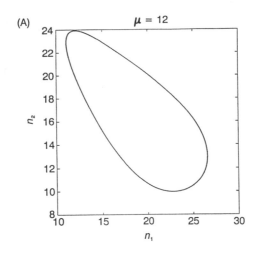

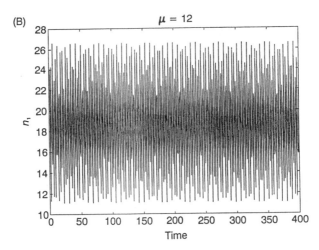

Figure 9.5: The quasiperiodic attractor (A) and an example of the dynamics of $n_1(t)$ on that attractor (B) for the system (9.71) with $\mu = 12$.

quasiperiodic attractor (Berge et al. 1984). The first, the *Ruelle-Takens-Newhouse route to chaos* (Ruelle and Takens 1971, Newhouse et al. 1978) occurs after a second Hopf bifurcation produces a third incommensurate frequency in the solution. The second, studied in a two-dimensional map by Curry and Yorke (1978), occurs directly from the invariant circle with two incommensurate frequencies. As μ is increased above some threshold value, the invariant circle becomes kinked. These kinks possess a complex fractal structure; their appearance signals that the attractor is no longer topologi-

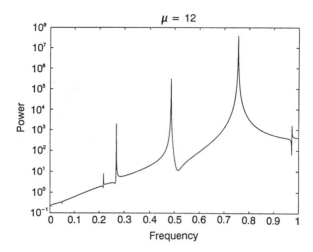

Figure 9.6: The power spectral density for $n_1(t)$ on the quasiperiodic attractor for $\mu = 12$.

cally a circle, but instead is a strange attractor. A third possibility, detected experimentally by Dubois and Berge (1981), occurs when the quasiperiodic attractor simply breaks up into a diffuse cloud of points (this seems to happen in the two-sex model of Caswell and Weeks 1986; see Chapter 10). A fourth possibility is a "crisis" (Grebogi et al. 1983), in which the quasiperiodic attractor collides with a coexisting unstable fixed point or limit cycle, and is abruptly replaced with a chaotic attractor.

Example 9.6 The two age-class model again

The two age-class model of Example 9.5 exhibits several of these phenomena. Figure 9.7 is a bifurcation plot, in which the value of n_1 on the attractor is plotted as a function of μ. For $\mu < 11.458$, the attractor is a fixed point. At $\mu = 11.458$ the Hopf bifurcation takes place; the points on the quasiperiodic attractor produce a solid vertical bar above the value of μ. Further increases in μ increase the size of the attractor.

The complex structure within Figure 9.7 appears to represent phase locking; a periodic band around $\mu = 12.6$ is especially clear. This internal structure is fascinating and relatively unexplored. Figure 9.8 shows a blow-up of the bifurcation plot for $11.79 < \mu < 11.81$.

As μ increases, there is an abrupt change in the attractor at $\mu \approx 15.6$, from an invariant circle to a limit cycle with a period of 12, which undergoes period-doubling, and eventually becomes chaotic (Figure 9.9).

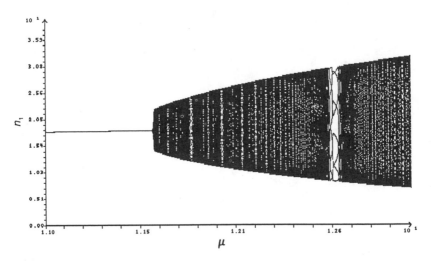

Figure 9.7: A bifurcation plot for the model of Example 9.5, plotting n_1 as a function of the bifurcation parameter μ for $11 < \mu < 13$. Five hundred iterations are plotted for each value of μ.

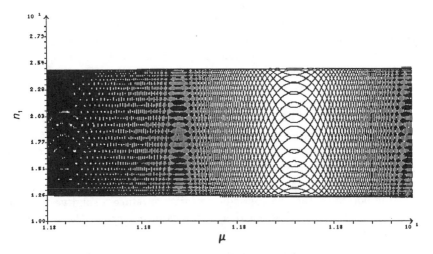

Figure 9.8: A blowup of the region from $11.79 < \mu < 11.81$ in Figure 9.7.

Windows of periodicity, with their own period-doubling cascades within them, are clearly visible within the chaotic region. Figure 9.10 shows the chaotic dynamics of $n_1(t)$, and a phase portrait of the attractor for $\mu = 18$. The attractor is clearly not a continuous curve, and this relatively low-resolution plot only hints at the complex structure within

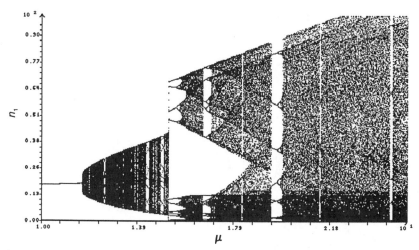

Figure 9.9: A bifurcation plot for the model of Example 9.5, plotting n_1 as a function of the bifurcation parameter μ for $10 < \mu < 25$. Five hundred iterations are plotted for each value of μ.

the attractor. Figure 9.11 shows the power spectrum of n_1. The noise level is increased dramatically compared to the quasiperiodic case (cf. Figure 9.6). The peak at a frequency of $\omega = 0.333$, corresponding to a period of 3, reflects the division of the attractor of Figure 9.10 into three pieces.

The coexistence of multiple attractors is always a possibility in nonlinear models, and is likely to be common for density-dependent matrix population models. Guckenheimer et al. (1977) studied a special case of (9.71), with $b_1 = b_2$ and $a_{21} = 1$. The symmetry imposed by setting $b_1 = b_2$ leads to a Hopf bifurcation through the cube root of unity, yielding a period-3 cycle, rather than the more typical quasiperiodic behavior, but there is a region of parameter space in which the stable 3-cycle coexists with the stable equilibrium.

The abrupt change in the attractor at $\mu \approx 15.6$ in Figure 9.9 is an example. The new period-12 attractor that appears there is actually the result of a series of period-doubling bifurcations from a period-3 attractor which coexists with the quasiperiodic attractor at least as early as $\mu = 13$. Figure 9.12 shows this period-doubling series for $13 < \mu < 17$. The change from the quasiperiodic attractor to the periodic attractor at $\mu \approx 15.6$ could reflect the disappearance of the invariant circle due to a crisis, or could be due to a shift in the domains of attraction of the two attractors. I have not attempted to map out those domains, so I do not know if the quasiperiodic

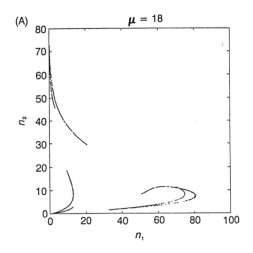

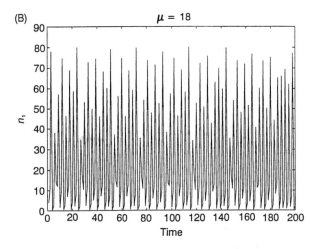

Figure 9.10: The chaotic attractor (A) and an example of the dynamics of $n_1(t)$ on that attractor (B) for the system (9.71) with $\mu = 18$. Compare with Figure 9.5.

attractor continues after it disappears from Figure 9.9.

The boundaries separating the domains of attraction of multiple attractors can be extraordinarily complex fractal structures (e.g., Grebogi et al. 1983, 1987; for a somewhat biological example see the discrete-time predator-prey system in Peitgen and Richter 1986, p. 125). The stunning computer graphics of the Mandlebrot set in Peitgen and Richter (1986) convey some of this complexity for the special case of two-dimensional maps expressed

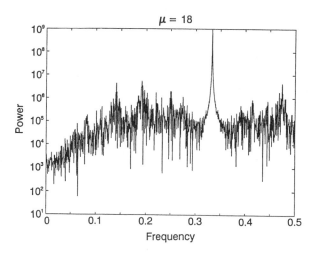

Figure 9.11: The power spectral density for $n_1(t)$ on the chaotic attractor for $\mu = 18$. Compare with Figure 9.6.

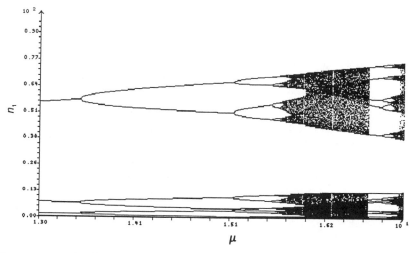

Figure 9.12: A bifurcation plot for the model of Example 9.5, plotting n_1 as a function of the bifurcation parameter μ for $13 < \mu < 17$. The period-3 attractor present here at $\mu = 13$ coexists with the quasiperiodic attractor at that value in Figure 9.9.

as quadratic mappings of the complex plane. This complexity can make it impossible to determine the ultimate fate of an initial condition specified with any finite precision.

9.4   Evolutionary Demography

We close this chapter with a brief discussion of selection in density-dependent structured populations. This theory is not as well developed as that for the density-independent case (Chapter 6). In particular, very little has been done on selection in populations undergoing quasiperiodic or chaotic fluctuations (Asmussen 1979, Auslander et al. 1978); it is possible that some approaches to stochastic environment models might be applicable in the latter case.

Density-dependent selection in populations without age structure has been extensively studied (e.g., MacArthur 1962, Roughgarden 1971, Anderson and King 1970, Charlesworth 1971; see review in Roughgarden 1979). Under many conditions, it can be shown that selection maximizes equilibrium population size; hence, this mode of selection has been termed K-selection, after the equilibrium population size in the logistic equation. Analogous results for age-classified populations have been obtained by Charlesworth (1976, 1980) and Hastings (1978b). The extension of these results to stage-classified models remains to be done.

9.4.1   Density-Dependent Selection

Charlesworth (1976, 1980) analyzed a one-locus age-classified selection model based on a discrete-time renewal equation of the form (2.34). He assumed that the vital rates depend on the total density $N(t)$ of some age class or group of age classes, referred to as the critical age group, in such a way that the net reproductive rate of each genotype is a strictly decreasing function of N (i.e., no depensation allowed). Assuming that selection is slow, so that population sizes will equilibrate before gene frequencies, he found that there is at most one equilibrium with all alleles present, that it maximizes $\hat{N}$, and that the invasion of a genotype requires that its carrying capacity exceed that of the genotypes present. In other words, the genotypic carrying capacities play the same role as the growth rate λ in density-independent selection, and selection maximizes the density of the critical age group.

These results rely on the assumption of slow selection, and on the absence of frequency dependence. They can also be altered by linkage relationships in multilocus models (Charlesworth 1980).

9.4.2   Evolutionary Stable Strategies

An *evolutionary stable strategy*, or ESS, is a strategy that, once established, cannot be invaded by any other. Hastings (1978a) introduced the distinction between ESS and *competitively stable strategies* (CSS), defining an ESS as stable against invasion by nearby strategies and a CSS as stable against invasion by any alternative strategy. If the genetic system is capable of producing it, selection should lead to an ESS or CSS.

Hastings (1978b) considers a density-dependent age-classified matrix model in which the F_i and P_i are functions of N. An equilibrium population $\hat{N}$ exists if and only if $R_0(\hat{N}) = 1$, where

$$R_0(\hat{N}) = \sum_{i=1}^{s} F_i(N) \prod_{j=1}^{i-1} P_j(N) \tag{9.73}$$

Hastings (1978b) proves that a life history leading to an equilibrium population size $\hat{N}$ is a CSS if and only if $R_0(\hat{N}) < 1$ for all other strategies. This is not difficult to see, since another strategy can invade the equilibrium $\hat{N}$ only if the dominant eigenvalue of its projection matrix, evaluated under the situation it is trying to invade, is greater than 1.

Now, make the additional assumptions that the equilibrium $\hat{n}$ is stable, and that $\partial R_0 / \partial N < 0$ at $N = \hat{N}$. Then Hastings shows that a strategy is an ESS if and only if it maximizes equilibrium population size.

To see this, write the fertility and survival terms as

$$F_i(N) = F_i(\mathbf{c}, N) \tag{9.74}$$
$$P_i(N) = P_i(\mathbf{c}, N) \tag{9.75}$$

where $\mathbf{c}$ is an m-vector of parameters (e.g., age-specific reproductive efforts) defining the life history strategy.

These parameters will be subject to constraints, which we assume can be written[3] as

$$H_k(\mathbf{c}) = 0 \quad \text{for } k = 1, 2, \ldots, q \tag{9.76}$$

The net reproductive rate function $R_0(N)$ implicitly defines a relationship between R_0 and the c_i:

$$R_0(c_1, c_2, \ldots, c_m, \hat{N}) = 1 \tag{9.77}$$

Differentiating implicitly yields

$$\frac{\partial R_0}{\partial c_i} + \frac{\partial R_0}{\partial \hat{N}} \frac{\partial \hat{N}}{\partial c_i} = 0 \quad \text{for } i = 1, \ldots, m \tag{9.78}$$

Since we have assumed that $\partial R_0 / \partial \hat{N}$ is not zero, it follows from (9.78) that $\partial R_0 / \partial c_i = 0$ if and only if $\partial \hat{N} / \partial c_i = 0$, i.e., extrema of R_0 and $\hat{N}$ coincide.

---

[3] Hastings also allows inequality constraints; these are reduced to equality constraints using Kuhn-Tucker theory; see Hastings (1978b).

Implicitly differentiating (9.78) leads to

$$\frac{\partial^2 \hat{N}}{\partial c_i \partial c_j} = \frac{\frac{\partial^2 R_0}{\partial c_i \partial c_j}}{\frac{\partial R_0}{\partial \hat{N}}} \tag{9.79}$$

Since we have assumed that $\partial R_0 / \partial \hat{N} < 0$, the signs of the second partials in (9.79) are the same. This proves that maxima of R_0 and $\hat{N}$ coincide.

Chapter 10

Two-Sex Models

Most demographic models are based on only one sex, usually the female. This practice can be justified by assuming either that the life cycles of the sexes are identical or that the dynamics of the population are determined by one sex independent of the relative abundance of the other. Neither assumption is generally valid; this chapter explores the dynamic consequences of relaxing them and including both sexes in demographic models of complex life cycles. First we examine some of the reasons for doubting the assumptions leading to one-sex models. Then we will develop and analyze a matrix population model (Caswell and Weeks 1986) incorporating both sexes and examine its dynamics.

10.1   Sexual Dimorphism in Demographic Traits

Sexual dimorphism in vital rates is well documented in a variety of species. In humans, male mortality almost always exceeds female mortality (e.g., Keyfitz and Flieger 1971, Cavalli-Sforza and Bodmer 1971, Wingard 1984); in the United States, the life expectancy of females at birth presently exceeds that of males by approximately 10%. Similar differences exist in countries with very different absolute levels of mortality. The dimorphism has existed for at least several centuries (e.g., data of Bourgeois-Pichat summarized in Cavalli-Sforza and Bodmer 1971, Wingard 1984), and there is now considerable debate over how much of it is due to social factors such as differences in cigarette smoking (Holden 1983, Trivers 1985).

Sexual dimorphism in mortality is well documented in other species. Darwin (1871) compiled anecdotal evidence on horses, sheep, cattle, fowl, fish, and insects (for a recent review, see Comfort 1979). The differences often greatly exceed those observed between male and female humans. The life expectancy of female ground squirrels (*Spermophilus beldingi*) exceeds that of males by 25% (Sherman and Morton 1984). The life expectancy of the female codling moth (*Carpocapsa pomonella*) exceeds that of the male by as much as 35% (MacArthur and Baillie 1932). In the black widow spider (*Latrodectus mactans*) the female advantage is 170% (Deevey and Deevey 1945). In the copepod *Pseudocalanus*, males and females require on the order of 40 days to reach maturity but after reaching maturity females live for more than 100 days, whereas males die in about 15 days (Corkett and McLaren 1978), a female advantage of over 250%.

Why male mortality should be generally greater is not clear. Geiser (1924) proposed that it is due to the expression of deleterious recessive genes carried on the sex chromosome. In species in which females are homogametic, such genes are expressed in males but not in females. On this hypothesis, the dimorphism in mortality should be reversed in species in which the male is the homogametic sex, e.g., birds and the lepidoptera. The available evidence, however, suggests that this is not the rule (MacArthur and Baillie 1932, Comfort 1979). Clutton-Brock et al. (1985) suggest that higher male mortality in mammals is a consequence of a greater susceptibility of young males to food shortage; this susceptibility is in turn a result of their higher growth rates and nutritional requirements. Maly (1970) found sex-specific predation rates on freshwater copepods (*Diaptomus* sp.) in experiments with salamanders and fish. Salamanders fed preferentially on female copepods whereas guppies fed preferentially on males. In ponds in which salamanders were the major predator the adult copepod sex ratio favored males (males/female 0.82–3.35) whereas in ponds in which fish were the major predators the adult sex ratio favored females (males/female 0.43–0.85).

Whatever its causes, sexual dimorphism in mortality responds to environmental factors and is subject to genetic variation. Dingle (1966) found that the dimorphism in mortality increased with population density in two species of Heteroptera (in which, incidentally, male mortality was less than female mortality). MacArthur and Baillie (1932) documented a clear latitudinal cline in the magnitude of the female advantage in the codling moth. Pearl (1928) documented genetic variation by comparing wild-type stocks of *Drosophila melanogaster* with stocks carrying a mutant gene for vestigial wings. The vestigial mutant not only increased overall mortality, but increased the sex differential from a 5% female advantage in the wild-type to a 40% female advantage in the vestigial strain.

Significant differences in age at maturity are also common. Females are 20% older than males at maturity in the lily *Chamaelirium luteum* (Meagher and Antonivics 1982a), males 150% older than females in the sperm whale *Physeter macrocephalus* (Allen 1980), and females 170–220% older than males in the turtle *Pseudemys scripta* (Gibbons et al. 1981). Data compiled by Bell (1980, his Figure 5) suggest that in freshwater fishes females are typically about 30% older than males at maturity, and that in mammals and birds males are typically about 40% older than females.

Finally, sexual dimorphism in fecundity is widespread. This is more complicated, since it depends strongly on the adult sex ratio. In particular, the variance in male and female fecundities may often differ, as demonstrated by Clutton-Brock et al. (1982) for the red deer (*Cervus elaphus*).

10.2   Dominance, Sex Ratio, and the Marriage Squeeze

One response to sexual dimorphism in the vital rates is to attempt parallel but separate treatment of the sexes, constructing and analyzing separate male and female life tables. Such separate life tables, however, are generally inconsistent, i.e., the rate of increase for females calculated from the female life table differs from that calculated for males from the male life table. Extrapolated, such inconsistency predicts that the relative abundance of one sex or the other will eventually decline to zero.

The simplest solution to the consistency problem is the assumption that one sex determines the population dynamics, in which case demographic calculations can be carried out based on the vital rates of that sex alone. The usual assumption is "female dominance": that there are always enough males to fertilize all the females.

When the assumption of dominance fails, distortions of the sex ratio result in a "marriage squeeze" (Schoen 1983), in which marriage, and by implication reproduction, is limited by the availabilty of the scarcer sex. Marriage squeezes are well known, even in large human populations, in which the overall sex ratio never deviates very far from unity. Patterns of preference for age and educational background (Goldman et al. 1984) in a mate can result in marked marriage squeezes (e.g., Long Island, New York, with an estimated 49.2 eligible men per 100 women, Anon 1985).

Fluctuations in the sex ratio affect reproduction in nonhuman populations in the laboratory (Wade 1984), and the use of such effects has been proposed as a component of biological control programs (Hamilton 1967, Robinson 1983). Seed production in some plants is known to be limited by pollen availability (see review by Willson and Burley 1983), which is in effect a shortage of males.

All other things being equal, marriage squeezes are most likely when the adult sex ratio differs substantially from unity. The sex ratio in human populations seldom does so; typical values in the compilation of Keyfitz and Flieger (1971) differ by only a few percent from a male:female ratio of unity. However, adult sex ratios in other species vary more widely. Willson (1983), for example, tabulates sex ratios for angiosperms which range from less than 0.1 to 191 males/female; values as low as 0.5 and as high as 3 are common. Sex ratios for aquatic animals (Altman and Dittmer 1962,

Maly 1970) range from less than 0.1 to over 10, for mammals from 0.25 to 2.7 (Altman and Dittmer 1962, Nevo 1979), and for birds from 0.35 to 3.3 (Altman and Dittmer 1962).

Nor are sex ratios constant within species. Maufette and Jobin (1985) found sex ratios from 0.46 to 1.99 in a sample of 13 local populations of the gypsy moth (*Lymantria dispar*). Alstad and Edmunds (1983) found sex ratios of local populations of the black pineleaf scale (*Nuculaspis californica*) from 0.005 to 0.320 in a sample of 18 trees measured over 3 years. Tande and Gronvik (1983) document a seasonal sex ratio cycle in the marine copepod *Metridia longa*: males are common in the winter (males/female $\approx$ 20) and rare in the summer (males/female $\approx$ 0). Marshall and Orr (1955, p. 29), speaking of the copepod *Calanus finmarchicus*, state:

> In plankton catches females usually out-number males greatly and although this is partly because of the shorter life of the males and partly because their maximum number occurs earlier in the breeding cycle than that of the females, it still remains a problem how all the females, especially those moulting late, can be fertilized.

Note that the collection and interpretation of such sex ratio data are complicated because demographic dimorphism is often associated with ecological and behavioral differences that make it hard to sample both sexes in comparable fashion (Ehrlich et al. 1984).

Mating squeezes resulting from fluctuating sex ratios may be more important, and will certainly be more complex, in species that exhibit more varied patterns of sexuality, such as sex reversal (Charnov 1982, Policansky 1982) or multiple mating strategies. In Atlantic salmon (*Salmo salar*), for instance, some males mature precociously without going to sea. These precocious males cannot mate with adult females, but sneak fertilizations from mating adult male-female pairs. Their reproductive output thus depends in a potentially complicated way on the relative frequency of females, precocious males, and adult males in the population. The frequency of precocious maturation varies in both space and time (Jones 1959, Caswell et al. 1984), and its adaptive significance depends on the relative fitnesses of each of the three types (cf. Caswell et al. 1984, Gross 1984). Similar alternative male strategies are well known in other species (e.g., Gross 1984). Such complications reach a baroque extreme in the basidiomycete fungi, populations of which may contain hundreds or even thousands of mating types (Raper 1966).

10.3 Two-Sex Models

If the life cycles of the sexes differ and the assumption of dominance fails, both sexes must be incorporated into demographic models. The resulting models are necessarily nonlinear, because only in a nonlinear model can reproduction depend on the relative abundance of males and females.

Human demographers have addressed the problem since the 1940s (see reviews by Keyfitz 1972c, Pollard 1977, Schoen 1988). Much of the human demographic literature focuses on the consistency problem (how to make the estimates of r based on male and female life tables agree; see the review in Das Gupta 1978) and ignores dynamics. The studies that have considered dynamics in any detail (e.g., Keyfitz 1968, Pollard 1973, Samuelson 1976, Yellin and Samuelson 1977, Luppova and Frisman 1983, Schoen 1984) have focused on models without age structure.

A very general framework called the "birth-matrix mating-rule" (BMRR) model for two-sex populations has been developed by Pollak (1986, 1987). It consists of a birth matrix, the (i, j) element of which is the number of offspring produced at $t + 1$ by a union of a female of age i and a male of age j at time t, and a mating rule that specifies the numbers of matings of different kinds as a function of the numbers of individuals in each age-sex category. Together with age-sex-specific survival probabilities, the birth matrix and the mating rule determine the dynamics of the age-sex distribution.

10.3.1 The Life Cycle Graph

We consider first a simple model based on the life cycle graph in Figure 10.1. Males are shown in the upper half of the graph, females in the lower half. Adults have age-independent survival probabilities of P_3 and P_5. Males require α time units and females β time units to reach maturity. Adult males and females produce sexually undifferentiated "zygotes" (n_1). The primary sex ratio (proportion males) is given by ρ; this fraction of the zygotes is assigned to n_2 and the complement to n_4. This description of reproduction is convenient, but the approach does not depend on it; we could write an equivalent graph showing the direct production of male and female offspring by males and females.

If the life cycle were time-invariant, the graph could be analyzed using the methods of Chapter 5. In a two-sex model, however, the life cycle graph will vary with time unless the population is at an equilibrium age-sex composition. I include the exponents in the graph anyway, although they will be of formal use only at equilibrium.

In Figure 10.1 the transition from the zygote stage (n_1) to n_2 or n_4 is assumed to require one time unit; this could be modified. Cases in which the sexes cannot be distinguished at birth, or where sex is determined envi-

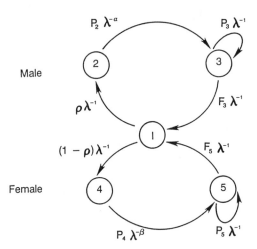

Figure 10.1: A life cycle graph for a two-sex population model. Stage 1 represents zygotes, which are produced jointly by adult males (n_3) and females (n_5), but which have not yet been assigned a sex. The P_i are survival probabilities, the F_i are fertilities, ρ is the primary sex ratio, and α and β are the male and female ages at maturity. From Caswell and Weeks (1986); ©University of Chicago.

ronmentally some time after birth (Adams et al. 1985), may be conveniently treated by increasing the lag in the transitions from n_1 to n_2 and from n_1 to n_4.

The per capita male and female fecundities F_3 and F_5 are nonlinear functions of the relative abundance of males and females, described in detail below.

The dynamics of this population can be described by a nonlinear projection matrix. For example, if $\alpha = 2$ and $\beta = 3$, the matrix corresponding to Figure 10.1 is

$$
\mathbf{A} = \left(
\begin{array}{c|ccc|cccc}
0 & 0 & 0 & F_3 & 0 & 0 & 0 & F_5 \\
\hline
\rho & 0 & 0 & 0 & 0 & 0 & 0 & 0 \\
0 & P_2 & 0 & 0 & 0 & 0 & 0 & 0 \\
0 & 0 & 1 & P_3 & 0 & 0 & 0 & 0 \\
\hline
1-\rho & 0 & 0 & 0 & 0 & 0 & 0 & 0 \\
0 & 0 & 0 & 0 & P_4 & 0 & 0 & 0 \\
0 & 0 & 0 & 0 & 0 & 1 & 0 & 0 \\
0 & 0 & 0 & 0 & 0 & 0 & 1 & P_5
\end{array}
\right)
\tag{10.1}
$$

The projection equation can be written in the standard fashion

$$
\mathbf{n}(t+1) = \mathbf{A_n} \mathbf{n}(t)
\tag{10.2}
$$

or as a nonlinear map

$$n(t + 1) = \pi[n(t)] \qquad (10.3)$$

The nonnegativity of the matrix $\mathbf{A}$ implies that the function $\pi()$ maps the set of all nonnegative vectors into itself.

10.3.2 The Birth and Fertility Functions

The per capita fertilities F_i in Figure 10.1 are functions $F_i(\mathbf{n})$ of the current population structure; they summarize the demographic interactions between the sexes. The fertility function is most easily derived from the birth function $B(\mathbf{n})$ (sometimes known in human demography as marriage function). $B(\mathbf{n})$ gives the number of births produced by the population $\mathbf{n}$. Biological considerations (cf. Frederickson 1971, McFarland 1972, Das Gupta 1972, Yellin and Samuelson 1974) suggest that $B(\mathbf{n})$ should satisfy certain criteria:

1. $B(\mathbf{n})$ should be well-defined and nonnegative for all nonnegative $\mathbf{n}$.

2. $B(\mathbf{n})$ should be a first-degree homogeneous function of its arguments, i.e., $B(k\mathbf{n}) = kB(\mathbf{n})$ for any nonnegative k.

3. Reproduction requires both males and females, so $B(\mathbf{n}) = 0$ for any $\mathbf{n}$ in which either males or females are absent.

4. $B(\mathbf{n})$ should be a nondecreasing function of the n_i.

Human demographers have examined a number of birth or marriage functions. Let n_m and n_f denote the numbers of males and females. Then $B(\mathbf{n})$ can be made proportional to

n_f	(female dominant)
n_m	(male dominant)
$an_m + (1-a)n_f$	(weighted mean)
$(n_m n_f)^{1/2}$	(geometric mean)
$\frac{2n_m n_f}{n_m + n_f}$	(harmonic mean)
$\min(n_m, n_f)$	(minimum)

Each of these functions has been rejected by human demographers (McFarland 1972) for one reason or another, but the harmonic mean is regarded as the least flawed. It produces a maximum number of births when males and females are equally abundant (Figure 10.2; see Caswell and Weeks 1986 for the case of multiple mates). Attempts to distinguish between them based on observed marriage rates have been frustrated by the limited range of sex ratios occurring in human populations (Keyfitz 1972c). I know of no attempts to distinguish them experimentally using other species in the laboratory.

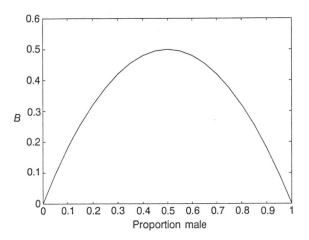

Figure 10.2: The harmonic mean birth function as a function of the relative abundance of males and females.

The per capita fertility functions $F_i(\mathbf{n})$ are derived from the birth function. Consider the life cycle graph of Figure 10.1. By definition,

$$B(\mathbf{n}) = n_3 F_3 + n_5 F_5 \tag{10.4}$$

Assuming that each zygote has exactly one parent of each sex, so that $n_3 F_3 = n_5 F_5$ (and thereby excluding such considerations as haplodiploidy), (10.4) can be rewritten as

$$F_3 = \frac{B(\mathbf{n})}{2n_3} \tag{10.5}$$

$$F_5 = \frac{B(\mathbf{n})}{2n_5} \tag{10.6}$$

For the harmonic mean birth function

$$B(\mathbf{n}) = \frac{2kn_3 n_5}{n_3 + n_5} \tag{10.7}$$

where k is clutch size, the female fertility function is

$$F_5 = \frac{kn_3}{n_3 + n_5} \tag{10.8}$$

(Figure 10.3) with a similar expression for males. The per capita fertility of a female increases hyperbolically with the abundance of males (for fixed n_5), and decreases with the abundance of females (for fixed n_3).

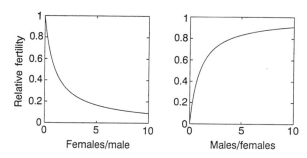

Figure 10.3: Per capita female fertility (F_3 in Figure 10.1) as a function of the relative abundance of males and females.

10.3.3 Frequency and Density Dependence

We can now distinguish frequency and density dependence. The nonlinear map (10.3) is said to be frequency dependent if $\pi(\mathbf{n})$ is homogeneous of degree one. The elements a_{ij} of the corresponding matrix model (10.2) are then homogeneous of degree zero in their arguments, i.e.,

$$a_{ij}(c\mathbf{n}) = a_{ij}(\mathbf{n}) \tag{10.9}$$

for any $c > 0$. The demographic properties of such a population depend only on the relative magnitude of the n_i, and not at all on their absolute magnitude. A matrix not satisfying this condition has at least some degree of density dependence. Requiring $B(\mathbf{n})$ to be homogeneous of degree one guarantees that the $F_i(\mathbf{n})$ are homogeneous of degree zero. Thus models based on the harmonic mean are strictly frequency-dependent. Caswell and Weeks (1986) discuss a nonhomogeneous model which might be generated by social facilitation of mating.

The Equilibrium Adult Sex Ratio

An equilibrium population structure, which automatically implies an equilibrium sex ratio, is given by any vector $\mathbf{w}$ satisfying

$$\mathbf{A}\mathbf{w} = \lambda\mathbf{w} \tag{10.10}$$

for some constant λ, which gives the growth rate of the population at equilibrium.

The zero vector is always a (trivial) solution to (10.10). The existence of a nontrivial solution is guaranteed if the matrix $\mathbf{A}$ is continuous and frequency-dependent, and if $\mathbf{A}$ does not map any nonzero vector directly to zero (Nussbaum 1986, 1988). To see this, define $\mathbf{x} = \mathbf{n}/\sum n_i$ as the vector of proportions in the different stages. Then define the map $\phi(\mathbf{x})$ by

$$\mathbf{x}(t+1) \ = \ \frac{\pi[\mathbf{x}(t)]}{\sum x_i(t)} \tag{10.11}$$

$$= \ \phi[\mathbf{x}(t)] \tag{10.12}$$

Since $\phi()$ is a continuous map from a closed, bounded set into itself, Brouwer's fixed point theorem guarantees the existence of a fixed point $\hat{\mathbf{x}}$ satisfying $\hat{\mathbf{x}} = \phi(\hat{\mathbf{x}})$. The homogeneity of $\pi()$ implies that any vector $\mathbf{w}$ proportional to $\hat{\mathbf{x}}$ satisfies (10.10), and represents an equilibrium population structure.

Any life cycle graph with a self-loop in the last stage within each sex (e.g., Figures 10.1 and 10.4) satisfies this condition, which is certainly more stringent than necessary.

If an equilibrium population structure $\mathbf{w}$ exists, its elements can be written down directly from the life cycle graph. Since $\mathbf{A}$ is homogeneous of degree zero, its variable elements become constant along the trajectory $\mathbf{n}(t+1) = \lambda \mathbf{n}(t)$, (10.10) reduces to a standard eigenvalue problem, and $\mathbf{w}$ is the right eigenvector of $\mathbf{A}$. Thus the population structure corresponding to the life cycle of Figure 10.1 is

$$\begin{aligned}
w_1 &= 1 \\
w_2 &= \rho\lambda^{-1} \\
w_3 &= \rho\frac{P_2\lambda^{-\alpha}}{\lambda - P_3} \\
w_4 &= (1-\rho)\lambda^{-1} \\
w_5 &= (1-\rho)\frac{P_4\lambda^{-\beta}}{\lambda - P_5}
\end{aligned} \tag{10.13}$$

The growth rate at equilibrium (λ) appears in $\mathbf{w}$ as a parameter; it is obtained from the characteristic equation

$$1 = \rho\frac{P_2F_3\lambda^{-(\alpha+1)}}{\lambda - P_3} + (1-\rho)\frac{P_4F_5\lambda^{-(\beta+1)}}{\lambda - P_5} \tag{10.14}$$

Since F_3 and F_5 are at equilibrium themselves functions of $\mathbf{w}$, (10.13) and (10.14) must be solved simultaneously to obtain λ and $\mathbf{w}$.

The equilibrium adult sex ratio $R = (n_3/n_5)$ is given by

$$R = \left(\frac{\rho}{1-\rho}\right)\left(\frac{P_2}{P_4}\right)\left(\frac{\lambda^{\beta-\alpha}(\lambda - P_5)}{\lambda - P_3}\right) \tag{10.15}$$

from which we see that the equilibrium sex ratio favors the sex with the higher juvenile survival, the shorter maturation time, and the higher adult survival. The maturation time effect is amplified by population growth rate; if $\lambda = 1$ it disappears, if $\lambda < 1$ it is reversed. The nonlinearity introduced by the fertility functions affects R only through the value of λ. Meagher (1981, 1982, Meagher and Antonovics 1982a,b) derives a similar formula, but makes the mistake of making the elements of the projection matrix functions of λ.

The reproductive values of each stage can also be written down directly from Figure 10.1

$$
\begin{aligned}
v_1 &= 1 \\
v_2 &= \frac{P_2 F_3 \lambda^{-\alpha}}{\lambda - P_3} \\
v_3 &= \frac{F_3}{\lambda - P_3} \\
v_4 &= \frac{P_4 F_5 \lambda^{-\beta}}{\lambda - P_5} \\
v_5 &= \frac{F_5}{\lambda - P_5}
\end{aligned}
\tag{10.16}
$$

The nonlinear fertility functions appear explicitly in $\mathbf{v}$, so that reproductive value depends directly on population composition through the F_i, as well as indirectly through λ. The reproductive value formulas can be used for sensitivity analysis of the population growth rate at equilibrium.

10.3.4 Stability of the Equilibrium Sex Ratio

When will a population with some other composition converge to an equilibrium structure $\mathbf{w}$? A number of two-sex models without age structure have been shown to be stable (e.g., Samuelson 1976, Yellin and Samuelson 1977, Schoen 1984, Pollard 1973, Keyfitz 1968), with the exception of some declining populations (Yellin and Samuelson 1977). Similar claims of stability have been made (Das Gupta 1972, Mitra 1978) for age-classified models that, at equilibrium, reduce to the classical renewal equation of the one-sex case. Those results, however, rely on the constancy of fertilities at equilibrium to eliminate the effects of the nonlinearity in the birth function. In fact, the characteristic equation of any frequency-dependent model reduces at equilibrium to the same form as that of a one-sex model, but this says nothing about convergence from initial conditions that do not lie on the equilibrium solution.

In this section, I present a theorem which gives sufficient conditions for the local stability of the equilibrium population structure. I have purposely phrased it so that it is not restricted to the life cycle shown in Figure 10.1. In fact, it applies to a very wide class of frequency-dependent population processes. Nussbaum (1986, 1988) provides a global stability analysis for a related class of models.

I assume that the elements a_{ij} of the matrix $\mathbf{A}$ are derived from generalized means of the elements of $\mathbf{n}$. Consider a set of variables x_i and a set of nonnegative weights p_i satisfying $\sum p_i = 1$. A generalized mean (Hardy et al. 1952) of the x_i is

$$M_r(x) = \left(\sum_i p_i x_i^r \right)^{1/r} \tag{10.17}$$

When $r = 1$, M_r is the arithmetic mean; $r = 0$ gives the geometric mean, and $r = -1$ the harmonic mean. The $\lim_{r \to \infty} M_r$ is the maximum and $\lim_{r \to -\infty} M_r$ the minimum of the x_i. This formulation is thus general enough to accommodate all of the commonly used birth functions.

I assume that each element of $\mathbf{A}$ is derived from a generalized mean of the entries of $\mathbf{n}$:

$$a_{ij} = \frac{k_{ij} M_{ij}(\mathbf{n})}{n_j} \tag{10.18}$$

where k_{ij} is a constant and M_{ij} is a mean, which may differ from one element of $\mathbf{A}$ to another. A constant a_{ij} follows from letting $M_{ij}(\mathbf{n}) = n_j$ in which case $a_{ij} = k_{ij}$. Our results also hold if the a_{ij} are derived from means of nonnegative linear combinations of the entries of $\mathbf{n}$. Caswell and Weeks (1986) used this to describe the effects of harem size when males mate with multiple females.

I will also assume that $\partial M_{ij}(\mathbf{n})/\partial n_j > 0$. That is, the mean involved in calculating the transition from n_j to n_i has some dependence on the abundance of the "source" stage. This assumption is stronger than necessary, as will be discussed below.

Equation (10.18) should be compared to the calculation of the fertility functions (10.5) and (10.6) from the birth function.

Since any mean is homogeneous of degree one, the a_{ij} defined by (10.18) are homogeneous of degree zero, and the system is frequency-dependent.

Theorem 10.1 *If the matrix $\mathbf{A}$ is defined by (10.18), with $\partial M_{ij}(\mathbf{n})/\partial n_j > 0$, and is primitive when evaluated along $\mathbf{n} = \mathbf{w}$, then any initial population near the stable population structure $\mathbf{w}$ converges to $\mathbf{w}$, and thus the sex ratio is locally asymptotically stable.*

The proof of this theorem relies on a generalization of the usual local stability analysis of nonlinear matrix models. Since the equilibrium population is not a constant solution of (10.2), we cannot directly apply the usual local stability analysis for equilibrium points of discrete nonlinear systems (Section 9.2.2). Instead, we combine the local stability analysis with the approach of Section 8.3.1 to convergence of population structure in variable environments.

Choose a reference solution $\mathbf{n}_s(t)$ to the nonlinear map

$$\mathbf{n}(t+1) = \pi[\mathbf{n}(t)] \tag{10.19}$$

and consider the nature of solutions that start near $\mathbf{n}_s$. (We are interested in reference solutions along which population structure is at equilibrium, so that $\mathbf{n}_s$ will be proportional to $\mathbf{w}$.)

Define the deviation $\boldsymbol{\delta}(t) = \mathbf{n}(t) - \mathbf{n}_s(t)$. The dynamics of this deviation are given by

$$
\begin{aligned}
\boldsymbol{\delta}(t+1) &= \mathbf{n}(t+1) - \mathbf{n}_s(t+1) \tag{10.20} \\
&= \pi[\boldsymbol{\delta}(t) + \mathbf{n}_s(t)] - \pi[\mathbf{n}_s(t)] \tag{10.21}
\end{aligned}
$$

Expanding $\pi()$ in a Taylor series about $\mathbf{n}_s$ and neglecting second-order terms gives a linear approximation for $\boldsymbol{\delta}$:

$$\boldsymbol{\delta}(t+1) = \left(\frac{\partial \pi}{\partial \mathbf{n}}\right)\boldsymbol{\delta}(t) \tag{10.22}$$

where the partial derivatives are evaluated along the reference solution $\mathbf{n}_s$.

In our case, the ith component of π is

$$\pi_i = \sum_k a_{ik} n_k \tag{10.23}$$

so

$$\frac{\partial \pi_i}{\partial n_j} = a_{ij} + \sum_k n_k \frac{\partial a_{ik}}{\partial n_j} \tag{10.24}$$

with both a_{ij} and the latter partial derivative being evaluated along $\mathbf{n}_s(t)$.

The resulting approximation for the deviation from the reference solution is

$$
\begin{aligned}
\boldsymbol{\delta}(t+1) &= [\mathbf{A}(t) + \mathbf{Q}(t)]\boldsymbol{\delta}(t) \tag{10.25} \\
&= \mathbf{B}(t)\boldsymbol{\delta}(t) \tag{10.26}
\end{aligned}
$$

where

$$q_{ij} = \sum_k n_k \frac{\partial a_{ik}}{\partial n_j} \tag{10.27}$$

If $\boldsymbol{\delta}(t)$ goes to zero, then the solution $\mathbf{n}(t)$ certainly converges to the reference solution. However, this convergence is stronger than necessary for convergence of population structure, which requires only that $\mathbf{n}(t)$ become proportional to $\mathbf{n}_s(t)$. An appropriate measure of the difference between the two solutions is thus the Hilbert projective metric (8.3.1).

Birkhoff's theorem (Section 8.3.1) states that multiplication by any positive (or nonnegative and primitive) matrix $\mathbf{D}$ is a strict contraction in terms of the projective metric. When $\mathbf{n}(t)$ is proportional to $\mathbf{n}_s(t)$, $d[\boldsymbol{\delta}(t), \mathbf{n}_s(t)] = 0$, so our proof of stability will apply Birkhoff's theorem to the projective distance between $\boldsymbol{\delta}$ and $\mathbf{n}_s$. We will assume that $\boldsymbol{\delta}(0)$ is positive, so that the projective metric can be calculated. We can always modify $n_s(0)$ to make it so, since the magnitude of the initial population along the reference vector $\mathbf{w}$ is arbitrary.

The applicability of Birkhoff's theorem depends on the nature of $\mathbf{B}(t)$. Since $\mathbf{A}$ is homogeneous of degree zero, it is constant along the reference solution. Since the derivative of a homogeneous function of degree zero is homogeneous of degree -1, the products $n_k \partial a_{ik}/\partial n_j$ that make up the elements of $\mathbf{Q}$ are also constant along $\mathbf{n}_s$. Thus $\mathbf{B} = \mathbf{A} + \mathbf{Q}$ is constant.

Consider $\mathbf{Bw} = \mathbf{Aw} + \mathbf{Qw}$. We know that $\mathbf{Aw} = \lambda \mathbf{w}$. Let $\mathbf{Qw} = \mathbf{g}$. Then

$$g_i = \sum_h \sum_k n_k w_h \left(\frac{\partial a_{ik}}{\partial n_h} \right) \tag{10.28}$$

Since $\mathbf{n}_s$ is proportional to $\mathbf{w}$, g_i is proportional to

$$\sum_k n_k \sum_h n_h \left(\frac{\partial a_{ik}}{\partial n_h} \right) \tag{10.29}$$

which, by Euler's theorem on homogeneous functions, equals zero. Thus $\mathbf{Bw} = \mathbf{Aw} + \mathbf{0}$, and both the deviation vector $\boldsymbol{\delta}$ and the reference solution vector $\mathbf{n}_s$ are being multiplied by the same matrix.

Since $\boldsymbol{\delta}(t)$ and $\mathbf{n}_s(t)$ are both multiplied by the same matrix $\mathbf{B}$, Birkhoff's theorem guarantees that the projective distance $d[\boldsymbol{\delta}(t), \mathbf{n}_s(t)]$ between them is strictly decreasing if $\mathbf{B}$ is nonnegative and primitive.

$\mathbf{A}$ is nonnegative and assumed to be primitive. Since $b_{ij} = a_{ij} + q_{ij}$, a sufficient (but stronger than necessary) condition for nonnegativity and primitivity of $\mathbf{B}$ is that $a_{ij} + q_{ij} > 0$.

Write q_{ij} as

$$q_{ij} = n_j \frac{\partial a_{ij}}{\partial n_j} + \sum_{k \neq j} n_k \frac{\partial a_{ik}}{\partial n_j} \tag{10.30}$$

$$= k_{ij} \frac{\partial M_{ij}(X_{ij})}{\partial n_j} - a_{ij} + \sum_{k \neq j} n_k \frac{\partial a_{ik}}{\partial n_j} \tag{10.31}$$

Thus $a_{ij} + q_{ij}$ is clearly nonnegative, and is strictly positive if, as we have assumed, $\partial M_{ij}(\mathbf{n})/\partial n_j > 0$. This completes the proof.

Note that the conditions of the theorem are sufficient but not necessary. In particular, if $\partial M_{ij}(\mathbf{n}) = 0$ for some (i,j), then $b_{ij} = 0$. This causes problems for the theorem only because it may render $\mathbf{B}$ imprimitive. If it does not do so (and this may be evaluated in specific cases by inspection of the life cycle graph) then the theorem still holds.

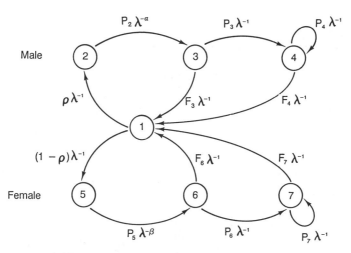

Figure 10.4: A life cycle graph incorporating two reproductive classes of males and females. The parameters are obvious extensions of those in Figure 10.1. From Caswell and Weeks (1986); ©University of Chicago.

The theorem also extends to cases in which a_{ij} is a positive linear combination of means. In this case, q_{ij} becomes a sum of terms, each of which is given by (10.31), and the nonnegativity results apply to each term individually.

10.4 Interstage Mate Competition

As general as the assumptions of Theorem 10.1 may be, one undeniably important factor is excluded from (10.18): interstage mate competition. According to (10.18), a_{ij} is negatively correlated with the abundance of only one stage (n_j). Thus the per capita production of stage i by stage j is reduced by competition *within* stage j, but not among different stages. Competition between males of different ages for access to females, or vice versa, is not included. Human demographers have criticized birth functions that leave out competition (Parlett 1972, McFarland 1972, Pollard 1977), because the rate of marriage between males and females of given ages depends not only on the relative abundance of those age groups, but on the abundance of other age groups as well. Interstage mate competition is probably even more important in many nonhuman species. Including it can dramatically alter the stability properties of the model.

To incorporate mate competition, the life cycle of Figure 10.1 must be modified to include two reproductive age classes of males and females (Figure 10.4). The fertility functions $F_i()$ must now incorporate the contributions of all possible combinations of male and female stages. Following Frederickson (1971), Das Gupta (1972, 1978), Parlett (1972), and Schoen (1981), we write the births $B(\mathbf{n})$ as a sum of the contributions of matings classified by male and female age:

$$B(\mathbf{n}) = \sum_i \sum_j B_{ij}(\mathbf{n}) \tag{10.32}$$

where i is the stage of the father and j the stage of the mother. The per capita fertility of a male of age x is then given by

$$F_x = \frac{1}{n_x} \left(\sum_j B_{xj}(\mathbf{n}) \right) \tag{10.33}$$

and that of a female of age y by

$$F_y = \frac{1}{n_y} \left(\sum_i B_{iy}(\mathbf{n}) \right) \tag{10.34}$$

If the birth functions in (10.33) and (10.34) have the form (10.18), the equilibrium sex ratio is still locally stable.

Interstage mate competition can be added by replacing (10.18) by

$$a_{ij} = \frac{\sum_h M_{ijh}(\mathbf{n})}{n_j + C_{ij}} \tag{10.35}$$

where h ranges over some set that produces a sum of birth contribution terms like those in (10.32). C_{ij} is a competition term. Define c_k as a measure of the competitive effect of n_k on n_j. Then

$$C_{ij} = \sum_k c_k n_k \tag{10.36}$$

Under these assumptions, $\mathbf{A}$ is still frequency-dependent. The difference between (10.35) and (10.18) is simply that per capita fertility of stage j is now reduced not only by its own abundance, but also by the abundance of all the other stages appearing in the competition term (10.36). This is a purely phenomenological description of the effects of interstage competition, with some analogies to competitive inhibition in models of enzyme kinetics. Pollard (1977) proposed a special case of (10.35) as a model for marriage competition without analyzing its dynamics.

The stability proof fails in the presence of interstage mate competition (Caswell and Weeks 1986). In the next section, I present numerical results showing that competition can actually destabilize the equilibrium population structure, and examine some of the resulting bifurcation patterns.

10.4.1 Numerical Results: Competition and Instability

The following numerical results use the life cycle in Figure 10.4, with fertilities given by

$$F_3 = \frac{k_{36}M(n_3, n_6) + k_{37}M(n_3, n_7)}{n_3 + Dn_4} \tag{10.37}$$

$$F_4 = \frac{k_{46}M(n_4, n_6) + k_{47}M(n_4, n_7)}{n_4 + Dn_3} \tag{10.38}$$

$$F_6 = \frac{k_{36}M(n_3, n_6) + k_{46}M(n_4, n_6)}{n_6 + Dn_7} \tag{10.39}$$

$$F_7 = \frac{k_{37}M(n_3, n_7) + k_{47}M(n_4, n_7)}{n_7 + Dn_6} \tag{10.40}$$

where the clutch size produced by a mating between a male of stage i and a female of stage j is $2k_{ij}$, $M()$ denotes the harmonic mean, and D is a competition coefficient. For simplicity, this competition was assumed to be symmetrical; this will certainly not be true in general.

For purposes of these simulations, males and females were assigned age-independent survival probabilities P_m and P_f. In terms of these probabilities, the coefficients in Figure 10.4 are $P_3 = P_4 = P_m$, $P_2 = P_m^\alpha$, $P_6 = P_7 = P_f$, and $P_5 = P_f^\beta$.

When $D = 0$, Theorem 1 applies and the equilibrium population structure is stable. Figure 10.5 shows the results of increasing D when the male and female development times (α and β) are identical; the adult sex ratio $(n_3 + n_4)/(n_6 + n_7)$ is plotted.

Between $D = 1.8$ and $D = 2.5$ the solution bifurcates to a stable oscillation of period 5. The amplitude, but not the period, of these oscillations increases with further increases in D. Between $D = 45.92$ and $D = 45.93$ the periodic solution becomes unstable and the system again converges to a stable equilibrium. Further increases in D do not seem to produce additional bifurcations.

More complex bifurcation patterns occur when males and females differ in development time as well as survival. Figure 10.6 shows some results when $\alpha = 2$, $\beta = 3$, $P_m = 0.5$, $P_f = 0.3$. At $D = 0.1$ the population still converges to a stable equilibrium (Figure 10.6A). Figure 10.6B shows a phase portrait, projecting the trajectory on a two-dimensional slice through the state space by plotting the proportion of adult males ($x_3 + x_4$) against the proportion of adult females ($x_6 + x_7$) in the population. (These proportions do not sum to 1 because there are other classes in the population.) The transient points shown in Figure 10.6B spiral in to the equilibrium sex ratio.

Between $D = 0.1$ and $D = 0.5$ a bifurcation to a quasiperiodic trajectory occurs (Figure 10.6C). The phase portrait of this trajectory (Figure 10.6D) is a continuous curve. Such quasiperiodic trajectories result from

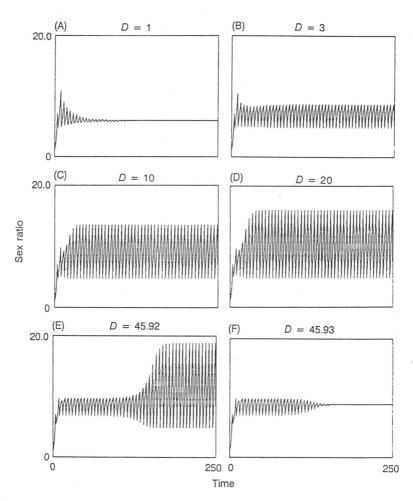

Figure 10.5: Bifurcation of the stable sex ratio as the interstage mate competition intensity D increases. The life cycle graph is as in Figure 10.4, with $\alpha = \beta = 3$, $P_m = 0.5$, $P_f = 0.3$, and $k_{ij} = 100$. From Caswell and Weeks (1986); ©University of Chicago.

the presence of two incommensurate frequencies in the solution. As D increases these frequencies converge, producing a decrease in the modulation frequency (Figure 10.6E) until, between $D = 6$ and $D = 7$ "phase locking" occurs, producing a stable period-5 solution (Figure 10.6F) of large amplitude.

The amplitude of this oscillation increases between $D = 7$ and $D = 360$. Between $D = 360$ and $D = 370$ another bifurcation occurs, producing another quasiperiodic solution (Figure 10.6G), with a more complex phase portrait (Figure 10.6H), which persists until $D \approx 6000$. At this point, an apparently chaotic solution emerges (Figure 10.6I), the attractor for which is not a closed curve (Figure 10.6J). Eventually ($D = 22,000$, Figure 10.6K–L) another quasiperiodic solution emerges. Again the modulation frequency decreases (Figure 10.6M) until phase locking occurs between $D = 25,000$ and $D = 26,000$ (Figure 10.6N) and a period-7 solution appears. This periodic solution remains stable until $D \approx 300,000$, at which point a complex, apparently quasiperiodic solution emerges (Figure 10.6O). The phase portrait for this solution (Figure 10.6P) does not appear to be a simple closed curve. It may be a very high period solution since the gaps between the points in Figure 10.6P are filled in very slowly if at all.

This entire range of parameter values is certainly not biologically relevant; these results are presented to show some of the possible patterns of behavior of two-sex models with mate competition.

The conclusions of these analyses are, first, that the assumptions that justify one-sex demographic models are unlikely to be universally satisfied, and, second, that the dynamics of two-sex models can be much more complicated than those of one-sex models. Interstage competition for mates can destabilize the equilibrium sex ratio may be unstable, leading to periodic, quasiperiodic, and chaotic behaviors.

The instability of population structure may have implications for studies of the evolutionary stability of the primary sex ratio using ESS methods, which assume the existence of an equilibrium background against which potential invading strategies may be evaluated. Selection on the primary sex ratio when there is no such equilibrium adult sex ratio is an unsolved question (cf. Auslander et al. 1978 for corresponding problems in a density-dependent model). Density-dependent nonlinearities are also known to produce bifurcations leading eventually to chaos. It is not clear how density-dependence and frequency dependence will interact.

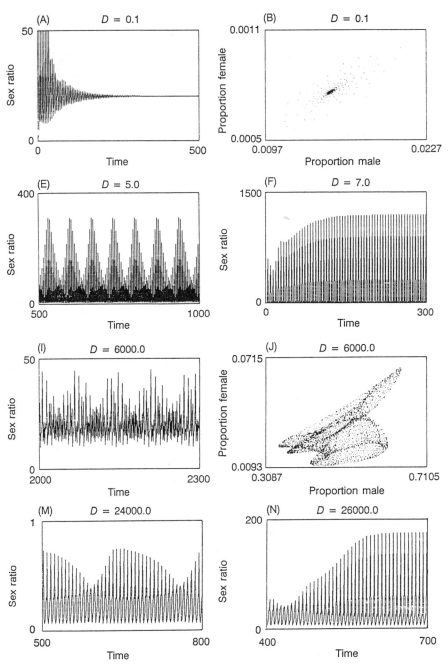

Figure 10.6: A study of the bifurcation of the equilibrium adult sex ratio as the interstage mate competition intensity D increases. The life cycle graph is as in Figure 10.4, with $\alpha = 2$, $\beta = 3$, $P_m = 0.5$, $P_f = 0.3$, $k_{46} = k_{47} = 1000$, and $k_{36} = k_{37} = 10$. Parameter values: (A): $D = 0.1$; (B): phase portrait for $D = 0.1$; (C): D=0.5; (D): phase portrait for $D = 0.5$; (E): $D = 5$; (F): $D = 7$;

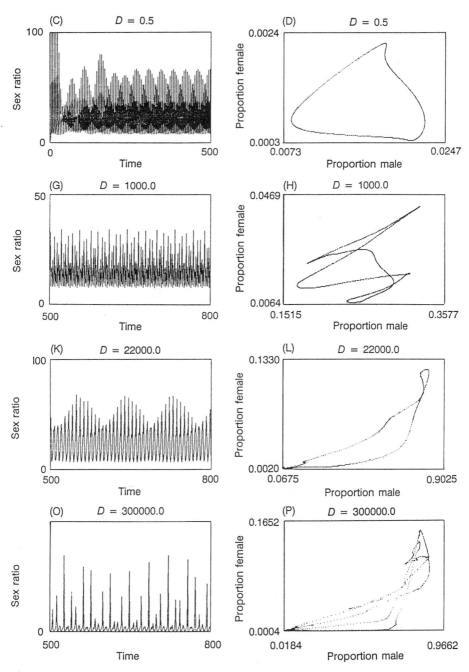

Figure 10.6: (G): $D = 1000$; (H): phase portrait for $D = 1000$; (I): $D = 6000$; (J): phase portrait for $D = 6000$; (K): $D = 22,000$; (L): phase portrait for $D = 22,000$; (M): $D = 24,000$; (N): $D = 26,000$; (O): $D = 300,000$; (P): phase portrait for $D = 300,000$. From Caswell and Weeks (1986; ©University of Chicago).

Appendix A

The Basics
of Matrix Algebra

The algebra of matrices and vectors follows a set of simple and consistent rules, obscure though they may seem at first. This appendix summarizes those aspects of matrix theory needed for matrix population models. The style is telegraphic, the coverage purposely selective, and the goal is to make it all reasonable.

A.1 Motivation

We begin with something you certainly understand: one equation in one unknown:

$$3x = 6$$

You know how to solve this (multiplying both sides by 3^{-1}) to obtain $x = 2$. Now consider two equations in two unknowns:

$$3x_1 + x_2 = 10$$
$$2x_1 - x_2 = 0$$

Given a minute, you could probably solve this by eliminating variables, obtaining $x_1 = 2$, $x_2 = 4$.

The next logical step is three equations in three unknowns

$$4x_1 + 3x_2 + 2x_3 = 0$$
$$2x_1 - 2x_2 + 5x_3 = 6 \qquad (A.1)$$
$$x_1 - x_2 - 3x_3 = 1$$

Solving systems of equations becomes more complex in practice, but not in principle, as the number of unknowns increases. Not only that, but the *labor* of writing down the equations is increasing. The set (A.1) required 9 x's, 6 plus or minus signs, and 3 equals signs, along with 12 coefficients. 10 equations in 10 unknowns would require 100 x's. However, it could be written without any loss of information as

$$\begin{pmatrix} 4 & 3 & 2 \\ 2 & -2 & 5 \\ 1 & -1 & -3 \end{pmatrix} \begin{pmatrix} x_1 \\ x_2 \\ x_3 \end{pmatrix} = \begin{pmatrix} 0 \\ 6 \\ 1 \end{pmatrix} \tag{A.2}$$

if an agreement could be made strictly defining the order of the variables and the positions of the coefficients. After all, what is needed is the names of the unknowns, the coefficients corresponding to each unknown in each equation, and the right-hand side of each equation. Equation (A.2) can be translated unambiguously to (A.1) *if* we have consistently arranged the unknowns in the same order in each equation, *if* that order is given by the order of the unknowns in the vertical column in (A.2), and *if* the order of the equations on the left-hand side of (A.1) corresponds to the order of the column on the right-hand side of (A.2).

Equation (A.2) is, however, more than a convenient way to write (A.1). It looks very much like some strange sort of multiplication might be going on: "multiply" the square array of numbers times the vertical array of unknowns and "get" the vertical array on the right-hand side. If you can look at (A.2) and see this analogy, congratulations. You have just invented matrix algebra.

Of course, your invention has its consequences. As soon as you give names to those arrays, they take on a life of their own; the "multiplication" process follows certain rules, and other strange and useful properties you haven't guessed at spring into existence. I am about to outline some of them. However, it is important to remember (especially if you are trying to learn this material for the first time) that *the rules of matrix algebra have only one purpose: to ensure that (A.2) is an accurate translation of (A.1)* .

A.2 Definitions

- A *matrix* is a rectangular array of symbols (numbers, variables, functions, etc.).

- The *dimensions* of a matrix are the number of its rows and columns. A matrix with m rows and n columns is of dimension $(m \times n)$.

- A *column vector* is an $(m \times 1)$ matrix. A *row vector* is a $(1 \times n)$ matrix.

- A *scalar* is an ordinary number, or, if you will, a (1×1) matrix.

A.3   Operations

Equation (A.2) seems to imply some operations on matrices and vectors, and the identification of (A.2) as a translation of (A.1) implies that these operations must correspond to operations on systems of equations.

A.3.1   Addition

To add equations, one adds the coefficients corresponding to the same unknowns. To add two matrices, one adds the corresponding elements.

$$\begin{pmatrix} a_{11} & a_{12} \\ a_{21} & a_{22} \end{pmatrix} + \begin{pmatrix} b_{11} & b_{12} \\ b_{21} & b_{22} \end{pmatrix} = \begin{pmatrix} a_{11} + b_{11} & a_{12} + b_{12} \\ a_{21} + b_{21} & a_{22} + b_{22} \end{pmatrix}$$

From this definition, it is obvious that $A + B$ is defined only if A and B are of the same dimension, and that, if they are defined, $A + B = B + A$.

A.3.2   Scalar Multiplication

When an equation is multiplied by a scalar, that scalar multiplies each coefficient. To multiply a matrix by a scalar, multiply each entry in the matrix by the scalar:

$$2 \begin{pmatrix} a & b \\ c & d \end{pmatrix} = \begin{pmatrix} 2a & 2b \\ 2c & 2d \end{pmatrix}$$

A.3.3   The Transpose and the Adjoint

The *transpose* of A, denoted by A', is obtained by switching the rows and columns:

$$\begin{pmatrix} 1 & 2 & 3 \\ 4 & 5 & 6 \end{pmatrix}' = \begin{pmatrix} 1 & 4 \\ 2 & 5 \\ 3 & 6 \end{pmatrix}$$

The transpose of a column vector is a row vector, and vice versa.

The *adjoint* (sometimes the Hermetian adjoint) of a matrix is the complex conjugate of the transpose, and is denoted by A^*. If A is real, $A^* = A'$, but this is not true if A is complex[1]:

$$\begin{pmatrix} 3 + 4i & 2 - 6i \end{pmatrix}^* = \begin{pmatrix} 3 - 4i \\ 2 + 6i \end{pmatrix} \tag{A.3}$$

A matrix is said to be *symmetric* if $A' = A$ and *skew-symmetric* if $A' = -A$, *Hermetian* if $A^* = A$, and *skew-Hermetian* if $A^* = -A$.

---

[1]We will have little occasion to consider complex vectors in this book, but they do arise as eigenvectors of projection matrices.

A.3.4 Scalar Product

The scalar product of two vectors is different from multiplication of a vector by a scalar. It is an operation on two vectors (of the same dimension) that produces a scalar result. It is defined by

$$\langle \mathbf{x}, \mathbf{y} \rangle = \mathbf{x}^* \mathbf{y} \tag{A.4}$$

If both $\mathbf{x}$ and $\mathbf{y}$ are real, then the scalar product is simply the sum of the products of the corresponding entries in the two vectors:

$$\langle \mathbf{x}, \mathbf{y} \rangle = x_1 y_1 + x_2 y_2 + \cdots + x_n y_n$$

Some properties of the scalar product:

$$\langle \mathbf{x}, \mathbf{y} \rangle = \overline{\langle \mathbf{y}, \mathbf{x} \rangle} \tag{A.5}$$
$$\langle c\mathbf{x}, \mathbf{y} \rangle = \bar{c} \langle \mathbf{x}, \mathbf{y} \rangle \tag{A.6}$$

A.3.5 Matrix Multiplication

Addition and transposition of matrices are quite natural operations, and even the scalar product seems pretty reasonable. Matrix multiplication usually causes the novice more difficulty. Remember that it is defined so that (A.1) and (A.2) are equivalent systems of equations. If you forget the rules, you can easily rederive them by writing out an example like that.

Multiplying a Vector by a Matrix

The equation

$$\begin{pmatrix} 1 & 2 \\ 3 & 4 \end{pmatrix} \begin{pmatrix} x_1 \\ x_2 \end{pmatrix} = \begin{pmatrix} 5 \\ 6 \end{pmatrix}$$

must be equivalent to

$$
\begin{aligned}
x_1 + 2x_2 &= 5 \\
3x_1 + 4x_2 &= 6
\end{aligned}
$$

Thus, the rule for multiplication must be (at least for 2×2 matrices, and in fact for matrices of any dimension)

$$\begin{pmatrix} a_{11} & a_{12} \\ a_{21} & a_{22} \end{pmatrix} \begin{pmatrix} x_1 \\ x_2 \end{pmatrix} = \begin{pmatrix} a_{11}x_1 + a_{12}x_2 \\ a_{21}x_1 + a_{22}x_2 \end{pmatrix}$$

An alternative expression for real matrices is, if $\mathbf{Ax} = \mathbf{b}$, then

$$
\begin{aligned}
b_1 &= \text{ scalar product of } \mathbf{x} \text{ and the first row of } \mathbf{A} \\
b_2 &= \text{ scalar product of } \mathbf{x} \text{ and the second row of } \mathbf{A} \\
&\vdots \\
b_n &= \text{ scalar product of } \mathbf{x} \text{ and the } n\text{th row of } \mathbf{A}
\end{aligned}
$$

To multiply $\mathbf{Ax}$, the number of rows of $\mathbf{x}$ must equal the number of columns of $\mathbf{A}$. In terms of equations, to be writing $\mathbf{Ax}$ as a shorthand for a system of equations, the number of coefficients in each equation must equal the number of unknowns.

Note that $\mathbf{Ax} \neq \mathbf{xA}$. In fact, $\mathbf{xA}$ is not even defined (the dimensions are wrong).

Multiplying Two Matrices

The product $\mathbf{AB}$ of two matrices $\mathbf{A}$ and $\mathbf{B}$ is obtained by treating each column of $\mathbf{B}$ as a column vector being multiplied by $\mathbf{A}$, and writing the resulting vectors side-by-side to form the product. Thus if

$$
\mathbf{A} = \left(\begin{array}{cc} a_{11} & a_{12} \\ a_{21} & a_{22} \end{array} \right)
$$

and

$$
\mathbf{B} = \left(\begin{array}{cc} b_{11} & b_{12} \\ b_{21} & b_{22} \end{array} \right)
$$

then

$$
\mathbf{AB} = \left(\begin{array}{cc} a_{11}b_{11} + a_{12}b_{21} & a_{11}b_{12} + a_{12}b_{22} \\ a_{21}b_{11} + a_{22}b_{21} & a_{21}b_{12} + a_{22}b_{22} \end{array} \right) \tag{A.7}
$$

To put it another way, suppose we let $a_i.$ denote the ith row of $\mathbf{A}$ and $b_{.j}$ the jth column of $\mathbf{B}$. Then, if we let $\mathbf{AB} = \mathbf{C}$,

$$
c_{ij} = \langle a_{i.}, b_{.j} \rangle \tag{A.8}
$$

The two matrices need not have the same dimension to be multiplied, but each column of $\mathbf{B}$ must be a vector of the appropriate size to be multiplied by $\mathbf{A}$. That is, the number of rows of $\mathbf{B}$ must equal the number of columns of $\mathbf{A}$.

In general, $\mathbf{AB} \neq \mathbf{BA}$, even if both products are defined (i.e., even if both matrices are square and of the same dimension). This is an important distinction between matrix and scalar multiplication.

A.4 Matrix Inversion

A.4.1 The Identity Matrix

A slight digression before getting to inversion. The *identity matrix* is a special square matrix with ones on the diagonal and zeros elsewhere, e.g.,

$$I = \begin{pmatrix} 1 & 0 & 0 \\ 0 & 1 & 0 \\ 0 & 0 & 1 \end{pmatrix}$$

It behaves like the number 1 in scalar arithmetic:

$$IA = AI = A$$
$$Ix = x$$

for any nonzero matrix A and vector x of the correct size to multiply.

A.4.2 Inversion and the Solution of Algebraic Equations

It is easy to solve one equation in one unknown

$$ax = b$$

by multiplying both sides by a^{-1}:

$$x = a^{-1}b$$

Solving n equations in n unknowns is harder, but perhaps it is possible to take advantage of their representation in matrix form. (Of course, it is or I wouldn't have mentioned it.) If

$$Ax = b$$

is it possible to find an inverse of the matrix A, call it A^{-1}, with the property that

$$x = A^{-1}b?$$

What we need is a matrix A^{-1} that satisfies $A^{-1}A = I$.

Such an inverse matrix can sometimes be found. You can find formulas in any matrix algebra text, and algorithms for carrying out the calculations in any numerical analysis text. You don't want to see them here. In practice, routines for matrix inversion are now widely available on both mainframe and microcomputers. It is, however, sometimes useful to be able to write down the inverse of a 2×2 matrix:

$$\begin{pmatrix} a & b \\ c & d \end{pmatrix}^{-1} = \frac{1}{(ad - bc)} \begin{pmatrix} d & -b \\ -c & a \end{pmatrix} \tag{A.9}$$

That is, you interchange the diagonal elements, change the signs of the off-diagonal elements, and divide the whole thing by $(ad - bc)$.

Which brings us naturally enough to the question of whether a matrix can always be inverted. Can every system of equations be solved? No. In the first place, if there are not the same number of equations as unknowns, the equations cannot be solved. Thus, nonsquare matrices cannot be inverted. However, not even all square matrices can be inverted. Those that cannot be are called *singular*; those that can be are called *nonsingular*. A 2×2 matrix is singular if and only if $ad - bc = 0$, in which case the formula above obviously won't work.

A.4.3 A Useful Fact about Homogeneous Systems

If its matrix is nonsingular, a homogeneous system of equations (i.e., one whose right-hand side is all zeros: $\mathbf{Ax} = \mathbf{0}$) has only one solution:

$$\mathbf{x} = \mathbf{A}^{-1}\mathbf{0} = \mathbf{0} \tag{A.10}$$

We'll use this later.

A.5 Determinants

The singularity or nonsingularity of a matrix is revealed by its determinant. The *determinant* is a scalar function of a square matrix, denoted by $\det(\mathbf{A})$ or $|\mathbf{A}|$, with the property that $\mathbf{A}$ is singular if and only if $|\mathbf{A}| = 0$.

Calculation of determinants, like inverses, rapidly becomes complex for large matrices, and is best left to machines. The formula for a 2×2 matrix is simple, though:

$$\det \begin{pmatrix} a & b \\ c & d \end{pmatrix} = ad - bc \tag{A.11}$$

Note that in (A.9) each element of the inverse is divided by $|\mathbf{A}|$; this can be done only if $|\mathbf{A}| \neq 0$.

What is the determinant, anyway? Consider the 2×2 matrix in (A.11), and consider the two rows as vectors (the same result would follow from taking the columns). Plot them in two dimensions (Figure A.1) and form the parallelogram defined by the two vectors. The area of this parallelogram is $\pm(ad - bc)$. In other words, the determinant of the matrix is (give or take a sign) the area of the parallelogram defined by its rows.

In higher dimensions, the determinant is (give or take a sign) the hyper-volume of the hyper-parallelogram formed in n-dimensional space by the n rows of the matrix.

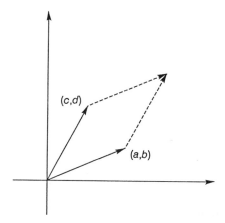

Figure A.1: The columns of the matrix in (A.11) plotted as vectors in the plane. The area of the parallelogram defined by the vectors is the determinant of the matrix.

Now consider two equations such as

$$2x_1 + x_2 = 2$$
$$4x_1 + 2x_2 = 4$$

These cannot be solved (try if you like) because the second equation is just a multiple of the first. This system is really just two copies of a single equation. Since there are two unknowns, the equation has an infinite number of solutions. In larger systems the same thing can happen and be much less obvious.

If we write these equations in matrix form and plot the rows as vectors, they are multiples of each other and the area of the defined parallelogram (and thus the determinant) is zero. Thus the determinant detects dependencies among the equations that a matrix represents. When the determinant is zero, the number of equations is not equal to the number of unknowns, and the equations have no unique solution.

A.5.1 Properties of Determinants

1. The determinant of the product of two matrices is the product of the determinants:

$$\det(\mathbf{AB}) = \det(\mathbf{A})\det(\mathbf{B})$$

2. The determinant of the inverse is the reciprocal of the determinant:

$$\det(\mathbf{A}^{-1}) = \frac{1}{\det(\mathbf{A})}$$

A.6   Eigenvalues and Eigenvectors

The eigenvalues (sometimes referred to as "latent roots" or "characteristic values") of a square matrix play a fundamental role in the solution of linear systems of difference or differential equations. They provide complete dynamic information (i.e., the solution to the difference or differential equations) from the solution to a set of static, algebraic equations. Since matrix population models are based on a set of matrix difference equations

$$n(t + 1) = An(t)$$

eigenvalues and eigenvectors are the basis on which most of demographic analysis rests. You need not just a mechanical understanding, but a real intuitive grasp of the slippery little suckers. This section will try to provide it.

A.6.1   Eigenvectors

Begin by considering what happens when you multiply an arbitrary vector **x** by a given matrix **A** to get some vector **y**; e.g.,

$$\begin{pmatrix} 3 & -6 \\ 2 & -5 \end{pmatrix} \begin{pmatrix} 4 \\ 1 \end{pmatrix} = \begin{pmatrix} 6 \\ 3 \end{pmatrix} \tag{A.12}$$

Note that there is no clear relationship between **x** and **y**; x_1 has increased by a factor of 1.5 while x_2 has increased by a factor of 3. If a different **x** vector had been chosen, the changes in x_1 and x_2 would have been different.

However, consider the special vector $\mathbf{x} = (1\ 1)'$. Then

$$\begin{pmatrix} 3 & -6 \\ 2 & -5 \end{pmatrix} \begin{pmatrix} 1 \\ 1 \end{pmatrix} = \begin{pmatrix} -3 \\ -3 \end{pmatrix} \tag{A.13}$$

This time, matrix multiplication multiplied both entries of **x** by the same factor (-3).

A vector **x** with the property that matrix multiplication is equivalent to scalar multiplication, so that

$$\mathbf{Ax} = \lambda\mathbf{x} \tag{A.14}$$

for some scalar λ, is called an *eigenvector* of **A**; the scalar λ is the *eigenvalue*. "Eigen" is from the German for "self," and you can see that the eigenvectors of a matrix retain their identity, in a sense, under the transformation defined by the multiplication by **A**.

A.6.2 Left Eigenvectors

The eigenvectors defined in the previous section are the *right eigenvectors* of **A**. By multiplying **A** on the left by a row vector, one can define the analogous *left eigenvectors*. Just to make life interesting, there are two definitions, not quite equivalent, of these eigenvectors. One (e.g., Wilkinson 1965) says that a vector **y** is a left eigenvector of **A** if

$$\mathbf{y}'\mathbf{A} = \lambda\mathbf{y}' \qquad (A.15)$$

and the other (e.g., Horn and Johnson 1985) says that **y** is a left eigenvector if

$$\mathbf{y}^*\mathbf{A} = \lambda\mathbf{y}^* \qquad (A.16)$$

The two definitions are equivalent for real eigenvectors, for which $\mathbf{y}' = \mathbf{y}^*$, but for complex eigenvectors they give complex conjugates of each other.

The same results can be obtained using either definition, but you have to be consistent. In this book, I will use (A.16).

Some natural questions arise. Are the eigenvectors unique, or are there others with the same property? If there are others, is the eigenvalue λ the same for all of them? Given a matrix, how does one find its eigenvectors and eigenvalues? We'll begin with the last question, and work toward the others.

A.6.3 The Characteristic Equation

We have a matrix **A**; we wish to find λ and **x** such that $\mathbf{A}\mathbf{x} = \lambda\mathbf{x}$. Thus λ and **x** will satisfy

$$\mathbf{A}\mathbf{x} - \lambda\mathbf{x} = \mathbf{0}$$

where **0** is a vector of zeros. Thus

$$(\mathbf{A} - \lambda\mathbf{I})\mathbf{x} = \mathbf{0} \qquad (A.17)$$

Here we have a homogeneous system of linear equations, the matrix for which $(\mathbf{A} - \lambda\mathbf{I})$ depends on an unknown parameter λ. Recall from A.4.3 that, if the matrix is nonsingular, there is only one solution: $\mathbf{x} = \mathbf{0}$. This, however, is a trivial solution to an eigenvector problem, since $\mathbf{A}\mathbf{0} = \mathbf{0}$ for *any* matrix **A**. We want something more useful.

In order for a nonzero solution **x** of (A.17) to exist, the matrix $\mathbf{A} - \lambda\mathbf{I}$ must be singular, that is

$$\det(\mathbf{A} - \lambda\mathbf{I}) = 0 \qquad (A.18)$$

This equation still contains the unknown parameter λ. Any value of λ satisfying (A.18) will be an eigenvalue, and permit us to find a nonzero eigenvector from (A.17). Equation (A.18) is called the *characteristic equation* of **A**.

What does the characteristic equation look like? For the 2×2 example above,

$$\mathbf{A} - \lambda\mathbf{I} = \begin{pmatrix} 3 - \lambda & -6 \\ 2 & -5 - \lambda \end{pmatrix}$$

and the determinant is

$$\begin{aligned} \det(\mathbf{A} - \lambda I) &= (3 - \lambda)(-5 - \lambda) - (2)(-6) \\ &= \lambda^2 + 2\lambda - 3 \end{aligned}$$

Setting this equal to zero gives the characteristic equation

$$\lambda^2 - 2\lambda - 3 = 0$$

For a 2×2 matrix, then, the characteristic equation is a second-order polynomial, and will have two (possibly repeated) roots, in this case $\lambda_1 = -3$ and $\lambda_2 = 1$ (as is standard practice in this book, I have numbered them in decreasing order of absolute magnitude). In general, the characteristic equation of an $n \times n$ matrix is an nth-order polynomial, with n solutions.

A.6.4   Finding the Eigenvectors

Now to find the eigenvectors. If we substitute $\lambda_1 = -3$ into (A.17) we obtain

$$\begin{pmatrix} 6 & -6 \\ 2 & -2 \end{pmatrix} \begin{pmatrix} x_1 \\ x_2 \end{pmatrix} = \begin{pmatrix} 0 \\ 0 \end{pmatrix}$$

Note that the rows of this matrix are not independent [as (A.18) says they shouldn't be]. Suppose we let $x_1 = 1$; the first equation reduces to

$$6 - 6x_2 = 0$$

or

$$x_2 = 1$$

Thus $\mathbf{x} = (1 \ 1)'$ is an eigenvector corresponding to $\lambda_1 = -3$. Are there others? Yes. If we let $x_1 = 2$ we obtain $x_2 = 2$, so $\mathbf{x} = (2 \ 2)'$ is also an eigenvector. In general, *any nonzero scalar multiple of an eigenvector is also an eigenvector.*

To find the eigenvector corresponding to $\lambda_2 = 1$, we substitute it in (A.17) and get

$$\begin{pmatrix} 2 & -6 \\ 2 & -6 \end{pmatrix} \begin{pmatrix} x_1 \\ x_2 \end{pmatrix} = \begin{pmatrix} 0 \\ 0 \end{pmatrix}$$

from which $\mathbf{x} = (3 \ 1)'$ or any multiple thereof.

A.6.5 Complications

The characteristic equation of an $n \times n$ matrix is an nth-order polynomial. Such a polynomial has n roots. The example considered here has avoided two complications. First, some of the roots may be (usually will be) complex conjugate pairs. The corresponding eigenvectors will also be complex conjugate pairs. Second, the characteristic equation may have repeated roots. This can cause complications in the calculation of the eigenvectors (see any matrix algebra text), but repeated roots essentially never arise in demographic applications, so they will not be discussed further here.

A.6.6 Linear Independence of Eigenvectors

If the eigenvalues are distinct (i.e., the characteristic equation has no repeated roots), the eigenvectors are also distinct. They are also linearly independent. A set of vectors $x_1, x_2, \ldots, x_n$ is linearly *dependent* if it is possible to write any of the vectors as a linear combination of the others:

$$x_j = \sum_{i \neq j} c_i x_i$$

for some set of constants c_i. The criteria for nonsingularity of a matrix (i.e., for a nonzero determinant) is that the rows (or columns) be linearly independent.

We will not make much use of the concept of linear independence, important though it is. We will, however, need the following information.

Consider the set of all n-dimensional vectors (an "n-dimensional vector space" as they say). A set of n linearly independent vectors forms a *basis* for this space, i.e., *any* n-vector can be written as a linear combination of those linearly independent vectors. That is, any vector can be written as a linear combination of the vectors in the basis set.

Since the n eigenvectors $x_1, x_2, \ldots, x_n$ of an $n \times n$ matrix with distinct eigenvalues are linearly independent, we can write any vector y as

$$y = \sum_{i=1}^{n} c_i x_i$$

for some set of coefficients c_i.

A.6.7 The Left Eigenvectors

The left eigenvectors v_i of A are defined by

$$v_i^* A = \lambda_i v_i^* \tag{A.19}$$

The eigenvalues λ_i for the left and right eigenvectors are identical. The left and right eigenvectors satisfy

$$\langle \mathbf{v}_i, \mathbf{w}_j \rangle = 0 \qquad \text{for } i \neq j \tag{A.20}$$

A.6.8 Computation of Eigenvalues and Eigenvectors

Numerical computation of eigenvalues and eigenvectors combines the worst of several difficult numerical problems: finding determinants, solving polynomials, and solving systems of equations with singular matrices. In practice, it is done on a computer if one wants numerical results; there are a number of powerful routines available (Chapter 4). A great deal of information about the eigenvectors can be obtained directly from the life cycle graph, as discussed in Chapter 5

A.7   Similarity of Matrices

Two matrices $\mathbf{A}$ and $\mathbf{B}$ are said to be *similar* if there exists a matrix $\mathbf{C}$ with the property

$$\mathbf{A} = \mathbf{CBC}^{-1} \tag{A.21}$$

Similarity is important in evaluating functions of matrices (Chapter 4) and in some aspects of sensitivity analysis (Chapter 6). To see where it comes from, consider the matrix $\mathbf{A}$ as defining a transformation of one vector into another. That is, the operation $\mathbf{Ax} = \mathbf{y}$ transforms the vector $\mathbf{x}$ into the vector $\mathbf{y}$; the rules of the transformation are embodied in the entries of $\mathbf{A}$.

Suppose we express $\mathbf{x}$ and $\mathbf{y}$ in some new units, so that $\mathbf{x}' = \mathbf{Cx}$ and $\mathbf{y}' = \mathbf{Cy}$, for some matrix $\mathbf{C}$. What new matrix will define the same transformation as $\mathbf{A}$, but expressed in the new units? We know that $\mathbf{x} = \mathbf{C}^{-1}\mathbf{x}'$ and $\mathbf{y} = \mathbf{C}^{-1}\mathbf{y}'$, so $\mathbf{Ax} = \mathbf{y}$ translates into

$$\mathbf{AC}^{-1}\mathbf{x}' = \mathbf{C}^{-1}\mathbf{y}' \tag{A.22}$$

or

$$\mathbf{CAC}^{-1}\mathbf{x}' = \mathbf{y}' \tag{A.23}$$

The matrix defining the transformation in the new coordinates is thus similar to that for the old coordinates. It may help to think of the set of all matrices similar to a given matrix $\mathbf{A}$ as describing the same transformation in all possible sets of coordinates.

A.7.1 Properties of Similar Matrices

1. Similar matrices have the same determinant.

$$\begin{aligned} \det(\mathbf{A}) &= \det(\mathbf{CAC^{-1}}) \\ &= \det(\mathbf{C})\det(\mathbf{A})\det(\mathbf{C})^{-1} \\ &= \det(\mathbf{A}) \end{aligned}$$

2. Similar matrices have the same characteristic equations, and thus the same eigenvalues.

3. Consider any function $f(\mathbf{A})$ of a matrix (e.g., $\mathbf{A}^t$, $\sin\mathbf{A}$, etc.). If $\mathbf{A}$ and $\mathbf{B}$ are similar, then

$$f(\mathbf{A}) = \mathbf{C}f(\mathbf{B})\mathbf{C}^{-1}$$

This holds for any function that can be expressed as a power series, $f(\mathbf{A}) = \sum_{i=0}^{\infty} c_i \mathbf{A}^i$.

A.8 The Kronecker Product

A special matrix product, the Kronecker product (also known as the tensor product or the direct product), appears in some applications. Suppose $\mathbf{A}$ is an $(m \times n)$ matrix and $\mathbf{B}$ is an $(r \times s)$ matrix. The Kronecker product of $\mathbf{A}$ and $\mathbf{B}$ is

$$\mathbf{A} \otimes \mathbf{B} = \begin{pmatrix} a_{11}\mathbf{B} & a_{12}\mathbf{B} & \cdots & a_{1n}\mathbf{B} \\ a_{21}\mathbf{B} & a_{22}\mathbf{B} & \cdots & a_{2n}\mathbf{B} \\ \vdots & \vdots & \vdots & \vdots \\ a_{m1}\mathbf{B} & a_{m2}\mathbf{B} & \cdots & a_{mn}\mathbf{B} \end{pmatrix} \tag{A.24}$$

The Kronecker product $\mathbf{A} \otimes \mathbf{B}$ is of dimension $(mr \times ns)$. It contains all possible combinations of the elements of $\mathbf{A}$ and $\mathbf{B}$. This is why, for instance, it shows up in Chapter 8 in an expression for the covariances among all possible combinations of the entries of a matrix.

The properties of the Kronecker product are discussed in detail by Graham (1981). Some of the more useful are

$$\begin{aligned} \mathbf{A} \otimes (c\mathbf{B}) &= c(\mathbf{A} \otimes \mathbf{B}) \quad \text{for any scalar } c \\ \mathbf{A} \otimes (\mathbf{B} + \mathbf{C}) &= \mathbf{A} \otimes \mathbf{B} + \mathbf{A} \otimes \mathbf{C} \\ (\mathbf{A} \otimes \mathbf{B})' &= \mathbf{A}' \otimes \mathbf{B}' \\ (\mathbf{A} \otimes \mathbf{B})(\mathbf{C} \otimes \mathbf{D}) &= \mathbf{AC} \otimes \mathbf{BD} \end{aligned}$$

If $\mathbf{A}$ has eigenvalues λ_i and eigenvectors $\mathbf{w}_i$ and $\mathbf{B}$ has eigenvalues μ_i and eigenvectors $\mathbf{u}_i$, then $\mathbf{A} \otimes \mathbf{B}$ has eigenvalues $\lambda_i\mu_i$ with eigenvectors $\mathbf{w}_i \otimes \mathbf{u}_i$.

A.9   Norms of Vectors and Matrices

The *norm* of a vector, denoted $\|\mathbf{x}\|$, is a measure of size. The two most commonly encountered norms are the taxicab or city block norm

$$\|\mathbf{x}\| = \sum_i |x_i| \tag{A.25}$$

and the Euclidean norm

$$\|\mathbf{x}\| = \left(\sum_i |x_i|^2\right)^{1/2} \tag{A.26}$$

These norms often appear in the literature as $\|\mathbf{x}\|_1$ and $\|\mathbf{x}\|_2$; in this book it will be clear from the context which one is intended.

The norm of a matrix is also a measure of matrix size. Imagine a matrix $\mathbf{A}$ multiplying a vector $\mathbf{x}$. The resulting vector $\mathbf{A}\mathbf{x}$ is either shrunken or magnified (in norm) relative to $\mathbf{x}$. The "size" of $\mathbf{A}$ is defined as the maximum amount by which it magnifies a vector:

$$\|\mathbf{A}\| = \sup_{\mathbf{x} \neq 0} \frac{\|\mathbf{A}\mathbf{x}\|}{\|\mathbf{x}\|} \tag{A.27}$$

The norm of a matrix thus depends on the norm used to measure the size of $\mathbf{x}$. The matrix norms $\|\mathbf{A}\|_1$ and $\|\mathbf{A}\|_2$, corresponding to the taxicab and Euclidean vector norms, are

$$\|\mathbf{A}\|_1 = \max_j \sum_i |a_{ij}| \tag{A.28}$$

$$\|\mathbf{A}\|_2 = \left(\lambda_1^{(\mathbf{A}^*\mathbf{A})}\right)^{1/2} \tag{A.29}$$

where $\lambda_1^{(\mathbf{A}^*\mathbf{A})}$ is the dominant eigenvalue of the matrix $\mathbf{A}^*\mathbf{A}$.

Any vector or matrix norm has the basic properties of a distance measure:

$$\|\mathbf{A}\| \geq 0 \tag{A.30}$$

$$\|\mathbf{A} + \mathbf{B}\| \leq \|\mathbf{A}\| + \|\mathbf{B}\| \tag{A.31}$$

$$\|a\mathbf{A}\| = |a|\|\mathbf{A}\| \quad \text{for any } a \tag{A.32}$$

Furthermore

$$\|\mathbf{A}\mathbf{x}\| \leq \|\mathbf{A}\|\|\mathbf{x}\| \tag{A.33}$$

A.10 Suggested Reading

There are many good texts on matrix algebra. I recommend that you find one that suits your tastes and needs, and become familiar with it. My current favorites are Franklin (1968) at the introductory level and Horn and Johnson (1985) at a slightly more advanced, but still very lucid and applicable level. Gantmacher (1959) is a classic source, but not all that easy to read. Wilkinson (1965) is the standard reference on eigenvalue and eigenvector computation; see also Coleman and Van Loan (1988). Graham (1981) is a good reference for Kronecker products. Seneta (1981) is the standard text on nonnegative matrices. Press et al. (1986) contains programs for many types of matrix calculations.

Bibliography

Adams, J., P. Greenwood, and I. Swingland. 1985. Sex in an unpredictable world. New Scientist, 7 February, pp. 32–34.

Allan, J. D. and R. E. Daniels. 1982. Life table evaluation of chronic exposure of *Eurytemora affinis* (Copepoda) to kepone. Marine Biology 66:179–184.

Allee, W. C. 1931. *Animal Aggregations*. University of Chicago Press, Chicago.

Allee, W. C. 1951. *Cooperation Among Animals*. Henry Schuman, New York.

Allee, W. C., A. E. Emerson, O. Park, and T. Park. 1949. *Principles of Animal Ecology*. W.B. Saunders, Philadelphia.

Allen, K. R. 1980. *Conservation and Management of Whales*. University of Washington Press, Seattle.

Alm, G. 1959. Connection between maturity, size, and age in fishes. Drottningholm Institution Freshwater Research, Report 40:5–145.

Alstad, D. N. and G. F. Edmunds, Jr. 1983. Selection, outbreeding depression, and the sex ratio of scale insects. Science 220:93–95.

Altman, P. L. and D. S. Dittmer. 1962. *Growth, Including Reproduction and Morphological Development*. Biological Handbooks, Federation of American Societies for Experimental Biology, Washington, DC.

Anderson, R. J. and J. R. Landis. 1980. CATANOVA for multidimensional contingency tables: Nominal-scale response. Communications in Statistical Theory and Methods A9:1191–1206.

Anderson, T. W. and L. A. Goodman. 1957. Statistical inference about Markov chains. Annals of Mathematical Statistics 28:89–110.

Anderson, W. W. and C. E. King. 1970. Age-specific selection. Proceedings of the National Academy of Sciences 66:780–786.

Andrewartha, H. G. and L. C. Birch. 1954. *The Distribution and Abundance of Animals*. University of Chicago Press.

Anon. 1985. Alas, for women of a certain age. The Economist, 12 January 1985, pp. 26–27.

Antonovics, J. 1976. The nature of limits to natural selection. Annals of the Missouri Botanical Garden 63:224–247.

Aronson, D. G., M. A. Chory, G. R. Hall, and R. P. McGehee. 1982. Bifurcations from an invariant circle for two-parameter families of maps of the plane: a computer-assisted study. Communications in Mathematical Physics 83:303–354.

Asmussen, M. A. 1979. Regular and chaotic cycling in models of ecological genetics. Theoretical Population Biology 16:172–190.

Auslander, D., J. Guckenheimer, and G. Oster. 1978. Random evolutionarily stable strategies. Theoretical Population Biology 13:276–293.

Beddington, J. 1974. Age distribution and the stability of simple discrete time population models. Journal of Theoretical Biology 47:65–74.

Bell, G. 1980. The costs of reproduction and their consequences. American Naturalist 116: 45–76.

Bellows, T. S., Jr. 1986. Impact of developmental variance on behavior of models for insect populations. I. Models for populations with unrestricted growth. Research in Population Ecology 28:53–62.

Bergé, P., Y. Pomeau, and C. Vidal. 1984. *Order Within Chaos*. Wiley, New York.

Bernardelli, H. 1941. Population waves. Journal of the Burma Research Society 31:1–18.

Bierzychudek, P. 1982. The demography of jack-in-the-pulpit, a forest perennial that changes sex. Ecological Monographs 52:335–351.

Birch, L. C. 1948. The intrinsic rate of natural increase of an insect population. Journal of Animal Ecology 17:15–26.

Birch, L. C. 1953. Experimental background to the study of the distribution and abundance of insects. Ecology 34(4):698–711.

Birch, L. C., T. Dobzhansky, P. O. Elliott, and R. C. Lewontin. 1963. Relative fitness of geographic races of *Drosophila serrata*. Evolution 17:72–83.

Birkhoff, G. 1957. Extensions of Jentzsch's theorem. Transactions of the American Mathematical Society 85:219–227.

Bishop, Y. M. M., S. E. Fienberg, and P. W. Holland. 1975. *Discrete Multivariate Analysis: Theory and Practice*. MIT Press, Cambridge.

Blythe, S. P., R. M. Nisbet, and W. S. C. Gurney. 1984. The dynamics of population models with distributed maturation periods. Theoretical Population Biology 25:289–311.

Bodenheimer, F. S. 1938. *Problems of Animal Ecology*. Oxford University Press, Oxford.

Boling, R. H., Jr. 1973. Toward state-space models for biological populations. Journal of Theoretical Biology 40:485–506.

Bonner, J. T. 1965. *Size and Cycle*. Princeton University Press, Princeton, NJ.

Botsford, L. W. 1984. Effect of individual growth rates on expected behavior of the nortern California Dungeness crab (*Cancer magister*) fishery. Canadian Journal of Fisheries and Aquatic Sciences 41:99–107.

Botsford, L. W. and D. E. Wickham. 1978. Behavior of age-specific, density-dependent models and the northern California Dungeness crab fishery. Journal of the Fisheries Research Board of Canada 35:833–843.

Boyce, M. S. 1977. Population growth with stochastic fluctuations in the life table. Theoretical Population Biology 12:366–373.

Bradshaw, A. D. 1965. Evolutionary significance of phenotypic plasticity in plants. Advances in Genetics 13:115–155.

Brown, L. A. 1927. Temperature characteristics for duration of an instar in cladocerans. Journal of General Physiology 10:111–119.

Burns, B. R. and J. Ogden. 1985. The demography of the temperate mangrove [*Avicennia marina* (Forsk.) Vierh.] at its southern limit in New Zealand. Australian Journal of Ecology 10:125–133.

Cabrera, L. B. A. 1982. Analisis demografico de la copa de *Pinus hartwegii* Lindl. Thesis, Universidad Nacional Autonoma de Mexico.

Campbell, A. and M. D. Eagles. 1983. Size at maturity and fecundity of rock crabs, *Cancer irroratus*, from the Bay of Fundy and southwestern Nova Scotia. Fishery Bulletin 81:357–362.

Carey, J. R. 1983. Practical application of the stable age distribution: analysis of a tetranychid mite (*Acari: Tetranychidae*) population outbreak. Environmental Entomology 12:10–18.

Caswell, H. 1978. A general formula for the sensitivity of population growth rate to changes in life history parameters. Theoretical Population Biology 14:215–230.

Caswell, H. 1980. On the equivalence of maximizing reproductive value and maximizing fitness. Ecology 61:19–24.

Caswell, H. 1981. Reply to comments by Yodzis and Schaffer. Ecology 62:1685.

Caswell, H. 1982a. Stable population structure and reproductive value for populations with complex life cycles. Ecology 63:1223–1231.

Caswell, H. 1982b. Optimal life histories and the maximization of reproductive value: a general theorem for complex life cycles. Ecology 63:1218–1222.

Caswell, H. 1982c. Life history theory and the equilibrium status of populations. The American Naturalist 120:317–339.

Caswell, H. 1982d. Optimal life histories and the age-specific costs of reproduction. Journal of Theoretical Biology 98:519–529.

Caswell, H. 1983. Phenotypic plasticity in life-history traits: demographic effects and evolutionary consequences. American Zoologist 23:35–46.

Caswell, H. 1984. Optimal life histories and age-specific costs of reproduction: two extensions. Journal of Theoretical Biology 107:169–172.

Caswell, H. 1985. The evolutionary demography of clonal reproduction. pp. 187–224 in J. B. C. Jackson, L. W. Buss, and R. E. Cook, eds. *Population Biology and Evolution of Clonal Organisms.* Yale University Press, New Haven.

Caswell, H. 1986. Life cycle models for plants. Lectures on Mathematics in the Life Sciences 18:171–233.

Caswell, H. 1988. Approaching size and age in matrix population models. pp. 85–105 in B. Ebenman and L. Persson, eds. *Size-Structured Populations.* Springer-Verlag, Berlin.

Caswell, H. 1989a. The analysis of life table response experiments. I. Decomposition of treatment effects on population growth rate. Ecological Modelling (in press).

Caswell, H. 1989b. Life history strategies. British Ecological Society 75th Anniversary Symposium (in press).

Caswell, H. and A. Hastings. 1980. Fecundity, developmental time, and population growth rate: an analytical solution. Theoretical Population Biology 17:71–79.

Caswell, H. and S. Twombly. 1989. Estimation of stage-specific demographic parameters for zooplankton populations: methods based on stage-classified matrix projection models. *Symposium on Estimation and Analysis of Insect Populations.* Springer-Verlag, New York (in press).

Caswell, H. and D. E. Weeks. 1986. Two-sex models: chaos, extinction, and other dynamic consequences of sex. The American Naturalist 128:707–735.

Caswell, H. and P. A. Werner. 1978. Transient behavior and life history analysis of teasel (*Dipsacus sylvestris* Huds.). Ecology 59:53–66.

Caswell, H., H. E. Koenig, J. A. Resh, and Q. E. Ross. 1972. An introduction to systems science for ecologists. pp. 3–78 in B. C. Patten, ed. *Systems Analysis and Simulation in Ecology,* vol. 2. Academic Press, New York.

Caswell, H., R. J. Naiman and R. Morin. 1984. Evaluating the consequences of reproduction in complex salmonid life cycles. Aquaculture 43:123–134.

Caughley, G. 1977. *Analysis of Vertebrate Populations.* Wiley, New York.

Cavalli-Sforza, L. L. and W. F. Bodmer. 1971. *The Genetics of Human Populations.* W.H. Freeman, San Francisco.

Chapman, A. R. O. 1986. Age versus stage: an analysis of age- and size-specific mortality and reproduction in a population of *Laminaria longecruris* Pyl. Journal of Experimental Marine Biology and Ecology 97:113–122.

Charlesworth, B. 1971. Selection in density-regulated populations. Ecology 52:469–474.

Charlesworth, B. 1976. Natural selection in age-structured populations. Lectures on Mathematics in the Life Sciences 8:69–87.

Charlesworth, B. 1980. *Evolution in Age Structured Populations.* Cambridge University Press, Cambridge.

Charnov, E. L. 1982. *The Theory of Sex Allocation.* Princeton University Press, Princeton, NJ.

Chen, W. K. 1976. *Applied Graph Theory: Graphs and Electrical Networks,* 2d Ed. North-Holland Publishing, New York.

Cheverud, J. M. 1984. Quantitative genetics and developmental constraints on evolution by selection. Journal of Theoretical Biology 110:155–171.

Chiang, C.L. 1968. *Stochastic Processes in Biostatistics.* Wiley, New York.

Clutton-Brock, T. H., F. E. Guinness, and S. D. Albon. 1982. *Red Deer: Behavior and Ecology of Two Sexes.* University of Chicago Press, Chicago.

Clutton-Brock, T. H., S. D. Albon, and F. E. Guinness. 1985. Parental investment and sex differences in juvenile mortality in birds and mammals. Nature 313:131–133.

Coale, A. J. 1972. *The Growth and Structure of Human Populations: A Mathematical Approach.* Princeton University Press, Princeton, NJ.

Coates, C. L. 1959. Flow-graph solutions of linear algebraic equations. IRE Transactions on Circuit Theory 6:170–187.

Cochran, M. E. 1986. Consequences of pollination by chance in the pink lady's-slipper, *Cypripedium acaule.* Ph.D. dissertation, University of Tennessee, Knoxville.

Cohen, J. E. 1976. Ergodicity of age structure in populations with Markovian vital rates, I: countable states. Journal of the American Statistical Association 71:335–339.

Cohen, J. E. 1977a. Ergodicity of age structure in populations with Markovian vital rates, II. General states. Advances in Applied Probability. 9:18–37.

Cohen, J. E. 1977b. Ergodicity of age structure in populations with Markovian vital rates, III: finite-state moments and growth rate; an illustration. Advances in Applied Probability 9:462–475.

Cohen, J. E. 1978. Derivatives of the spectral radius as a function of non-negative matrix elements. Mathematical Proceedings of the Cambridge Philosophical Society 83:183–190.

Cohen, J. E. 1979a. Comparative statics and stochastic dynamics of age-structured populations. Theoretical Population Biology 16:159–171.

Cohen, J. E. 1979b. Contractive inhomogeneous products of non-negative matrices. Mathematical Proceedings of the Cambridge Philosophical Society 86:351–364.

Cohen, J. E. 1979c. Ergodic theorems in demography. Bulletin of the American Mathematical Society 1:275–295.

Cohen, J. E. 1979d. The cumulative distance from an observed to a stable age structure. SIAM Journal of Applied Mathematics 36(1):169–175.

Cohen, J. E. 1979e. Long-run growth rates of discrete multiplicative processes in Markovian environments. Journal of Mathematical Analysis and Applications 69:243–251.

Cohen, J. E. 1986. Population forecasts and confidence intervals for Sweden: a comparison of model-based and empirical approaches. Demography 23:105–126.

Cohen, J. E. 1987. Stochastic demography. Encyclopedia of Statistical Sciences, Vol. 8.

Cohen, J. E. 1988. Subadditivity, generalized products of random matrices and operations research. SIAM Review 30:69–86.

Cohen, J. E., S. W. Christensen, and C. P. Goodyear. 1983. A stochastic age-structured population model of striped bass (*Morone saxatilis*) in the Potomac River. Canadian Journal of Fisheries and Aquatic Sciences 40:2170–2183.

Cole, L. C. 1954. The population consequences of life history phenomena. Quarterly Review of Biology 19:103–137.

Cole, L. C. 1958. Sketches of general and comparative demography. Cold Spring Harbor Symposia on Quantitative Biology 22:1–15.

Coleman, T. F. and C. Van Loan. 1988. *Handbook for Matrix Computations*. SIAM, Philadelphia.

Collet, P. and J. P. Eckmann. 1980. *Iterated Maps of the Interval as Dynamical Systems*. Birkhauser, Boston.

Comfort, A. 1979. *The Biology of Senescence*, 3rd Ed. Elsevier, New York.

Cook, R. E. 1980. Germination and size-dependent mortality in *Viola blanda*. Oecologia 47:115–117.

Cook, R. E. 1983. Clonal plant populations. American Scientist 71:244–253.

Cook, R. E. 1985. Growth and development in clonal plant populations. pp. 259–296 in J. B. C. Jackson, L. W. Buss, and R. E. Cook, eds. *Population Biology and Evolution of Clonal Organisms*. Yale University Press, New Haven.

Cooper, W. S. 1984. Expected time to extinction and the concept of fundamental fitness. Journal of Theoretical Biology 107:603–629.

Corkett, C. J. and I. A. McLaren. 1978. The biology of *Pseudocalanus*. Advances in Marine Biology 15:1–231.

Crouse, D. T., L. B. Crowder, and H. Caswell. 1987. A stage-based population model for loggerhead sea turtles and implications for conservation. Ecology 68:1412–1423.

Cull, P. and A. Vogt. 1973. Mathematical analysis of the asymptotic behavior of the Leslie population matrix model. Bulletin of Mathematical Biology 35:645–661.

Cull, P. and A. Vogt. 1974. The periodic limit for the Leslie model. Mathematical Biosciences 21:39–54.

Cull, P. and A. Vogt. 1976. The period of total population. Bulletin of Mathetical Biology 38:317–319.

Curry, J.H. and J.A. Yorke. 1978. A transition from Hopf bifurcation to chaos: computer experiments with maps on R^2. pp. 48–68 in *The Structure of Attractors in Dynamical Systems*. Springer-Verlag, New York.

Cushing, J. M. 1989. A strong ergodic theorem for some nonlinear matrix models for the dynamics of structured populations. Natural Resource Modeling (in press).

Cvetkovic, D. M., M. Doob, and H. Sachs. 1979. *Spectra of Graphs: Theory and Application*. Academic Press, New York.

Cvitanovic, P. 1984. *Universality in Chaos*. Adam Hilger Ltd., Bristol.

Daniels, R. E. and J. D. Allan. 1981. Life table evaluation of chronic exposure to a pesticide. Canadian Journal of Fisheries and Aquatic Sciences 38(5):485–494.

Darwin, C. 1859. *On the Origin of Species*. John Murray, London.

Darwin, C. 1871. *The Descent of Man and Selection in Relation to Sex*. John Murray, London.

Darwin, J. H. and R. M. Williams. 1964. The effect of time of hunting on the size of a rabbit population. New Zealand Journal of Science 7:341–352.

Das Gupta, P. 1972. On two-sex models leading to stable populations. Theoretical Population Biology 3:358–375.

Das Gupta, P. 1978. An alternative formulation of the birth function in a two-sex model. Population Studies 32:367–379.

Davis, C. S. 1984. Interaction of a copepod population with the mean circulation on Georges Bank. Journal of Marine Research 42:573–590.

de Kroon, H., A. Plaisier, J. van Groenendael, and H. Caswell. 1986. Elasticity: the relative contribution of demographic parameters to population growth rate. Ecology 67:1427–1431.

De Roos, A. M., O. Diekmann, and J. A. J. Metz. 1989. The escalator boxcar train: basic theory and an application to *Daphnia* population dynamics. Submitted.

DeAngelis, D. L., L. J. Svoboda, S. W. Christensen, and D. S. Vaughan. 1980. Stability and return times of Leslie matrices with density-dependent survival: applications to fish populations. Ecological Modelling 8:149–163.

Deevey, E. S., Jr. 1947. Life tables for natural populations of animals. Quarterly Review of Biology 22:283-314.

Deevey, G. B. and E. S. Deevey, Jr. 1945. A life table for the black widow. Transactions of the Connecticut Academy of Arts and Sciences 36:115–134.

Demetrius, L. 1969. The sensitivity of population growth rate to perturbations in the life cycle components. Mathematical Biosciences 4:129–136.

Demetrius, L. 1971. Primitivity conditions for growth matrices. Mathematical Biosciences 12:53–58.

Demetrius, L. 1974a. Demographic parameters and natural selection. Proceedings of the National Academy of Sciences USA 12:4645–4647.

Demetrius, L. 1974b. Natural selection and age-structured populations. Genetics 79:535–544.

Demetrius, L. 1983. Statistical mechanics and population biology. Journal of Statistical Physics 30:709–753.

Demetrius, L. 1985. The units of selection and measures of fitness. Proceedings of the Royal Society of London B 225:147–159.

Desharnais, R. A. and J. E. Cohen. 1986. Life not lived due to disequilibrium in heterogeneous age-structured populations. Theoretical Population Biology 29:385–406.

Desharnais, R. A. and L. Liu. 1987. Stable demographic limit cycles in laboratory populations of *Tribolium castaneum*. Journal of Animal Ecology 56:885–906.

Desoer, C. A. 1967. Perturbations of eigenvalues and eigenvectors of a network. pp. 8–11, Fifth Annual Allerton Conference on Circuit and System Theory. University of Illinois, Urbana.

Devaney, R. L. 1986. *An Introduction to Chaotic Dynamical Systems*. Benjamin-Cummings, Menlo Park.

Diaconis, P. and B. Efron. 1983. Computer-intensive methods in statistics. Scientific American 248:116–130.

Dickerson, G. E. 1955. Genetic slippage in response to selection for multiple objectives. Cold Spring Harbor Symposia on Quantitative Biology 20:213–224.

Dingle, H. 1966. The effect of population density on mortality and sex ratio in the milkweed bug, *Oncopeltus*, and the cotton stainer, *Dysdercus* (Heteroptera). American Naturalist 100: 465–470.

Dingle, H. and J. P. Hegmann. 1982. *Evolution and Genetics of Life Histories*. Springer-Verlag, New York.

Doyle, R. W. and W. Hunte. 1981. Demography of an estuarine amphipod (*Gammarus lawrencianus*) experimentally selected for high "r": a model of the genetic effects of environmental change. Canadian Journal of Fisheries and Aquatic Sciences 38:1120–1127.

Dubois, M. and P. Bergé. 1981. Instabilites de couche limite dans un fluide en convection. Evolution vers la turbulence. Le Journal de Physique 42:167.

Easterlin, R. 1961. The American baby boom in historical perspective. American Economic Review 51:860–911.

Ebert, T. A. 1985. Sensitivity of fitness to macroparameter changes: an analysis of survivorship and individual growth in sea urchin life histories. Oecologia 65:461–467.

Efron, B. 1982. *The Jackknife, the Bootstrap and Other Resampling Plans*. Society for Industrial and Applied Mathematics, Philadelphia.

Efron, B. and R. Tibshirani. 1986. Bootstrap methods for standard errors, confidence intervals, and other measures of statistical accuracy. Statistical Science 1:54–77.

Ehrlich, P. R., A. E. Launer, and D. D. Murphy. 1984. Can sex ratio be defined or determined? The case of a population of checkerspot butterflies. American Naturalist 124:527–539.

Emlen, J. M. 1970. Age specificity and ecological theory. Ecology 51:588–601.

Enright, N. and J. Ogden. 1979. Applications of transition matrix models in forest dynamics: *Araucaria* in Papua New Guinea and *Nothofagus* in New Zealand. Australian Journal of Ecology 4:3–23.

Euler, L. 1970. A general investigation into the mortality and multiplication of the human species. Theoretical Population Biology 1:307–314. (Originally published 1760).

Faddeev, D. K. 1959. The conditionality of matrices ("Ob obuslovlennosti matrits"). Matematicheskii institut Steklov, Trudy No. 53:387–391.

Faddeev, D. K., and V. N. Faddeeva. 1963. *Computational Methods of Linear Algebra*. W. H. Freeman, San Francisco.

Fahrig, L. and G. Merriam. 1985. Habitat patch connectivity and population survival. Ecology 66:1762–1768.

Fahrig, L., L. P. Lefkovitch, and H. G. Merriam. 1983. Population stability in a patchy environment. pp. 61–67 in W. K. Lauenroth, G. V. Skogerbol, and M. Flug, eds. *Analysis of Ecological Systems: State-of-the-Art in Ecological Modelling*. Elsevier, New York.

Falconer, D. S. 1981. *Introduction to Quantitative Genetics*, 2nd Ed. Longman, New York.

Feller, W. 1968. *An Introduction to Probability Theory and its Applications*. Wiley,New York.

Fetcher, N. 1983. Optimal life-history characteristics and vegetative demography in *Eriophorum vaginatum*. Journal of Ecology 71:561–570.

Fienberg, S. E. 1977. *The Analysis of Cross-Classified Categorical Data*. MIT Press, Cambridge.

Fingleton, B. 1984. *Models of Category Counts*. Cambridge University Press, Cambridge.

Fisher, R. A. 1930. *The Genetical Theory of Natural Selection*. Clarendon Press, Oxford.

Fitzmayer, K. M., J. G. Geiger, and M. J. Zan Den Avyle. 1982. Effects of chronic exposure to semazine on the cladoceran, *Daphnia pulex*. Archives of Environmental Contamination and Toxicology 11:603–609.

Forbes, R. D. 1930. Timber growing and logging and turpentining practices in the southern pine region. Technical Bulletin 204, U.S. Department of Agriculture.

Frank, P. W., C. D. Boll, and R. W. Kelly. 1957. Vital statistics of laboratory cultures of *Daphnia pulex* DeGeer as related to density. Physiological Zoology 30:287–305.

Franklin, J. N. 1968. *Matrix Theory*. Prentice-Hall, Englewood Cliffs.

Frederickson, A. G. 1971. A mathematical theory of age structure in sexual populations: random mating and monogamous marriage models. Mathematical Biosciences 10:117–143.

Frisch, R. E. 1984. Body fat, puberty and fertility. Biological Reviews 59:161–188.

Furstenberg, H. and H. Kesten. 1960. Products of random matrices. Annals of Mathematical Statistics. 31:457–469.

Gantmacher, F. R. 1959. *Matrix Theory*. Chelsea Publishing Company, New York.

Gause, G. F. 1934. *The Struggle for Existence*. Dover Publications, Inc., New York.

Geiser, S. W. 1924. The differential death-rate of the sexes among animals. Washington University Studies 12:73.

Gentile, S. M., J. H. Gentile, J. Walker, and J. F. Heltshe. 1982. Chronic effects of cadmium on two species of mysid shrimp: *Mysidopsis bahia* and *Mysidopsis bigelowi*. Hydrobiologia 93:195–204.

George, V. S. 1985. Demographic evaluation of the influence of temperature and salinity on the copepod *Eurytemora herdmani*. Marine Ecology Progress Series 21:145–152.

Gibbons, J. W., R. D. Semlitsch, J. L. Greene, and J. P. Schubauer. 1981. Variation in age and size at maturity of the slider turtle (*Pseudemys scripta*). American Naturalist 117:841–845.

Gibbons, J. W., J. L. Greene, and K. K. Patterson. 1982. Variation in reproductive characteristics of aquatic turtles. Copeia 1982(4):776–784.

Gillespie, J. H. 1974. Natural selection for within-generation variance in offspring number. Genetics 76:601–606.

Gillespie, J. H. 1977. Natural selection for variances in offspring numbers: a new evolutionary principle. American Naturalist 111:1010–1014.

Glass, L., M. R. Guevara, J. Belair and A. Shrier. 1984. Global bifurcations of a periodically forced biological oscillator. Physical Review A29:1348– 1357.

Gleeson, S. K. 1984. Medawar's theory of senescence. Journal of Theoretical Biology 108:475–479.

Gleick, J. 1987. *Chaos: Making a New Science.* Viking Penguin, New York.

Goldman, N., C. F. Westoff, and C. Hammerslough. 1984. Demography of the marriage market in the United States. Population Index 50:5–25.

Gollub, J. P. and S. V. Benson. 1980. Many routes to turbulent convection. Journal of Fluid Mechanics 100:449–470.

Golubitsky, M., E. B. Keeler, and M. Rothschild. 1975. Convergence of the age structure: applications of the projective metric. Theoretical Population Biology 7:84–93.

Goodman, D. 1982. Optimal life histories, optimal notation, and the value of reproductive value. American Naturalist 119:803–823.

Goodman, D. 1987. The demography of chance extinction. pp. 11–34 in M. E. Soulé, ed. *Viable Populations for Conservation.* Cambridge University Press, Cambridge.

Goodman, L. A. 1967. On the reconciliation of mathematical theories of population growth. Journal of the Royal Statistical Society 130:541–553.

Goodman, L. A. 1969. The analysis of population growth when the birth and death rates depend upon several factors. Biometrics 25:659–681.

Goodman, L. A. 1971. On the sensitivity of the intrinsic growth rate to changes in the age-specific birth and death rates. Theoretical Population Biology 2:339–354.

Goodman, L. A. and W. H. Kruskal. 1954. Measures of association for cross classifications. Journal of the American Statistical Association 49:732–764.

Gould, S. J. 1983. *Hens' Teeth and Horses' Toes.* W.W. Norton, New York.

Gourley, R. S. and C. E. Lawrence. 1977. Stable population analysis in periodic environments. Theoretical Population Biology 11:49–59.

Graham, A. 1981. *Kronecker Products and Matrix Calculus: With Applications.* Halstead Press, New York.

Graham, A. 1987. *Nonnegative Matrices and Applicable Topics in Linear Algebra.* Halstead Press, New York.

Gray, L. N. and J. S. Williams. 1975. Goodman and Kruskal's tau b: multiple and partial analogs. Proceedings of the Social Statistics Section, American Statistical Association. pp. 444–448.

Grebogi, C., E. Ott, and J. A. Yorke. 1983. Fractal basin boundaries, long-lived chaotic transients, and unstable-unstable pair bifurcation. Physical Review Letters 50:935–938.

Grebogi, C., E. Ott, and J. A. Yorke. 1987. Chaos, strange attractors, and fractal basin boundaries in nonlinear dynamics. Science 238:632–638.

Gross, K. L. 1981. Predictions of fate from rosette size in four "biennial" plant species: *Verbascum thapsus, Oenothera biennis, Daucus carota,* and *Tragopogon dubius.* Oecologia 48:209–213.

Gross, M. R. 1984. Sunfish, salmon, and the evolution of alternative reproductive strategies and tactics in fishes. pp. 55–76 in G.W. Potts and R.J. Wootton, eds. *Fish Reproduction: Strategies and Tactics.* Academic Press, New York.

Guckenheimer, J. and P. Holmes. 1983. *Nonlinear Oscillations, Dynamical Systems, and Bifurcations of Vector Fields.* Springer-Verlag, New York.

Guckenheimer, J., G. Oster, and A. Ipaktchi. 1977. The dynamics of density dependent population models. Journal of Mathematical Biology 4:101–147.

Gurtin, M. E. and R. C. MacCamy. 1974. Non-linear age-dependent population dynamics. Archive for Rational Mechanics and Analysis 54:281–300.

Haberman, S. J. 1977. Log-linear models and frequency tables with small expected cell counts. Annals of Statistics 5:1148–1169.

Haig, I. T., K. P. Davis, and R. H. Weidman. 1941. Natural regeneration in the western white pine type. U.S. Department of Agriculture Technical Bulletin 767.

Hajnal, J. 1976. On products of non-negative matrices. Mathematical Proceedings of the Cambridge Philosophical Society 79:521–530.

Haldane, J. B. S. and S. D. Jayakar. 1963. Polymorphism due to selection of varying direction. Journal of Genetics 58:237–242.

Hamilton, W. D. 1966. The moulding of senescence by natural selection. Journal of Theoretical Biology 12:12–45.

Hamilton, W.D. 1967. Extraordinary sex ratios. Science 156:477–488.

Hardy, G. H., J. E. Littlewood, and G. Polya. 1952. *Inequalities,* 2nd Ed. Cambridge University Press, Cambridge.

Harper, J. L. 1977. *Population Biology of Plants.* Academic Press, New York.

Hartshorn, G. S. 1975. A matrix model of tree population dynamics. pp. 41–51 in F. B. Golley and E. Medina, eds. *Tropical Ecological Systems.* Springer-Verlag, New York.

Harvell, C. D., H. Caswell, and P. Simpson. 1989. Density dependence in clonal populations: experimental studies with a marine bryozoan (*Membranipora membranacea* L.). Oecologia (in press).

Hassell, M. P. 1978. *The Dynamics of Arthropod Predator-Prey Systems.* Princeton University Press, Princeton, NJ.

Hastings, A. 1978a. An evolutionary optimization principle. Journal of Theoretical Biology 75:519–525.

Hastings, A. 1978b. Evolutionarily stable strategies and the evolution of life history strategies: I. Density dependent models. Journal of Theoretical Biology 75:527–536.

Hayssen, V. 1984. Basal metabolic rate and the intrinsic rate of increase: an empirical and theoretical reexamination. Oecologia 64:419–424.

Hennemann, W. W., III. 1983. Relationship among body mass, metabolic rate, and the intrinsic rate of natural increase in mammals. Oecologia 56:104-108.

Heron, A. C. and E. E. Benham. 1985. Life history parameters as indicators of growth rate in three salp populations. Journal of Plankton Research 7:365–379.

Heyde, C. C. and J. E. Cohen. 1985. Confidence intervals for demographic projections based on products of random matrices. Theoretical Population Biology

27:120–153.

Hines, A. H. 1982. Allometric constraints and variables of reproductive effort in brachyuran crabs. Marine Biology 69:309–320.

Hirose, T. and N. Kachi. 1982. Critical plant size for flowering in biennials with special reference to their distribution in a sand dune system. Oecologia 55:281–284.

Hirshfield, M. F. and D. W. Tinkle. 1975. Natural selection and the evolution of reproductive effort. Proceedings of the National Academy of Sciences 72:2227–2231.

Holden, A. V. 1986. *Chaos.* Manchester University Press, Manchester.

Holden, C. 1983. Can smoking explain ultimate gender gap? Science 221:1034.

Hoogendyk, C. G. and G. F. Estabrook. 1984. The consequences of earlier reproduction in declining populations. Mathematical Biosciences 71:217–235.

Horn, R. A. and C. A. Johnson. 1985. *Matrix Analysis.* Cambridge University Press, Cambridge.

Horst, T. J. 1977. Use of the Leslie matrix for assessing environmental impact with an example for a fish population. Transactions of the American Fisheries Society 106:253–257.

Horvitz, C. C. and D. W. Schemske. 1986. Seed dispersal and environmental heterogeneity in a neotropical herb: a model of population and patch dynamics. pp. 169–186 in A. Estrada and T. H. Fleming, eds. *Frugivores and Seed Dispersal.* Junk Publishers, Dordrecht.

Hourston, A. S., V. Haist, and R. D. Humphreys. 1981. Regional and temporal variation in the fecundity of Pacific herring in British Columbia waters. Canadian Technical Report of Fisheries and Aquatic Sciences No. 1009.

Hubbell, S. P. and P. A. Werner. 1979. On measuring the intrinsic rate of increase of populations with heterogeneous life histories. American Naturalist 113:277–293.

Huenneke, L. F. and P. L. Marks. 1987. Stem dynamics of the shrub *Alnus incana ssp. rugosa*: transition matrix models. Ecology 68:1234–1242.

Huggins, W. H. and D. R. Entwisle. 1968. *Introductory Systems and Design.* Blaisdell, Waltham, MA.

Hughes, T. P. 1984. Population dynamics based on individual size rather than age: A general model with a reef coral example. American Naturalist 123:778–795.

Hughes, T. P. and J. H. Connell. 1987. Population dynamics based on size or age? A reef-coral analysis. American Naturalist 129:818–829.

Hughes, T. P. and J. B. C. Jackson. 1985. Population dynamics and life histories of foliaceous corals. Ecological Monographs 55:141–166.

Hummon, W. D. and M. R. Hummon. 1975. Use of life table data in tolerance experiments. Tome 16:743–749.

Hutchinson, G. E. 1978. *An Introduction to Population Ecology.* Yale University Press, New Haven.

Iooss, G. 1979. *Bifurcation of Maps and Applications.* North-Holland Publishing Company, New York.

Istock, C. A. 1983. The extent and consequences of heritable variation for fitness characters. pp. 61–96 in C. E. King and P. S. Dawson (eds.) *Population Biology: Retrospect and Prospect.* Columbia University Press, New York.

Jackson, J. B. C. 1985. Distribution and ecology of clonal and aclonal benthic invertebrates. pp.297–355 in J. B. C. Jackson, L. W. Buss, and R. E. Cook, eds. *Population Biology and Evolution of Clonal Organisms.* Yale University Press, New Haven.

Jackson, J. B. C., L. W. Buss, and R. E. Cook. 1985. *Population Biology and Evolution of Clonal Organisms.* Yale University Press, New Haven.

Jacobi, C. J. G. 1846. Uber ein leichtes Verfagren die in der Theorie der Sacularstorungen Vorkommenden Gleichungen numerisch aufsulosen. J. Reine Angew. Math. 30:51–95.

Janzen, D. H. 1976. Why bamboos wait so long to flower. Annual Review of Ecology and Systematics 7:347–391.

Jimenes, J. A. and A. E. Lugo. 1985. Tree mortality in mangrove forests. Biotropica 17:177–185.

Jones, J. W. 1959. *The Salmon.* Harper & Bros., New York.

Jury, E. I. 1964. *Theory and Application of the z-Transform Method.* Wiley, New York.

Karlin, S. and U. Lieberman. 1974. Random temporal variation in selection intensities: case of large population size. Theoretical Population Biology 6:355–382.

Kato, T. 1982. *A Short Introduction to Perturbation Theory for Linear Operators.* Springer-Verlag, New York.

Keller, E. L. 1980. Primitivity of the product of two Leslie matrices. Bulletin of Mathematical Biology 42:181–189.

Kendall, M. G., and A. Stuart. 1958. *The Advanced Theory of Statistics,* vol 1. Hafner, New York.

Keyfitz, N. 1967. Reconciliation of population models: matrix, integral equation and partial fraction. Journal of the Royal Statistical Society 130:61–83.

Keyfitz, N. 1968. *Introduction to the Mathematics of Population.* Addison-Wesley, Reading, MA.

Keyfitz, N. 1971a. Linkages of intrinsic to age-specific rates. Journal of the American Statistical Association 66:275–281.

Keyfitz, N. 1972a. On future population. Journal of the American Statistical Association 67:347–363.

Keyfitz, N. 1972b. Population waves. pp. 1–38 in T. N. E. Greville, ed. *Population Dynamics.* Academic Press, New York.

Keyfitz, N. 1972c. The mathematics of sex and marriage. Proc. 6th Berkeley Symposium on Mathematical Statistics and Probability 4:89–108.

Keyfitz, N. 1977. *Applied Mathematical Demography.* Wiley, New York.

Keyfitz, N. 1980. Multistate demography and its data: a comment. Environment and Planning A 12:615–622.

Keyfitz, N. and J. A. Beekman. 1984. *Demography through Problems.* Springer-Verlag, New York.

Keyfitz, N. and W. Flieger. 1968. *World Population: an Analysis of Vital Data.* The University of Chicago Press, Chicago.

Keyfitz, N. and W. Flieger. 1971. *Population: Facts and Methods of Demography.* W.H. Freeman, San Francisco.

Kim, Y. J. and Z. M. Sykes. 1976. An experimental study of weak ergodicity in human populations. Theoretical Population Biology 10:150–172.

King, C. E. 1967. Food, age, and the dynamics of a laboratory population of rotifers. Ecology 48:111–128.

Kingman, J. F. C. 1976. Subadditive processes. Lecture Notes in Mathematics 539:167–223. Springer-Verlag, New York.

Kingsland, S. 1985. *Modeling Nature*. University of Chicago Press, Chicago.

Klinkhamer, P. G. L., T. J. de Jong, and E. Meelis. 1987a. Delay of flowering in the 'biennial' *Cirsium vulgare*: size effects and devernalization. Oikos 49:303–308.

Klinkhamer, P. G. L., T. J. de Jong, and E. Meelis. 1987b. Life-history variation and the control of flowering in short-lived monocarps. Oikos 49:309–314.

Kostitzin, V. A. 1939. *Mathematical Biology*. George G. Harrap & Company Ltd., London.

Lacey, E. P., L. Real, J. Antonovics, and D. G. Heckel. 1983. Variance models in the study of life histories. American Naturalist 122:114–131.

Lack, D. 1947. The significance of clutch size. Ibis 89:302–352.

Lack, D. 1954. The evolution of reproductive rates. pp. 143–156 in F. B. Huxley, A. C. Hardy, and E. B. Ford, eds. *Evolution as a Process*. George Allen and Unwin, London.

Land, K. C. and A. Rogers. 1982. *Multidimensional Mathematical Demography*. Academic Press, New York.

Lande, R. 1982a. A quantitative genetic theory of life history evolution. Ecology 63:607–615.

Lande, R. 1982b. Elements of a quantitative genetic model of life history evolution. pp. 21–29 in H. Dingle and J. P. Hegmann, eds. *Evolution and Genetics of Life Histories*. Springer-Verlag, New York.

Lande, R. 1988. Demographic models of the northern spotted owl (*Strix occidentalis caurina*). Oecologia (Berlin) 75:601–607.

Lande, R. and S. H. Orzack. 1988. Extinction dynamics of age-structured populations in a fluctuating environment. Proceedings of the National Academy of Sciences USA 85:7418–7421.

Lanford, O. E., III. 1973. Bifurcation of periodic solutions into invariant tori: the work of Ruelle and Takens. pp. 159–192 in I. Stakgold, D. D. Joseph, and D. H. Sattinger, eds. *Nonlinear Problems in the Physical Sciences and Biology*. Springer-Verlag, New York.

Larntz, K. 1978. Small sample comparisons of exact levels for chi-square goodness-of-fit statistics. Journal of the American Statistical Association 73:253–263.

Law, R. 1983. A model for the dynamics of a plant population containing individuals classified by age and size. Ecology 64:224–230.

Law, R. and M. T. Edley. 1989. Transient dynamics of populations with age- and size-dependent vital rates. Ecology (in press).

Lawrence, J. M. 1987. *A Functional Biology of Echinoderms*. Johns Hopkins University Press, Baltimore.

Lee, R. 1974. The formal dynamics of controlled populations and the echo, the boom and the bust. Demography 11:563–585.

Lefkovitch, L. P. 1963. Census studies on unrestricted populations of *Lasioderma serricorne* (F.) (Coleoptera: Anobiidae). Journal of Animal Ecology 32:221–231.

Lefkovitch, L. P. 1965. The study of population growth in organisms grouped by stages. Biometrics 21:1–18.

Lefkovitch, L. P. 1971. Some comments on the invariants of population growth. pp. 337–360 in G. P. Patil, E. C. Pielou, and W. E. Waters, eds. *Statistical Ecology*, vol. 2. Pennsylvania State University Press, University Park, Pennsylvania.

Lefkovitch, L. P. and L. Fahrig. 1985. Spatial characteristics of habitat patches and population survival. Ecological Modelling 30:297–308.

Lenski, R. E. and P. M. Service. 1982. The statistical analysis of population growth rates calculated from schedules of survivorship and fecundity. Ecology 63:655–662.

Lerner, I. M. 1958. *The Genetic Basis of Selection*. Wiley, New York.

Leslie, P. H. 1945. On the use of matrices in certain population mathematics. Biometrika 33:183–212.

Leslie, P. H. 1948. Some further notes on the use of matrices in population mathematics. Biometrika 35:213–245.

Leslie, P. H. 1959. The properties of a certain lag type of population growth and the influence of an external random factor on a number of such populations. Physiological Zoology 32:151–159.

Leslie, P. H. and T. Park. 1949. The intrinsic rate of natural increase of *Tribolium castaneum* Herbst. Ecology 30:469–477.

Leslie, P. H. and R. M. Ranson. 1940. The mortality, fertility and rate of natural increase of the vole (*Microtus agrestis*) as observed in the laboratory. Journal of Animal Ecology 9:27–57.

Leslie, P. H., J. S. Tener, M. Vizoso, and H. Chitty. 1955. The longevity and fertility of the Orkney vole, *Microtus orcadensis*, as observed in the laboratory. Proceedings of the Zoological Society of London 125:115–125.

Leverich, W. J. and D. A. Levin. 1979. Age-specific survivorship and repreoduction in *Phlox drummondii*. American Naturalist 113:881–903.

Levin, L. A., H. Caswell, K. D. DePatra, and E. L. Creed. 1987. Demographic consequences of larval development mode: planktotrophy vs. lecithotrophy in *Streblospio benedicti*. Ecology 68:1877–1886.

Levin, S. A. 1981. Age-structure and stability in multiple-age spawning populations. pp. 21–45 in T. L Vincent and J. M. Skowronski, eds. *Revewable Resource Management*. Springer-Verlag, Heidelberg.

Levin, S. A. and C. P. Goodyear. 1980. Analysis of an age-structured fishery model. Journal of Mathematical Biology 9:245–274.

Lewis, E. G. 1942. On the generation and growth of a population. Sankhya: The Indian Journal of Statistics 6:93–96.

Lewis, E. R. 1972. Delay-line models of population growth. Ecology 53:797–807.

Lewis, E. R. 1976. Applications of discrete and continuous network theory to linear population models. Ecology 57:33–47.

Lewis, E. R. 1977. *Network Models in Population Biology*. Springer-Verlag, New York.

Lewontin, R. C. 1965. Selection for colonizing ability. pp. 77–94 in H. G. Baker and G. L. Stebbins, eds. *The Genetics of Colonizing Species*, Academic Press, New York.

Lewontin, R. C. and D. Cohen. 1969. On population growth in a randomly varying environment. Proceedings of the National Academy of Sciences 62:1056–1060.

Liaw, K.-L. 1980. Multistate dynamics: the convergence of an age-by-region population system. Environment and Planning A 12:589–613.

Liebetrau, A. M. 1983. *Measures of Association.* Quantitative Applications in the Social Sciences 32. Sage, Beverly Hills.

Light, R. J. and B. H. Margolin. 1971. An analysis of variance for categorical data. Journal of the American Statistical Association 66:534–544.

Liu, L. and J. E. Cohen. 1987. Equilibrium and local stability in a logistic matrix model for age-structured populations. Journal of Mathematical Biology 25:73–88.

Loeschcke, V. 1987. *Genetic Constraints on Adaptive Evolution.* Springer-Verlag, New York.

Longstaff, B. C. 1977. The dynamics of collembolan populations: a matrix model of single species population growth. Canadian Journal of Zoology 55:314–324.

Longstaff, B. C. 1984. An extension of the Leslie matrix model to include a variable immature period. Australian Journal of Ecology 9:289–293.

Lopez, A. 1961. *Problems in Stable Population Theory.* Princeton University Press, Princeton, NJ.

Lotka, A. J. 1924. *Elements of Physical Biology.* Williams and Wilkins, Baltimore. (Reprinted in 1956 by Dover Publications, New York, as *Elements of Mathematical Biology.*)

Lotka, A. J. 1939. A contribution to the theory of self-renewing aggregates, with special reference to industrial replacement. Annals of Mathematical Statistics 10:1–25.

Lotka, A. J. 1945. Population analysis as a chapter in the mathematical theory of evolution. pp. 355–385 in W. E. LeGros Clark and P. B. Medawar, eds. *Essays on Growth and Form.* Oxford University Press, Oxford.

Luppova, E. P. and E. Ya. Frisman. 1983. Stationarity and stability of a dynamical system describing the behavior of a dioecious population. pp. 84–92 in *Differential and Operator Equations in Function Spaces*, USSR Academy of Sciences, Fareast Science Center, Vladivostok.

MacArthur, J. W. and W. H. T. Baillie. 1932. Sex differences in mortality in *Abraxas*-type species. Quarterly Review of Biology 7:313–325.

MacArthur, R. H. 1962. Some generalized theorems of natural selection. Proceedings of the National Academy of Sciences 48:1893–1897.

Maly, E. J. 1970. The influence of predation on the adult sex ratios of two copepod species. Limnology and Oceanography 15:566–573.

Manning, A. 1972. *An Introduction to Animal Behavior.* Addison-Wesley, Reading, MA.

Marsden, J. E. and M. McCracken. 1976. *The Hopf Bifurcation and its Applications.* Springer-Verlag, New York.

Marshall, J. S. 1962. The effects of continuous gamma radiation on the intrinsic rate of natural increase on *Daphnia pulex.* Ecology 43(4):598–607.

Marshall, S. M. and A. P. Orr. 1955. *The Biology of a Marine Copepod, Calanus finmarchicus* (Gunnerus). Oliver & Boyd, Edinburgh.

Mason, S. J. 1953. Feedback theory—some properties of signal flow graphs. Proceedings of the IRE 41:1144–1156.

Mason, S. J. 1956. Feedback theory—further properties of signal flow graphs. Proceedings of the IRE 44:920–926.

Mason, S. J. and H. J. Zimmermann. 1960. *Electronic Circuits, Signals, and Systems.* Wiley, New York.

Maufette, Y. and L. Jobin. 1985. Effects of density on the proportion of male and female pupae in Gypsy-moth populations. Canadian Entomologist 117:535–539.

May, R. M. 1974. Biological populations with nonoverlapping generations: stable points, stable cycles, and chaos. Science 186:645–647.

May, R. M. 1976. Simple mathematical models with very complicated dynamics. Nature 261:459–467.

May, R. M. and G. F. Oster. 1976. Bifurcations and dynamic complexity in simple ecological models. American Naturalist 110:573–599.

McFarland, D. D. 1972. Comparison of alternative marriage models. pp. 89–106 in T.N.E. Greville, ed. *Population Dynamics*. Academic Press, New York.

McGraw, J. B. 1989. Age- and size-specific shoot life histories and shoot population growth in *Rhododendron maximum*. American Journal of Botany (in press).

McGraw, J. B. and J. Antonovics. 1983. Experimental ecology of *Dryas octopetala* ecotypes. II. A demographic model of growth, branching, and fecundity. Journal of Ecology 71:899–912.

McKendrick, A. G. 1926. Applications of mathematics to medical problems. Proceedings of the Edinburgh Mathematical Society 40:98–130.

McKenzie, W. D., Jr., D. Crews, K. D. Kallman, D. Policansky, and J. J. Sohn. 1983. Age, weight and the genetics of sexual maturation in the platyfish, *Xiphophorus maculatus*. Copeia 3:770–774.

McLaren, I. A. 1978. Generation lengths of some temperate marine copepods: estimation, prediction, and implications. Journal of the Fisheries Research Board of Canada 35:1330–1342.

Meagher, T. R. 1981. Population biology of *Chamaelirium luteum*, a dioecious lily. II. Mechanisms governing sex ratios. Evolution 35:557–567.

Meagher, T. R. 1982. The population biology of *Chamaelirium luteum*, a dioecious member of the lily family: two-sex population projections and stable population structure. Ecology 63:1701–1711.

Meagher, T. R. and J. Antonovics. 1982a. The population biology of *Chamaelirium luteum*, a dioecious member of the lily family: life history studies. Ecology 63:1690–1700.

Meagher, T. R. and J. Antonovics. 1982b. Life history variation in dioecious plant populations: a case study of *Chamaelirium luteum*. pp. 139–154 in H. Dingle and J.P. Hegmann, eds. *Evolution and Genetics of Life Histories*. Springer-Verlag, New York.

Medawar, P. B. 1952. *An Unsolved Problem in Biology*. H. K. Lewis, London.

Menges, E. S. 1986. Predicting the future of rare plant populations: demographic monitoring and modeling. Natural Areas Journal 6:13–25.

Menges, E. 1990. Stochastic modeling of extinction in plant populations. In P. L. Fiedler and S. Jain, eds. *Conservation Biology; The Theory and Practice of Nature Conservation, Preservation, and Management*. Chapman and Hall, New York (in press).

Mertz, D. B. 1971. Life history phenomena in increasing and decreasing populations. pp. 361–399 in G. P. Patil, E. C. Pielou, and W. E. Waters, eds. *Statistical Ecology. II. Sampling and Modeling Biological Populations and Population Dynamics*. Pennsyvania State University Press, University Park.

Metz, J. A. J. 1977. State space models for animal behavior. Annals of System Research 6:65–109.

Metz, J. A. J. and O. Diekmann. 1986. *The Dynamics of Physiologically Structured Populations*. Springer-Verlag, Berlin.

Meyer, J. S., C. G. Ingersoll, L. L. McDonald, and M. S. Boyce. 1986. Estimating uncertainty in population growth rate: jackknife vs. bootstrap techniques. Ecology 67:1156–1166.

Meyer, J. S., C. G. Ingersoll, and L. L. McDonald. 1987. Sensitivity analysis of population growth rates estimated from cladoceran chronic toxicity tests. Environmental Toxocology and Chemistry 6:115–126.

Michod, R. E. and W. W. Anderson. 1980. On calculating demographic parameters from age frequency data. Ecology 61:265–269.

Mitra, S. 1978. On the derivation of a two-sex stable population model. Demography 15:541–548.

Moloney, K. A. 1986. A generalized algorithm for determining category size. Oecologia 69:176–180.

Moloney, K. A. 1988. Fine-scale spatial and temporal variation in the demography of a perennial bunchgrass. Ecology 69:1588–1598.

Murray, B. G. and L. Garding. 1984. On the meaning of the parameter x of Lotka's discrete equations. Oikos 42:323–326.

Nevo, E. 1979. Adaptive convergence and divergence of subterranean mammals. Annual Review of Ecology and Systematics 10:269–308.

Newhouse, S., D. Ruelle, and F. Takens. 1978. Occurrence of strange axiom-A attractors near quasi-periodic flows on T^m, $m \geq 3$. Communications in Mathematical Physics 64:35.

Nisbet, R. M. and W. S. C. Gurney. 1982. *Modelling Fluctuating Populations*. Wiley, New York.

Nour, E.-S. and C. M. Suchindran. 1984. The construction of multi-state life tables: comments on the article by Willekens et al. Population Studies 38:325–328.

Nussbaum, R.D. 1986. Convexity and log convexity for the spectral radius. Linear Algebra and its Applications 73:59–122.

Nussbaum, R. D. 1988. *Hilbert's Projective Metric and Iterated Nonlinear Maps*. Memoirs of the American Mathematical Society 391, Providence, RI.

Odum, H. T. and W. C. Allee. 1954. A note on the stable point of populations showing both intraspecific cooperation and disoperation. Ecology 35:95–97.

Orzack, S. H. 1985. Population dynamics in variable environments V. The genetics of homeostasis revisited. American Naturalist 125:550–572.

Orzack, S. H. and S. Tuljapurkar. 1989. Population dynamics in variable environments. VII. The demography and genetics of iteroparity. American Naturalist (in press).

Oster, G. 1976. Internal variables in population dynamics. Lectures on Mathematics in the Life Sciences 8:37–68.

Oster, G. and Y. Takahashi. 1974. Models for age-specific interactions in a periodic environment. Ecological Monographs 44:483–501.

Palmer, J. O. 1985. Life-history consequences of body-size variation in the milkweed leaf beetle, *Labidomera clivicollis* (Coleoptera: Chrysomelidae). Annals of the Entomological Society of America 78:603–608.

Parlett, B. 1972. Can there be a marriage function? pp. 107–135 in T.N.E. Greville, ed. *Population Dynamics*. Academic Press, New York.

Pearl, R. 1928. *The Rate of Living*. Alfred A. Knopf, New York.

Pearl, R. 1940. *Medical Biometry and Statistics*. W. B. Saunders, Philadelphia.

Pearl, R. and L.J. Reed. 1920. On the rate of growth of the population of the United States since 1790 and its mathematical representation. Proceedings of the National Academy of Sciences, USA 6:275–280.

Pearl, R., J. R. Miner, and S. L. Parker. 1927. Experimental studies on the duration of life. XI. Density of population and life duration in *Drosophila*. American Naturalist 61:289–318.

Peitgen, H.-O. and P. H. Richter. 1986. *The Beauty of Fractals: Images of Complex Dynamical Systems*. Springer-Verlag, Berlin.

Pennycuick, L. 1969. A computer model of the Oxford great tit population. Journal of Theoretical Biology 22:381–400.

Pennycuick, C. J., R. M. Compton, and L. Beckingham. 1968. A computer model for simulating the growth of a population, or of two interacting populations. Journal of Theoretical Biology 18:316–329.

Peterson, C. H. 1986. Quantitative allometry of gamete production by *Mercenaria mercenaria* into old age. Marine Ecology 29:93–97.

Pinero, D., M. Martinez-Ramos, and J. Sarukhan. 1984. A population model of *Astrocaryum mexicanum* and a sensitivity analysis of its finite rate of increase. Journal of Ecology 72:977–991.

Policansky, D. 1982. Sex change in plants and animals. Annual Review of Ecology and Systematics 13:471–495.

Pollak, R. A. 1986. A reformulation of the two-sex problem. Demography 23:247–259.

Pollak, R. A. 1987. The two-sex problem with persistent unions: a generalization of the birth matrix-mating rule model. Theoretical Population Biology 32:176–187.

Pollard, J. H. 1966. On the use of the direct matrix product in analysing certain stochasic population models. Biometrika 53:397–415.

Pollard, J. H. 1969. Continuous-time and discrete-time models of population growth. Journal of the Royal Statistical Society 132:80–88.

Pollard, J.H. 1973. *Mathematical Models for the Growth of Human Populations*. Cambridge University Press, Cambridge.

Pollard, J.H. 1977. The continuing attempt to incorporate both sexes into marriage analysis. International Population Conference, Mexico, 1977, pp. 291–309. International Union for the Scientific Study of Population.

Potts, D. C. 1983. Evolutionary disequilibrium among Indo-Pacific corals. Bulletin of Marine Sciences 33:619–632.

Potts, D. C. 1984. Generation times and the quaternary evolution of reef-building corals. Paleobiology 10:48–58.

Press, W. H., B. P. Flannery, S. A. Teukolsky, and W. T. Vetterling. 1986. *Numerical Recipes: the Art of Scientific Computing*. Cambridge University Press, Cambridge.

Price, G. R. 1970. Selection and covariance. Nature 227:520–521.

Price, G. R. 1972. Extension of covariance selection mathematics. Annals of Human Genetics, Lond. 35:485–490.

Rabinovich, J. E. 1969. The applicability of some population growth models to a single-species laboratory population. Annals of the Entomological Society of America 62:437–442.

Rago, P. J. and R. M. Dorazio. 1984. Statistical inference in life-table experiments: the finite rate of increase. Canadian Journal of Fisheries and Aquatic Sciences 41:1361–1374.

Rago, P. J. and C. P. Goodyear. 1987. Recruitment mechanisms of striped bass and Atlantic salmon: comparative liabilities of alternative life histories. American Fisheries Society Symposium 1:402–416.

Rao, T. R. and S. S. S. Sarma. 1986. Demographic parameters of *Brachionus patulus* Muller (Rotifera) exposed to sublethal DDT concentrations at low and high food levels. Hydrobiologia 139:193–200.

Raper, J.R. 1966. Life cycles, basic patterns of sexuality, and sexual mechanisms. pp. 473–512 in G.C. Ainsworth and A.A. Sussman, eds. *The Fungi: An Advanced Treatise.* vol. II. Academic Press, New York.

Real, L. A. 1980a. Fitness, uncertainty, and the role of diversification in evolution and behavior. American Naturalist 115:623–638.

Real, L. A. 1980b. On uncertainty and the law of diminishing returns in evolution and behavior. pp. 37–64 in J. E. R. Straddon, ed. *Limits to Action.* Academic Press, New York.

Resh, J. A. 1967a. Improvements in the state axioms. Tenth Midwest Symposium on Circuit Theory. pp. V-3-2 – V-3-11.

Resh, J. A. 1967b. On the construction of state spaces. Fifth Annual Allerton Conference on Circuit and System Theory. University of Illinois, Urbana, pp.112–118.

Robertson, A. 1968. The spectrum of genetic variation. In R. C. Lewontin, ed. *Population Biology and Evolution.* Syracuse University Press, Syracuse.

Robinson, A. S. 1983. Sex-ratio manipulation in relation to insect pest control. Annual Review of Genetics 17:191–214.

Robinson, J. G. and K. H. Redford. 1986. Intrinsic rate of natural increase in neotropical forest mammals: relationship to phylogeny and diet. Oecologia 68:516–520.

Rogers, A. 1966. The multiregional matrix growth operator and the stable interregional age structure. Demography 3:537–544.

Rogers, A. 1968. *Matrix Analysis of International Population Growth and Distribution.* University of California Press, Berkeley.

Rogers, A. 1975. *Introduction to Multiregional Mathematical Demography.* Wiley, New York.

Rogers, A. 1985. *Regional Population Projection Models.* Sage Publications, Beverly Hills, CA.

Rorres, C. 1976. Stability of an age specific population with density dependent fertility. Theoretical Population Biology 10:26–46.

Rose, M. R. 1982. Antagonistic pleiotropy, dominance, and gentic variation. Heredity 48:63–78.

Rose, M. R. 1984a. Genetic covariation in *Drosophila* life history: untangling the data. American Naturalist 123:565–569.

Rose, M. R. 1984b. The evolution of animal senescence. Canadian Journal of Zoology 62:1661–1667.

Rose, M. R. and B. Charlesworth. 1981. Genetics of life-history in *Drosophila melanogaster*. II. Exploratory selection experiments. Genetics 75:709–726.

Rose, M. R., P. M. Service, and E. W. Hutchinson. 1987. Three approaches to trade-offs in life-history evolution. pp. 91–105 in V. Loeschcke, ed. *Genetic Constraints on Adaptive Evolution*. Springer-Verlag, New York.

Rosenblatt, D. 1957. On the graphs and asymptotic forms of finite Boolean relation matrices and stochastic matrices. Naval Research Logistics Quarterly 4:151–167.

Roughgarden, J. 1971. Density-dependent natural selection. Ecology 52:453–468.

Roughgarden, J. 1979. *Theory of Population Genetics and Evolutionary Ecology: An Introduction*. Macmillan, New York.

Ruelle, D. and F. Takens. 1971. On the nature of turbulence. Communications in Mathematical Physics 20:167–192.

Saether, B.-E. and H. Haagenrud. 1983. Life history of the moose (*Alces alces*): fecundity rates in relation to age and carcass weight. Journal of Mammology 64:226–232.

Salthe, S. N. and J. S. Mecham. 1974. Reproduction and courtship patterns. pp. 310–521 in B. Lofts, ed. *Physiology of the Amphibia*, vol. II. Academic Press, New York.

Samuelson, P. A. 1976. Time symmetry and asymmetry in population and deterministic dynamic systems. Theoretical Population Biology 9:82–122.

Sarukhán, J. and M. Gadgil. 1974. Studies on plant demography: *Ranunculus repens* L., *R. bulbosus* L. and *R. acris* L. III. A mathematical model incorporating multiple modes of reproduction. Journal of Ecology 62:921–936.

Sarukhán, J., M. Martinez-Ramos, and D. Piñero. 1984. The analysis of demographic variability at the indevedual level and its population consequences. pp. 83–106 in R. Dirzo and J. Sarukhán, eds. *Perspectives on Plant Population Ecology*. Sinauer Associates, Sunderland.

Sauer, J. R. and N. A. Slade. 1985. Mass-based demography of a hispid cotton rat (*Sigmodon hispidus*) population. Journal of Mammology 66:316–328.

Sauer, J. R. and N. A. Slade. 1986. Size-dependent population dynamics of *Microtus ochrogaster*. American Naturalist 127:902–908.

Sauer, J. R. and N. A. Slade. 1987. Uinta ground Squirrel demography: Is body mass better acategorical variable than age? Ecology 68:642–650.

Schaffer, W. M. 1974. Selection for optimal life histories: the effects of age structure. Ecology 55:291–303.

Schaffer, W. M. 1981. On reproductive value and fitness. Ecology 62:1683–1685.

Scheiner, S. M. and C. J. Goodnight. 1984. The comparison of phenotypic plasticity and genetic variation in populations of the grass *Danthonia spicata*. Evolution 38:845–855.

Schenker, N. 1985. Qualms about bootstrap confidence intervals. Journal of the American Statistical Association 80:360–361.

Schlichting, C. D. 1986. The evolution of phenotypic plasticity in plants. Annual Review of Ecology and Systematics 17:667–693.

Schmidt, K. P. and L. R. Lawlor. 1983. Growth rate projection and life history sensitivity for annual plants with a seed bank. American Naturalist 121:525–539.

Schmidt, K. P. and D. A. Levin. 1985. The comparative demography of reciprocally sown populations of *Phlox drummondii* Hook. I. Survivorships, fecundities, and finite rates of increase. Evolution 39:396–404.

Schoen, R. 1981. The harmonic mean as the basis of a realistic two-sex marriage model. Demography 18:201–216.

Schoen, R. 1983. Measuring the tightness of a marriage squeeze. Demography 20:61–78.

Schoen, R. 1984. Relationships in a simple harmonic mean two-sex fertility model. Journal of Mathematical Biology 18:201–211.

Schoen, R. 1988. *Modeling Multigroup Populations*. Plenum Press, New York.

Schuster, H. G. 1984. *Deterministic Chaos*. Physik-Verlag, Weinheim.

Schwarz, R. J. and B. Friedland. 1965. *Linear Systems*. McGraw-Hill, New York.

Sebens, K. P. 1987. The ecology of indeterminate growth in animals. Annual Review of Ecology and Systematics 18:371–407.

Semlitsch, R. D. and J. P. Caldwell. 1982. Effects of density on growth, metamorphosis, and survivorship in tadpoles of *Scaphiopus holbrooki*. Ecology 63:905–911.

Seneta, E. 1981. *Non-Negative Matrices and Markov Chains*, 2nd Ed. Springer-Verlag, New York.

Sharpe, F. R. and A. J. Lotka. 1911. A problem in age-distribution. Philosophical Magazine 21:435–438.

Sherman, P. W. and M. L. Morton. 1984. Demography of Belding's ground squirrels. Ecology 65:1617–1628.

Shryock, H. S. and J. S. Siegel. 1976. *The Methods and Materials of Demography*. Academic Press, New York.

Sibly, R. and P. Calow. 1982. Asexual reproduction in protozoa and invertebrates. Journal of Theoretical Biology 96:401–424.

Sibly, R. and P. Calow. 1983. An integrated approach to life-cycle evolution using selective landscapes. Journal of Theoretical Biology 102:527–547.

Sibly, R. and P. Calow. 1984. Direct and absorption costing in the evolution of life cycles. Journal of Theoretical Biology 111:463–473.

Sibly, R. M. and P. Calow. 1986. *Physiological Ecology of Animals*. Blackwell, Oxford.

Silander, J. A., Jr. 1978. Density-dependent control of reproductive success in *Cassia biflora*. BioTropica 10:292–296.

Simpson, E. H. 1951. The interpretation of interaction in contingency tables. Journal of the Royal Statistical Society, Series B 13:238–241.

Sinko, J. W. and W. Streifer. 1967. A new model for age-size structure of a population. Ecology 48:910–918.

Sinko, J. W. and W. Streifer. 1969. Applying models incorporating age-size structure of a population to *Daphnia*. Ecology 50:608–615.

Skellam, J. G. 1966. Seasonal periodicity in theoretical population ecology. Proceedings of the 5th Berkeley Symposium on Mathematical Statistics and Probability 4:179–205.

Slobodkin, L. B. 1961. *Growth and Regulation of Animal Populations*. Holt, Rinehart, and Winston, New York.

Smith, B. T., J. M. Bouyle, J. J. Dongarra, B. S. Garbow, Y. Ikebe, V. C. Klema, and C. B. Moler. 1976. *Matrix Eigensystem Routines EISPACK Guide.* Springer-Verlag, New York.

Smith, D. and N. Keyfitz. 1977. *Mathematical Demography.* Springer-Verlag, New York.

Smith, F. E. 1952. Experimental methods in population dynamics: a critique. Ecology 33:441–450.

Smouse, P. E. and K. M. Weiss. 1975. Discrete demographic models with density-dependent vital rates. Oecologia 21:205–218.

Solbrig, O. T. 1981. Studies on the population biology of the genus *Viola.* II. The effect of plant size on fitness in *Viola sororia.* Evolution 35:1080–1093.

Somerton, D. A. 1981. Regional variation in the size and maturity of two species of tanner crab (*Chionoecetes bairdi* and *C. opilio*) in the eastern Bering Sea, and its use in defining management subareas. Canadian Journal of Fisheries and Aquatic Sciences 38:163–174.

Somerton, D. A. and R. A. MacIntosh. 1983. The size at sexual maturity of blue king crab, *Paralithodes platypus,* in Alaska. Fishery Bulletin 81:621–628.

Stearns, S. C. and J. C. Koella. 1986. The evolution of phenotypic plasticity in life-history traits: predictions of reaction norms for age and size at maturity. Evolution 40:893–913.

Stiven, A. E. 1962. The effect of temperature and feeding on the intrinsic rate of increase of three species of Hydra. Ecology 43(2):325–328.

Streifer, W. 1974. Realistic models in population ecology. pp. 199–266 in A. MacFadyen, ed. *Advances in Ecological Research.* Academic Press, New York.

Strong, D. R. 1986. Density vagueness: abiding the variance in the demography of real populations. pp. 257–299 in J. Diamond and T. J. Case, eds. *Community Ecology.* Harper & Row, Publishers, New York.

Sutton, S. L., M. Hassell, R. Willows, R. C. Davis, A. Grundy, and K. D. Sunderland. 1984. Life histories of terrestrial isopods: a study of intra- and interspecific variation. Symposia of the Zoological Society of London 53:269–294.

Svirezhev, Y. M. and D. O. Logofet. 1983. *Stability of Biological Communitites.* Mir Publishers, Moscow.

Swick, K. E. 1976. A model of single species population growth. SIAM Journal of Mathematical Analysis 7:565–576.

Swick, K. E. 1981. Stability and bifurcation in age-dependent population dynamics. Theoretical Population Biology 20:80–100.

Sykes, Z. M. 1969. On discrete stable population theory. Biometrics, June 1969:285–293.

Takasu, H. 1987. Life history studies on *Arisaema* (Araceae) I. Growth and reproductive biology of *Arisaema urashima* Hara. Plant Species Biology 2:29–56.

Tande, K.S. and S. Gronvik. 1983. Ecological investigations on the zooplankton community of Balsfjorden, Northern Norway: sex ratio and gonad maturation cycle in the copepod *Metridia longa* (Lubbock). Journal of Experimental Marine Biology and Ecology 71:43–54.

Tantawy, A. O. and M. O. Vetukhiv. 1960. Effects of size on fecundity, longevity and viability in populations of *Drosophila pseudoobscura.* American Naturalist 94:395–403.

Taylor, F. 1979. Convergence to the stable age distribution in populations of insects. American Naturalist 113:511–530.

Taylor, G. C. 1985. Primitivity of products of Leslie matrices. Bulletin of Mathetical Biology 47:23–34.

Taylor, H. M., R. S. Gourley, C. E. Lawrence, and R. S. Kaplan. 1974. Natural selection of life history attributes: an analytical approach. Theoretical Population Biology 5:104–122.

Templeton, A. R. 1980. The evolution of life histories under pleiotropic constraints and r-selection. Theoretical Population Biology 18:279–289.

Thompson, J. M. T. and H. B. Stewart. 1986. *Nonlinear Dynamics and Chaos.* Wiley, New York.

Thompson, R. J. 1979. Fecundity and reproductive effort in the blue mussel (*Mytilus edulis*), the sea urchin (*Strongylocentrotus droebachiensis*), and the snow crab (*Chionoecetes opilio*) from populations in Nova Scotia and Newfoundland. Journal of the Fisheries Research Board of Canada 36:955–964.

Thompson, W. R. 1931. On the reproduction of organisms with overlapping generations. Bulletin of Entomological Research 22:147–172.

Trivers, R. 1985. *Social Evolution.* Benjamin-Cummings, Menlo Park, CA.

Tuljapurkar, S. D. 1982a. Population dynamics in variable environments. II. Correlated environments, sensitivity analysis and dynamics. Theoretical Population Biology 21:114–140.

Tuljapurkar, S. D. 1982b. Population dynamics in variable environments. III. Evolutionary dynamics of r-selection. Theoretical Population Biology 21:141–165.

Tuljapurkar, S. D. 1982c. Why use population entropy? It determines the rate on convergence. Journal of Mathematical Biology 13:325–337.

Tuljapurkar, S. D. 1985. Population dynamics in variable environments. VI. Cyclical environments. Theoretical Population Biology 28:1–17.

Tuljapurkar, S. D. 1986. Demography in stochastic environments. II. Growth and convergence rates. Journal of Mathematical Biology 24:569–581.

Tuljapurkar, S. D. 1989. An uncertain life: demography in random environments. Theoretical Population Biology (in press).

Tuljapurkar, S. D. and S. H. Orzack. 1980. Popualtion dynamics in variable environments I. Long-run growth rates and extinction. Theroetical Population Biology 18:314–342.

Usher, M. B. 1966. A matrix approach to the management of renewable resources, with special reference to selection forests. Journal of Applied Ecology 3:355–367.

Usher, M. B. 1969a. A matrix approach to the management of renewable resources, with special reference to selection forests—two extensions. Journal of Applied Ecology 6:347–348.

Usher, M. B. 1969b. A matrix model for forest management. Biometrics 25:309–315.

Usher, M. B. 1972. Developments in the Leslie matrix model. pp. 29–60 in N. R. Jeffers, ed. *Mathematical Models in Ecologly.* Blackwell, Oxford.

Usher, M. B. 1976. Extensions to models, used in renewable resource management, which incorporate an arbitrary structure. Journal of Environmental Management 4:123–140.

van Sickle, J. 1977a. Analysis of a distributed-parameter population model based on physiological age. Journal of Theoretical Biology 64:571–586.

van Sickle, J. 1977b. Mortality rates from size distributions. Oecologia 27:311–318.

Vance, R. R., W. I. Newman, and D. Sulsky. 1988. The demographic meanings of the classical population growth models of ecology. Theoretical Population Biology 33:199–225.

Vandermeer, J. 1978. Choosing category size in a stage projection matrix. Oecologia 32:79–84.

Via, S. 1987. Genetic constraints on the evolution of phenotypic plasticity. pp. 47–71 in V. Loeschcke, ed. *Genetic Constraints on Adaptive Evolution*. Springer-Verlag, New York.

Via, S. and R. Lande. 1985. Genotype-environment interaction and the evolution of phenotypic plasticity. Evolution 39:505–522.

Volterra, V. 1926. Variazioni e fluttuazioni del numero d'individui in specie animali conviventi. Memorie della R. Accademia dei Lincei 2:31–113.

Volterra, V. 1938. Population growth, equilibria, and extinction under specified breeding conditions: a development and extension of the theory of the logistic curve. Human Biology 10:1–11.

von Foerster, H. 1959. Some remarks on changing populations. pp. 382–407 in F. Stohlman, Jr., ed. *The Kinetics of Cellular Proliferation*. Grune & Stratton, New York.

Wachter, K. W. 1988. Elusive cycles: Are there dynamically possible Lee-Easterlin models for U.S. births? Sloan-Berkeley Working Papers in Population Studies, Institute of International Studies, University of California, Berkeley.

Wachter, K. W. and R. D. Lee. 1988. U.S. births and limit cycle models. Sloan-Berkeley Working Papers in Population Studies, Institute of International Studies, University of California, Berkeley.

Wade, M. J. 1984. Variance-effective population number: the effects of sex ratio and density on the mean and variance of offspring numbers in the flour beetle, *Tribolium castaneum*. Genetical Research 43:249–256.

Wagner, T. L., H.-I. Wu, P. J. H. Sharpe, R. M. Schoolfield, and R. N. Coulson. 1984. Modeling insect development rates: A literature review and application of a biophysical model. Annals of the Entomological Society of America 77:208–225.

Walton, W. E., S. M. Compton, J. D. Allan, and R. E. Daniels. 1982. The effect of acid stress on survivorship and reproduction of *Daphnia pulex* (Crustacea: Cladocera). Canadian Journal of Zoology 60:573–579.

Wan, Y.-H. 1978. Computation of the stability condition for the Hopf bifurcation of diffeomorphisms on R^2. SIAM Journal of Applied Mathematics 34:167–175.

Warner, R. R. and T. P. Hughes. 1988. The population dynamics of reef fishes. Proceedings of the 6th International Coral Reef Symposium (in press).

Watt, K. E. F. 1960. The effect of population density on fecundity in insects. Canadian Entomologist 92:674–695.

Weatherley, A. H. and S. C. Rogers. 1978. Some aspects of age and growth. pp. 52–74 in S. D. Gerking, ed. *Ecology of Freshwater Fish Production*. Wiley, New York.

Weinberg, J. R., H. Caswell, and R. B. Whitlatch. 1986. Demographic importance of ecological interactions: How much do statistics tell us? Marine Ecology

93:305–310.

Werner, P. A. 1975. Predictions of fate from rosette size in teasel (*Dipsacus fullonum* L.). Oecologia 20:197–201.

Werner, P. A. and H. Caswell. 1977. Population growth rates and age versus stage-distribution models for teasel (*Dipsacus sylvestris* Huds.). Ecology 58:1103–1111.

Wilkinson, J. H. 1965. *The Algebraic Eigenvalue Problem*. Clarendon Press, Oxford.

Wilkinson, J. H. and C. Renisch. 1971. *Linear Algebra*. Springer-Verlag, New York.

Williams, G. C. 1957. Pleiotropy, natural selection, and the evolution of senescence. Evolution 11:398–411.

Williams, G. C. 1966. Natural selection, the costs of reproduction, and a refinement of Lack's principle. American Naturalist 100:687–690.

Williamson, M. H. 1959. Some extensions of the use of matrices in population theory. Bulletin of Mathematical Biophysics 21:13–17.

Willson, M.F. 1983. *Plant Reproductive Ecology*. Wiley, New York.

Willson, M.F. and N. Burley. 1983. *Mate Choice in Plants*. Princeton University Press, Princeton, NJ.

Wingard, D. L. 1984. The sex differential in morbidity, mortality, and lifestyle. Annual Review of Public Health 5:433–458.

Winner, R. W. and M. P. Farrell. 1976. Acute and chronic toxicity of copper to four species of *Daphnia*. Journal of the Fisheries Research Board of Canada 33:1685–1691.

Yellin, J. and P. A. Samuelson. 1974. A dynamical model for human population. Proceedings of the National Academy of Sciences USA 71:2813–2817.

Yellin, J. and P.A. Samuelson. 1977. Comparison of linear and nonlinear models for human population dynamics. Theoretical Population Biology 11:105–126.

Yodzis, P. 1981. Concerning the sense in which maximizing fitness is equivalent to maximizing reproductive value. Ecology 62:1681–1682.

Zadeh, L. A. 1964. The concept of state in system theory. pp. 39–50 in M. D. Mesarovic, ed. *Views on General Systems Theory*. Wiley, New York.

Zadeh, L. A. 1969. The concepts of system, aggregate, and state in system theory. pp. 3–42 in L. A. Zadeh and E. Polak, eds. *System Theory*. McGraw Hill, New York.

Zadeh, L. A. and C. A. Desoer. 1963. *Linear System Theory*. McGraw-Hill, New York.

Zon, R. 1915. Seed production of western white pine. Bulletin No. 210, U.S. Department of Agriculture.

Index